D1563193

Thunder from the Prairie

Thunder from the Prairie
The Life of Harold E. Hughes

Jerry Harrington

 University Press of Kansas

Published by the University Press of Kansas (Lawrence, Kansas 66045),
which was organized by the Kansas Board of Regents and is operated and
funded by Emporia State University, Fort Hays State University, Kansas State
University, Pittsburg State University, the University of Kansas, and Wichita
State University.

Library of Congress Cataloging-in-Publication Data

Names: Harrington, Jerry, author.
Title: Thunder from the prairie : the life of Harold E. Hughes / Jerry
    Harrington.
Other titles: Life of Harold E. Hughes
Description: Lawrence, Kansas : University Press of Kansas, 2023. |
    Includes bibliographical references and index.
Identifiers: LCCN 2022050618 (print)
    LCCN 2022050619 (ebook)
    ISBN 9780700634699 (cloth)
    ISBN 9780700634705 (ebook)
Subjects: LCSH: Hughes, Harold E. (Harold Everett), 1922–1996. |
    Politicians—United States—Biography. | Legislators—United
    States—Biography. | United States. Congress. Senate—Biography. |
    United States—Politics and government—1969–1974. | Iowa—Politics and
    government—20th century. | Iowa—Biography. | Recovering
    alcoholics—United States—Biography.
Classification: LCC E840.8.H83 H37 2023 (print) | LCC E840.8.H83
    (ebook) | DDC 973.92092 [B]—dc23/eng/20221026
LC record available at https://lccn.loc.gov/2022050618.
LC ebook record available at https://lccn.loc.gov/2022050619.

British Library Cataloguing-in-Publication Data is available.

Printed in the United States of America

10 9 8 7 6 5 4 3 2 1

The paper used in this publication is acid free and meets the minimum
requirements of the American National Standard for Permanence of Paper
for Printed Library Materials Z39.48-1992.

I dedicate this book to my seven grandchildren—Laila, Mira, Yousef, Kai, Jack, Arlo, and Penny. May they grow to know the active compassion reflected in the career of Harold E. Hughes.

Contents

A photo gallery follows page 148.

Preface

The year 1968 marked the first time I recall paying attention to national news coverage. And what an astonishing year it was. As a thirteen-year-old growing up on a farm in northeastern Iowa, I found that I was a citizen of a nation experiencing violent clashes on urban streets, political assassinations, campus riots, racial conflicts, a presidential campaign filled with upheavals almost every month, and a controversial, seemingly endless war in Vietnam. All this was capped in December by a picture of the earth taken by the crew of Apollo 8, which was orbiting the moon, of a beautiful, bright globe amidst the darkness of space, reminding us that despite the intense divisions seen that year, we all inhabit the same magnificent planet.

It was also during that year that I first noticed Harold Hughes, the governor of Iowa. I watched him on television as he gave the nominating speech for Senator Eugene McCarthy at the 1968 Democratic convention in Chicago, cast against the struggles on the convention floor and the brutal battles between antiwar demonstrators and police outside. I was captivated by this handsome man with a deep, rich voice talking about the possibilities of peace. As an Iowa native, I was proud we came from the same state. I have been fascinated with him ever since.

This interest of mine blossomed into a more intense curiosity about the history of my state while I was a student at Cornell College in Mount Vernon, Iowa. This was helped by two classes I took in my junior year. One was a twentieth-century US history course taught by Professor Richard Thomas, who was also chair of the State Historical Society of Iowa and promoted the study of Iowa history among students, including me. The other was a twentieth-century American literature course taught by Professor Richard Martin, where I was introduced to the works of William Faulkner. Faulkner spent nearly his entire literary career writing about a single mythical county in Mississippi, and studying him made me realize that the universal can be found in the local. I applied that to my interest in history. Iowa became my Yoknapatawpha County.

Immersing myself in the history of Iowa, I have become well versed in the literature—particularly works dealing with political history, my

first love. Over the years, I have written articles—both popular and ac-
ademic—about Iowa history for magazines, journals, and newspapers.
All that led me to this book on Harold Hughes.

Many individuals helped me along this journey. First, I want to thank
those who took the time to talk with me in person or over the phone
about their memories of Harold Hughes. I especially want to thank
Dwight Jensen of Iowa City and Bill Hedlund of Des Moines, both of
whom worked on Hughes's staff in Iowa and Washington, DC. They
spent long hours with me on several occasions. Phyllis Hughes Ewing,
Hughes's surviving daughter, was also kind enough to share information about her father. I hope they gained as much from the exchange
as I did.

Those at the University of Iowa Special Collections and Archives,
which houses the Hughes gubernatorial and senatorial papers, were
more than helpful—pulling out box after box of documents, day after
day, week after week. They answered my questions about source material and other aspects of research collection. I also want to thank the
University of Iowa library staff, who provided me with spools of micro-
film containing daily newspaper accounts from the 1960s and 1970s.

Both the Iowa City and Des Moines offices of the State Historical
Society of Iowa provided assistance. I particularly want to thank Mary
Bennett and Charles Scott of Iowa City, who offered wise counsel and
direction in my research.

John Liepa, retired professor of history at the Des Moines Area Community College, reviewed a draft of the manuscript and provided sage
advice. At a table off the kitchen in his Des Moines home, we spent
several Monday mornings reviewing each page as he regaled me with
personal stories from his career in Iowa Democratic politics and tale
after tale of baseball history, his obvious passion.

I am deeply indebted to Linda Lotz, copyeditor for the University
Press of Kansas, who applied her professional skills to nearly every page
of the manuscript. She made this a better work and, as I reviewed her
edits, made me a better writer. I could not have asked for a more skilled
editor.

Last, I want to thank my wife, Leslie, who was with me throughout
this journey of researching, interviewing, and writing. She encouraged
me in this endeavor, and I could not imagine doing it without her.

Introduction

On the day Harold Everett Hughes was born—February 10, 1922—a fire destroyed the farm rented by his family outside Ida Grove, Iowa. Recent arrivals in western Iowa from the hills of Kentucky via Illinois, the Hughes family of four survived with only the clothes on their backs. With little money before the blaze and now totally destitute, they relied on the kindness of kin, their religious faith, and their indomitable will.[1]

Born into poverty, Harold Hughes had a special perspective on how life's burdens can affect individuals through no fault of their own. As a young man, he faced additional hardships—the violent death of a beloved brother, brutal conflict on the battlefields of Europe, and the severe alcoholism that nearly destroyed him. Overcoming these hurdles, Hughes used his unique leadership talent to become governor of his state in the 1960s and a US senator from 1969 to 1974.

But political office is not Hughes's only legacy. It is what he did and how he did it. As Iowa governor, he led a reform of state government with a dynamism not seen in decades, modernizing it to accommodate mid-twentieth-century needs. Hughes shares that heritage with a select group of Iowa governors who significantly altered the state's political landscape: James Grimes in the 1850s, who led the reform movement for a new Iowa Constitution and helped found the Iowa Republican Party; Albert Baird Cummins, who initiated Progressive Era reforms in the early twentieth century; and Robert Ray, who continued to renovate state government as Hughes's successor.

Hughes's significant and impactful Democratic governorship stands in stark contrast to the tradition he inherited in Iowa—a generally conservative Republican state. Elected to three consecutive two-year terms—a first in Iowa history for a member of his party—Hughes led and also benefited from the postwar growth of the Democratic Party in Iowa. At the same time, he stood out as a unique, charismatic leader who rose above mere party mechanics and organization. Indeed, he often found himself at odds with Democratic political leaders in Iowa, and he established a reputation among voters as a singular independent voice. Often in defiance of Iowans' conservative attitudes, he not only spoke about caring for the downtrodden but also aggressively acted on their behalf.

As a single-term US senator, Hughes vigorously raised the issue of alcoholism as a disease to the national level, spearheading the first federal programs to aid sufferers. He was a relentless critic of the Vietnam War and American military deception. As a politician, Hughes was an inspirational leader who fearlessly addressed controversial issues. His captivating presence on the national stage compelled supporters to initiate a presidential campaign on his behalf, only to have Hughes end it.

Aside from these singular accomplishments, why is it important to examine the political career of a governor of a small midwestern state and one-term US senator? What makes Hughes significant to historians and to others who may not be particularly interested in Iowa or midwestern history? The answer is that his life provides a distinct perspective into a unique and colorful era in American history. Hughes's time in politics spans the period called by some historians the "Long Sixties," extending from the birth of the modern civil rights movement in the late 1950s, through the Vietnam War and its domestic divisiveness, and ending with the Watergate scandal in the early 1970s. As a spirited political actor, Hughes was deeply immersed in the era's myriad and complex issues and events. Scholars and others can gain special insight into this period by reviewing the life of Harold Hughes.[2]

Hughes clearly established himself within the postwar liberal tradition—supporting an activist government domestically and anticommunism abroad—until this consensus became frayed in the late 1960s by the war in Southeast Asia. He began his governorship during the forward-looking optimism of John Kennedy's New Frontier. In fact, Hughes's successful run for governor in 1962 was similar to Kennedy's presidential campaign two years earlier, applying the theme of "getting the country moving again" to Iowa. Like Kennedy, Hughes was a charismatic politician who pledged to revive robust government, which, he claimed, had been left slumbering by the prior Republican administration. Hughes supported the overall thrust of Lyndon Johnson's Great Society programs, marking the high point of postwar liberalism, although he criticized specific implementations. But Hughes's liberalism was not that of policy wonks or academics—indeed, he attended only one year of college. Instead, it stemmed from the Christian Social Gospel he learned as a youth, using government to help those in need. As a liberal politician, Hughes initiated activist government programs at the state level, such as the Iowa Manpower Development Council and a program to aid alcoholics. This included using government to enhance economic development, a tactic used by other liberals. A clear example was the creation of the Iowa community college system, an idea Hughes advanced in campaign after campaign until it finally came to fruition in 1965. To support these ends, Hughes increased state taxes. He reformed state government so that it met the goals advanced by liberals more efficiently. As governor of an overwhelmingly white state, Hughes reached out to Iowa's Black community and fought racism in an almost crusade-like fashion.

As the nation became increasingly divided over the Vietnam War, Hughes, too, struggled over the conflict. He was hesitant to criticize President Johnson, to whom he had grown close. Like others in this period, Hughes finally came out strongly against the war and became one of its leading opponents. Taking this opposition to Washington, DC, as a US senator, Hughes opposed not only the Nixon administration's Vietnam policy but also many aspects of its domestic policies, criticizing cutbacks of federal aid to the needy. Like other Nixon critics, Hughes denounced the Watergate affair, but surprisingly, he brought into his close circle one of its conspirators: Charles Colson.

In many ways, the political life of Harold Hughes is a study in microcosm of the "Long Sixties," providing a prism through which to see this important period in American history.

Hughes was a man of unusual candor and directness. But it was how he expressed himself that so impressed people. He was a large (six-foot-three, 230 pounds), handsome man gifted with a deep, booming voice, and his speeches could bring vast crowds to tears as he expressed empathetic compassion for the less fortunate. He spoke eloquently about the suffering of others, applying, in one writer's words, "the compassion of one who has known and overcome despair."[3]

According to Nick Kotz and James Risser of the *Des Moines Register*, who covered Hughes in both Iowa and Washington, DC, "the trademark of the Hughes political style has been an outspoken forthrightness on issues, presented with all the charismatic advantages of rugged good looks, imposing physique, deep bass voice, and compelling personal intensity." This is the man Iowans saw year after year and rewarded with five statewide electoral victories over a decade.[4]

Residing within this individual was an uneasy soul of immense contradictions. Hughes was a recovered alcoholic who fought to expand legal liquor sales in Iowa, a college dropout who could easily discourse with intellectuals, a sincere Christian who swore like a vulgar stable hand, and an ambitious politician who walked away from political power to follow his own inner calling. Compounding these contradictions was a man willing to learn and change as his political career advanced, reflecting not opportunism but a capacity for growth. Changing his position on Vietnam is only one example. His outlook on Black Iowans is another, gained by meeting with them week after week in their neighborhoods to understand their lives. And on an intensely personal level, Hughes continually reexamined his religious outlook, altering his theological beliefs throughout his life. This trait alone—his ability to reflect internally and modify strongly held beliefs—makes Hughes a political actor worth studying.[5]

This is the individual born on that day of flames in western Iowa in 1922. But fire may not be the best image to mark this man. Perhaps a better one is thunder, a deep, rumbling sound heralding the passion of an Old Testament God. This metaphor—thunder from the prairie—illustrates Harold Hughes, a man of weight and depth who dramatically impacted countless lives, moved others to take productive action, and made a positive difference in the way we live today.

This is his story.

1 | Youth, War, and Alcohol

Harold Hughes's parents, Lewis and Etta Kelly Hughes, were born in Pulaski County, in the hills of south-central Kentucky, where poverty was a common condition. The Hughes family was large. Lewis's grandfather had two wives; the first bore ten children before she died, and the second gave birth to eight, so Lewis had a slew of great-aunts and great-uncles when he was growing up. Etta's family was smaller, and her lineage included a great-grandmother who was Cherokee, although the details are scarce. She grew up on a small, hardscrabble farm and dropped out of school in fourth grade to work on the farm. The Hugheses traced their European ancestry to Wales, and the Kellys traced theirs to Northern Ireland.[1]

Lewis and Etta met while attending Cabin Holler Baptist Church. Etta had previously been engaged to another young man who died of tuberculosis, prompting her to vow never to wed, but Lewis Hughes persuaded her otherwise. They were married at the Kelly family farm, called "Strawberry," consisting of a few rocky acres on the side of a Kentucky mountain. Etta's uncle, a Baptist minister, performed the ceremony on February 4, 1912, Lewis's twenty-first birthday.[2]

Seeing no future in Pulaski County, the young couple thought moving west would be an improvement. Lewis's cousin Norman Hughes, who had already migrated to Ida County, Iowa, wrote to them and said if they came to west-central Iowa "they could starve slower here." So the pair loaded up what little they had in their car and headed west. The automobile broke down in Bloomington, Illinois, and without the cash to carry on, they stayed there for the next five years. Lewis got a job as foreman at the McLean County Poor Farm, and the couple saved their money. During that time their first son, Jesse, was born.[3]

Lewis and Etta finally scraped enough money together to travel with their infant son to rural Ida County, Iowa. Lewis borrowed funds to rent a small farm, where he planted crops and purchased feed for hogs and sows. Etta became pregnant with their second child soon after they arrived.[4]

Harold Everett Hughes was named after another child—Harold Everett Jones—whom Etta had cared for at the Illinois poor farm and remembered fondly. During her pregnancy, Etta's diet was poor, due to limited family finances. As a consequence, Harold weighed only five pounds at birth and suffered from jaundice. The doctor who delivered him apparently commented that the newborn "wasn't much to look at."[5]

A fire on the day of Harold's birth destroyed everything the family owned, although years later, Etta would recall that the only thing she regretted losing in the blaze was her light blue wedding dress. The entire Hughes clan, including family members from both Iowa and Kentucky, helped the young family get back on its feet. They now had two children to feed—Jesse was not yet three years old. Lewis labored as a farmhand and then as a construction worker for a firm that erected buildings in western Iowa. Etta worked scrubbing floors, cleaning houses, and washing dishes for the dining room at a local hotel. She also raised chickens, butchered them, and sold them door-to-door.[6]

Lewis and Etta also found comfort in their strong Christian beliefs. Their Kentucky roots were firmly Baptist, but there was no Baptist church in Ida Grove, so the family attended the Methodist church in town.[7]

Poverty was never far from the Hughes household. By the mid-1920s, the rural Midwest was suffering from an agricultural depression. When the 1929 stock market crash launched the Great Depression, it only compounded the economic problems in rural America. The Hughes family was already living on a limited income, and this became a hand-to-mouth existence as hard times hit. They often went without meat unless Lewis loaded his Stevens twelve-gauge shotgun and managed to shoot a rabbit or two for the evening meal.[8]

Financial hardship affected the family's health. Lewis suffered from stomach ulcers, and when Harold was thirteen years old, his father started to hemorrhage. Lewis was denied admission to the Ida Grove hospital because of the family's lack of funds. A couple of local doctors gave Lewis little chance to live, but he was finally admitted to a hospital in nearby Sioux City, where he improved. "It was one of those cases," recalled Harold, "where if you didn't have the money, you didn't get help."[9]

Harold knew firsthand about life on "the other side of the tracks," but lessons from his mother gave him a special empathy for the underdog, the downtrodden, and the poor. Etta instilled in her son a compassion for the less fortunate and a lifelong drive to extend a helping hand to others. Often she would tell her son about the despondent, indigent

YOUTH, WAR, & ALCOHOL | 7

people she had seen on the poor farm in Illinois, poverty-stricken, down-on-their-luck individuals and families who depended on government aid to live. Etta, a deeply religious woman, taught her son that the fundamental core of Christ's teachings was helping others. Hughes recalled that, despite the family's poverty, Etta always reminded him "there were other people worse off than we were, and we ought to be doing something to help them." According to Etta's granddaughter and Harold's daughter, Phyllis Hughes Ewing, "Her form of Christianity was very evolved social consciousness, fighting for the right thing, fighting for the underdog."[10]

As Harold and Jesse grew up, they contributed to the limited family income by trapping animals and selling their pelts. They would get $1 for muskrat fur, $2 for skunk, and $10 for mink. The boys got up at three o'clock in the morning, regardless of the weather, to check their trapping lines next to the Maple River. They were back home at five for breakfast, and at eight they rushed off to school.[11]

Eventually, the family borrowed $600 from Lewis's father and bought a house on the edge of town. Over time, Lewis and Etta saved enough money to open a commercial greenhouse in Ida Grove, where they managed their own successful business.[12]

Jesse and Harold were inseparable. Three years older, Jesse was graced with auburn hair, freckles, and Irish humor, which he inherited from the Kellys. Harold took after his father's side of the family, with a darker, more ruggedly handsome look. The brothers played, hunted, and worked together, including jobs as caddies at the local country club. Both of them played on the school football team, and their size prompted people to say they looked like two elephants on the field. A local sportswriter agreed, describing them as "two pachyderms." The nicknames stuck: Jesse was called "Big Pack" and Harold "Little Pack." Harold was known as Pack for the rest of his life.[13]

Jesse was just as big, but his younger brother was the more aggressive football player at right guard. Harold excelled in track and field as well, and in 1938 he won the Iowa state discus championship. The next year he was selected to the all-state football team. The *Des Moines Register* called him one of "the best guards in the state," with "brilliant play on both offense and defense." Harold was "big, tough and rough and really handed out the punishment to the opposing forwards by his fierce talking and hard blocking." Ida Grove teammate Jim Lindsay recalled playing opposite Hughes during practice. "He was a nice guy, but on the football field he was mean . . . I can tell you that I remember well being cannon-fodder for a future United States Senator."[14]

Hughes's talents included music as well. In 1939 he was selected to the all-state band as a tuba player. He did well academically, too—"I had my share of B's and high Cs," he said. But he had to work to achieve those grades. "I studied at night when I got home," Hughes remembered, "but it was labor for me."[15]

At Ida Grove High School, Hughes was a popular student, respected and admired by most. Said Ramona Barry of nearby Danbury, "he excelled in everything he did—football, track, arguing, the tuba . . . drinking."[16] That was when Hughes's drinking began. While attending a dance as a sophomore, he and several friends paid an elderly man to buy them a bottle of liquor, and they consumed the whole thing outside the dance. The alcohol helped the young Hughes—tongue-tied around girls—get over his shyness that evening. He later wrote, "I never really liked the taste of the burning stuff . . . I drank because it lifted my inhibitions and made me relaxed and easygoing at dances and social affairs. Whenever a bottle was passed around . . . it stayed the longest with me."[17]

In part, drinking was a trait he inherited from his father. As a boy, Harold recalled his father coming home drunk. Once, Lewis drove the family car into a ditch while inebriated. Sometimes, the boy found liquor bottles in the outhouse and other places where the elder Hughes hid them. This led to arguments between Etta and Lewis over his drinking. "There was never anything rough. It was just my mother's carrying on that made it bad," Harold recalled. But these experiences failed to leave an impression on the son.[18]

Drinking helped ease the younger Hughes through social situations, but he did not find it pleasant. As he recalled years later, "I was not like people that seemed to get a glow on and a smile on their face. And then everything is rosy in life when they drink. I don't remember that as being a part of my drinking at all. It was not a happy experience for me." Even as a youth, Hughes showed signs of emerging alcoholism. "I also had a physical addiction when I drank. I never wanted to stop. Some sort of chemical process set up in my body that I wanted to drink three for every drink that someone else drank. I still don't know what it was. It was there all during the period of my drinking."[19]

Hughes's drinking did not go unnoticed at home. When he came home drunk at night, he would often bang into the furniture and wake the family. Jesse warned his younger brother that their parents, who were well aware of his habits, were concerned, but Harold dismissed these warnings. One reason was that his drinking was not affecting his schoolwork and after-school activities. He took home statewide honors in athletics and band. In 1940 Hughes graduated from Ida Grove High School, wearing the first suit he had ever owned, ordered from a Sears & Roebuck catalog. His all-state football and athletic honors had earned him a football scholarship to the University of Iowa in Iowa City that fall.[20]

Immediately after high school graduation, Hughes shared a ride to Iowa City, where he lived in a private home and worked that summer at the university as a steamfitter's helper for $18 a week, half of which went toward tuition. He also worked at the Downtown Café in the evening, cleaning the floors and tables to earn dinner, and he got a job with the New Deal's National Youth Administration (NYA), which helped pay his rent. When school started in the fall, Hughes turned to his studies and training with the football team. Committed to staying in shape for athletics, he later wrote, "I tried not to drink much."[21]

Returning home for Christmas break, Hughes attended a holiday party in Ida Grove, where he noticed an attractive young lady. Though he did not talk to her that evening, he asked others about her and discovered that her name was Eva Mercer and she was the sister of a girl Hughes had dated earlier. Her family, originally from nearby Holstein, had recently moved to Ida Grove. The youngest of four children, Eva grew up in dire poverty. Said Hughes's daughter Phyllis, "My dad used to say about himself, 'We were poor growing up, but your mother was really poor.'" Eva's father, a small-town newspaperman, died of cancer at the beginning of the Depression, forcing Eva's mother to depend on charity from her siblings. At times, the family had no food in the house.[22]

Hughes thought of Eva frequently during his second semester at Iowa. While attending a carnival later that summer in Ida Grove, he saw her and struck up a conversation. They dated and eventually fell in love. Not one to ponder a decision for long, he asked for her hand, and they were married in a small ceremony in August 1941. She was seventeen and he was nineteen.[23]

Hughes returned to the University of Iowa that fall and got into a conflict with the athletic department over financial aid he believed was owed him. Deciding he would rather be a married man in Ida

Grove than a college student in Iowa City, Hughes dropped out and hitchhiked home. The decision to leave college greatly disappointed his mother, who scolded him severely; Hughes's father expressed his displeasure with silence. The young couple, however, were seemingly happy together.[24]

With few jobs in Ida Grove, Harold and Eva moved to Des Moines, where he eventually got a construction job, helping to build a defense plant outside the city. He later took a better-paying job with the Des Moines Department of Public Works. Soon, Eva was pregnant with their first child. But family life was jolted by the bombing of Pearl Harbor on December 7, 1941, launching America into World War II. This meant that Hughes could expect to be drafted into military service soon.[25]

Before that happened, Hughes had to grapple with a deep tragedy. On June 1, 1942, Jesse Hughes and three friends were driving to Storm Lake, north of Ida Grove, to attend a dance. It was supposed to be one final fling before the elder Hughes brother reported for military service. On the way, they were caught in a severe thunderstorm and struck a bridge abutment, throwing the car into a raging stream. All four passengers were killed. Hughes's Uncle Oscar in Des Moines called Harold at work to break the news. Harold then drove to Coon Rapids, where his father was working as a construction foreman, to tell him about Jesse. In Ida Grove, the local undertaker called Etta—who knew nothing of the tragedy—and asked her about funeral details. Stunned, Etta collapsed. The undertaker immediately called a doctor, who found her in shock and near death in her home.[26]

Jesse's death devastated his family. Harold could barely imagine life without the vigorous, laughing older brother who had been his constant companion. Hughes later wrote that his mother "was a different person after Jesse's death. Gone was the fun-loving joking woman who always had a happy remark or laugh." Hughes's father "sank within his grief, but didn't say much."[27]

Life moved on. In July 1942 a girl, named Connie, was born to Harold and Eva Hughes. Later that year, they moved back to Ida Grove, and Harold got a job building bridges. Anticipating military induction in a few months, he wanted Eva and Connie to be around family instead of in the unfamiliar environs of Des Moines. By the end of the year, Hughes received his draft notice, and he left to begin his military service on December 28. After bidding farewell to the rest of the family,

Hughes climbed into this father's car, and the two drove to Des Moines. With a short "Good-bye, son, God go with you" from his father, Harold Hughes walked into world history on that cold, icy day.[28]

As 1943 dawned, Hughes was starting army training at Camp Sibert, Alabama, located on 37,035 acres in the central part of the state, straddling Etowah and St. Clair Counties. The newly created camp had officially been dedicated on Christmas Day 1942, only weeks before Hughes arrived, and many sections were still incomplete. Sibert, consisting of bleak, white-painted barracks in red-mud fields, was, in Hughes's words, "where civilian-soft men were transitioned into toughened soldiers."[29]

The United States had been at war for over a year and was well on its way to transforming a nascent, ill-equipped military into a powerful force aimed at defeating the Axis threat. Under President Franklin Roosevelt's leadership, the United States had adopted a "Germany first" policy, opting to defeat Nazi Germany before concentrating on Japan. The thinking was that, once Germany was beaten, the Soviet Union—then fighting for its life against the Nazi onslaught—would join Allied forces to crush Japan. In November 1942 the United States linked with its British ally in Operation Torch, landing troops in North Africa to remove the German army from that continent. When Hughes began basic training, US and British armies were marching toward Tunisia to accomplish that goal. By May 1943, German and Italian troops had surrendered in northern Tunisia, providing the Allies complete control of North Africa.[30]

Hughes and the rest of the raw recruits in Alabama knew they were preparing for the next stage of the conflict: attacks into Sicily and the Italian peninsula. Hughes found the eighteen weeks of basic training "almost enjoyable," given that he loved the outdoors, and he thought marksmanship practice was "fun." Even getting up at 5:00 a.m., he later recalled, was "a fairly normal hour to me." In late March Hughes was transferred to the Eighty-Third Chemical Battalion in Camp Gordon, Georgia, where he was trained to use the Browning automatic rifle (BAR). This portable machine gun required two operators—one to fire it, and another to carry the ammunition and hand it over during combat. Hughes assumed he would be given the job of carrying and firing the twenty-one-pound gun because of his size.[31]

Training did not last long. By April, Hughes's company received the order to ship overseas. It happened so quickly that Hughes's furlough home, promised at the end of basic training, was canceled. He had been looking forward to ending the months of separation from Eva and his infant daughter. Amidst his anger and disappointment, Hughes raced from sergeant to sergeant, trying to arrange extended time to see his family; he even toyed with the idea of having Eva come to Georgia for a day, but to no avail. Hughes was in the army now, and with the nation at war, troops were needed overseas immediately. It did not help his homesick soul when, after traveling by troop train to Fort Stanton, Massachusetts, Hughes witnessed officers pulling rank so their wives could meet them at the base. The Iowan seethed at the unfair privilege.[32]

Hughes and the rest of the Eighty-Third continued on to New York City, where they boarded a navy ship with thousands of others for the voyage to Oran, Algeria, in preparation for the Allied invasion of Sicily. After arriving, Hughes gave in to his alcoholic demons while awaiting orders. He and a friend went to town, got drunk, and missed the last truck back to camp. Opting to continue their drinking, the pair eventually got into a fight with the military police. Hughes woke the next morning in a stockade, charged with being drunk and disorderly and attacking an officer. With no choice but to plead guilty, Hughes faced a two-thirds pay cut for six months. As he walked away, the military judge said, "You can go back to regular duty—where you'll probably get killed anyway."[33]

The killing began soon enough. In the dark, early-morning hours of July 10, 1943, Hughes sat aboard a troop transport ship off the southern shore of Sicily at Gela. He was part of the initial US assault—primarily against Italian defenders supported by German divisions—to establish a foothold in Europe under the command of General George Patton. Carrying two cartridge belts with 250 rounds of ammunition and the automatic rifle—both of which bit into his shoulder—Hughes waited for the order to disembark. Once it was given, he scrambled down the sagging net and jumped onto the landing barge that would carry the troops into the hell of battle.[34]

The landing commenced just after 3:30 a.m., and Hughes joined it on the Sicilian beach as the Italian defenders fired bullets, bombs, and grenades at the Americans as they pushed forward onto land. Wave after wave of troops emerged from the barges as chaos surged around them. Fueled with adrenalin, Hughes hit the shore and, as fellow fighters were being killed left and right, crawled on his elbows and knees to a grassy hill. Attempting to fire, he realized his BAR was jammed with sand. He tried to take it apart and reassemble it in the dark, but a mortar shell exploded nearby, tossing the parts away. Hughes then grabbed ammunition from a dead GI and moved forward amidst the bedlam. At one point, an enemy tank rolled over Hughes as he took cover in a foxhole; he survived by hugging the earth.[35]

Hughes managed to live through the day and reconnected with his outfit at nightfall. By this time, the Americans had taken control of the beach. Then, through no fault of his own, Hughes took part in one of the Allies' gravest and darkest errors of World War II. In the pitch black of night, paratroopers from the Eighty-Second Airborne Division jumped from planes roaring above the troops who had just spent the day defying death. The ground soldiers assumed these were Germans coming to the aid of the Italian defenders and blasted away at the helpless parachuters. According to military historian Rick Atkinson, "At last the shooting ebbed, the guns fell silent, and an awful epiphany seeped across the beachhead . . . that men-at-arms had done what men-at-arms most fear doing: they had killed their own." Owing to miscommunication among American military leaders, the ground troops had received no signal that Allied paratroopers would be landing. According to later investigators, the response demolished twenty-three Allied planes and severely damaged another twenty-three; more important, an estimated 410 men died. Atkinson calls it "among the worst friendly fire episodes in modern warfare."[36]

Once they had recovered, Hughes's group linked up with the First Battalion of the American Rangers and began the ninety-mile march up western Sicily toward Palermo. Although most of the American soldiers did not know it at the time, they were part of a competition between American general Patton and British field marshal Bernard Law Montgomery to see who could reach northern Sicily first. Patton prevailed, taking Messina at the northern tip of Sicily after relentlessly driving his troops across the island under the hot Mediterranean sun.[37]

With Axis forces driven from Sicily, the Allied soldiers rested, although it was an uneasy respite. They all knew the island would serve as a launching pad for the invasion of Italy. In late August Hughes received a cable from Eva, telling him that their second child, a girl, had been born. Not yet named, the baby was doing well, as was the mother. This would be the last message Hughes received from home for some time.[38]

The Allied landing on Italian soil began on September 9 in a wave of assaults around Salerno on the west coast, south of Naples. Hughes found himself attached to a British commando group, providing support with his hefty BAR. This group's mission was to land at Vietri sui Mare west of Salerno and capture the coastal highway. The goal was to cut off German reinforcements and hold them until Fifth Army moved west from Salerno. Leaving Sicily on stormy waters, Hughes and his shipmates headed into the Gulf of Salerno, where they could see the main invasion on the horizon. The dark sky was brilliantly lit by anti-aircraft fire, along with the glow from burning ships. Sailing past the main action, Hughes's group landed on the Italian shore early the next morning, where they found open shops and business as usual.[39]

The peace did not last long. By afternoon, Germans had started to shell the unit, driving it back to its battle stations on the shore. The Allied troops fought back and moved inland but still faced continuous shelling. During one barrage, mortar shells exploded all around Hughes, knocking him to the ground; he landed next to a man whose skull had been blown open, and he could only turn away and vomit. The soldiers collected themselves and fought their way to the village, battling the Germans house to house and then room to room. After several days they were able to drive the Germans away and secure the highway. Fifth Army finally advanced to Vietri, and Hughes's unit left the decimated town seventeen days after landing.[40]

The group advanced eight miles and then collapsed in a small stone church. An exhausted Hughes attempted to sleep but could not. A severe headache of several days' duration intensified, and he was shaken by chills. He participated in another day of fighting and then collapsed. Medics found Hughes delirious and with a fever of 106 degrees. He was transferred to a British hospital ship bound for North Africa. Hughes had contracted malaria, which is transmitted by mosquitoes. This was a common problem among soldiers fighting in the Mediterranean theater. In all, about ten thousand men suffered from malaria in US Seventh Army and nearly twelve thousand in Eighth Army.[41]

For days, the Iowan slipped in and out of consciousness at a British hospital in North Africa. Once the worst was over, Hughes hardly recognized himself. He had lost forty pounds in a month. It took several weeks before he could walk again. Slowly recovering and regaining his strength, Hughes was finally well enough by February 1944 to rejoin the Eighty-Third Chemical Battalion, now stationed around Bagnoli.

It was then that he learned he had probably cheated death, as most of those he knew in Company D had been killed in combat. Hughes's spirits were uplifted, however, when he discovered a large packet of letters waiting for him at company headquarters. The army had lost track of Hughes while he was in a British hospital, and he found sixty-three letters and two telegrams in the package. Among the news was that his second daughter's name was Carol. He raced through the rest of the correspondence and wrote his first letter home to Eva in months.[42]

As the war continued, Hughes's company was transferred to the Italian front and eventually to the Anzio beachhead, established to take pressure off fronts elsewhere in Italy. One day, after completing a patrol, Hughes once again experienced chills and a high fever: his malaria had returned. Checking into the evacuation hospital on the beachhead, Hughes began his second recovery. As he slowly regained strength, he checked regularly with the replacement center, expecting to be sent back into combat. One morning, however, he was greeted with some welcome news: "Get ready, Hughes. You'll be leaving for the States tomorrow morning at five o'clock." The medical review board had determined that the Iowan had seen enough combat and should be sent home and assigned to other duties.[43]

Hughes left Italy on June 1, 1944. Days into the trek across the Atlantic, crew members learned of the D-day invasion at Normandy, launching a second front against Germany. Upon landing at Newport News, Virginia, he received orders to report to Camp Butner in North Carolina, where he would serve in the military police unit. But first he had earned a three-week furlough. Hughes caught the first train to Des Moines and arrived there two days later. He then hitchhiked to Ida Grove to be with Eva and his two daughters.[44]

Upon reporting to North Carolina, Hughes was transferred to a military police unit at Fort Benjamin Harrison in Evanston, Indiana. Ironically, despite being responsible for enforcing military law, Hughes and two fellow soldiers went out drinking, got into a fight with local police, and ended up in jail. Hughes was arrested on similar charges in Columbus, Ohio; Morganfield, Kentucky; and, in his words, "other places I can't remember." At the time, he dismissed these incidents as youthful drinking sprees, but Hughes's uncontrollable alcoholic binges would soon consume his life.[45]

Hughes was discharged from the military in July 1945 and returned to civilian life in Ida Grove. With a wife and two children to support, he dismissed the idea of returning to college and plunged into the job market to earn money for his family. His first job was pumping gas at a local filling station, followed by a position at Wilkens Hardware Store. Obtaining a loan through the GI Bill, Hughes bought a house at 701 North Main in Ida Grove, and the family was featured in the local newspaper as the first in town to take advantage of the federal program for veterans. Needing to earn more money to make the monthly mortgage payments, Hughes got a job at A&P Creamery in Ida Grove, picking up cans of milk every day from dairy farmers. One winter morning he slipped on the ice while carrying a heavy milk can, severely injuring his back. Fearing the loss of his job if he sought medical treatment, Hughes simply soldiered on with what would later be diagnosed as a broken back.[46]

Like many combat veterans, Hughes still lived with the horrors of war. Often, when a loud bang or holiday fireworks erupted in the neighborhood at night, Hughes would jump out of bed and kneel, as if preparing to shoot his BAR. This would later be diagnosed as post-traumatic stress disorder (PTSD). Whenever this happened, Eva would console him until he could return to bed.[47]

When the job at the creamery proved insufficient to cover his family's expenses, Hughes took a job with a small, independent trucking firm run by Gordon Hinrichs in Ida Grove. Hinrichs contracted with farmers and grain elevators to haul grain and livestock to market, as well as transporting farm machinery to customers throughout the Midwest. This launched Hughes's career in the trucking industry. After a brief training period behind the wheel, he was hauling goods around the country. Prior to one trip to Sioux City, Hinrichs warned Hughes that, in order to pass under a viaduct on the route, he would need to stop and let some air out of the tires for clearance. Driving a truck loaded with steel girders, Hughes did that and cleared the overpass. On the way back, however, Hughes crashed the top of the trailer into the bridge, wrecking it. He had not figured that—without the load—the truck would be several inches higher. His new boss was forgiving, simply patting him on the back and saying, "Next time, look *both* ways."[48]

Hughes had attached himself to a growing enterprise. Hinrichs eventually expanded the livestock transportation business throughout the Midwest to include moving hogs from collection centers to packing plants and calves to regional feeders for fattening. Hughes also drove to Chicago once a week, taking cattle to the stockyard; for the return trip, he loaded the empty semitruck with goods needed in western Iowa, such as construction materials. The expanding business prompted Hinrichs to buy land outside Ida Grove for an office and a few livestock pens, and he added another semi, five livestock trailers, and five regular trucks. The firm was also selling and transporting fertilizer and feed.[49]

As Hinrichs's business grew, Hughes took on new tasks and assumed more responsibilities. He became increasingly involved with customers, which included making deals and signing contracts. This also meant more socializing—and drinking. Hughes contended that his drinking did not interfere with his work, but it impacted his marriage. He frequently came home drunk on Friday and Saturday nights, as well as some nights during the week. To avoid disturbing Eva and his daughters after a binge, Hughes would often sleep on the couch in his small office. From time to time, Hughes promised Eva he would give up drinking, and he would be successful for a while. But then a business meeting would call for a drink to celebrate and he would think, "What the hell. One drink won't hurt." This frequently led to Hughes drinking himself senseless and staying out all night.[50]

Hughes later wrote, "One of the reasons I avoided going home was that I discovered that Eva was afraid of me. I couldn't understand it until one night I saw the two little girls cowering behind a closet door. It was then that I realized how angry and belligerent I had become." Finally, Eva had had enough. After her husband indulged in yet another drinking binge, she contacted the Ida County Sanity Commission and had the sheriff serve papers on Hughes demanding that he show cause why he should not be committed to the state asylum as an inebriate.[51]

The subpoena, signed by Eva, shocked Hughes. With a lawyer at his side, he faced four members of the Ida County Sanity Commission, which included Arthur Johnson, a University of Iowa alumus and county Republican chairman who had helped Hughes get his scholarship. Johnson interrogated Hughes, asking whether his drinking had affected his job and his family life. Hughes replied that it had not. With his voice breaking, he said, "Art, if we can get this thing dropped, I promise; I won't take a drink for a year." Eva, who was present in the room, consulted with Johnson and agreed.[52]

Hughes and his wife eventually reconciled. One of the painful truths Eva told her husband was that the idea for the subpoena had originated with Harold's father, Lewis. The incident, no doubt, became common knowledge in the small town of Ida Grove, and perhaps this helped Hughes keep his word. He did not drink for fourteen months, taking his sobriety into late 1951. Then, while at a truckers' gathering in Ames, Hughes relapsed and woke up in a Des Moines hotel room two days later, with no memory of taking that first drink. But the telltale signs of vomit in the toilet and the stale taste in his mouth told Hughes that he had been on an alcoholic binge. Next to his bed was a nearly empty bottle of bourbon. He called home and begged for forgiveness, earning a reluctant pardon from his wife.[53]

The forgiveness was premature. Hughes soon returned to his old habits and often came home drunk. He later claimed that he was never physically violent, but his verbal abuse was intense, causing Eva to "cringe like a beaten kitten" and his two daughters to cry and huddle in fear. "By then," he later wrote, "I had decided that drinking was an inevitable part of my life and I no longer made claims about trying to stop. Anyone who tried to talk to me about it was curtly rejected for I would always tell them I could control it."[54]

He could not. His alcoholism was wrecking his life, and he knew it. He was having difficulty sleeping, and when he did sleep, he would have nightmares about the war and often woke up screaming. He continued to get arrested for drinking and fighting. "I was powerless to stop doing the one thing that caused it all," Hughes wrote. "It was as if a malignant force was whirling me toward a frightening precipice."[55]

That precipice emerged on a cold morning in January 1952 when Hughes left his Ida Grove home for a daylong meeting with other truckers in another town. He had promised Eva that he would be home in time for a dinner engagement with friends that evening. He was quite proud that he had not taken a drink in two weeks. As the business meeting concluded, someone suggested they go to the bar, and Hughes imposed a one-drink limit on himself. That did not happen. After downing glass after glass, Hughes realized it was eleven o'clock at night. In his drunken state, he jumped into his car and raced home, only to find the house abandoned. Eva had taken their daughters and fled to her mother's, a refuge she had used before to escape his drinking.[56]

Hughes descended into a dark despair as he wandered around his empty house. As he slowly sobered up, he could not escape his "horrible self-loathing" and felt "a sense of blackness closing in on me," asking himself, "What was the point of living?" As this deep melancholy seized his soul, Hughes later recalled that a "cold feeling of logic overcame me," and his thoughts turned to suicide. "The more I thought about the disorder in my life and the inability to control it, the more I wanted to end it." Hughes reached for his twelve-gauge, single-barrel Remington shotgun, loaded three shells into it, and pumped the chamber. To avoid the anticipated mess, he climbed into the bathtub, positioned the barrel in his mouth, and aimed the deadly weapon upward toward his brain. Then he hesitated. Tumbling out of the tub, he fell to his knees and prayed, sobbing and pleading with God. Eventually, Hughes recalled, a "warm peace seemed to settle deep within me, filling the terrible emptiness, driving out the self-hate and condemnation." He felt a bond with the divine and was filled with a joy "so intense it seemed to burst my breast." Driven by despair and hopelessness, he felt he had only two choices: suicide or a transformed, born-again life.[57]

Harold Hughes chose the latter.

2 | Business Success and Statewide Office

The morning after his near suicide, Hughes called his mother-in-law's home and begged Eva for forgiveness. He promised to reform and asked her to come home and bring the two children with her. Eva responded that he had better get to work. He did, and when he got home that evening, the family was there.[1]

Hughes had promised to change in the past, but this episode was different. With one significant exception, there is no evidence that Hughes ever took another alcoholic drink. He did not make this transition to sobriety entirely by himself, although his own determination was the primary force behind his reform. One person Hughes relied on was the new minister of the Methodist church in Ida Grove, Wayne Shoemaker. Hughes attended church with his family on a regular basis and got to know Reverend Shoemaker well. A Nebraska native about the same age as Hughes, Shoemaker counseled the recovering alcoholic during his struggle to give up drinking. "He was a man I could talk to, a man I could question and get answers," said Hughes. "He was understanding and tolerant."[2] The two men had a pact: Hughes would not drink alcohol, and Shoemaker agreed to give up coffee. For the rest of his life, Shoemaker drank only hot water in the morning, honoring his pledge to Hughes.[3]

Another person who helped Hughes was Russell Wilson, a student minister at the Ida Grove Church of God. Wilson noticed that alcoholism kept many male members from coming to church with their families, and he discussed the situation with Shoemaker, who told him to talk to Hughes for a firsthand understanding of the problem. He did, and during the four years Wilson served at the church, the two became fast friends. As Wilson noted, "I thought of him as a big brother." Wilson found serving a congregation emotionally challenging, and he used Hughes as a sounding board; Hughes, in turn, shared his burdens with the young ministry student. "We spent long evenings in his kitchen or mine," Wilson recalled, "drinking coffee and talking alcoholism and religion."[4]

Hughes had one setback that would later impact his political career. After two years of sobriety, he went on what he later called "an errand of mercy" to help a close family friend. Jack, who had a drinking problem, had left his family and was living in Kissimmee, Florida. In 1954 Hughes drove to Florida to try to convince Jack to return to his family. While the two men were eating at a local café, Jack ordered drinks for them. Hughes, not wanting to alienate his friend by refusing the drink and feeling "the need to relate to him," thought he would have "just one drink."[5] That was a mistake. As Hughes should have known from experience, once alcohol touched his lips, he lost control. Hours later, Hughes's car was resting on railroad tracks somewhere in rural Florida, and he and Jack were thrown in jail.

The next morning, Hughes learned that he and Jack would have to wait several days until the judge arrived to hear their case. He opted to pay $125 bond for the two of them and then forfeited the bond by driving home to Iowa with his friend. Four months later, he received a notice from the Florida Public Safety Commission that his driver's license—a necessity if he hoped to continue making a living as a truck driver—had been revoked for driving while intoxicated. He contacted the Iowa Motor Truck Association and, through the Iowa Safety Commission, converted the revocation to a sixty-day suspension from the date of his arrest. Since the sixty days had already passed, he applied for a new license and received one. The arrest, however, remained on the books in Florida. Hughes had initially hoped to hide the incident from Eva, but he told her the truth when he needed to renew his license. Sensing that he had sincerely changed this time, she forgave him again.[6]

In addition to Shoemaker and Wilson, Hughes was helped by Alcoholics Anonymous (AA), a mutual aid fellowship of alcoholics dedicated to sobriety. Once his own struggles with alcoholism became well known in the community, Hughes was often asked to help fellow alcoholics, and he responded to these pleas for the rest of his life. Shortly after the Florida incident, Hughes encountered a high school friend whose drinking jeopardized both his job and his family. Initially hesitant to offer assistance—especially after the disastrous consequences in Florida—Hughes finally talked with his friend and suggested that the two of them attend an AA meeting in nearby Storm Lake. That night, Hughes met many of the men he had gotten drunk with in the past—now sober and healthy looking. That gathering was just one of countless other meetings around the nation where alcoholics shared their problems and challenges with one another. Impressed by the experience, Hughes and his friend attended a second meeting the following week. Although AA meetings did not become a regular part of Hughes's recovery at this time, he would eventually make it a practice to attend meetings in different cities.[7]

Hughes's involvement in Hinrichs's business was expanding, and he was now managing much of the company's trucking and livestock operations. He was also becoming more aware of industry issues, particularly the setting of trucking rates. Hughes knew that some independent truckers were slashing their rates below standard levels, undercutting their competitors to get more jobs. The Iowa State Commerce Commission—headed by a three-member elected board—was responsible for maintaining industry-wide rates, but it was extremely lax at enforcing them. After hearing Hughes complain about the unfairness of this practice, Hinrichs suggested that he get involved with the Iowa Motor Truck Association, composed of corporate fleet owners and independent truckers. Hinrichs was a director of the association, and Hughes became a prominent speaker at its meetings, calling for reform. For the first time, the future politician began to polish his considerable rhetorical abilities, although his speaking style was often crude and vulgar when talking to his fellow truckers.[8]

Talking was not enough for Hughes, however. Because so many independent truckers cut their rates to attract more business in an effort to keep up with the insurance and loan payments on their trucks, overall rates suffered, and some truckers simply could not stay in business. In an act that would later define his leadership style, Hughes called a meeting of independent truckers in and around Ida County. Working with a local inspector from the Iowa State Commerce Commission, Hughes gathered about fifty truckers who agreed to maintain standard rates to avoid undercutting one another.[9]

Hinrichs kept the Iowa Motor Truck Association informed of Hughes's activities. Impressed, the board offered Hughes a part-time job as an organizer, which he accepted, splitting his time between those activities and his job with Hinrichs. Soon, the position with the association expanded into a full-time effort, so Hughes left Hinrichs's company to work on tariff and trucker rates in eighteen counties in northwestern Iowa. One result of the new job was that Hughes's network of regional contacts expanded—connections that would later form part of his nascent political organization.[10]

While working for the Iowa Motor Truck Association, Hughes discovered that independent truckers had immense difficulty competing with the major trucking lines. These corporate organizations were larger and much better equipped to pay drivers higher rates. Hughes brooded over the unfairness, and in late 1955 he collected a list of names and addresses of independent truckers in western Iowa and mailed hundreds of postcards, inviting them to the Ida Grove Armory on a Saturday to discuss forming a group to represent their interests. To Hughes's surprise, nearly six hundred men showed up, along with two directors from the Iowa Motor Truck Association. As the discussion progressed throughout the day, there was plenty of arguing and shouting as tempers flared among the gruff truck-driving veterans. But at the end of the day, thanks to Hughes's leadership, the Iowa Better Trucking Bureau was created to fight for better terms for independent truckers. Hughes set up an office in Ida Grove, with himself as the bureau's full-time employee, earning $125 a week plus expenses for travel.[11]

Hughes's personal life was changing as well. In 1952 his third daughter, Phyllis, was born. Hughes also engaged in a short-lived flirtation with the ministry. At the suggestion of Reverend Shoemaker, Hughes spoke on "layman's Sunday" at the Ida Grove Methodist Church. "It was a critical experience for me," Hughes recalled. "I felt that many of the people in the congregation might view me as a sinner rather than someone who could speak of spiritual things."[12]

Hughes started taking correspondence courses through the Methodist Church's denominational headquarters, with the goal of becoming an accredited lay minister. Once he achieved that goal, he began studying for the full ministry via correspondence courses through Southern Methodist University. His trucking work, however, took precedence, and he eventually abandoned the effort. But his lay ministry work and preaching, combined with his frequent oratory before his fellow truckers, helped transform this awkward working-class man into a more polished and confident public speaker. Said Russell Wilson, "I had him preach in my church. The guy had this booming voice, but he'd get nervous and sweat like crazy and wipe his brow." Hughes used these opportunities to develop a stirring speaking style that would come to define his political career. The lay ministry also helped Hughes establish connections around Iowa when he filled in for vacationing Methodist ministers—contacts that would later prove valuable.[13]

"These were growing years for me, speaking, understanding, pursuing the Spirit, and things began to happen in my personal life," said Hughes. In addition to Shoemaker and Wilson, Hughes befriended Carl Sinning, a local Presbyterian minister, and all of them became lifelong friends. He often called on them later whenever he needed help in his various endeavors. "And as a result, all the years of my life in one way or another, we have been working on spiritual programs and social programs."[14]

Although he stayed sober throughout this period, it was a struggle for Hughes, and he realized he needed help from others. He later wrote, "I was really learning to live one day at a time." Recalling his favorable impression of the Storm Lake AA meeting, Hughes and others started a similar group in Ida Grove, holding regular meetings in the basement of the Better Trucking Bureau office. In addition, the group turned outward and offered advice to local physicians and ministers on how to treat those in need, based on their personal experiences.[15]

Hughes also faced challenges in his marriage. Eva suffered from mental illness, later described by daughter Phyllis as bipolar disorder. Sometime before Phyllis was born, Eva had a nervous breakdown and was admitted to a mental hospital in a nearby city. Facing shock treatments, she called her husband and demanded that he come get her. Against the advice of the institution, Hughes picked her up, carried her out of the hospital, and took her home to Ida Grove. After that, the family dealt with Eva's mental challenges on their own. She became pregnant with Phyllis while still suffering from psychological instability. Hughes considered having his mother care for the baby, but according to Phyllis, "When I was born, she snapped out of it and was more like her normal self."[16]

For the rest of her life, however, Eva continued to suffer bouts of mental illness. Recalls Phyllis, "She would have herself all whipped up in a frenzy. She would believe in conspiracies, crazy things, and we would have to keep her calm." Often major life changes would cause these episodes, such as Hughes's first year as governor in Des Moines and as senator in Washington, DC. But, for the most part, the family managed to keep Eva's struggles out of the public eye. "It was a deep, dark secret to be covered up," said Phyllis.[17]

Eventually, Hughes expanded the Iowa Better Trucking Bureau beyond its base in northwestern Iowa to encompass the rest of the state. Driving a new Ford car, Hughes traveled throughout Iowa with a list of independent operators, going from town to town and talking to trucker after trucker, building the organization until it eventually had more than fifteen hundred members. By binding these independent truckers into a group, Hughes was able to initiate insurance programs they could not have afforded individually. While on his travels, he connected with AA members in towns throughout the Hawkeye State, building connections and expanding his personal network. "He didn't intend that, but it gave him a political base," said Russell Wilson.[18]

Despite this extensive work, Hughes and his allies still faced an uphill battle against the larger trucking firms, which could offer lower rates. One obstacle was the Iowa State Commerce Commission. Although it was charged with regulating carrier rates through a statewide network of inspectors, the commission's board often sided with the corporate firms, and even when decisions favored the smaller truckers, the rulings were not always enforced. Also, there were rumors that some commissioners and inspectors were taking under-the-table bribes for decisions that favored the bigger truckers. This infuriated Hughes, who felt he could do little in the face of this corruption.[19]

Frustrated and with nowhere else to turn, Hughes decided to take his case to Iowa governor Herschel Loveless in Des Moines. The governor, thought Hughes, seemed like a person who would be sympathetic to the needs of the independent truckers. Only the third Democrat to be elected Iowa's governor in the twentieth century, Loveless had launched his political career as mayor of Ottumwa in southeastern Iowa. First elected governor in 1956, he benefited from significant support by labor, which had grown more politically active in postwar Iowa, and an increasingly sophisticated Democratic Party organization, especially in centrally located Polk County. Both factors reflected the state's growing urbanization. In many ways, Loveless shared personal characteristics with Hughes. Born to the working class, the governor had no formal education beyond high school and had worked in the railroad and meatpacking industries. As a politician, he was not known as a particularly good speaker, but compensated with his energy and aggressiveness.[20]

Hughes connected with the governor's office through a friend and got an appointment with Loveless. Face-to-face with the governor, Hughes poured out his complaints, primarily about the unfairness and corruption of the Commerce Commission. But the governor was not the most important person Harold Hughes met that day. It was his aide.[21]

Park Rinard, Governor Loveless's executive assistant, sat in on this important meeting, gently puffing his pipe and, from time to time, asking a question of the rough-hewn truck driver from Ida Grove. No doubt, he was sizing Hughes up, and he became more impressed as the raw western Iowan made a forceful case for honesty and fairness on behalf of his fellow truckers. This first meeting between the two would blossom into a bond that changed both their lives. Hughes later said of Rinard, "If there was any one person in the world who had an impact on my life it was Park Rinard."[22]

The contrast between the two men, however, could not have been starker. Born in 1912 in Thompson Falls, Montana, Rinard was raised in Mason City, Iowa, and graduated from the University of Iowa with an English degree during the Great Depression. He later earned a master's degree in creative writing there. These degrees would serve him well as he developed his polished, graceful speechwriting style. Rinard befriended local artist Grant Wood, who lived down the street and had risen to prominence with his painting *American Gothic* a few years earlier. The two often spent time together, in Rinard's words, "talking about life and art and one thing or another." By 1935, Rinard was working for Wood in Iowa City as a general secretary, helping with the artist's business affairs. This lasted until Wood's death in 1942 of liver cancer. After World War II, Rinard returned to Mason City, started his own construction business, and became involved in Democratic politics in the otherwise Republican stronghold.[23]

Rinard's liberal political ideology was shaped by his father's support of Theodore Roosevelt's Bull Moose Progressive Party earlier in the century and by President Franklin Roosevelt's New Deal reforms. Rinard saw many of these progressive traits in Loveless during his campaign for governor in 1956; the two met in Mason City, and Rinard impressed the candidate. Once in office, Loveless's single assistant was overwhelmed by paperwork and needed someone to answer mail and write speeches, so the governor invited Rinard to join his staff. By the time he met Hughes, Rinard had begun to establish himself as a powerful force for progressive change in Iowa politics. A quiet, thoughtful man, Rinard nevertheless possessed an inner toughness that prepared him well for bare-knuckled political battles.[24]

In the governor's office that day, Rinard no doubt saw a forceful yet untamed natural leader, later saying that Hughes "looked like a porpoise in a fishbowl" as the giant of a man poured out his complaints against "the goddamn big truckers." Hughes's friend Vance Bourjaily of the University of Iowa Writers Workshop noted, "Quite simply, Harold Hughes is an overpowering man." Describing Hughes's organic magnetism, Bourjaily continued, "Harold Hughes has more of it than any man I've ever met," and "I sometimes wonder if he realizes the strength of his own magnetism." Certainly, Rinard recognized the truck driver's unmolded potential.[25]

During the meeting, Hughes mentioned that he was a Republican. As Rinard listened to Hughes and dissected his political thinking, he concluded that the man talked like a Democrat and asked why he was a Republican. Hughes simply laughed and said, "I grew up a Republican. I don't know any Democrats in Ida Grove." The meeting concluded, and little had been resolved. But at least Hughes had expressed his complaints to someone of influence who was willing to listen. After the meeting, Loveless told Rinard to look out for Hughes—which he did.[26]

Rinard's comment about political parties planted a seed in Hughes's mind. Up to that point, he had been a lifelong Republican, campaigning for local Republican candidates and even going to the state Republican convention representing Ida County. However, at the convention in Des Moines, Hughes's credentials had somehow been misplaced, and he was not allowed to sit on the floor; instead, he was forced to view the convention from the balcony, which left him furious and fuming—an affront that stirred a passion to leave the party.[27]

Still another push toward the Democrats came during Hughes's second contact with Loveless a month after the Des Moines meeting. During a festival in Spirit Lake in northwestern Iowa, Loveless took Hughes aside and suggested that he run for one of the two commerce commissioner seats open in 1958, a year and a half away. "If you're really concerned about the truckers," the governor said, "why don't you consider running for one of the seats on the Commission?" Then he added, "You might want to consider changing parties, too."[28]

During the drive home from the festival, Hughes thought long and hard about the governor's suggestion. He had no idea what a campaign would cost, but he certainly knew he could not afford to pay for it himself, given that he and his family were living paycheck to paycheck. He would have to raise money, a task that was foreign to him. And if he ran, his work for the trucking association would suffer, along with the growing insurance business he was developing. Also, running as a Democrat in an overwhelmingly Republican state like Iowa could be a quixotic mission. Another consideration was his past; his alcoholism could be an issue with voters, and there was a risk that a high-pressure statewide campaign might cause him to drink again. When he got home that evening, he talked it over with Eva, and they agreed to sleep on it. Slumber did not come easy to Hughes that night. By morning, however, the couple agreed that he would run.[29] As Hughes later explained:

> I felt there was a strong purpose in running even though victory wasn't assured. The running itself serves a good purpose. It helps to increase the public discussion, the debate, on the critical issues and the needs of our time. . . . In the final analysis, I had to accept the fact that we were running against the odds that were overwhelming and the possibility of winning was quite remote. We lived with that reality constantly and that every step of the way was uphill. I had to do it.[30]

Hughes next talked with Edith Hansmann Julius, a local teacher and chair of the Ida County Democrats—a somewhat lonely position—to test the waters and see whether the party was interested in him. In a conversation on her porch, she candidly revealed what many had already seen in Hughes and many more would acknowledge in the future: he had a natural gift for leadership. That talent, she argued, could compel Iowans to rally around him. As Hughes later wrote, "It was all I needed." He raced to the Ida County courthouse to change his party registration to Democrat—to the wide-eyed astonishment of the county clerk.[31] This small action led to a dramatic change in Iowa politics that would ripple through the state and the nation for decades.

The upstart Hughes was hardly the first choice of establishment Democrats. Soon after he declared his candidacy for commerce commissioner, old-line Democrats lined up a candidate of their own, and a third joined the race to make it a three-way primary. The party's candidate, Bernard Martin of Des Moines, had a formidable resumé that included a background in both trucking and railroads. He had worked for the Minneapolis and St. Louis Railroad and the Rock Island Railroad, as well as the Western Weighing and Inspection Bureau. Martin was also terminal manager and traffic manager for Brady, Bruce, and Merchants Motor Freight Lines.[32]

Hughes's campaign, however, was fueled by a network of his own creation. In addition to support from Loveless, he had an array of trucking association supporters who formed a strong and enthusiastic organization. They made cash contributions and, perhaps more importantly, placed "Hughes for Commerce Commissioner" signs in strategic locations along Iowa's roads and highways where motorists could easily see them. In addition, Hughes relied on a network of AA members he was acquainted with; his connections through membership in the American Legion, Masons, and Abu Bekr Shrine; and contacts through his lay ministry work at Methodist churches throughout the state.[33]

This proved to be enough. In the 1958 Democratic primary, Hughes collected 50,502 votes as the leading commerce commissioner candidate; Martin finished second with 44,875. In the general election, the pair faced off against the two Republican incumbents, Dave Long and John Ropes, for the two open posts.[34]

The general election was an entirely new experience for the novice candidate. Hughes canvassed the state, giving speeches to large audiences and small as he developed the unique speaking style that would serve him so well. On a hot day in August, he was asked to stand in as a surrogate for Loveless, who was running for reelection, in Lyon County in the northwestern corner of the state. Loveless's opponent, Republican Bill Murray, a professor of history and economics at Iowa State University, made a standard speech and received enthusiastic applause from the audience. When Hughes started to speak, few showed any interest, and crowd members drifted away, talking among themselves. But Hughes's solemn, deep baritone brought them back to the podium, especially when he began to talk about poor people who could not help themselves and those suffering from "neglect and indifference." The gathering quieted down and paid attention. An orator was born.[35]

He took his unique speaking style to all corners of the state, impressing people wherever he appeared. Building on his experience in front of both church congregations and truckers, he could command any stage. John Culver, who later served as an Iowa congressman and senator, said, "There was an awesome power behind Harold Hughes. He could make the telephone book sound like Shakespeare."[36]

Hughes also applied his personal touch to a new medium that was becoming increasingly important: television. His campaign scraped together enough money to buy two live fifteen-minute broadcasts where

Hughes looked into the camera and spoke spontaneously. He recalled that he "managed to pull through with no grievous errors."[37]

On election night, watching from his Ida Grove home, Hughes celebrated his win. He received the most votes among the four candidates running for commissioner—407,193. Martin finished second with 399,896, giving the two Democrats the majority on the three-member commission. Loveless had invited Hughes to a victory party in Des Moines, but that would have meant renting a hotel room, something Hughes could not afford.[38]

Hughes was now a state official with a steady income, but money was still tight for the family. He had gone into debt to create the trucking association and insurance business. With his election to the Commerce Commission, Hughes suddenly found himself in direct conflict with these businesses, and he was forced to sell his interest in them—as he later put it, "everything that I had built my life on to that point"—to take a state job that paid $7,200 a year. Hughes sold his house in Ida Grove and managed to pull together $1,500 and buy a house in the western part of Des Moines, after renting a home in the capital city for the first six months of his tenure as commissioner.[39]

As he began his political career, Harold Hughes found himself overseeing the commerce of a state that was changing dramatically at midcentury.

3 | Running for Governor

Harold Hughes's job as commerce commissioner became an advanced course on the economy of Iowa. Through hearings, discussions with business and political leaders, contacts with farmers, and economic reports, the former truck driver immersed himself in the multifaceted fabric of the state, gaining insight into how Iowa functioned commercially and politically. What he found was a state in transition—economically, politically, and demographically—although these changes were not moving at the same speed.[1]

Iowa had long been an agricultural state, but this was shifting dramatically in the postwar years. Iowa's population was moving from rural to urban areas. At the dawn of the twentieth century, about one-fourth of Iowa's population lived in towns of twenty-five hundred or more, defined by the US census as "urban." In 1940, based on this definition, Iowa's urban population had grown to 40 percent. The 1960 census showed that, for the first time in the state's history, more Iowans were living in urban areas than rural. This was part of a larger transition in the post–World War II Midwest that saw people moving to cities—both large and small—attracted by jobs created by the growth of industry.[2]

While the promise of jobs was a powerful incentive to some rural residents, another cause of this urban shift was farming technology itself—advanced machinery, improved pesticides and fertilizers, enhanced plant and animal genetics, better agronomic practices and livestock management, and modern transportation. This agricultural revolution—begun in the late nineteenth century and accelerating after World War II—dramatically increased farmer efficiency and allowed individual producers to expand their farming operations over more acres. Federal and state support through land-grant universities and research stations offered farmers improved production techniques through local extension outreach. Farmers also benefited from federal government aid in the form of direct payments, loan deficiency disbursements, and commodity purchase programs that varied in type and level of success. Federal crop insurance programs and disaster relief protected farmers from occasional crop damage or loss. In short, Iowa needed fewer farmers to produce the bounty on its land, and many sons and daughters of farmers chose to move to the city.[3]

This trend was intensified by higher wages and better working conditions in urban occupations. Between 1939 and 1947 the number of Iowans involved in manufacturing increased by 59 percent. By 1949, Iowa's gross industrial product matched the revenue produced by agricultural goods. A decade later, the industrial output in Iowa exceeded that of farming by a ratio of 2.5 to 1. Although agriculture was still a significant industry and would remain so, manufacturing and nonfarm businesses in Harold Hughes's Iowa were growing by leaps and bounds. In particular, meatpacking operations and farm machinery manufacturers—part of the "agro-industrialization" that characterized Iowa's commerce—blossomed and expanded in all corners of the state.[4]

Iowa was part of an industrial boom in the Midwest that began with World War II and continued through the next several decades, even in rural areas. From 1947 to 1972 the number of manufacturing establishments in Iowa increased from 2,965 to 3,388, the number of businesses with one hundred or more employees grew from 241 to 393, and the average number of production workers increased from 112,490 to 157,000. According to historian Wilson Warren, postwar industrial growth in rural midwestern counties outpaced that in neighboring urban counties. This expansion was aided by lower labor costs, improved transportation access, increased government incentives, and new sources of workers. The industrial boom also led to the growth of urban areas throughout the state. Des Moines, Iowa's capital city in centrally located Polk County, was the largest municipality in the state, but significant business operations were widely distributed among Iowa's fifteen largest cities, which accounted for half the state's population.[5]

The increased urbanization of Iowa contributed to a shift in its political makeup. Changes in political alignments and electoral coalitions were nothing new to the Hawkeye State. In fact, they had been part of the state's history since its inception. At statehood in 1846, Iowa politics was dominated by the Democratic Party, ideologically bent toward limited government, low taxes, and opposition to banks, which mirrored Democratic president Andrew Jackson's belief that banks were elite institutions that exerted undue economic control over the average citizen. The party's strength was bolstered by an early surge of immigrants from the American South, where Jackson's ideology flourished. In opposition were the minority Whigs, who supported banks to aid economic growth and more aggressive government investment in the economy. Consequently, the ideology of the Democratic Party dominated the convention that wrote Iowa's first constitution at statehood, which included a clause outlawing banks. The first two Iowa governors—Ansel Briggs and Stephen Hempstead—were both Democrats.[6]

The tumultuous decade of the 1850s dramatically changed American politics. The debate over slavery and other issues destroyed the Whig Party, but from its ashes rose the Republican Party, fusing the Whigs' business orientation with abolitionism, temperance, and other political movements. In Iowa, this Republican coalition came together under the leadership of charismatic James Grimes, a New Hampshire native who had arrived in Iowa in 1836 and pursued careers in farming, business, banking, law, and finally politics. Elected as a Whig in 1854, Grimes became Iowa's third governor, and he combined his immense energy with shrewd political tact. Shortly after becoming governor, he and his allies benefited from the dramatic influx of people from areas to the east and overseas, forming the Republican Party base and outpolling the Democrats. Grimes's leadership cemented the Republican alliance with Iowa business and agricultural constituencies, creating a powerful political partnership that dominated the state for most of the next century. Grimes also led the political battle in 1857 to rewrite and pass by popular vote Iowa's second constitution, which still governs the state today. This document removed the prohibition against banks, freeing the state's financial institutions to more aggressively seek economic investment. For these reasons, Grimes stands as one of the more impactful and significant governors in Iowa history.[7]

Republicans continued to dominate Iowa politics for the rest of the nineteenth century, generally offering conservative, safe governance during the Gilded Age. One exception was William Larrabee, a Republican governor in the late 1880s who led a surprisingly progressive—and successful—effort to regulate railroad abuses in Iowa. Only one Democrat was elected governor of Iowa between 1854 and 1932—Horace Boies of Waterloo, a former Republican who split with his party over its support for prohibition.[8]

Lording over Iowa politics during this period was US senator William Boyd Allison of Dubuque. Elected to the Senate in 1873, he served until his death in 1908. A conservative who was open to compromise, Allison became one of the more powerful politicians in Washington, DC, through his leadership on the Senate Appropriations and Finance

Committees, shaping both federal spending and taxation. In Iowa, politicians looked to him for leadership and advice. Allison led an Iowa delegation in Washington that included David Henderson, also of Dubuque, who became Speaker of the House, and several other congressmen who headed influential committees. Iowa at this time had eleven representatives in Washington, and because Iowa Republicans faced little opposition in their reelection bids, the congressional seniority system rewarded them with powerful committee posts. It was said that anyone who wanted something from the federal government simply had to "Ask Iowa."[9]

On the state level, political clashes generally emerged not between Republicans and Democrats but within the Iowa Republican Party itself. By the early twentieth century, the party had split into two ideological factions—progressives and standpatters—over the role of government and the need for reform. Progressives, led by Albert Baird Cummins of Des Moines, believed in more activist government, regulation to curb abusive business practices, open party primaries, and the direct election of senators, among other issues. Standpatters, led by Senator Allison, generally opposed these reforms.[10]

A wealthy corporate attorney who attained fame as counsel in a suit against a barbed wire monopoly, Cummins was consumed by political ambition but ran into opposition from the Iowa Republican establishment. Several times he tried and failed to get elected to the US Senate (at the time, senators were elected by state legislators). Turning directly to Iowa voters, Cummins won the governorship in 1901 as a Republican and was reelected twice. His time as governor ignited one of the more explosive eras of legislative reform in Iowa history. Cummins and his legislative allies worked to curb abusive business practices and make corporate actions more transparent. Their efforts included reforms in railroad regulation, food and drug safety, child labor, grain elevator operations, and insurance. The latter established Iowa as a magnet for insurance companies wanting to do business in a trustworthy state and made Des Moines one of America's insurance capitals. Cummins and the Iowa progressives also established a statewide primary, allowing people to vote directly for their party's candidates rather than their being selected by party leaders. Like Grimes, Cummins stands out as one of Iowa's more important governors. With Allison's death in 1908, Cummins finally won the US Senate seat he had long sought and served until his own death in 1926.[11]

Despite their internal squabbles, Republicans continued to dominate Iowa politics through the first third of the twentieth century, electing governors, holding majorities in the General Assembly in Des Moines, and, for the most part, sending GOP members of Congress to Washington, DC. The most colorful political character during this time was Senator Smith Wildman Brookhart, a fiery prairie populist who defied the Republican establishment by gaining popular support in primary contests. He formed links with Iowa's small farmers in the 1920s by supporting federal efforts to subsidize farm income, seen as a radical effort by some. Brookhart was finally defeated in the 1932 Senate primary by a more conservative Republican.[12]

The Great Depression of the 1930s brought an end to Republican dominance in Iowa. In the 1932 election, Iowans reacted to a decade of low farm prices and high unemployment by removing GOP members from office. They elected Democrats Clyde Herring of Des Moines as governor and Louis Murphy of Dubuque as US senator, while Democratic presidential candidate Franklin Roosevelt carried the state over native son Herbert Hoover. Democrats also gained majorities in the Iowa house and senate. This trend continued as Roosevelt carried the state again in 1936 and Democrats won three straight governor and US Senate races during the 1930s. By the end of the decade, however, Iowans turned back to their Republican roots and, with some exceptions, elected GOP politicians to state and national offices.[13]

By the mid-1950s, the state's growing urbanization had created constituencies that were supportive of Democrats who offered city residents more government services. One early indication of this shift was Democrat Harry Truman's surprise win in Iowa in the 1948 presidential election; the tenacious campaigner took Iowa by combining urban support with farmers' concern that Republicans would discontinue popular farm programs. Likewise, Democrat Herschel Loveless of Ottumwa used a tireless campaign style to propel himself into the governor's office in 1956, defeating incumbent Republican Leo Hoegh despite Republican Dwight Eisenhower's handy win in the presidential race. A major factor in Loveless's win—and his reelection two years later—was the rise of labor unions in Iowa, reflecting the state's growing urbanization. Union leaders had turned to the Democratic Party in the hope that it would support favorable legislation for their membership, such as repeal of the right-to-work law. They simply had no confidence that the Republican Party could achieve these goals, given its strong links to business through the Iowa Manufacturers Association (IMA). The 1956 merger of the American Federation of Labor (AFL) and Congress of Industrial Organizations (CIO) created a more politically united labor movement at the state and local levels. Especially important to Loveless's victory were counties with strong union populations such as Black Hawk (home of John Deere and Rath Packing) and Wapello (home of John Morrell and Company).[14]

Another significant factor in Loveless's success was factionalism within the Iowa Republican Party, caused largely by controversial positions taken by Governor Hoegh. Both as Iowa attorney general and as governor, Hoegh strongly opposed "liquor by the drink," an issue that was gaining support among Iowans. Also, he courted organized labor by supporting pro-union legislation, flying in the face of opposition from the IMA. He further irritated Republican legislators by publicizing the votes of those he accused of failing to support the Republican platform. Finally, Hoegh signed a bill containing an unpopular sales tax increase—from 2 to 2.5 percent—and then campaigned against it. Loveless jumped on the tax increase and Republican divisions to win the governorship in 1956 and reelection in 1958.[15]

Iowa political writer Frank Nye wrote of Loveless's victory in 1956, "Something different was in the Iowa political wind." According to scholar Thomas Ryan, "Herschel Loveless's triumphs in 1956 and 1958 contributed significantly to a subsequent realignment of the Iowa electorate." He argues that Loveless captured a larger percentage of the vote than all but two previous Democratic gubernatorial candidates since the mid-1880s; the exceptions came in 1932 and 1934, and these Democratic wins were largely attributed to voter anxiety about the Great Depression. Unlike the wins by Democrat Horace Boies in 1889 and 1891 and their triumphs in the 1930s, Democrats in the 1950s and 1960s continued to enjoy success. From 1956 to 1966 Democrats won five of six gubernatorial races. Indeed, the Iowa political landscape was changing.[16]

Another change was taking place in the mid-1950s in Polk County, Iowa's most populous. Several young Des Moines attorneys—Wade Clarke, Lex Hawkins, and Neal Smith, among others—revived the county's Democratic Party from its decades-long languor and, through deft political organizing, house-to-house campaigning, and plain hard work, dramatically increased Democratic voter registration. One constituency they recruited was returning World War II veterans, who had lived through depression and war under Democratic leadership and were willing to break with Republican family tradition. In 1954 their efforts culminated in a Democratic takeover of the Polk County Board of Supervisors and all the administrative offices and legislative seats in the county.[17]

Hawkins was a particularly significant figure in this movement. A charismatic individual who could, in the words of historian James Larew, "create the heroic from the mundane," Hawkins brought excitement to party meetings. He stirred enthusiasm and made party members feel important, and he brought crowds to their feet when applauding members' accomplishments. In 1958 Hawkins played a key role in replacing longtime state Democratic Party chairman Jake More with the more activist Dick "Duke" Norberg. More represented the old-fashioned, slumbering Democratic Party that more active players like Hawkins wanted to push out of the way. Two years later, Hawkins himself took over as state Democratic chair.[18]

This network of party activists expanded their reach beyond Polk and into neighboring counties. One sign of their success was Neal Smith's election to Congress in 1958, where he would serve his central Iowa congressional district for thirty-four years. Three other Democrats— Leonard Wolf, Stephen Carter, and Melwin Coad—were also elected to Congress that year, making up half of Iowa's eight-member congressional delegation. One reason for the Iowa Democrats' success that year was the widespread unpopularity of Republican secretary of agriculture Ezra Taft Benson and his restrictive federal policies. However, unlike Smith, these three were defeated when running for reelection in 1960. Still, Democrats had proved that they could turn out the vote, and Iowa's days as a single-party state were coming to an end.[19]

This was what the political world looked like when Harold Hughes assumed his post on the Commerce Commission. He later wrote that he believed he had been successful in his mission. "Through it all, we did get transportation rates under control and hired honest and qualified inspectors to enforce regulations." According to Nick Kotz and James Risser, who covered Hughes for the *Des Moines Register*, "He did a fair job of ending discrimination against the small truckers and stopped, by his mere hulking presence, the most obvious political corruption on the Commerce Commission."[20]

Hughes attended AA meetings regularly in Des Moines, making no effort to hide the fact that he was a recovered alcoholic. One evening, seven-year-old Phyllis asked her father, "Daddy, why are you going to these meetings? You never drank." Hughes's jaw dropped, and he did not know how to respond. Finally, he explained that he had had a drinking problem before she was old enough to remember. At the meeting that evening, Hughes related this story to his fellow AA members. Her question, said the proud father, showed how far he had come.[21]

As 1960 approached, Hughes's ambitions grew. The Commerce Commission post was a four-year term, so he was not running for re-election that year. Most other state executive posts consisted of two-year terms, including the governorship. Loveless decided to forgo another term as governor and run for US Senate instead, leaving the Democratic gubernatorial nomination open. Lieutenant Governor Edward "Nick" McManus of Keokuk declared his candidacy and was the odds-on favorite to win the Democratic nomination. But as Hughes evaluated McManus and the overall direction of state government, he concluded that the Hawkeye State needed a more aggressive, positive force that could modernize Iowa. The United States was coming out of a recession in the late 1950s, and other midwestern states were "moving forward," in Hughes's words, but Iowa was not. Hughes believed that Iowa's political leadership was failing to meet the needs of a more urbanized economy, operating within an antiquated system of state government that hindered rather than helped attract new businesses and new opportunities to the state. According to Hughes, Iowa needed someone to shake off the cobwebs of decades-long inaction and stir the political pot. Many saw McManus as part of the older, more established wing of the Democratic Party and thought he was not the right person to move the state in this positive direction. As Hughes discussed his views with others, a run for governor became more of a reality.[22]

Other Democrats agreed that Hughes could be an asset at the top of the ticket in 1960. Loveless saw Hughes as a worthy successor and supported him behind the scenes, as did Democratic state chairman Norberg. With this backing, Hughes declared himself a candidate.[23]

Hughes's decision to plunge into the primary for governor did not sit well with all the party faithful, partly because he had been a Republican only two years earlier. He explained that he was "a Democrat by principle, not by accident of birth." He rejected the idea of the party as a "snobbish club requiring a pedigree for membership" and added, "I believe that a great deal of the present strength of the Democratic party in Iowa comes from people like me." In other words, the party needed Republican converts if it hoped to win in Iowa. Undeterred, Hughes traversed the state and, in his words, "tried to attend every county dinner I could." His opponent McManus stressed his long membership in the Democratic Party, reminding people that he was a lifelong Democrat and had gone to his first Democratic convention as a four-year-old. But Hughes was making progress. Bill Sueppel, a young attorney in Iowa City, attended a rally where he heard Hughes speak. Afterward, he commented to his wife, "I don't think he's going to win, but I think we've just seen a future leader in Iowa politics."[24]

McManus defeated Hughes in the June 6, 1960, primary by a vote of 74,990 to 46,542, only to lose in the general election in November. The vote showed, however, that the former trucker could attract significant support. When Iowa Democrats held their state convention later that summer, Hughes addressed party members as commerce commissioner. He was becoming an impressive orator, taking advantage of his direct speaking style and deep voice. In the speech, he brought up the issues he had raised during the campaign, challenging the party to be more aggressive in addressing the needs of the modern state and stressing—as he would for the rest of his political life—the obligation to care for the young, old, sick, and poor. He was greeted with a thunderous ovation. This assembly of Democratic loyalists was impressed, and Hughes had established himself as a significant force in the party.[25]

As 1962 approached, several Democrats in northwestern Iowa urged Hughes to run for Congress, but national office did not interest him. However, the attention got him thinking about another run for governor. By this time, he had developed a close relationship with Park Rinard, who was now executive director of the Iowa League of Municipalities. That group represented Iowa cities on the state level, and its outlook was in sync with Hughes's views on modernizing Iowa government. The pair spent several evenings in Hughes's living room talking about the possibility of his candidacy. Rinard pledged to help Hughes "in any way I can," which translated to political consultation, speechwriting, and acting as a policy sounding board, duties he would perform for the rest of Hughes's political career.[26]

In the spring of 1962 Hughes declared his candidacy for governor. Soon he would be presented with an issue that dominated the race.

On Sunday, May 6, 1962, the front page of the state's largest newspaper, the *Des Moines Sunday Register*, blared with the headline "'Liquor by Drink' in 2/3 of Iowa!" The story, written by veteran journalist George Mills (assisted by a staff of investigative reporters), described widespread violation of the law against serving liquor by the glass over the counter in Iowa. Investigators found that "sale of liquor by the drink has been more or less commonplace in even small towns." Reporters uncovered illegal liquor sales in sixty-six of Iowa's ninety-nine counties and discovered that local law enforcement officials often looked the other way because many citizens either opposed the law or did not care. Wrote one reporter, "All you need is the money, and courage enough to walk into a club and ask for bourbon, after telling the bartender you are sick of beer [which was exempt from the law]."[27]

The sale of liquor and its prohibition have a long and colorful history in Iowa, and the liquor-by-the-drink issue was only the latest in a lively legal debate that involved ethnic identity, religion, and freedom of choice. Iowans had toyed with prohibition on and off in the nineteenth and early twentieth centuries, always facing the challenge of how to enforce a law that many simply disregarded. After national Prohibition's repeal in 1933, Iowans decided to allow liquor sales in the state, but only in bottles sold through a state-operated liquor monopoly. No liquor could be served in glasses over the counter or "by the drink." Only beer, limited to 3.2 percent alcohol, could be served by the glass in taverns.[28]

Iowa politicians debated whether to legalize liquor by the drink in the 1950s but refused to change the law. In 1961 a bill in the Iowa house was soundly defeated by a vote of 72 to 22, despite popular support for the effort to legalize liquor sales. A *Des Moines Register* poll in May 1962 showed that 55 percent of Iowans supported allowing liquor by the drink, with 37 percent opposed. The same poll showed 62 percent of "city" residents and 52 percent of "town" residents favored a change in the law, but only 42 percent of "farm" residents responded positively.[29]

This urban-rural divide explained why the issue had gotten nowhere politically. The stalemate stemmed from the rural bias of the Iowa legislature, where representation in the house was based on geography, and urban voters were dramatically underrepresented in the senate. With rural citizens generally opposed to liquor by the drink, the legislature refused to act. (See chapter 4 for an explanation of rural domination in the Iowa legislature.)[30]

Given the *Register*'s exposure of widespread violation of the law and support for reform among the majority of Iowans, backing liquor by the drink seemed a ready-made issue for a candidate like Harold Hughes. However, there were two reasons for Hughes to be hesitant. One was the reality of resistance within the rural-based Iowa legislature and the uphill battle required to pass legislation. The other was Hughes's alcoholism. He made no effort to hide his past, and when asked about it, he replied that he had overcome the demon and had not had a drink in nearly a decade. Still, to some people, a recovered alcoholic advocating the sale of alcohol would seem like the peak of hypocrisy and the very reason why liquor sales should be limited. Among Hughes's political advisers, the consensus was that he should avoid taking a stand. Iowa politicians, they said, had been getting elected for years by gliding over the issue and merely promising to enforce the law as best they could. The topic was simply too hot to raise, they claimed.[31]

That, however, was not the way Harold Hughes operated. Soon after the *Register*'s exposé appeared, Hughes declared his support for legalizing liquor by the drink. He argued that looking the other way and accepting widespread violations showed disrespect for the concept of law itself. Other states, he said, sold liquor by the drink and managed to implement effective controls, and he expected that Iowa could do so as well. Indeed, all the states around Iowa allowed over-the-counter liquor sales. In addition, collecting taxes on drinks sold legally would add $10 million to state revenue.[32]

Taking on controversial issues and honestly expressing his thoughts had become a feature of Hughes's style. Many noted there was little difference between what Hughes said privately behind closed doors and what he said in public. Nick Kotz of the *Des Moines Register* covered Hughes during the 1962 campaign and often traveled with him across Iowa. He later said, "I was impressed with Hughes's straight-forward courage. He said what was on his mind." Said Sherwin Markman, a Des Moines attorney who knew Hughes well, "The man had no falsity in him at all."[33]

Although there were other issues facing Iowa's gubernatorial candidates in 1962, the liquor issue consumed most of the oxygen in the campaign. Virtually all Iowans had views on the subject, which they discussed with their neighbors, over the kitchen table, in their living rooms, and at work. The issue certainly did not hurt Hughes on his way to the Democratic nomination. Whereas he had been the underdog challenger in the 1960 Democratic primary, he was the favorite this time and overwhelmed his single primary opponent—Lewis E. Lint of Winterset, a Methodist minister and former Tax Commission secretary—winning by a vote of 66,624 to 17,770. Hughes then turned his efforts toward defeating the Republican incumbent, Norman Erbe of Boone.[34]

An Iowa native and World War II veteran, Erbe rose through the Republican ranks, serving as county Republican chairman prior to his election as state attorney general in 1956. In his second term as the state's chief lawyer, he sought to raise his profile by invoking an 1886 law and banning forty-two "girlie" magazines as obscene literature. The action had little effect on the magazines' availability, but the controversy and the ensuing publicity helped Erbe win a close GOP gubernatorial primary in 1960 and then beat McManus in the general election.[35]

On the liquor issue, Erbe felt constrained by the legislature and the Republican Party. The legislature makes the laws, he argued, not the governor. "I don't want to come out whole hog for this position or that if it doesn't materialize in the Legislature," he said. "There's no use doing this unless you know you have the votes." He saw the governor as an administrator who simply carries out the laws, noting that "it's impossible for the governor to impress his will if the Legislature or government departments don't want to follow." The 1962 Iowa Republican platform stated that the liquor issue should only be "studied," and Erbe refused to go further than that.[36]

This attitude was contrary to Hughes's concept of leadership. In his acceptance speech at the state Democratic convention held in July in Des Moines, Hughes called the liquor debate a moral issue of "official hypocrisy that shames the entire state." In his booming voice he declared that "every honest person in Iowa knows that we have liquor-by-the-drink in this state now." He defined the issue as follows: "Shall we straight-forwardly legalize the sale of liquor-by-the-drink, enforce the law and really control the liquor traffic in this state? Or shall we perpetuate the present wide-open key club system that subsidizes the bootleggers and racketeers with revenues that rightfully belong to the taxpayers of Iowa?"[37]

As the campaign moved into the fall, the conservative stance of no action seemed like a safe bet for Erbe. In the first *Register* poll released on October 7, Erbe led Hughes 49 to 42 percent. However, when Iowans were asked who would do the best job on "liquor," Hughes led 46 to 30 percent—an ominous sign for Erbe.[38]

An energized Hughes crusaded around the state, relying on his personal charisma and distinctive speaking style to change voters' minds. Jumping in his old Ford and heading out the driveway at 5:30 in the morning, Hughes drove from town to town, where he spoke at gatherings, talked to local newspaper reporters, and greeted voters. He found the traditional handshaking uncomfortable at first. He considered it a waste of time and preferred to stop and talk with voters about issues, but he managed to incorporate pressing the flesh into his campaign style.[39]

On the stump, Hughes aggressively attacked his opponent on the liquor-by-the-drink issue. In Erbe's hometown of Boone, Hughes asked, "Why hasn't Mr. Erbe done anything about the shocking statewide, open violations of the state liquor laws?" In Davenport he said, "Since we have it [liquor] anyway, why not have the profits go to the taxpayers?" By this time, Hughes had raised the estimated state revenue available by taxing legal over-the-counter liquor sales to $15 million; however, the centerpiece of his argument was not revenue but morality, honesty, and respect for the law. Consistent with that stand, Hughes pledged in early October that, despite his support for legalization, he would enforce the current law prohibiting liquor-by-the-drink sales. The law is the law, he asserted.[40]

Businesspeople, who were typically loyal to the Republican Party, were reaching a consensus that it was time for a change on the liquor issue. This was especially true of restaurant owners. Ermol Loghry of Iowa City, newly elected treasurer of the Iowa Restaurant Association, said, "The way we're bringing up children now to wink at the law is not right. . . . We've had 30 years of handling liquor the way it is now. Thirty years is long enough to see if it can be enforced." Other members of the association noted that it was unfair for businesses located close to the rivers on either side of the state because restaurants in Nebraska and Illinois could serve liquor legally.[41]

Although the liquor question was a central issue, Hughes integrated it into his aggressive campaign to advance Iowa into a bold, progressive future. He positioned himself and the Democratic Party as offering new, modern ideas and programs and linked them with President John Kennedy's New Frontier. Similar to Kennedy's presidential campaign two years earlier, Hughes depicted himself as the candidate of growth; he promised to get the state "moving again" and contrasted his lively activism with the lethargic Republican leadership. This message, combined with Hughes's charismatic and handsome presence and direct speaking style, distinguished the Democrats from the hesitant conservatism of the Republicans. Hughes said, "The Republican leadership is concerned with Iowa's past—with a past of their own making, but yet beyond their comprehension and control. But the Democratic leadership is concerned with Iowa's future—and they are better equipped to meet this future, for they understand the past, are not afraid of the present, and welcome the future with confidence."[42]

The Democratic candidate for governor offered new programs to match an increasingly urban Iowa. Hughes said, "Iowa is heading into the jet age with a horse and buggy," referring to Iowa's antiquated state and county governments that failed to address modern needs. He called for property tax reform to counter rising rates that caused industries to leave Iowa, as well as greater investment in education, particular postsecondary vocational schools, to encourage young people to stay in the state. Hughes advocated flexibility among local governments to aid industrial development. He urged the passage of legislation to withhold state income tax from paychecks, which would add to state revenue by thwarting tax evaders. "Where money is needed for programs vital to the state's future, I believe we must support those programs." If that meant higher state income taxes, concluded Hughes, that is what he would recommend.[43]

Countering Erbe's argument that the governor's hands were tied by law, Hughes called it a "milquetoast concept to the high responsibilities of government" and "a curious spineless concept of the governor's role." Leadership was needed, and Hughes boldly offered it. "If the laws are unfair or inadequate, or unenforceable, then it is the governor's responsibility to lead the way to change," Hughes declared. "If new legislation is needed, the governor is the legislative leader of the state." Hughes called Erbe the "Great Vacillator" for failing to generate a plan for property tax relief or enforce the state's liquor laws.[44]

Knowing that he needed to campaign every day if he hoped to catch and surpass Erbe, Hughes was greatly irritated when he was invited to a "command performance" for Democratic candidates with President Kennedy and Vice President Lyndon Johnson in Washington, DC, along with three other Iowa politicians. The four climbed into an old station wagon and drove through the night to avoid paying for a hotel room. Meeting Kennedy in the Rose Garden reception line, the candidate for governor simply said, "I'm Hughes from Iowa." Kennedy responded with a smile, a firm handshake, and a remark: "I'm really expecting you to perform out there." The Iowa group then climbed back into the station wagon and sped home, complaining about the lost campaign time for most of the return trip.[45]

As Election Day neared, Iowa's "dry" forces sensed that the tide was turning on the liquor issue, and they decided to take a stand in the debate. In late October, the Greater Des Moines Evangelical Ministers Association, representing fifty churches, passed a resolution opposing liquor by the drink. On October 21 the Temperance Legislative Council, a lobbying group that included members from the Iowa Women's Christian Temperance Union, the Iowa Temperance League, and the Iowa Council of Churches, announced its support for Erbe, based primarily on the liquor issue. Responding to the potential opposition from church pulpits, in October the Hughes campaign sent a letter signed by the candidate to more than a thousand Iowa clergy, explaining his stand. Addressing the "thousands of good people who oppose any change in the liquor laws because of temperance convictions," Hughes wrote that his advocacy of liquor by the drink was not "simply another chapter in the wet-dry issue. . . . It is an issue of law and order over crime and confusion. It is an issue of honesty over hypocrisy." More directly, Hughes said in a speech in Corning, "It is time that the temperance people in Iowa opened their eyes and looked at reality."[46]

The *Des Moines Sunday Register* endorsed Erbe on October 28. This was significant because it was the only statewide newspaper, and its Sunday edition had an extensive circulation. The *Register* believed the incumbent could get more done because Republicans dominated the legislature—and presumably would continue to do so in 1963—and they would block any efforts supported by Hughes. Other newspapers endorsed Hughes. The *Davenport Morning Democrat* noted that Hughes "faces the facts realistically" and "has shown the kind of courage and clarity of thinking as a candidate that would make him a good governor."[47]

Beneath the editorials and headlines, Hughes appeared to be making inroads, even among those who disagreed with him. Reflecting the opinion of many Iowans, Harry Beardsley of West Des Moines, who was opposed to liquor by the drink, wrote in a letter to the editor of the *Register*, "I respect Harold Hughes for the intelligence and integrity he has shown in trying to think honestly about the liquor problem, and for his willingness to state clearly, unequivocally and forthrightly what he believes should be done about it." The final opinion poll issued by the *Register* the weekend before the election showed Hughes behind but gaining. Erbe had a narrow 52 to 48 percent lead among those who had already decided, but the candidates were tied, 46 to 46 percent, among key city voters.[48]

After spending the bulk of the year running for governor, Hughes returned to Ida Grove on election eve to vote the next day and await the results. That evening, Hughes left his house and attended an AA meeting.[49]

The result on Election Day—November 6, 1962—was a solid victory for Hughes over Erbe, 430,899 to 388,602. In the lightest turnout since 1946, Hughes cruised to victory by carrying Iowa's population centers; he won in Polk County by more than 23,000 votes, which accounted for more than half his victory margin. Among the five counties with populations greater than 100,000, Hughes carried all but one (Scott County), winning seven of the top ten counties and fourteen of the top twenty. The irony was that the Democratic candidate from one of Iowa's least populous counties—Ida County—won with an overwhelmingly urban vote. His victory was a personal one; all other statewide officials elected in 1962 were Republican, and Republicans maintained their majority in both the Iowa house and senate.[50]

The banner headline in the *Cedar Rapids Gazette* after the election was "Hughes—Liquor Mandate." That immediate judgment may have been too simplistic, although the liquor law had clearly been the major issue in the campaign. Many, including Hughes, said he won the election because he took a strong stand on issues—certainly on liquor, but also on property tax relief, capital improvements, and other concerns. "We won because we had a program," said Hughes, "and because a majority of the voters believe that we had every intention of putting this program into effect, if elected." He added, "The liquor issue was to our campaign as a tail is to a dog. The tail is an important part of the dog, but the tail does not wag the dog—it is the other way around."[51]

Another important factor in Hughes's victory was a strong Democratic organization, especially in urban areas, continuing Iowa's transition from a one-party state to a more competitive two-party one. Led by the aggressive Lex Hawkins, the Iowa Democrats solidified voter registration and turnout. In Polk County alone, Democrats went from matching Republican Party registrations to a seven thousand–voter lead in 1962. On Election Day, Democratic Party workers in large counties were out at 6:00 a.m., getting voters to the polls. By the early 1960s, the

Iowa Democratic Party had cemented an expanding political relationship with organized labor that brought more working-class voters to the party; in 1962 Democrats worked with labor leaders to register union members in sixteen Iowa cities and get them to the polls on Election Day. This increasingly effective Democratic organization, combined with Hughes's aggressiveness and Erbe's lackluster campaign and refusal to take a firm position on important issues, gave the governorship to the Democrat.[52]

Hughes promised to modernize Iowa government in line with the fast-moving 1960s. Yet he faced an overwhelmingly Republican legislature that Iowans had also elected to set the pace of the state—a body filled with members who were diametrically opposed to many of these efforts. With this reality in mind, the new governor-elect and the Iowa Republicans turned to 1963.

4 | 1963's Political Battles
Liquor by the Drink and the Shaff Plan

After winning the election, Hughes spent several days hunting in southwestern Iowa with friends and then returned to Ida Grove for a celebration and parade on November 14. At the event, local Republican state representative J. W. Graham noted that Hughes had "leap frogged in the few years from an unknown personality in politics to the top office in state government. About two more jumps and he will be dealing with the Kennedy boys and they will be as dumbfounded as the Republicans are at the present time."[1]

If some were dumbfounded by Hughes, he made his intentions clear in his first postelection remarks in Ida Grove that day. Said Hughes, "I hope illegal sale of liquor comes to a stop before I become governor. It will make things simpler for everybody if that happens." *Des Moines Register* reporter George Mills wrote, "Hughes in effect invited Iowa Attorney General Evan Hultman and the 99 county attorneys to begin enforcement now of the ban on sale of liquor by the drink."[2]

The governor-elect's strategy was transparent. Enforcing the current liquor law was a heavy club designed to show Iowans what it actually meant. Anticipating an outcry among citizens who were used to easy access to liquor by the glass, Hughes and his allies worked to light a hot fire under the feet of recalcitrant legislators and encourage them to legalize liquor by the drink. But reform forces still faced a stiff challenge in the legislature. After the 1962 election, Republicans controlled 78 of 108 Iowa house seats and 38 of 50 state senate seats. Nick Kotz of the *Register* estimated that the more urban-oriented senate seemed on the verge of approving legalization, but the house was about ten votes short.[3]

Opinion within the Iowa GOP, however, was starting to change. Hughes's victory based on the liquor issue was the most obvious sign that attitudes—and voters—were shifting. A secret poll taken for the Republican Party in the fall of 1962 showed that 63 percent of Iowans favored liquor sales, with only 30 percent opposed; within their own party,

Republicans favored legalization 49 to 45 percent. State Republican Party chairman George Nagle of Iowa City publicly endorsed change and convinced the Republican State Central Committee to support the effort too, although the vote was not unanimous. Even Governor Erbe had a change of heart and came out for reform. In a postelection newspaper interview, he said he "personally felt there should be some liquor-by-the-drink system in Iowa," and if he had to do it over again, he would have supported change. But during the campaign he had felt bound by the GOP platform, which called only for a review of liquor laws.[4]

State law enforcement took note of the incoming administration's attitude. On December 10 Iowa safety commissioner Carl Pesch, anticipating an order from Hughes to crack down on illegal liquor traffic, announced that twenty-seven state agents would be taking "refresher courses" in raiding techniques, "search and seizure," preservation of evidence, and other subjects related to liquor law enforcement. He acknowledged that "new and novel responsibilities soon may be thrust upon this department." Hughes and Pesch appeared together at a Des Moines press conference on January 3 to announce a state crackdown on illegal liquor sales. The *Register* covered the event under the headline "Hughes Set to 'Dry up' Iowa." The governor-elect said he hoped he would not have to use state manpower; he would prefer to rely on local law enforcement to ensure that businesses complied with the current law. "I believe that adequate warning has been given that I expected voluntary enforcement before taking office," he said. "And we are not going to wait two months and see what the legislature will do with the liquor laws."[5]

The effect was immediate throughout the state. In community after community, establishments that had been serving liquor illegally "dried up," either voluntarily or after warnings by local law enforcement. In some cases, this resulted in job losses. The president of the Dubuque Tavern Keepers Association estimated that two hundred people would be out of work. Sales at Iowa liquor stores in traditionally "wet" counties on Iowa's eastern and western borders—the source of liquor for illegal sales—plunged significantly. Most business owners who had been selling illegal drinks saw this as a temporary situation and tacitly agreed to stop doing so until the legislature legalized it. The president of the Tavern Owners Association in Clinton said, "The dry-up is to show Hughes we are willing to co-operate. We want liquor by the drink."[6]

In the meantime, Hughes prepared to assume the governorship. It was common knowledge that Hughes's principal adviser was Park Rinard. Under Rinard's leadership, the Iowa League of Municipalities had supported Hughes's push to modernize state government, and Rinard was now engaged in hiring staff for the governor's office. *Register* reporter Dwight Jensen called Rinard in mid-December 1962 and asked, "When are you gonna put together a staff? You haven't even got a chief of staff yet." "Well," responded Rinard, "we thought about you, but we knew you wouldn't take it." "Well, ask me," the reporter replied, to Rinard's surprise. After spending an evening with Rinard and discussing it with his wife, Pat, the thirty-two-year-old Jensen accepted the position as executive assistant to Hughes, a job he kept for the entire six years of the administration.[7]

Jensen's selection was immediately controversial among many Democrats, especially those in Polk County, who vigorously voiced their objections. Jensen was a registered independent and a newspaper reporter, not an administrator. A native of West Branch, Jensen had graduated with a journalism degree from the University of Iowa, where he was editor of the *Daily Iowan* and was named outstanding journalism graduate in 1955. He was hired in 1956 by the *Des Moines Register*, where he covered local government, city hall, the courthouse, and the police. Jensen had reported on the 1962 campaign and got to know Hughes, who was impressed with the journalist. In a move that reflected their standard practice, Hughes and Rinard ignored criticism from establishment Democrats and hired Jensen anyway.[8]

The two men continued their disregard for political norms and hired another newspaperman, twenty-eight-year-old Kirk Boyd, as administrative assistant in February. A native of Davenport, Boyd had worked as a reporter for the *Des Moines Tribune* in 1957 and as city editor and political reporter for the *Davenport Democrat* in 1958 and 1959. At the time he was hired, Boyd was a Ph.D. student at the University of Iowa. Together, Jensen and Boyd made up the entire gubernatorial staff, not including clerical assistance.[9]

Jensen and Boyd operated with very little guidance from the previous administration; Governor Erbe had left few files, so the two-man staff made up their duties as they arose. Jensen was overwhelmed with paperwork because so many people wrote to Hughes, believing he was a governor who would listen. "The mail just flowed in and we had to figure out how to manage it," recalled Jensen, who often worked late into the night handling correspondence. "We considered part of our job to keep as much as possible out of his [Hughes's] hair. One of us would go into his office with a list of things and got 'yes,' 'no,' 'do this,' and we'd go do it."[10]

Although the governor's small staff helped execute policy, it was the team of Hughes and Rinard that developed strategy. During the Hughes administration, the two men often spoke on the phone every day. Hughes later said Rinard "gave me a catechism class on government and how it worked." Just as important, Rinard contributed grace and polish to Hughes's ideas through his speechwriting—and most of the governor's speeches were delivered at the last minute. Rinard's mastery of the English language, combined with Hughes's commanding presence and voice, equaled the power to persuade in public forums. Rinard's speechwriting was a closely guarded secret, although it was, no doubt, common knowledge throughout the Iowa political establishment. Rinard doubled as a lobbyist for the Iowa League of Municipalities, which constituted a potential conflict of interest; however, it never became a serious issue during the Hughes administration.[11]

Rinard's rhetorical flourish was on display in Hughes's inaugural speech, given shortly after he took the oath of office at noon on January 17, 1963. With Eva and their three daughters looking on, Hughes faced the overwhelmingly Republican Iowa legislature, gathered in the packed house chamber, and addressed the partisan divide early on. The citizens of Iowa "expect us to do our jobs regardless of party labels," he said, and pledged "an atmosphere of good will and cooperation." Hughes left no doubt, however, that he meant to shake up state government, saying, "the hand of the past lies heavy upon many of the departments of state government." Statistics showed that forty-six of the fifty states were growing faster than Iowa, so he made state economic development a priority, pushing for a strengthened Iowa Development Commission, increased financial aid to business, and more aggressive economic and agricultural research. Turning to legislative reapportionment, a fiercely contentious issue among the rural legislators, Hughes called on members to create a program to "meet the responsibility of developing a sound and equitable plan." This last plea generally fell on deaf ears.[12]

Hughes also recommended abolishing the death penalty in Iowa, claiming that it "inflicts severe spiritual damage upon all of the citizens of our state." As expected, Hughes supported liquor-by-the-drink legislation as "a more enforceable system of liquor control." Until then, he promised, "the new administration will exert its best effort to enforce the law." In all, Hughes articulated nearly forty specific areas for reform. The most controversial one—and an issue that had not been prominent during the campaign—was Hughes's endorsement of allowing private school students, most of whom attended religious schools, to be transported by public school buses. His reasoning was that the parents of private school students paid local taxes that financed the buses, so they had a right to use them. This issue caused the most conversation after the speech and revived the debate on separation of church and state.[13]

As Hughes ended his thirty-three-minute speech, he acknowledged that Iowa was a conservative state, but it was a conservatism of "prudence, rather than fear and inertia." He told the audience there are times to watch and wait, and there are times for action. Hughes admitted that he hoped to "experiment and make some mistakes" and added, "It is sometimes said that the knack of skillful government is to hang back, do as little as possible, and make no mistakes. I hope there is another way—for between you and me, this prospect does not invite my soul."[14]

After the address, the political elite of the Hawkeye State retired to Veterans Auditorium in downtown Des Moines for the inaugural ball. An estimated five thousand people waited in line to shake hands with Hughes and the new First Lady of Iowa.[15]

The new governor's family—Hughes, Eva, and their youngest daughter, Phyllis—moved into the governor's mansion, then located at 2900 Grand Avenue in Des Moines. Hughes's oldest daughter, Connie, was married to Dennis Otto by then, and the couple had moved into the family's vacated house at 317 Fifty-Eighth Street, Des Moines. Hughes told reporters he did not plan to sell his old house "because I may need it again some day." Hughes's middle daughter, Carol, was going to business college in Des Moines and living in her own apartment.[16]

Hughes wasted little time communicating his priorities to Iowans. As early as January 25, he started recording regular radio speeches—dubbed the Tall Corn Network—which his staff mailed to stations around the state. The five-minute spots were welcomed by stations that needed to fill airtime. Tall Corn topics included the governor's stands on reapportionment, the death penalty, liquor-by-the-drink legislation, and other key issues. These weekly addresses allowed Hughes to bypass other Iowa political leaders, pressuring state legislators and setting the state's political agenda.[17]

Hughes also scheduled regular sessions with the media. He met with journalists in his office every Wednesday at 9:00 a.m. during the legislative session. The reporters gathered informally around the governor's desk and were free to ask off-the-record questions, although Hughes frequently granted permission for them to use the information they had learned. These sessions cemented a positive relationship between Hughes and the Iowa media that lasted throughout his administration.[18]

As promised, Hughes prioritized the enforcement of current liquor laws. After a week on the job, the governor met with Republican attorney general Evan Hultman—newly reelected to a second term and a potential rival in 1964—to discuss the issue. In a joint news conference afterward, Hultman pledged his full cooperation in enforcing the prohibition of over-the-counter liquor sales. The attorney general's support sent a firm message to county attorneys that there was bipartisan agreement on liquor law enforcement, and they were expected to act accordingly.[19]

By the end of January, undercover agents were combing the state, investigating more than sixty potential violators, and clamping down on lawbreakers. The governor's office received several private letters exposing illegal liquor sales at specific sites and demanding action. Hughes and his aides passed them on to safety commissioner Pesch. In late February and early March state agents and local officials raided taverns and other establishments that were violating the law in Davenport and Clinton in eastern Iowa and Carter Lake in the west. State law enforcement agencies initiated another wave of arrests in Davenport in early May. All these raids were well publicized, demonstrating to Iowans—and state legislators—that there was a new sheriff in town, and he intended to enforce the law.[20]

In the legislature, the fracture between "wets" and "drys"—that is, supporters and opponents of liquor reform, respectively—was mostly an urban-rural split rather than a partisan divide. Most Democrats favored change, but those Democratic legislators who did not were brusquely informed by Hughes in late January that failure to support liquor by the drink "may determine the amount of consideration their recommendations for appointments in state jobs may get." Given that threat, most of them toed the line. The biggest battle was within the Republican

Party. Some in the GOP were leery about passing liquor reform and giving Hughes a political victory; others realized that his win in November meant that it was time for change. They feared that if they failed to pass liquor reform, Hughes and the Democrats would carry the issue into the 1964 elections, with potentially disastrous results for Republicans.[21]

The strategy adopted by Hughes and the Democrats was to avoid introducing liquor legislation that could be labeled a "Democratic bill"—sure to be a losing proposition in the Republican-dominated legislature. Instead, they opted for a bipartisan approach. They also decided to begin in the state senate, where a liquor reform bill had a greater chance of passage because, with larger districts, more senators represented urban constituencies. Senator Jack Schroeder, a Republican from Davenport, a strong supporter of liquor by the drink, and chairman of the Judiciary Committee, took charge of drawing up the legislation.[22]

Hughes encouraged citizens to pressure legislators for change. Against the background of lobbying efforts by some religious groups and others to halt liquor reform, Hughes said in a press conference in mid-January, "Persons who want the law changed must organize in conveying their feelings to legislators." Supporters heeded his call. In less than a month, nearly 100,000 Iowans had petitioned their state representatives, with only about 6,000 against reform. Legislators were overwhelmed by letters from voters, prompting *Register* reporter Mills to call it the "biggest mail session in modern times."[23]

By mid-February, Hughes was regularly meeting with a bipartisan group of legislators, including Schroeder and the state senate and house majority leaders, to count the votes on the liquor legislation. At a Democratic Party speech in Perry in late March, Hughes stressed that legislators needed to "start taking action—and soon—on a sensible liquor control bill." He warned that, despite enforcement efforts, it did not "mean we have made Iowa 'dry' or halted the intemperate use of alcohol. It only means we have driven bootlegging in this state further underground. Make no mistake about it. If the people of Iowa do not wish Iowa to be 'dry,' a few state police agents cannot make it dry." He repeated his campaign prediction that, without reform, "we will soon see this state drift into an atmosphere of cynicism where there will be little respect for any law."[24]

On April 4 the Senate Judiciary Committee voted 7–0 to approve proposed legislation allowing liquor by the drink in Iowa. The bill set a 10 percent tax on gross receipts from the sale of beverages and set license fees for various classes of businesses serving drinks; city and town councils and county boards of supervisors were authorized to grant final approval for liquor licenses. Backers coyly waited several days before bringing the bill to the senate floor, hoping to avoid an avalanche of phone calls to wavering legislators. At midmorning on Wednesday, April 10, supporters introduced the liquor bill, and debate began immediately. As deliberations continued throughout the day, it became obvious to supporters that they lacked sufficient votes for passage. At the center of the battle were three undecided senators, including Leigh Curran of Mason City. As news of the debate spread through the state via radio, other senators were called off the floor to take phone calls, pro and con, from constituents. By late afternoon, Curran was the focus of the pressure tactics, both inside and outside the legislature, answering phone calls and holding hushed conversations with fellow senators. Then, at 4:41 p.m., talk stopped abruptly and the senate secretary started to read the roll call in alphabetical order. When Curran voted "Aye," an anonymous voice from the floor cried, "That does it!" At the end of the roll call, the Iowa senate had passed its liquor-by-the-drink bill by a vote of 26–24.[25]

The senate vote seemed to take the wind out of the opposition in the more rural-based Iowa house. In addition, by the end of April, members had received petitions from 143,022 constituents favoring liquor by the drink and only 29,208 opposed. With minor amendments and less drama, on May 3 the house voted 68–40 to pass its liquor-by-the-drink bill—a more lopsided result than anyone would have predicted months earlier. The senate adopted the house amendments on May 9, and the bill went to Hughes for his signature. Acknowledging the long, bruising battle, Hughes noted at the May 14 signing, "It is the peculiar genius of democracy that persons with diverse points of view can get together and work out solutions to complex problems that are in the public interest. In my opinion, this is exactly what happened with this liquor bill."[26]

The bipartisan cooperation noted—and led—by Hughes resulted in more than passage of a law allowing over-the-counter liquor sales. It marked the end of more than a century of liquor-related debate in Iowa. The demise of this debate marked Iowa's transition from a state with powerful rural interests that kept liquor restrictions alive as a political issue to one with more urban sensibilities and tolerance for alcohol consumption. The irony is that this transformation was led by a man with personal and painful knowledge of the self-destructive potential of alcoholism. On this issue, however, Harold Hughes believed the more important focus was respect for law in a functioning democracy.[27]

Other than the liquor-by-the-drink legislation, the Sixtieth General Assembly—at 125 days, the longest session to date in Iowa history—had little to show in terms of accomplishments. It did, however, approve the largest budget in state history at more than $206 million for each of the next two years, yet this was nearly $24 million less than Hughes wanted and far less than state agencies and departments had originally requested. Calling it a "bare bones budget," Hughes contemplated calling the legislature back into session if more money was needed, but he reluctantly concluded, "I think it will be possible to carry on our operations without any tax increase."[28]

A major disappointment for Hughes was the lack of tax reform. The legislature adjourned on May 18 without passing any of the tax laws recommended by Hughes in his inaugural address. His push for state tax withholding, property tax relief through higher state income tax rates, and expanded aid for primary and secondary schools failed completely. The only tax bill that passed was an increase in the cigarette tax, from four to five cents per pack. The legislature also failed to enact several of Hughes's recommendations designed to modernize government, such as annual legislative sessions and four-year terms for state officeholders. And, on an issue that Hughes considered a fundamentally moral one, legislators did not abolish the death penalty. Likewise, Hughes's push to give parochial school students access to public school buses went nowhere.[29]

The legislature did act on some of the reforms advocated by Hughes. It increased workers' compensation and unemployment benefits, eased restrictions on home rule for cities, approved substantial funding increases for Iowa universities, increased benefits under the Iowa public employment retirement system, and passed a fair employment practices act that barred discrimination by unions and employers. Lawmakers also enacted legislation to foster industrial development in Iowa.[30]

The greatest defeat for Hughes was the early passage of the constitutional amendment known as the Shaff Plan, an attempt to reapportion the legislature to preserve rural power. The battle over the Shaff Plan involved the very concept of representative democracy itself, or how Iowans chose their lawmakers.

At the dawn of Iowa statehood in 1846, seats in each chamber of the legislature were divided among districts of generally equal population, and for forty years, the Iowa legislature reapportioned districts based on the number of residents, as determined by the decennial census. After 1886, however, this effort stopped, and districts remained unchanged owing to legislative inaction. In the meantime, populations in urban areas grew, without the appropriate increase in representation in the legislature. Grappling to address this unfairness, urban and rural factions compromised in 1904, agreeing on a constitutional amendment creating a 50-seat senate based on population and a 108-member house based on geography; each county was entitled to one house member, and each of the nine most populous counties received an extra representative. A 1928 amendment limited counties to a single senator, regardless of population; as the number of residents grew in some senate districts, urban voters were underrepresented in that chamber. Consequently, both houses became dominated by rural interests.[31]

By the mid-1950s, pressure was building to change the system. Groups such as the Iowa Federation of Labor (Iowa's AFL-CIO), the Iowa League of Women Voters, the Iowa League of Municipalities, and chambers of commerce from Iowa's largest cities supported apportionment reform to more fairly represent urban residents. Seeking to address the issue while retaining rural influence, the Iowa Farm Bureau Federation offered the Shaff Plan, a constitutional amendment named after its chief legislative sponsor, Senator David Shaff from Clinton. Drafted at the federation's headquarters in Des Moines, it called for a return to a state senate based on population and a ninety-nine-member house based on geography, with each Iowa county having only one representative. Supporters argued that the plan was fair because it gave urban voters a majority in the senate and rural interests a majority in the house. It was, they said, the federal system in reverse.[32]

The Shaff Plan also picked up support from the Iowa Manufacturers Association (IMA), consisting of business leaders from more than five hundred manufacturers throughout the state. This alliance between farm and business was spawned by the IMA's fear of increased labor power in urban areas. In particular, the group feared labor would support repeal of the right-to-work law, as well as work to pass more liberal worker benefit programs and intrusive rules on working conditions. For the IMA, the rural house would serve as a check on potential union power.[33]

Others saw the Shaff Plan as an unwelcome compromise. Many perceived the geography-based house as a permanent refuge for conservative rural interests that could stifle reforms needed to modernize the state. Opponents of the plan argued that it would give the Farm Bureau Federation and the IMA veto power over legislation. After debating the Shaff Plan during several sessions, legislators in both houses finally passed the plan as a constitutional amendment in 1961; as required by the Iowa Constitution, both houses passed it again in 1963, over Governor Hughes's objection. The next stage was a special election set for December 3, 1963, when Iowans would take part in an up-or-down vote on the reapportionment plan.[34]

Hughes could have simply deferred to the wisdom of the Iowa voters and sat out the debate over the Shaff Plan in silence. But that was not in his character. According to Martin Jensen, then covering state government for WMT News of Cedar Rapids, "Hughes was an active, decisive leader, quite uncommon for Iowa governors who tended to defer to the Iowa General Assembly in making laws. That certainly applied to the Shaff Plan." Resistance to liquor by the drink and the failure of other legislative goals showed Hughes that a conservative, rural-based legislature was a bulwark against the government reform demanded by the overwhelming majority of the population. The Shaff Plan would only cement that barricade within the Iowa Constitution. Using population figures from the 1960 census, critics pointed out that, under the Shaff Plan, control of the Iowa house could be vested in only 23.5 percent of the population. Hughes decided to take early, aggressive action against passage of the amendment, using the full powers of his office and his persuasive rhetorical abilities to that end.[35]

Immediately after the legislature approved the Shaff Plan for the second time and scheduled the statewide vote, Hughes blasted it in a radio address, emphasizing the unjustness of one house controlled by a minority of the state's population. Behind the scenes, aides were planning an aggressive campaign to defeat the plan. Staffer Kirk Boyd wrote in an internal memo, "Harold Hughes can have more influence over the outcome than can any other single factor." The strategy, he argued, was not to offer an alternative plan but to make the case against the Shaff Plan.[36]

Hughes, however, chose to accentuate the positive. In speech after speech, he stressed the optimistic goal, reminiscent of his earlier campaign rhetoric, of aggressively moving the state forward through fairer representation, positioning the Shaff Plan as an obstacle to that objective. In an address in September in northwestern Iowa, Hughes said the scheme would drive a wedge between rural and urban groups. "Neither rural nor urban Iowa can progress without the other," he said. "It's this simple: either we work together, plan together, and understand one another's problems or we will fail together to enjoy the better life." In another speech in Pottawattamie County he said, "My biggest objection to this plan is that it will deadlock the Legislature at a time when Iowa needs a Legislature that can get things done—in the form of programs that will expand her economy and strengthen Iowa agriculture." In Sioux City in late September he said, "I am firmly convinced that, if we pass this constitutional amendment, we may obstruct progress in our state for another 30 years."[37]

Some Iowans criticized Hughes for taking such an aggressive stand against the Shaff Plan, but he would hear none of it. He felt it was his duty. "I don't intend to fight the Shaff Plan as a Democrat, but as governor. This is not a partisan political issue. My interest is in the State of Iowa and its future."[38]

Officially, the two political parties remained neutral on the issue. Both Republican state chairman George Nagle and Democratic state chairman Lex Hawkins claimed their respective state central committees had taken no position on the plan. However, it was obvious that many conservative Republicans supported the preservation of a rural-based house; it was equally obvious that Iowa Democrats wanted the Shaff Plan defeated. The Iowa legislature's vote in early 1963 to pass the Shaff Plan had been overwhelmingly Republican in both the house and the senate. Although Hawkins pledged neutrality for the Democratic Party, he was very clear on his personal position: "If you want 25 percent of the people in Iowa to control how your state tax dollars are spent, then vote for the Shaff Plan. If you want the Farm Bureau and the Iowa Manufacturers Association to keep running this state, then vote for the Shaff Plan."[39]

Two organizations, officially nonpartisan, rose in mid-1963 to wage battle over the Shaff Plan. In early September Robert K. Beck, a newspaper publisher from Centerville, announced the creation of a thirty-member committee in favor of passage of the amendment, called Citizens for Reapportionment, December 3. By this time, foes of the amendment had already formed a committee called Iowans Against the Shaff Plan Inc., headed by Duane Dewel, former majority leader in the state senate and publisher of the *Kossuth County Advance*. Other prominent organizations were using their considerable political muscle to educate voters and get out the vote, including the Iowa League of Women Voters and Iowa Federation of Labor, which were against the plan, and the Iowa Farm Bureau, which was for it.[40]

Few individuals or organizations, however, carried the political weight or rhetorical power of the governor. In a speech before the Iowa Bankers Association in Des Moines on October 23, Hughes assailed the amendment in what the *Des Moines Tribune* called "one of his strongest attacks on the Shaff plan." He described it as a "blue-print for stalemate that would put a lid on economic growth and move the state backward" and claimed that it "sells both urban and rural people down the river and seeks to foreclose on the bright potential of Iowa's future." He compared the amendment to a crawdaddy, a crustacean that propels itself on land by moving backward. Using a contemporary Cold War metaphor, Hughes said the Shaff Plan would "erect a permanent Berlin wall between rural people and townspeople." He added, "The interests who want to foist the Shaff plan upon the people of Iowa are conducting an unprecedented campaign of fear in this state" by claiming that, without it, labor unions would take over. To that assertion he responded, "The plain truth is that there are only 70,000 members of organized labor in the entire state of more than 2,800,000 people. Neither now nor in the farthest reaches of the future is it conceivable that organized labor could dominate our legislators."[41]

By early November, it was clear that the nonpartisan masquerade was over. Republican leaders issued a firm statement in favor of the Shaff Plan. They included Lieutenant Governor W. L. Moody, Iowa house speaker Robert Naden (Webster City), senate majority leader Robert Rigler (New Hampton), house majority leader John Mowry (Marshalltown), and house speaker pro tempore Marvin Smith (Paulina). Blaming Hughes for politicizing the issue, they said:

> We feel the time has come when the legislative leadership of the Republican party can no longer remain silent on the reapportionment issue, which Governor Hughes has chosen to make a partisan issue. . . . Governor Hughes has chosen to put it in the political field and having done so, we feel that a statement should be made. . . . We feel that the Shaff Plan should be approved by the voters.[42]

Beck of the Citizens for Reapportionment claimed that Hughes was "injecting a strong element of political partisanship in the Shaff campaign," which was "something we had hopes of avoiding." In mid-November Beck accused Hughes of carrying out "one of the most irresponsible campaigns ever conducted by a high state official in Iowa history," adding that his actions are not "fitting to his high office." David Shaff himself maintained that Hughes "has made a basic mistake getting involved in this matter. His experience in government or legislative matters has not been sufficient to give him reason to use his office to influence people."[43]

Hughes disagreed. In addition to opposing the Shaff Plan in speech after speech, he directed his staff to work vigorously to influence the December vote. Principally under the direction of Kirk Boyd, they generated materials and contacted supporters around the state. On a near-daily basis from mid-November until the vote, the staff generated press releases summarizing Hughes's speeches against the plan; they also produced sample letters that constituents could send to local newspapers. Dwight Jensen surveyed the fifteen radio stations regularly running Hughes's Tall Corn Network speeches and reported that nearly all of them would "be glad to hear about the Shaff Plan and would accept two tapes on it if they were given in advance." Jensen proposed that they "hit it hard" in a tape planned for November 15; then, depending on how the campaign was going, make a November 29 tape "a little softer and place more stress on the need for people to be interested and get out and vote on Dec. 3." Hughes marked "OK" on Jensen's memo.[44]

Ahead of December 3, Shaff Plan opponents were taking no chances, in case the vote on apportionment did not go their way. They looked to the courts as their allies. In 1962 the US Supreme Court had determined in *Baker v. Carr* that federal courts have jurisdiction in matters involving state legislative apportionment; in other words, those who feel discriminated against under an unfair plan can turn to the federal courts for justice. The Iowa Federation of Labor filed suit in federal court in Des Moines several months before the December vote, claiming that the current apportionment arrangement was unconstitutional and asking the court to rule on the Shaff Plan. The court declared that the current system was unconstitutional and proclaimed that the present makeup of the legislature discriminated against a majority of Iowans because a minority could control both houses. The three-judge panel did not rule on the Shaff Plan, since the referendum was coming up, but it held open the possibility of doing so after the vote. This gave opponents another argument against the plan: do not vote for Shaff because the federal court will throw it out anyway.[45]

In the week before the vote, Hughes canvassed the state, making speeches against the Shaff Plan in Mason City, Fort Dodge, Ames, Muscatine, and Sioux City before arriving in Ida Grove, where he voted. Hughes paid for the tour out of his own pocket. Senator Shaff followed the governor with a "Truth Squad" to counter Hughes's messages. The pair joined an extensive network of speakers around the state—both pro and con.[46]

The sound and the fury of the campaign culminated on a chilly December 3 as voters rejected the Shaff Plan, 191,421 in favor and 271,214 against. The proposed amendment carried the vote in sixty-four of Iowa's ninety-nine counties, but urban numbers overwhelmed rural support. Voters in populous Polk County rejected the plan by 84 percent. The seventeen largest counties, with 50 percent of the state's population, voted it down by more than 114,000 votes. Wrote Mills, "Defeat of the plan apparently reflects in some measure the fact that Iowa has evolved from a rural state to an urban state in the last few years." The earlier passage of liquor by the drink seemed to corroborate that statement.[47]

Deeming the vote "a victory for all of the people of Iowa," Hughes called on both sides to forget their differences and work together "so all people may have fair play and equality of citizenship wherever they might live." Hours after the governor spoke, US district court judge Roy Stephenson called for a pretrial conference of opposing attorneys to establish the issues for debate when the federal court reopened the case. It was becoming obvious that the courts would join the voters in deciding how Iowans were represented in their own legislature.[48]

This battle had only just begun.

5 | Helping the Downtrodden

Liquor reform and legislative reapportionment were not the only issues on Harold Hughes's mind during his first year in office. Another was the governorship itself. Hughes detested many of the ceremonial duties that came with the job. Frank Nye, veteran *Cedar Rapids Gazette* reporter, wrote that Hughes "isn't much of one to go along with all the folderol a governor has to put up with in office—the back-slapping and glad-handing and ribbon-cutting and building-dedicating and fair-attending."[1] And Hughes was not afraid to say so in public. At a gathering in Des Moines in late September 1963 he remarked:

> I didn't realize that the people of Iowa expected their governor to be a darn fool—running around the state cutting ribbons and dedicating supermarkets all night and then getting back to the office to run the state in the day time. . . . But I'm hooked by what my predecessors did. They ran around the state shaking hands everywhere on the theory that a hand shaken was a vote in the next election. . . . For instance, I'm down here tonight when I'd rather be home with my family. We had a fine meal here but I'd rather have a hamburger at home.[2]

When chief aide Dwight Jensen read these well-publicized comments in the *Des Moines Register* the next morning, he rushed into Hughes's office and asked if he had really made the "hamburger" remark. When Hughes replied in the affirmative, an angry Jensen said, "Well, then, I quit!" Hughes spent the next several minutes convincing him to stay. If it was any consolation to Jensen, the *Cedar Rapids Gazette* ran an editorial the next day titled "The Governor Is Right." It said, "After watching governor after governor wear himself down physically in an effort to please the people by appearing at various functions," the state should have two governors, one "ceremonial" and the other "working." Until then, the current arrangement would have to do.[3]

Another, much more serious issue was on Hughes's mind in 1963: the death penalty. In his inaugural address, Hughes had made it clear that he favored abolishing capital punishment in Iowa, saying that it "inflicts severe spiritual damage upon all of the citizens of our state." These words showed that this was more than a policy question to Hughes. Transcending mere politics, it was a deeply felt position based on the core of his religious faith; he often cited the sixth commandment, "Thou shalt not kill," as an argument against the death penalty. According to *Register* reporter Nick Kotz, Hughes "trembled with revulsion at the impending taking of life on Iowa gallows."[4]

Hughes failed to convince Republican lawmakers to outlaw the practice during the 1963 session, but he worked behind the scenes on another level to prevent the execution of Victor H. Feguer, scheduled for March. Feguer had been convicted of the 1960 kidnap-murder of Dr. Edward Bartels of Dubuque. The defense had claimed that Feguer was mentally ill, but the prosecution won the argument that he was "legally sane" and knew the difference between right and wrong. Feguer was the first Iowan convicted under the so-called Lindbergh law—the federal crime of kidnapping. And only the president of the United States can commute the sentence of a person convicted of a federal crime.[5]

Knowing Hughes's stand on capital punishment, Feguer's attorneys approached the governor and asked him to appeal to President Kennedy. "I'll try," said Hughes, "but I probably won't get past his first secretary." To his surprise, Hughes got through to Kennedy almost immediately, and after a few minutes of banter, he got to the point. Kennedy explained that he was familiar with the Feguer case and had studied the trial transcript. "Mr. President," said Hughes, "I would ask you to consider clemency in this case. I can only speak from my personal convictions. I am opposed to the taking of life and to capital punishment. I cannot see where this does any good. To me executions are senseless. In this case, there also is strong evidence that this man is mentally unbalanced." Hughes told the president he was "just making a plea from one man to another." Kennedy agreed to review the case a second time.[6]

The next week, Dubuque native Edward McDermott, director of the US Office of Emergency Planning and Kennedy's 1960 campaign coordinator in Iowa, flew to Des Moines and met with Hughes in the governor's mansion. McDermott explained that the president had been unable to find a reason to grant clemency and that no official linked to the case had recommended it. Hughes called Kennedy again to say that although he disagreed with the conclusion, he respected the president's judgment.[7]

Kotz, who covered this story for the *Register*, later recalled that Hughes "was very unhappy with Kennedy's answer. . . . I think this says a lot about Hughes. Not just that he was opposed to the death penalty. I mean, he was really very deeply committed against the death penalty."[8]

Feguer was executed on March 15, 1963, and it affected Hughes profoundly. "I remember that day as one of his worst days in office," said Dwight Jensen. Hughes did not want to talk to the press about it, so he and members of his staff left the capitol for a coffee shop and spent most of the morning there. Feguer had been told about Hughes's and Kennedy's efforts, and he was surprised that such prominent political leaders had taken an interest. A half hour before the execution, he wrote a note to Hughes: "Dear Sir: Thank you for your efforts in my behalf. God bless you and yours. Peace. Sincerely, Victor H. Feguer."[9]

Two years later, newly elected to his second term, Hughes faced a capital punishment verdict under Iowa law, where he had more control. In January 1965 Hughes commuted the death sentence of twenty-four-year-old Leon Tice Jr. to a life term at the state penitentiary in Fort Madison, Iowa. On June 21, 1963, Tice had brutally murdered two boys, aged two and thirteen. In a statement announcing the commutation, Hughes acknowledged the "ghastly crime" committed by Tice and said his "heart is heavy with grief for the bereaved family." Nevertheless, he continued, "the taking of another life will not bring back their loved ones. Nor will it, as I see it, strengthen us in the efforts we must make to prevent further tragedies of this nature by removing the basic causes that tend to produce such crimes." Privy to information that had not been available to the jury, Hughes described Tice's life as one "lived in a twilight atmosphere of poverty, sub-normal levels among the family members, personal delinquency, and emotional maladjustment born of deep feelings of inadequacy to cope with life." Hughes added, "Society itself bears some stern responsibility in the tragic events for which the defendant stands convicted."[10]

The action was controversial. Pottawattamie County attorney Norman Davis, who had prosecuted the case, said Hughes's decision was "another example of going contrary to the law and letting personal feelings stand in the way of what the people have decreed." Sheriff Roy Wichael declared, "It doesn't seem right to give one man the power to change it." But the person closest to capital punishment—warden John Bennett at the state penitentiary—was relieved. In his more than thirty years as a prison official, he had seen at least eighteen people die on the gallows. That, he said, is "something . . . you never get used to," and in his opinion, "everybody would be contented if we never had any more" such deaths.[11]

The Iowa prison system—and, most important for Hughes, those incarcerated by the system—became a prime concern for the governor. Hughes had been getting five to ten letters a day from inmates in these institutions, principally the state training school for boys in Eldora, the men's reformatory in Anamosa, and the Fort Madison state penitentiary. Writers either complained about conditions or asked for commuted sentences. On May 29, 1963, Hughes visited the Fort Madison penitentiary to, in his words, "get a feel of things" and talk to every lifer who had been there for more than fifteen years, with an eye toward commuting their sentences. It was the first time in history that an Iowa governor had visited the penitentiary with the express purpose of personally meeting with prisoners.[12]

Accompanied by Benjamin Baer, the Iowa director of corrections, Hughes talked with about twenty prisoners, eight of whom had been sentenced to life imprisonment. Hughes later described the experience as "unforgettable." The first man he interviewed had been imprisoned since 1922, causing Hughes to fall back in his chair when he heard the date. As they talked, the old man broke down and cried, saying he had appealed to every governor for the last forty years, and "no one has ever responded until you." Another inmate was a fifteen-year-old who had been sentenced to life for shooting his grandfather; he would soon be transferred to an institution for minors. Hughes also took part in a therapy session with nine inmates, where he assured them that some people do "give a damn about you fellows. You can rehabilitate yourselves. I really believe that." Before he left, the governor looked at the site of the old gallows, noting with approval that it had been dismantled, and he asked, "Can we get some gasoline while I'm here and burn it?"[13]

The letters pouring into the governor's office reflected severe problems in the state's correction system. These deficiencies exploded into two protests by prisoners in late 1963. The first occurred at the reformatory at Anamosa. On October 31 complaints about food escalated into a riot, and inmates set fires in three buildings, resulting in more than $275,000 in damage. Hughes pressed the three-member Board of Control, which managed state institutions, to fully investigate conditions at Anamosa, bluntly saying, "It seems inconceivable that a disturbance of this type could take place without officials of the institution being aware of dissatisfaction among the inmates."[14]

One of those board members was sent to negotiate with the Anamosa inmates on his first day on the job. Hughes had appointed thirty-four-year-old Russell Wilson, the Methodist minister he had known in Ida Grove, to the Board of Control because of his compassion. He said to the minister, "Wilson, I know you don't know a damn thing about running institutions, but you care about people. And they need that, too." On his first day as a board member, Wilson had no sooner parked his car in the capitol parking lot than he was told to go to Anamosa. "I hadn't even gotten my clothes out of the car and didn't have a place to stay," he recalled. Before 10:00 that morning, Wilson joined the other two board members, Joe Henry and Carroll Price, in the state plane and flew to the prison.[15]

One of the inmates' complaints, abuse by reformatory staff, was soon resolved with the resignation of a guard who was the source of much of the problem. Other complaints included lack of proper shower scheduling, no continuing education, minor concerns about overall physical and mental health, and other mistreatment. The board quickly prepared a report on conditions in Anamosa, including recommendations to upgrade the facility and its mission.[16]

At a subsequent press conference, Hughes emphasized that it was time to treat inmates as human beings, not simply as wards of the state. He promised to "broaden the program of modern penology," concentrating on rehabilitation, training, and treatment. In the past, none of these things had been given priority, but according to Hughes, that would change under his administration.[17]

A much larger and more dangerous uprising took place days later at the state penitentiary in Fort Madison, in southeastern Iowa. On Friday, November 8, 1963, between two hundred and three hundred men were involved in a flare-up at the prison. Prisoners looted the canteen, taking cigarettes, candy, and other items valued at $3,500, and broke about twenty-five windows. Although no one was hurt and no one attempted to escape, the looters isolated themselves in a cell block and demanded to talk to Governor Hughes about their problems.[18]

Both Baer and Bennett strongly advised Hughes not to meet with the prisoners. Instead, Hughes issued a recorded statement over the public address system, telling the men to obey orders from prison management. But the prisoners refused to believe it was really the governor. Then, against the counsel of his advisers, Hughes arranged a phone hookup in the warden's office so he could speak to the inmates directly. He listened to complaints from prisoner Raymond C. Lumadue, aged thirty-two, of Des Moines. The list of grievances included discrimination against Black inmates by prison personnel and claims that some prison employees wrote letters to prisoners' wives, recommending that they get divorced. Other complaints involved injustices in the parole system, high prices and lack of variety at the commissary, low pay for prison labor, and lack of a doctor at the infirmary. Hughes promised to act on complaints that had merit and advised the prisoners to select two men to represent them. After additional back-and-forth discussion, the men ended their siege and returned to their cells.[19]

As a follow-up, Hughes sent Jensen to Fort Madison to meet with the prisoners' committee for further discussions. Also, the Board of Control hired two professional penologists—Dr. Garrett Heyns of Olympia, Washington, and Myrl Alexander of Carbondale, Illinois, both veterans in their field—to study conditions at Anamosa and Fort Madison and recommend changes.[20]

It was clear that the impetus to reform Iowa's prisons was coming from the top. Speaking before the Iowa League of Municipalities in Des Moines in mid-November, Hughes called for a "more enlightened" approach to corrections policy. "Much as I am shocked by what has happened, I believe we must move ahead in the light of the vast professional and scientific information available to us." Hughes described the prison experts he intended to consult as "tough-minded practitioners," not "soft-headed do-gooders." As a practical matter, he argued, the state cannot afford to imprison every offender, and most of those convicted of crimes must be released at some point. "To send them back to society without having administered the best treatment and therapy available is to fall short of our essential goal—the protection of society."[21]

Reform of the prison system would not be accomplished overnight, nor would it be easy. The Heyns-Alexander report was completed and made public in early 1964. The two penologists cited several deficiencies in Iowa's system, including low pay, poor staff training, and management confusion; the latter stemmed from having just three individuals on the Board of Control to supervise the complex state network. The report applauded Hughes's positive attitude toward modernizing the prison system, noting that it was "unusual and most fortunate for

Iowa," but it also criticized his invitation to have inmates write to him directly, uncensored, about their personal problems and complaints, which the staff saw as "a lack of confidence in [prison] personnel." The report recommended the immediate expansion of corrections staff in three critical areas: personnel, operations, and industries. In addition, it strongly suggested higher base salaries, expanded training, additional counselors, and investment in pre-release programs.[22]

Hughes said he agreed "wholeheartedly" with the report and encouraged the Board of Control to implement the experts' recommendations as "rapidly as is possible within our financial limitations." Pushback came from a powerful voice on the interim legislative committee on corrections, Republican senator John Shoeman of Atlantic, an old-school advocate who believed the primary purpose of prisons is to punish. "I'm not opposed completely to rehabilitation," said Shoeman, "but when discipline and custody are secondary to treatment and rehabilitation, then the custody people at the institutions lose control." Shoeman's committee was influential in directing the Board of Control and setting its budget, and the senator was a controlling force in limiting the salaries of counselors and mental health professionals hired by the prison system.[23]

On overall prison reform, Hughes was undeterred. In a speech at Drake University in Des Moines in mid-May, he stressed that he would continue to push for reform, even though his "strong position in support of modern correction and probation procedures is not popular with some people." He said he would "stand by the program and the principles and will run on my record in this area, as in other areas in 1964."[24]

One casualty of the conflict was Benjamin Baer, who had been Iowa's director of corrections since 1960. An Illinois native with a master's degree in social work from the University of Southern California, Baer was firmly in the so-called modern school of penology and believed that rehabilitation of prisoners was of prime importance. On Monday, June 8, Baer resigned, claiming that he had been "deliberately and subtly undermined" by "certain members" of the Board of Control and had been accused of "coddling" prisoners. His efforts had also been opposed by Shoeman. However, the specific issue prompting his resignation was the hiring of a new warden at the Anamosa reformatory, a man that Baer felt was unqualified.[25]

In the middle of June, Hughes met with members of the Board of

Control in a seventy-five-minute closed session to work out a policy everyone could live with. Afterward, he dismissed Baer's resignation as "a lack of communication and a clash of personalities." Hughes stressed that reform would continue. "The Republican-controlled board of control and I are committed to the continuation of the modern corrections program we have underway in Iowa," he said. "In due time I will defend this program and my own role in support of it against all critics and political adversaries."[26]

Until Hughes could accumulate more political capital, the parties simply agreed to disagree, and this uneasy conflict lasted through the end of Hughes's administration. One victory was lawmakers' acceptance of the difference between healthy inmates and those who were mentally ill; having acknowledged that, the key was providing treatment to those who needed it. Hughes, through the University of Iowa and its medical school, obtained forty acres of land west of Iowa City to build a hospital for the evaluation and treatment of mentally ill inmates. The legislature allocated funds for this project, which became the Iowa Medical and Classification Center in Coralville, also known as Oakdale.[27]

Another issue that Hughes stood firm on was civil rights. The African American population in Iowa was small and largely concentrated in urban areas such as Des Moines and Waterloo. National attention was centered on the American South, but Hughes believed he could not criticize other states unless Iowans got their own house in order. In a July 1963 radio address, he acknowledged that people in Iowa "are denied employment opportunities and decent housing because of the color of their skin or their religion." In an effort to sell civil rights to white Iowans, Hughes placed it in the context of economic growth. "It leads to a dismal and distressing squandering of human resources. It does not allow many Iowans to fulfill their economic potential, thus making all Iowans the poorer for it." Later that month, he announced the creation of a thirty-five-member Human Rights Commission. A bipartisan group headed by Donald Boles, political science professor at Iowa State, the commission included businessmen, industrialists, labor union leaders, college professors, ministers, and individuals active in civil rights organizations. Said Hughes, "It is my hope that the commission will gather data and investigate complaints not only where they concern businesses and labor unions, but also where they concern units of government."[28]

Hughes knew, of course, that appointing a commission on civil rights would not alleviate deep-seated racial or religious prejudices. Civil rights reforms would require constant and continuous support from Iowa leaders like himself. For instance, in a late July press conference, he urged the Iowa Highway Patrol, composed entirely of white officers, to hire Black employees. When the Human Rights Commission urged the adoption of local ordinances to prohibit racial discrimination in housing, Hughes said, "I agree with them 100 percent." His push for advances in civil rights would continue more intensely later in his administration.[29]

The governor's concern for the downtrodden of society also extended to Iowa's poor. In a late September 1963 radio broadcast, Hughes defended the Aid to Dependent Children (ADC) program, which granted funds to low-income mothers. Acknowledging that supporters of such programs "are not particularly popular these days," he said, "no one gets a good living from ADC payments." The governor was referring to a report that 2 percent of ADC recipients were obtaining the funds fraudulently. He defended the 98 percent who used ADC funds "legally and properly to feed and clothe their children and send them to school."[30]

Hughes was also anticipating a crisis in ADC funding. In the proposed budget he sent to the legislature in 1963, he recommended a $1.25 million increase in state funding for ADC, but Republicans increased the allotment by only $250,000. (The ADC program combined federal, state, and county contributions.) State welfare officials reported that, beginning in November, they would be forced to cut payments to about thirty-eight hundred Iowa families. Where to place the blame, said Hughes, was clear. "There is no one else responsible but the Legislature for the payment cuts." Blasting Republicans at a press conference, the governor also announced efforts to improve the collection of child-support payments from deserting fathers and to strengthen laws requiring parents to support their children. In early October Hughes met with more than a dozen ADC recipients in his office—many of whom brought their children—to hear their protests about the cuts. Given the budget limitations, he could offer little more than a sympathetic ear and the hope for a more supportive legislature in the future.[31]

Hughes, feeling that the formality of the governor's office had cut him off from average citizens, announced on August 19, 1963, that he was establishing a weekly session—Wednesdays from 9:30 a.m. to noon—

for ordinary Iowans to talk to him on a first-come, first-served basis. He hoped to listen to them and address whatever concerns they might have. "I'm sure I won't be able to help all of them, but the least I can do is to see them and help as many as I can," he said. Hughes had gotten the idea from Michigan governor George Romney at a recent governors' conference.[32]

On September 4 nearly two dozen people—and half as many reporters—gathered at the governor's office at the state capitol. Hughes opened his door and began each session by setting a five-minute egg timer on his desk and let each visitor talk until their time ran out. Some asked Hughes to look into paroling their relatives. Others complained about low ADC payments. A week later, two guards from the Fort Madison penitentiary came to thank the governor for improving working conditions there. One man waltzed into Hughes's office with no agenda at all; he simply wanted to see a governor up close, so he was invited to plop his feet on the governor's desk and chat with the state's top executive for five minutes.[33]

Most of his weekly visitors came from the "lower economic class" of society, said Hughes, and he could not help all of them. "They've exhausted every other source and believe that I can help them, but in most cases there's nothing that I can do," he said. Much of the actual work was done by Hughes's limited staff, whose workload was increased by the necessary follow-up, letter writing, and contact with other state departments. As Hughes's schedule and speaking engagements took up more of his time, he canceled some of these Wednesday sessions and ultimately did away with them. But as 1963 ended, one thing was clear: this was not an ordinary governor who simply sat behind his desk and ran state government. He meant to use his post and the tools it provided to interact with and aid those on society's outer edges.[34]

6 | Reapportionment and Reform

After the Shaff Plan's defeat at the polls, Iowa's reapportionment battle moved to the courts. In January 1964 a federal three-judge panel in Des Moines unanimously ruled that the present reapportionment arrangement was unconstitutional, and it strongly urged that a special session of the legislature be called to create a new plan. If the legislators failed in that endeavor, the court would draw up a plan of its own. In fact, two plans were needed: a temporary statutory plan to cover the upcoming 1964 elections, and a permanent plan implemented through a constitutional amendment. The court mandated that representation in one house be based on population; in the other house, strict adherence to a population basis was not required, but any departure had to be "rational." This nebulous caveat confused many lawmakers, but most took it to mean that they could consider other factors, such as area or county units.[1]

Hughes and legislative leaders agreed that the special session would begin on February 24 to tackle both the interim and the permanent plans. As governor, Hughes had official sway over only the temporary plan for the 1964 elections. Since this would consist of a law passed by the Iowa house and senate, he had the power to veto a proposal he disliked or that, in his opinion, would not pass judicial muster; he could use that power to shape the final bill. On the constitutional amendment process to create the permanent plan, Hughes had little input other than personal persuasion. Iowa law mandated that constitutional amendments pass both houses in two consecutive legislative sessions, followed by approval or rejection by the general population; the governor had no official role.[2]

Facing the Republican-controlled legislature on the opening day of the special session, Hughes addressed the lawmakers and, referring to the Shaff Plan battle, asked that "bygones be bygones." But he warned against passing "another minority-controlled reapportionment plan," saying that legislators were "deluding themselves" if they thought this would be possible. Hughes said he favored "a bicameral legislative pattern with the House [based] on population and the Senate [based] on population and area factors," but he coyly declined to specify further details, knowing that any plan of his would probably die at the hands of the Republican majority. Instead, he proclaimed only that he was "open-minded about the mechanics of the actual apportionment." Repeating earlier themes in the Shaff Plan debate, Hughes declared that fairer representation would have "a magnetic influence" and would keep "a reasonable share of our talented young people in Iowa," contributing to "a magnificent era of potential progress and economic development." The not-so-hidden meaning behind this idea was that urban elements would blossom in the new legislature, overriding the more conservative rural forces and creating a more progressive government.[3]

With that, the legislators plunged into committee consultations, making the temporary plan for the 1964 elections their top priority. All Iowa house members and half the senate would be running for reelection under that plan, and the primaries were just around the corner in June. The Iowa Constitution currently mandated that district boundaries not cross county lines; districts had to be entirely within one county or include two or more contiguous counties. This meant that counties with large populations, such as Polk, had to either create subdistricts within counties or elect representatives at large. During the debate, the at-large argument won.[4]

Debate on the temporary plan continued into March, with legislators offering multiple plans and different sizes for both houses. They engaged in intense and often emotional discussions, mostly within the Republican Party. Entering the legislative debate from outside, Iowa Republican Party chairman Robert Ray and Republican attorney general Evan Hultman offered a plan that clashed with elements of the GOP that wanted to keep rural representation strong. Ray hoped to avoid alienating urban voters from the Republican Party, and Hultman, already a declared candidate for governor, hoped to curry favor with urban voters in the fall. Some GOP lawmakers claimed that Hultman was abandoning rural Iowa and pledged not to support him for governor, despite the lack of other candidates. In fact, Ray and Hultman, both attorneys, knew what would be acceptable to the court and were fighting for the best possible outcome for rural Iowans.[5]

The Ray-Hultman plan walked a fine line between political factions. They advocated an Iowa house of 129 members and a senate of 58 members, with a majority of the house representing 47 percent of the Iowa population and a majority of the senate representing 40 percent. The Iowa Republican State Central Committee endorsed the plan, but it was opposed by the Iowa Farm Bureau, the Iowa Manufacturers Association, and many rural legislators.[6]

Democratic legislators—without Hughes's input—presented a similar plan, but they lacked the votes to pass it and saw the Ray-Hultman proposal as an acceptable option. This presented an interesting situation: Republican Party chairman Ray was asking Democrats to support a plan opposed by significant Republican lobbying groups and members of his own party. Overriding all this was the threat of a Hughes veto.[7]

On March 11 the Iowa senate approved a temporary plan that created house districts based on equal population but preserved a clear rural majority in the senate. Hughes flatly stated that he would veto it. He offered to meet with Republican leaders, but they were reluctant to talk with the Democratic governor and risk increased grassroots hostility among Republicans. Some urban Republican leaders were actually pleased that Hughes had clearly stated his intention to veto the bill. They believed this gave them more leverage to convince rural members to vote for a more equitable plan.[8]

By mid-March, negotiations seemed to be at a standstill. When legislators left Des Moines for home on Friday, March 14, one of them said, "Well, we certainly finished this week in a blaze of nothing."[9]

Early the next week, however, Republicans were ready to face reality. Most of them realized that failure to compromise and agree on a temporary plan—under the threat of a Hughes veto—meant that the court would create a system with less protection for rural areas. On March 17, the twenty-fifth day of the special session, a newly created joint house-senate conference committee recommended a 124-member house and a 59-member senate for 1964. Under this plan, a majority of the senate would potentially be controlled by senators from districts with 38.9 percent of the state's population, compared to 35.6 percent under the current 50-member senate. The house would potentially be controlled by legislators from districts representing 47.5 percent of the population, compared to the present 37 percent. Keeping the at-large policy in the house, the plan gave Polk County eleven representatives; the next sixteen largest counties received two to five representatives each, depending on population; and all other counties had one representative each.[10]

Legislators passed this temporary plan on March 18, after it became clear that Hughes would sign the bill. He did so on March 23 in the presence of forty legislators and state officials. Four days later, the three-judge federal panel unanimously approved the temporary plan.[11]

The next task was to create a permanent plan in the form of a constitutional amendment. The political matrix of this process was different, since there was no threat of a Hughes veto. However, the plan was still subject to judicial oversight. It also required a second passage in the next legislature, which would no doubt have greater urban representation after the 1964 elections conducted under the temporary plan. None of that stopped Republican lawmakers from creating a permanent plan with rural control of the legislature as its focus. After much debate, the legislature passed a plan with a 50-member senate, based largely on area, and a 114-member house based on population. This meant that a majority of the senate could be elected by less than 32 percent of the Iowa population, and half the state could elect half the house. It seemed very similar to the Shaff Plan, which Iowans had recently rejected. But, with the permanent plan passed, Republican lawmakers adjourned the special session and went home.[12]

Hughes called the proposal "a nightmare of galloping apportionment." Whereas the temporary plan had been a "beacon of hope," he said "that light went out" with passage of the permanent plan. He compared it to creating a British House of Commons and House of Lords—with the proposed senate being the latter. Claiming that the plan showed an inability to face reality, Hughes said, "Apparently a majority of the Legislators chose to believe that the Shaff Plan was *not* defeated on December 3, that the courts did *not* rule against minority control of the Legislature, and that the people of Iowa do *not* want to move forward." He added, "The majority party had an opportunity to make history—they chose to make politics."[13]

The governor promised to take the issue into the fall campaign. However, it would not be a point of contention between the two major-party candidates for governor. Hultman, recognizing the plan's legal failings and its dismissal of urban voters, said, "This is not a plan that I can or will" support. He stated that, if elected governor, he would work against the plan in the 1965 legislature.[14]

All the arguments in favor of rural representation came crashing down on June 15, 1964, when the US Supreme Court declared in *Reynolds v. Sims* that state legislatures must be entirely apportioned by population. The court instructed federal judges to proceed slowly in implementing this order and asked them to consider the proximity of upcoming elections and the mechanics and complexities of state election laws. For Iowans, this meant that the temporary plan for the November election would probably stand, but the permanent plan would be ruled unconstitutional.[15]

Hughes announced that he was "pleased" with the decision and said it was "obvious the permanent Iowa reapportionment plan will not meet the standards set out by the U.S. Supreme Court." The next important step was electing legislators in 1964 who would write their own version of the permanent reapportionment plan.[16]

Reapportionment was not the only task on Hughes's agenda in early 1964. He was also tackling the overall reorganization and modernization of the state government, an effort that would continue throughout his governorship. Hughes created a ninety-two-member commission, headed by Park Rinard, to promote and increase cooperation between state and local government. In addition to state and local officials, the group included public school representatives and other interested parties. The commission was charged with reviewing home rule (granting cities and towns the power to make their own governing decisions), state aid, better public understanding of government, economy in government, small-town development, and joint government planning for metropolitan areas.[17]

In February Hughes initiated regular meetings with heads of fifteen major state agencies to facilitate the exchange of ideas and to review problems and programs. The goal was to use the existing framework to drive government reform by unifying operations and increasing efficiency where possible. In May Hughes announced a series of nonpartisan conferences with community and industrial leaders to solicit their advice on state administrative and financial matters for "the common cause of Iowa's development." Hughes also sent Iowa business representatives around the country—and eventually internationally—to promote Iowa commerce. Hughes was the first Iowa governor to initiate these international visits.[18]

Hughes's reform efforts included education, particularly the need for vocational schools. He had repeatedly emphasized this issue during the 1962 campaign and continued to do so as governor. At a careers conference at the University of Iowa in February 1964, he cited the need to train Iowans to compete in the highly technical and specialized workplace, both industrial and agricultural, to keep people in the state.

He highlighted vocational training to aid workers who were displaced by automation and to provide alternatives to high school dropouts. Hughes complained that the last three sessions of the legislature have "barely been keeping up with the minimum demands of education" and admitted that the state has "not been facing up to the challenges of the future in education."[19]

Hughes was correct about the lack of action in the legislature, despite the studies it generated. In 1959 legislators granted $25,000 to the Legislative Research Bureau for a comprehensive study on higher education in Iowa. That study underscored the need for vocational schools to train workers in the skills necessary to participate in increasingly complex businesses and to provide options for those choosing not to go to a four-year college. In 1961 the legislature commissioned a second study on vocational and technical education, resulting in a report titled "Education beyond High School Age: The Community College." Despite the results of these two studies, the 1963 legislature took no action.[20]

The main problem was funding. Creating a vocational education system was going to be expensive, and the governor knew it. "Sure, it will cost more to provide this training," Hughes said to a Cedar Rapids audience in February, "but that cost will be nothing in comparison with the loss in productivity of these people if we don't provide it. We must equip our children to meet the challenges of the age in which they will live."[21]

It was up to the legislature to create these schools and fund them. But that would have to wait until after the 1964 elections—for both lawmakers and the governor.

7 | LBJ's "Favorite Governor" and Reelection

Republican attorney general Evan "Curly" Hultman's campaign for governor had an inauspicious start. He planned to declare his candidacy in his Des Moines office on the morning of Monday, December 20, 1963. He rose early that day for the long drive from his home in Waterloo, but his car stalled about fifty miles into the journey. He hitchhiked to the nearest large town, rented a car, and hired someone to pick up his disabled auto. His campaign did not improve much after that.[1]

In an informal press conference after his announcement, Hultman admitted that Hughes had created a "positive image" by taking tough stands on controversial issues, but he intended to take some tough stands, too. Thirty-eight years old and standing five feet five inches tall, Hultman was a former Golden Gloves bantamweight boxing champion. Born in Albia, Iowa, he had attended public schools in Ottumwa and Waterloo and obtained a law degree from the University of Iowa in 1952. Elected Iowa's attorney general in 1960, he was now serving his second two-year term and was ready to take the next step in his career. He had dreamed of becoming governor since he was a child.[2]

One problem Hultman faced was resistance within his own party because of his stance on reapportionment. Even Republican Party chairman Robert Ray admitted early in 1964 that some members were "miffed" at Hultman's opposition to the rural faction, but with no other candidate in the running, Ray thought objecting to Hultman was "the height of contradictory reasoning." Nevertheless, support for Hultman among rural Republicans was less than enthusiastic.[3]

Another problem was Harold Hughes. In a *Des Moines Register* poll released in mid-January, Hughes had a 57 percent approval rating among Iowans, the highest for a governor in four years. By mid-March, during the reapportionment battle, this had risen to 67 percent, an all-time high. At the same time, in a direct matchup between the two contenders, a poll showed Hughes leading 51 to 21 percent; even among traditionally Republican rural voters, Hughes led 50 to 19 percent, and among small-town residents he led 42 to 24 percent. That same month, the UPI news service named Hughes Iowa's "Man of the Year" for the second consecutive time; he was the unanimous choice of Iowa newspaper editors and radio and television news directors. Hughes had clearly established a love affair with Iowans through his forthrightness, his bold stand on issues, and his unflinching willingness to fight for fair-minded policies.[4]

Hughes declared himself a candidate for reelection on Saturday, January 18, at a Des Moines press conference in advance of a Democratic fund-raiser at Veterans Auditorium. "It has been my conviction that public officials should take clear stands on the major issues," Hughes said in his announcement. "I believe the record will show that I have never hesitated to place my political future on the block for what I believed to be in the public interest. I have no intention of changing this policy."[5]

On a personal level, Hughes and Hultman got along quite well. On a policy level, they saw eye to eye on liquor by the drink and reapportionment, removing these issues from campaign debates. During a well-publicized private meeting between the two men early in January to discuss a state legal issue, they talked for more than an hour. Afterward, Hughes said, "We agreed that if we are political opponents our responsibilities as state officials will have priority over everything else. We also agreed to keep an open line of communications between our offices." The governor added that he had always been on friendly terms with Hultman and expected to remain so during the campaign.[6]

Of course, these "friendly terms" came to an end once the campaign kicked into high gear shortly after the special legislative session adjourned. At that point, Hultman accused Hughes of promoting tax hikes by calling for increased government spending. The attorney general, in contrast, advocated dramatic tax cuts. Hughes's response was to position himself as the advocate for fiscal responsibility and critical state services. "Are we to cut state taxes at the expense of vital services such as education, mental health, or old age assistance?" He pointed out that "talking about reducing state taxes without talking about local property taxes is like discussing Little Red Riding Hood without even mentioning the wolf." The danger in reducing state taxes, Hughes said, was that property taxes might have to be increased to take up the slack.[7]

To support his reelection effort, Hughes actively recruited other candidates to run for state office on the Democratic ticket. "There weren't a lot of people in the pipeline because Democrats weren't winning a lot of state offices," said Dwight Jensen. Hughes took to the phone in an effort to recruit a quality lineup for the state slate. According to Jensen, Hughes tried to convince Gary Cameron, a Fairfield attorney, to run for secretary of state. "I remember him saying, 'Well, Gary, all you need to do is just go to campaign events, get on the platform and say a few things.' I don't remember if he said you don't need to worry about getting elected, but it was implicit in the conversations. . . . Of course, everyone got elected, including Gary Cameron." According to journalist Martin Jensen of WMT in Cedar Rapids, "These were not accidental candidates. These were very capable, strong, influential, and savvy, smart people, too."[8]

As the 1964 campaign moved into the summer months, Hughes sought an advantage by linking himself with the popular Lyndon Johnson, who was running for his first full term as president after assuming the office following Kennedy's assassination. Hughes had first met Johnson in 1959, when the Texan was majority leader of the US Senate and had come to Iowa to make speeches in Des Moines and Marshalltown. In a letter to a friend, Hughes called Johnson "a very strong and capable personality." At a governors' conference in Miami Beach in July 1963, the two met again, but this time, Hughes was the governor of Iowa and Johnson was the vice president. The two later exchanged letters, saying how pleased they had been to see each other again.[9]

In mid-January 1964, shortly after Johnson became president, Hughes—along with aide Jensen and Democratic chairman Lex Hawkins—visited him at the White House for half an hour. In addition to politics, they talked about "everything from deer hunting in Texas to cattle raising," according to Hughes, and Johnson, he noted, "knows a lot about both."[10]

It was clear that Hughes and Johnson were building a close relationship based on traits they shared, including their strong personalities. Both Johnson and Hughes were liberal Democratic officeholders at one of the high points of American liberalism. As postwar prosperity generated greater tax revenue—especially after the federal tax cut in 1964, which prompted further growth—liberals believed that government could improve the quality of life for citizens and raise the standard of living for lower-income Americans. To the latter end, Johnson declared a "war on poverty" in his first State of the Union address in early 1964, marking the beginning of his ambitious Great Society initiatives. A master at pressuring Congress to bend to his will, Johnson aggressively pursued a massive explosion of federal programs that included Medicare, antipoverty efforts, civil rights advances, funding for cultural initiatives, and aid to education. The man in the White House who achieved all these goals with his near-limitless energy was someone Hughes clearly admired.[11]

The feeling was mutual. Hughes soon became known as "LBJ's favorite governor," a label the president himself promoted. On July 28 Hughes and Eva were guests at the White House, where they attended a state dinner honoring the president of the Malagasy Republic. The Hugheses stayed in a three-room suite overlooking the front lawn of the executive mansion and were ushered into the White House by Johnson's wife, Lady Bird. The couple had the additional honor of being seated at the same table as the president during the dinner. At the after-dinner reception, President Johnson danced with Eva. The evening marked a sterling moment for the couple from Ida Grove.[12]

Several weeks prior to the 1964 Democratic convention in Atlantic City, New Jersey, Hughes got a call from White House aide Cliff Carter asking him to make a seconding speech at the convention. A startled Hughes immediately agreed. Weeks later, Hughes, Eva, and twelve-year-old Phyllis joined another Iowa couple and drove to the World's Fair in New York and then on to Washington for another presidential event prior to the convention. When the Hughes family arrived, they discovered that they would be spending the night in the White House; Phyllis even had her own room. Lady Bird herself gave Eva and Phyllis, along with other governors' wives who were attending the event, a tour of both the public and family quarters of the White House. Treated to a performance of the musical *Oklahoma* on the White House lawn, Hughes and Eva enjoyed a pleasant chat with the president.[13]

Some of these presidential pleasantries would vanish at the 1964 Democratic convention in Atlantic City. During the preceding months, Johnson had been playing a coy game building up to his nomination, acting presidential and using his special talents to drive the Civil Rights Act of 1964 and the first wave of his Great Society programs through Congress. He delayed the announcement of his candidacy until the convention, although few doubted that he would run and would get the nomination by acclamation. He wanted a flawless convention to show Americans a united Democratic Party fully behind its president. That goal faced potential disruption due to the controversy involving the Mississippi Freedom Democratic Party (MFDP). By most outsiders' standards, the state's regular Democratic delegation to the convention had been chosen through a racist process, resulting in an all-white group. Shut out of the delegate selection system and fueled by the organizational energy of Freedom Summer, Mississippi Blacks, along with white civil rights supporters, created a parallel procedure and elected their own delegates, following the rules of the Democratic Party and often risking their lives as they endured bombings, beatings, and bullets. Dubbed the MFDP, this group also arrived in Atlantic City and demanded to be seated at the convention. Faced with a potential crisis, President Johnson ordered his allies at the convention—in no uncertain terms—to work out a compromise.[14]

The MFDP presented its case to the convention's credentials committee through civil rights attorney Joseph Rauh and demanded to be seated. Behind the scenes in Atlantic City and at the White House, intense and passionate negotiations got under way to broker a deal between the civil rights movement and the southern delegations. Many southern delegates considered any concession at all to the MFDP intolerable, and significant numbers threatened to walk out of the convention if that happened. Participating in the negotiations was Des Moines attorney and credentials committee member Sherwin Markman, whom Hughes had recommended to the White House as an able mediator. (President Johnson took notice of his work, and Markman became a White House staffer in 1965.) After days of tense parleys, a tentative agreement emerged: the MFDP would get two at-large delegates to join Mississippi's all-white delegation.[15]

The compromise first required the approval of the convention's credentials committee. Standing in the way of acceptance was another Iowan on the committee, Mrs. James Dunbar of Cedar Falls. "I am satisfied these [MFDP] delegates have complied with the rules and regulations of the party but they have been refused recognition in their own state," she said. Dunbar intended to sign the minority report that would take the MFDP's protest to the floor of the convention, a move that was gaining support. "As I see it, justice is color blind," she added.[16]

Dunbar's position caught the attention of the president, who placed a call to Hughes at his hotel suite. In blunt language, Johnson told the governor that Dunbar was not supporting the compromise and warned Hughes, "You all are going to have to do something about that." Hughes protested that Dunbar was a "civil rights person," and he did not want to "apply undue pressure on my people." After a chilling moment of silence, LBJ said, "Governor, I expect you to control these things; when we get people on these committees, we expect them to do what we want them to do. Now I want you to take care of it." Hughes again tried to explain his position, but a cold, steely LBJ responded, "Governor, I expect you to take care of it and I don't want to have any more problems with that woman." With that, the president of the United State hung up on the perspiring governor of Iowa.[17]

Hughes summoned Dunbar to his suite the next morning and talked to her about the issue. As it happened, she had walked up to a group of civil rights leaders to tell them how much she admired them, and the group, late for a meeting, had brushed her aside, greatly offending her. Thanks to this social gaffe, she was now willing to support the compromise, saving Hughes from Johnson's wrath. This episode, however, provided insight into the powerful, intense personality of Lyndon Johnson. Although the compromise was angrily rejected by the MFDP, it prevented a massive walkout by the South and helped LBJ preserve a relatively united Democratic Party.[18]

On Wednesday evening, August 26, Hughes strolled into the national spotlight with a four-minute seconding speech for President Johnson. At the time, all three national television networks broadcast virtually every minute of the quadrennial political conventions. In his flowery political speech, Hughes bragged that Iowa had produced its first billion-dollar corn crop, and in November it was "going to produce a bumper crop of Democratic votes." Eva Hughes listened to her husband's speech with Lady Bird Johnson in the presidential box seats. The next evening, when Johnson entered the convention to give his acceptance speech, Hughes was part of the nominee's traditional escort to the speaker's stand. According to the *Des Moines Tribune*'s Drake Mabry, Hughes had emerged as the principal party spokesman for midwestern Democratic governors.[19]

Hughes pronounced the convention "tremendously successful" and said he believed the party platform was "acceptable to both Democrats and moderate Republicans." In a remark reflecting both his public and private interactions with the president, Hughes stated in a postconvention press release, "If Lyndon Johnson dominated the convention—as indeed he did—then I think we can say this is the kind of leadership we need in the difficult days ahead. He didn't get his amazing legislative program through the Congress by playing solitaire in an ivory tower."

Iowa's Democratic nominee for governor looked forward to a fall campaign with a popular president at the top of the ticket and a united party behind him.[20]

The opposite was true for Curly Hultman. The 1964 primary season marked the rise of the conservative movement in the Republican Party with the candidacy of Arizona senator Barry Goldwater. Running on a platform of limited government, anticommunism, and strong defense, Goldwater defied the liberal postwar consensus, and this suited his energetic and vocal base just fine. One problem, however, was Goldwater's often ill-suited and ill-timed quotes, which cast him as unsteady and unqualified for the presidency. His call to privatize Social Security and cavalier remarks about using nuclear weapons gave strong ammunition to his opponents—both inside and outside the Republican Party—depicting him as a potential disaster at the top of the ticket in the fall. But Goldwater continued to collect delegates through the primaries, and as the Republicans' convention in San Francisco loomed that summer, it seemed that nothing could stop the well-organized Goldwater bandwagon.[21]

The presidential nomination battle split the leadership of the Iowa Republican Party. At the convention, Hultman and party chairman Ray announced that they would be voting for Governor William Scranton of Pennsylvania, a late entry in the race in an attempt to stop Goldwater. Both strongly believed that Goldwater would lose heavily in November and take the state ticket down with him. Opposing them in the Iowa delegation were the Old Guard Republicans, represented by Iowa US senators Bourke Hickenlooper and Jack Miller, who both supported Goldwater. After an Iowa caucus voted 14–10 for Goldwater, a Goldwater delegate poked Hultman and said, "That one's for you." With that, the Republican nominee for governor angrily stalked out of the room.[22]

When the dust settled after Goldwater's nomination, there appeared to be two Republican campaigns in Iowa—one for Goldwater and the other to salvage Iowa Republicans' chances in November. Both efforts were facing Democrats at the top of the ticket—President Johnson and Governor Hughes—who had commanding leads at the polls. Hultman was running against Hughes with a badly divided Republican Party in Iowa and an increasingly unpopular figure leading the national party.[23]

Hughes sought to link Goldwater with Iowa Republicans, forcing them
to carry the negative weight of his candidacy into November. At the Iowa
Democratic convention in Des Moines, Hughes lashed out at the nominee with special flourish. Referring to Goldwater's vote against the 1964
Civil Rights Act and his militaristic statements, Hughes said:

> What has happened to America that one of our two major political parties
> should nominate a man whose beliefs repeal the idealism of the American
> dream of equality and justice for all? What has happened to America when
> we see a man nominated for the presidency who is a brash, nostalgic saber
> rattler amid the stark realities of an age that exists under the black cloud of
> possible nuclear war?

Hughes highlighted his own groundbreaking accomplishments, such
as liquor by the drink and the temporary reapportionment plan, and
asked, "Is anyone naïve enough to believe the Republicans would have
made these progressive moves voluntarily without the prodding of Democratic leadership and the forces of enlightened public opinion?"[24]

With both gubernatorial candidates back from their respective national conventions, the Iowa campaign for governor started on Labor
Day weekend. Hughes officially opened his campaign for reelection
with a speech in Mason City in northern Iowa, emphasizing that there
were still major changes he wanted to make. The most important was
tax reform to reduce the growing property tax burden by redirecting
state funds to local governments. He also continued to advocate for
expanded educational opportunities for young Iowans, particularly vocational training.[25]

Hughes benefited from a well-financed campaign. Finance chair Joseph Rosenfield, head of the Younkers department stores and a Hughes
confidant, said raising money for Hughes was "relatively easy." He
added, "We've had a lot of Republican contributors—and we don't have
to pressure them to get money either. . . . We could get more Republican money if we would only ask. Many usually Republican businessmen
are mighty impressed with Hughes." Additional money for the campaign was hardly needed, however. A July *Des Moines Register* poll showed
Hughes ahead of Hultman, 52 to 35 percent. By mid-August, Hughes
had increased his lead to 61 to 35 percent; in Iowa cities, Hughes was
ahead 75 to 21 percent.[26]

As the fall campaign began, Hultman came out swinging by accusing
Hughes of planning tax increases across the board. The charge had

merit because the governor's goals of expanded educational opportunities and property tax relief through state aid would both cost money. In contrast, the Republican candidate called for tax reductions of $17 million, declaring that no increases were needed. In a September debate between the two candidates before the Iowa Press Association, Hughes said, "Bluntly, my opponent has made the wildest and most irresponsible statements about fiscal matters of any gubernatorial candidate in my memory." Hughes asked Hultman how he would make up for his tax reductions, declaring that cuts in state taxes would mean higher local taxes. "To advocate reduction in state taxes that would result in local property tax increases is an insult to the intelligence of the people of Iowa," Hughes charged. Hultman did not change his position.[27]

Hultman's strategy was to target rural and small-town voters, who traditionally fell into the Republican camp, despite his stand against pronounced rural representation in the reapportionment debate. He did not believe that Hughes had won in 1962 by attracting a strong urban vote; rather, he believed the rural Republican vote had declined, and Hultman was determined to win it back. This meant campaigning vigorously throughout rural Iowa. At one point, Hultman said, "Man, I've seen the inside of more barns in the last few days than I thought existed." In the can't-get-a-break department, Hultman's plane was forced down by storms as he flew from Des Moines to make an appearance in Spencer in northwestern Iowa; he then rented a car to complete the trip, which got a flat tire.[28]

In mid-October Hughes began a helicopter tour of Iowa, designed to speed up travel and attract crowds that had never seen such an aircraft. The plan was to cover fifteen hundred miles and visit forty cities in one week. On this stretch, Hughes continued to emphasize vocational education to complement economic growth and a pay-as-you-go tax policy, combined with property tax relief from the state. As he neared the finish line and polls continued to show a large lead (63 to 35 percent) over Hultman, it appeared that Hughes was heading for overwhelming victory in November.[29] Then the issue of his past drinking arose.

About a year before the election, the editors of *Look* magazine, which had a circulation of several million and was published by Cowles Magazines of Des Moines, approached Hughes and asked him to authorize an article featuring his triumph over alcoholism. Hesitant at first, Hughes decided to grant an interview, reasoning that publicity about his recovery could be a positive example to others suffering from alcoholism. Up to that point, there had been little discussion of Hughes's alcoholism in the media, but he had freely answered questions when asked, proclaiming that he had not had a drink in more than a decade. For the *Look* article, he was interviewed by Fletcher Knebel, nationally famous as the coauthor of the novel *Seven Days in May*, about a threatened military overthrow of the US government.[30]

Hughes was told that the article would appear in an April 1964 issue, well before the election, but editorial delays pushed it to October 6, 1964, just a month before the vote. Entitled "One Man's Triumph," it was an affirmative, uplifting story about a recovered alcoholic who had overcome his drinking problem and become governor of Iowa. However, Hughes had been less than truthful about the end of his drinking days. He chose not to mention his near-suicide attempt and instead said he had taken his last drink after waking up in a Des Moines hotel room following a two-day binge. Nor did he mention his 1954 relapse in Kissimmee, Florida, where he was arrested for public intoxication. Most damaging, however, was the date: Hughes was quoted as saying his last drink had been in 1952, not 1954. He later wrote to Knebel, pointing out the error, and the writer replied, "My notes said 1952, but of course, I could have misunderstood you." Hughes later wrote that it could have been his fault as well. *Look* did not issue a correction.[31]

The initial reaction to the article was generally positive. Hughes received dozens of letters from people all over the country, complimenting his candor and thanking him for being an example to others. But he also received several media inquiries about the 1954 Kissimmee incident. His response was, "No comment." Two reporters even visited the governor's mansion to ask about the arrest, but Hughes's silence quelled the media's interest.[32]

David Herrick, retired chief of the Iowa Highway Patrol, had learned about the Florida arrest through his law enforcement contacts and alerted the media. He was angry at Hughes after being pushed out of his job and replaced. When media inquiries failed to generate publicity, Herrick turned to the Hultman campaign, and the Republican candidate decided to use the information to throw a last-minute Hail Mary pass.[33]

On the Friday before Election Day, the candidates for governor traditionally conducted a luncheon debate before the Greater Des Moines Chamber of Commerce at the downtown Hotel Savery. That morning,

Bill Sueppel, the commissioner of public safety and a close friend of Hughes, received a phone call from a Republican contact: Hultman had information about Hughes's 1954 arrest for intoxication and was going to raise it at the debate. Sueppel quickly passed the information on to Hughes, who was prepared for the attack.[34]

Prior to the debate, Hultman took Hughes aside and, after confirming the facts of the Florida arrest, said he intended to bring it up during the debate. With a knot in his stomach, Hughes said, "Well, Curly, you do what you have to do. You know there's nothing I can do to stop you and I'm sorry you feel that you must do it. But you do what you have to do." Hughes later wrote that Hultman's eyes "had the look of a desperate man, ready for a final fight."[35]

The two candidates took their seats, and a coin flip determined the first speaker. Hultman won. In front of the audience of 285 people, Hultman launched into the details of the 1954 arrest and the inconsistency with Hughes's claim in *Look* that he had taken his last drink in 1952. Calling it clear deception, Hultman warned that if it happened once, it could happen again. To the hushed, stunned audience, the Republican claimed that he regretted bringing this incident up, but Hughes "had interjected this personal issue into the campaign" by cooperating with the *Look* article. Hultman thought Iowans should know the truth about a man who was claiming integrity but in fact had none.[36]

When Hultman finished, Hughes rose to speak, leaving his prepared remarks at his plate. Turning to the silent audience, Hughes said:

> At this eleventh hour of the political campaign, my opponents have come up with an item out of the past which they hope will blacken my reputation and influence the outcome of the election. . . . Well, ladies and gentlemen, I regret that the subject of my alcoholism had been brought up. But now that it has, I want to respond. The answer is yes. Yes, I was in Kissimmee, Florida. I did get drunk there. I was drunk driving my car. I was thrown in jail where I spent the night. I posted bond and left the city because there was no judge available the next day to appear in court. I did nothing to clear the files of the State Safety Commission. Whatever was on the records then is there today.

He started to choke up as he continued. "But I want to explain one thing and I'll never talk about it again. And this is, I regret that my family has to continue to suffer because of my alcoholism. It is bad enough that I suffer but it's worse that my wife and children have to suffer because of it. I'm deeply hurt that they have to be dragged through this again." Hughes paused. "I am an alcoholic and will be until the day that I die. But with God's help, I'll never touch a drop of alcohol again. Now can we talk about the issues of this campaign?"[37]

With that, the audience rose in sustained applause. Sherwin Markman, Hughes's campaign manager, was listening from the back of the room and recalled, "I thought that Curly's campaign died at that instant."[38]

As Hultman's accusation and Hughes's response reverberated around the state, the Iowa Republican Party headquarters in Des Moines was inundated with phone calls. A GOP spokesman said, "We have had a tremendous number of calls and most of them were very critical of Hultman." The Republican candidate for lieutenant governor, William Moody, condemned Hultman and issued a statement that said, "It is regrettable that an outdated personal matter has been injected into the campaign for governor." A Republican candidate for state representative from Polk County said that many "must have felt shock and dismay at the personal attack made on Governor Hughes last Friday by our Republican gubernatorial candidate." Hughes's office received an avalanche of phone calls, including one from a man who said he was a "damn good Republican, but just became a damn good Democrat." Another had a message for Hughes: "Tell him there is one more Republican that is going to vote for him. I never saw such a damn-fool stunt in my life." As the days passed, the office was flooded with letters, nearly all of them supporting Hughes. Many of them were from lifelong Republicans. Typical was one from Dr. Charles Logan of Keokuk, "a long time rather staunch Republican," who wrote to Hultman and copied Hughes: "In my opinion, the supposed strategy you [Hultman] used yesterday before the Greater Des Moines Chamber of Commerce was cheap, disgusting, and far below a level befitting any man aspiring to the governorship of our state."[39]

As Iowa State University professor James Socknat put it, "In the Bible Belt one may attack sin, but woe to the man who attacks the converted sinner."[40]

On Tuesday, November 3, 1964, Iowans elected Harold Hughes to a second term by the largest vote ever cast for governor and the biggest margin of victory over his opponent. He also had the distinction of running ahead of LBJ in Iowa: Hughes received 69 percent of the vote (794,610 to Hultman's 365,131), while 62 percent of Iowans voted for Johnson. (The latter was noted by the chief occupant of the White House, and not entirely positively.)[41]

Just as important was the Democrats' sweep throughout the Hawkeye State, winning significant majorities in both the Iowa house and senate and all seven statewide executive offices. Not since the 1930s had the Iowa Democrats held such power. The 1965 Iowa legislature would be the most heavily Democratic in the state's history, with 101–23 control in the house and 34–25 control in the senate. The temporary reapportionment plan—giving additional seats to urban counties, which were now electing Democrats—and the popular candidates at the head of the ticket proved a winning combination for Iowa Democrats. Another factor was that legislators were elected at large from each county, not from individual districts; for instance, Polk County elected eleven representatives, all Democrats. Among statewide offices, of particular significance was the election of Robert Fulton of Waterloo as lieutenant governor; he would play a major role in managing legislation as head of the Iowa senate.[42]

As Iowa Democrats celebrated their victories on election night in 1964, there was a broad feeling among Iowans that the floodgates controlled by conservatives for generations were about to break open, initiating a wave of reform under Harold Hughes. They were right.

8 | The Historic 1965 Iowa Legislature

When Harold Hughes cast his eyes over the Iowa legislature as he gave his State of the State address on January 12, 1965, it was a very different group from the one he had worked with two years earlier. It was the most heavily Democratic legislature in the state's history and much more reflective of urban Iowa. In the prior legislature, the state's five largest counties—Polk, Linn, Black Hawk, Scott, and Woodbury—had only ten representatives among them in the Iowa house; now they had thirty-two. The *Des Moines Register* declared on the first day of the session, "Rural power in the Iowa Legislature drops to an all-time low today," and "the new balance of power reflects the increased growth of cities and towns and the decline of the rural population in this age of increased industrialization of agricultural-minded Iowa."[1]

Sixty-five percent of the 128 Iowa house members and 37 percent of the 50 senators were new, compared with only 20 percent of the house and 15 percent of the senate two years earlier. Political commentator Frank Nye wrote that the gathering "may have been the most inexperienced legislature to meet in Iowa since the 1st General Assembly convened in 1846." Also, for the first time in Iowa history, two African Americans took the oath as house members: Mrs. Willie Glanton, an attorney from Polk County, and James Jackson, a high school science teacher from Black Hawk County. At twenty-five, Jackson was the youngest member of the legislature.[2]

Along with a dramatic change in composition, the new legislature cast aside barriers against reform that had been building for decades. Change was in the air, and the governor of Iowa now had the numbers, the allies, and the new attitudes to make change happen.

One significant engine of change was the *Des Moines Register*, Iowa's only statewide newspaper, thanks to the artful assistance of Hughes confidant Park Rinard through reporter Nick Kotz. "Somewhere on the east side of Des Moines was a bar where Park and I had a number of beers at noon and they served free food," recalled Kotz:

Park would tell me about changes needed in the state and I set about writing all these Sunday stories about the issues—the need for fair employment, civil rights, three or four other topics. These meetings with Park helped set me up with stories on issues that Hughes and Park wanted to push through the state. . . . I was barely aware that he had anything more on the line than giving me a good story. He was working his agenda which became Hughes's agenda.[3]

The *Register*'s editorial page also expressed support for reform.

Hughes captured this change in attitude in his State of the State address. "At long last, I believe we have begun to free ourselves from the bullheaded prejudices that have cramped our spirit and retarded our growth in years gone by." Though he made no specific legislative proposals, he hailed the past two years as a period of unprecedented prosperity for most Iowans, with record industrial and economic growth.[4]

Indeed, Iowa's industrial production had reached $8 billion for the first time in its history. Employment hit record highs in both of the last two years, and new industries, branches, and expansions totaled 168 in 1963 and leaped to 278 in 1964. Capital investment in plants and equipment—a major source of state and local revenue—exceeded $134 million in 1964, nearly double the 1963 record of more than $70 million. Iowa was part of the ongoing postwar economic boom, and its government had to accommodate the state's growing economy.[5]

Although his initial speech to the legislature was general, Hughes's inaugural address days later was more specific and detailed. He touched on thirty-two areas of possible legislative activity. A significant focus of the message was education, a critical issue as the baby boomers moved from crib to classroom, placing unprecedented pressure on schools. Hughes recommended creating at least four vocational schools around the state and increasing the funding for all educational levels from primary school through college. He also called for significant government reform to meet modern needs; specifically, he sought a shift from three-member state boards to more efficient professional management systems, and he outlined a nine-point program that included annual legislative sessions, four-year terms for governor, and state executive posts that were appointed rather than elected. Hughes again called for abolition of the death penalty. In addressing labor relations, he took a stand against repeal of the right-to-work law and instead came out for a "union shop," an issue that would inflame debate for the rest of the session.[6]

He ended his ambitious second inaugural address—no doubt written by Rinard—on a positive note, declaring that Iowa had swung "from a negative to an affirmative point of view." He stated, "We have, I think, reached a clearer distinction between what is right and what is only self-righteous." We Iowans, he said, have "regained our poise, our sense of venture, and our faith in the future. . . . In short, we have gained maturity and unity of purpose as a society. And this bodes well for Iowa's future."[7]

Now it was up to the newly empowered Iowa Democrats to implement this ambitious agenda. The first task was organization. And Iowa Democrats were finding that Hughes intended to be as involved in this process as he was in setting legislative priorities. One legislative leader had already been selected by the Iowa voters: Lieutenant Governor Robert Fulton. The Iowa Constitution gave the lieutenant governor the additional task of being president of the Iowa senate, a job at which Fulton, an attorney, proved particularly adept. He had a fine political sense and knew how to work with legislators, such as when to bring up a piece of legislation and when not to. A smart politician and a popular networker, Fulton ensured that the 1964 Iowa Democratic platform was transformed into Iowa law. Said Hughes aide Dwight Jensen, Fulton "was magnificent. He was responsible for a lot of the legislative achievements, I think. It took Hughes, of course, but Fulton managed to work them through."[8]

Selection of the rest of the Democratic leadership took place shortly after the November election. At a caucus of Democrats at the Hotel Fort Des Moines, state representative Vince Steffen of New Hampton, president of a grain drying equipment company, was elected Iowa house speaker. At thirty-five, he was the youngest person to hold the post since 1935. Hughes himself took part in the meeting and expressed a preference for Steffen, who was serving only his second term but had obviously impressed the governor with his leadership abilities. The *Des Moines Register*'s article on his selection was headlined, "Hughes Man Is Elected Speaker of the House." On the senate side, Andrew Frommelt of Dubuque, a more flamboyant politician than Fulton, was elected majority leader, following his service as minority leader in 1961 and 1963.[9]

When the legislature convened in early January 1965, it was presented with the final report from the Governor's Commission on State and Local Government, appointed a year earlier and headed by Rinard.

Many of the recommendations paralleled the Democratic platform, but they benefited from the support of groups that had studied state government outside the partisan realm. The proposals included increasing the governor's term to four years; authorizing the governor to reorganize and merge state agencies, pending legislative approval; permitting the governor to appoint state officials, rather than having the voters elect them; and allowing the governor a line-item veto on appropriation bills. The *Register* lauded the commission for producing "a long and impressive list of recommendations for legislation."[10]

The first wave of reforms from the Democrats involved process and structure, designed to enhance efficiency and openness. On the first day of the 1965 session, both the house and the senate adopted rules to open all committee meetings and mandated that all votes on bills in those committees be recorded. Prior to this, sessions and votes could be secret. The people's elected officials now had to operate with transparency.[11]

Democratic leaders also streamlined the committee system in both chambers, cutting senate committees from thirty-one to fifteen and house committees from forty-three to fifteen. With the same number of committees in both chambers, joint deliberation on issues became easier. "Not in several decades at least has an incoming party applied the axe to the legislative committee system with such sweeping effect," wrote George Mills of the *Register*. Fashioned through Fulton's leadership, the plan was reviewed and approved by Hughes.[12]

With the legislative machinery now in motion, Iowa Democrats began to reform the state government on a scale not seen in generations. However, not all the measures supported by Hughes sailed smoothly through the legislature. One such issue was Hughes's support for transporting parochial school students on public school buses. At the time, about 100,000 primary and secondary students attended private schools in Iowa—with about three-quarters of them attending Catholic schools. Since the 1940s, these students had been prohibited from using public school buses through both legislative and court action. The main argument justifying this position—a strong one among Iowans—was the concept of separation of church and state; busing of these students was seen as state support for church-run schools. Others opposed the increased costs for local schools.[13]

Both party platforms were silent on the issue in 1964, but Hughes strongly supported the use of public school buses for parochial school students, citing pleas from parents. His argument was that because the parents of parochial school students paid taxes that supported the buses, their children deserved to ride on them. But the church-state dispute raised hot emotions. Mills wrote, "Few bills in the 1965 legislative session are as controversial as the bus measure." Frank Nye of the *Cedar Rapids Gazette* called it "the hottest subject this legislature will face." Some legislators were receiving 150 letters a day on the topic. The issue also led to Catholic-Protestant conflicts. One legislator, Democrat C. E. Hutchins of Belle Plaine, changed his vote from support to opposition after receiving letters from Protestants expressing anti-Catholic bigotry, saying that the approval of busing would destroy two-thirds of the goodwill developed between Catholics and Protestants. "I feel the hate generated by such a bill is not worth it," he said.[14]

In early April the Iowa house passed the bus bill, 66–55. As the senate prepared to vote later in the month, Hughes called several members into his office to lobby for the bill, although one senator said there was no arm-twisting or political pressure. The senate ultimately rejected the measure, 39–19, with sixteen Democratic senators voting against it. Nye called the vote "the worst blow suffered by Gov. Harold Hughes since he took the oath of office in 1963."[15]

The outcome was entirely different on another education-related issue—the creation of a network of community colleges. At the time, Iowa had sixteen two-year junior colleges administered locally through individual school districts and supported by local taxes, state aid, and tuition. There were also sixteen "area schools" that provided vocational and technical education, operating with federal and state aid. Some of these area schools were affiliated with existing community or junior colleges, some were operated by local high schools, and one was run by a four-year university. With the exception of the latter, they were administered by local school districts. However, these schools were underfunded, were often inadequate to meet vocational training needs, and failed to follow a coordinated statewide effort to address educational demands.[16]

Given the Iowa legislature's failure to advance the issue in its 1963 session, despite years of study and debate, Hughes had made the creation of vocational training schools a major part of his reelection campaign in 1964. With solid Democratic majorities in both houses in 1965, he pushed for passage of the vocational school program. One of the key sponsors of the legislation was Democratic senator Jack Kibbie of Emmetsburg, who guided the measure through the legislature and credited Hughes's strong support for its passage. "The program would not have happened without Governor Harold Hughes," said Kibbie later.[17]

The Area Schools Act, signed by Hughes on June 7, 1965, led to the creation of a network of fifteen colleges across Iowa providing vocational training, two-year degrees, and adult education. Thirteen were organized as community colleges and two as vocational schools; all the community colleges also offered vocational and technical training. No state resident had to travel more than fifty miles for access to a postsecondary education. One of the key features of the legislation was merging junior colleges and vocational education programs into a single system.[18]

These institutions worked with industry and businesses such as John Deere, General Motors, and others, as well as community organizations, state agencies, and other key stakeholders, to become engines of economic development—realizing the vision Hughes and other supporters had for these schools. They trained a workforce for increasingly complex technical careers. This network also fed students into the state's four-year institutions through the transfer of credits, allowing students to obtain two years of higher education at a lower cost. The system gave marginal students a pathway to a four-year degree, offering life-changing opportunities for multiple generations of Iowans.[19]

According to Janice Nahra Friedel, who researched the history of Iowa community colleges, the resource "developed and grew into a system which fostered local flexibility, responsiveness, resourcefulness, collaboration, and partnerships with both the public and private sectors." During "good times," it provided "customized training and retraining for workers in the knowledge and skills needed for adoption of new technologies and processes, and in worker skills upgrading." During economic downturns, the system offered retraining for the thousands who lost their jobs; this was particularly important for Iowans during the farm crisis of the 1980s. The community colleges created in Iowa in 1965, according to Friedel, "emerged as powerful economic tools, demonstrating an agility to provide quality customized training for new and existing employees of companies looking to locate or to expand in the state."[20]

This was exactly what Hughes and his allies were working toward, and it remains one of the crowning achievements of the governor and the 1965 Iowa legislature.

The recurring debate over reapportionment returned in 1965, but in a different political matrix. Instead of a dominant rural Republican legislature, the Democrats, with significant urban representation, held the power. Also, the US Supreme Court's decision in *Reynolds v. Sims*, mandating that both chambers of state legislatures be apportioned based on population, meant that Iowa's 1964 permanent plan, with a geography-based senate, was unconstitutional. In February 1965 the federal district court in Des Moines went one step further, ruling that even the temporary plan of 1964 did not represent population closely enough and needed to be changed to meet those requirements for the 1966 elections.[21]

The legislators took up the task of the constitutional amendment first, shaping a general blueprint rather than drawing up specific districts. By mid-April, both houses had passed a permanent plan calling for a house of not more than one hundred members and a senate of not more than fifty, with representation based on population in both chambers. A bipartisan commission appointed jointly by legislators and the governor was tasked with dividing the state into districts. This amendment would have to be approved by the next legislature and then affirmed through a statewide vote.[22]

By late May, both houses had agreed on a temporary plan for the 1966 elections, with a 61-member senate and a 124-member house. One factor complicating the mix was the Iowa Constitution's prohibition against creating districts that crossed county lines or divided counties, which the courts had allowed to stand. Given this stipulation, plus the need to create equal-population districts, the Legislative Research Bureau, which was tasked with drawing up districts, sought computer help from the University of Iowa and Iowa State University. A *Register* editorial called the temporary plan far from ideal and observed that it was "based more on expediency and practical politics than on principle" but conceded that it "probably would meet court requirements"[23]

Still another debate was whether to create legislative districts within large-population counties (called subdistricting) or to elect representatives at large within counties. The former would require a constitutional amendment mandating subdistricting. In the 1964 elections, voters in populous counties—often with large Democratic majorities—had cast ballots for multiple at-large candidates; consequently, Democrats won all the at-large seats, shutting out Republicans. Subdistricting would give

Republicans an opportunity to win targeted seats. Early in the session, Hughes favored subdistricting. Otherwise, he said, it would be difficult for voters to choose when several candidates were vying for multiple offices. Also, he believed at-large voting violated the one-man, one-vote directive of the courts because it allowed high-population counties to control multiple representatives, compared with smaller counties that voted for only one. This pitted Hughes against many house Democrats and on the side of the Republicans. "The Hughes position," wrote reporter Mills early in the session, "is not expected to be popular with some members of his own party."[24]

The amendment to divide counties into legislative districts passed both houses in the 1964 special session and passed the senate again in 1965; it needed only house passage to advance to a statewide vote. That was not to be. On June 3 the house killed the amendment, 64–53, which was seen as a feud between Hughes and "large-population Democrats." "They made a horrible mistake and they'll bear the responsibility for it," said Hughes. (This would not be the last word on the subject. Legislative districts of equal population could later cross county lines, with each voter selecting only one representative.)[25]

The constitutional amendment on permanent reapportionment was only one of nine amendments passed by the 1965 legislature—a record number for a single session. Some of the amendments originated from the Committee on Government Reorganization appointed by Hughes and headed by Rinard. In addition to reapportionment, other significant amendments granted "home rule" to cities and towns; mandated annual sessions of the legislature; gave the governor line-item veto power on appropriation bills; approved four-year terms for the governor and lieutenant governor and required them to run as a team; and permitted the governor to appoint executive posts, pending senate approval.[26] These changes represented a significant modernization of the Iowa government.

By far, the most heated debate between Governor Hughes and Iowa lawmakers in 1965 was over labor legislation—in particular, the effort by labor Democrats to repeal the state's right-to-work law. In 1947 Congress had passed the Taft-Hartley Act, which allowed states to establish a worker's right to refrain from joining a union as a condition of employment. Shortly thereafter, the Iowa legislature passed a right-to-work law for businesses operating within the state's borders. By 1965, Iowa had outlawed the union shop, where an employee was required to join a union after being hired; the closed shop, where a person had to be a union member before being hired; and the agency shop, where an employee was not required to join the union but had to pay dues to the union for representing him or her in dealings with the employer.[27]

Labor supporters, counting on expanded Democratic support in the legislature, wanted to repeal these prohibitions to provide a psychological boost to union organizing efforts. Knowing that Iowans were suspicious of organized labor, union leaders argued that this would not increase union membership. Instead, they said, repeal would improve labor's status among the public by removing the stigma of union membership and giving labor representatives more prestige when dealing with plant managers. Another goal was to get more workers to pay their union dues, which ranged from $2 a month in small factories to as much as $7 in the building trades.[28]

In the mid-1960s about 112,000 Iowans belonged to some 1,200 local unions, accounting for approximately 15 percent of the state's nonfarm workforce. Three major employers in Iowa were unionized: Firestone Tire & Rubber Company in Des Moines—1,800 workers organized by the United Rubber Workers Union; John Deere Tractor in Waterloo—6,400 workers organized by the United Auto Workers; and Rath Packing Company in Waterloo—3,400 workers, represented mostly by the United Packinghouse Workers Union.[29]

Iowa business owners and managers, particularly those in the construction industry, were absolutely opposed to any change in the law. Boosting unions' ability to organize would raise labor costs, but for public consumption, the business leaders positioned their opposition as freedom of choice for workers. The Master Builders of Iowa and the Associated General Contractors of Iowa sent a joint letter to Hughes and legislators in early January: "Stripped of all its emotionalism, the controversy boils down to one simple question: Should each individual citizen of this state be permitted to decide for himself whether or not he will join a union, or should he be forced to join a union in order to keep his job?" This attitude was shared by most Iowa business managers.[30]

Hughes stood firmly against repeal of the right-to-work law in Iowa and favored only an amendment to permit the union shop, which he saw as a middle ground between mandatory union membership prior to hiring and no obligation to join a union. His opposition to repeal was also a response to the possibility that Congress would repeal the federal right-to-work law. He wanted to maintain a prohibition against the closed shop in Iowa, repeal of which could hinder business investment in the state. "We're all one family, and the well-being of one depends on the other," Hughes said. "Somewhere in between there is a middle ground so that neither side is alienated. I'm not the governor of special interests, regardless of who it is." In the middle of the debate in March, Hughes frankly admitted in one of his daily press conferences that he did not want outright repeal because he did not want to offend the traditionally Republican business and industrial community, which had given him significant support last November. This statement prompted one of his aides to feel "like crawling under the table." Wrote the *Des Moines Tribune*'s Drake Mabry, "Such political frankness often is heard only in the back rooms."[31]

Early in the session, all eleven Democratic representatives from Polk County supported repeal of the right-to-work law. Party members passed the bill out of the Industrial Relations Committee, earning the ire of the Democratic governor. This prompted Hughes to address Democratic house leaders in a private meeting on January 28, where he "very lucidly"—according to those present—spoke of his opposition to the bill. At a press conference after the meeting, he refused to say what he had discussed, admitting only that "I was mad."[32]

The governor's temper was also tested in February at a tense meeting at Democratic national headquarters in Washington, DC, between Hughes (who was in the capital on other business) and labor leaders. The gathering's goal was to pressure Hughes to back full repeal of Iowa's right-to-work law. Those present included Charles Davis, president of the Iowa Federation of Labor; Jack Lewis, secretary-treasurer of that group; Alexander Barkin, national director of the AFL-CIO's Committee on Political Education; and Cliff Carter, executive director of the Democratic National Committee and President Johnson's personal aide on political matters. If these men thought they could force Hughes to cave on the issue, they were badly mistaken. In the words of the *Register*'s Nick Kotz, who wrote about the meeting months later, the Iowa governor said "in no uncertain terms that labor had been pushing him too hard, that he didn't like the pressure tactics, and that he wasn't going to budge." Hughes claimed repeal would be devastating for both Democrats and labor in Iowa, and it would endanger other measures being considered in the state legislature, such as worker safety, workers' compensation, and unemployment benefits. The result was that everyone agreed to support Hughes's compromise position of a union shop. "The labor union men probably were swayed in terms of practical politics of the possible," wrote Kotz, "rather than by complete agreement with Hughes's ideas of legislation."[33]

Despite the agreement between Hughes and labor Democrats in Iowa, the path forward was not easy. Few Republicans and some Democrats saw no difference between the union shop and the closed shop; both required union membership at some point. By mid-March, supporters drew up a "package plan" labor bill to legalize the union shop, and it passed the respective committees in the Iowa house and senate. The bill also created a state mediation and conciliation service to handle intrastate disputes between unions and companies, and it limited the issuance of injunctions by judges in labor disputes. Its supporters claimed that the bill helped define a fair and just relationship between workers and employers.[34]

Not everyone in Iowa agreed. The *Des Moines Register*, normally supportive of Hughes, opposed the legislation, calling it a "one-sided labor bill." It pointed out that a union would be able to determine who should continue working by virtue of its control over union membership policies. A dozen businessmen who had planned to accompany Hughes on a "Sell Iowa" trip to Europe in June withdrew from the delegation, citing the governor's support for the labor measure. Accusing Hughes of creating an "anti-industry climate," Peter H. Kuyper, president of the Rolscreen Company in Pella, wrote, "Dozens of good-will trips to Europe, and to the American centers of industry, will not off-set the damage that will be done Iowa's industrial growth by the main features of pending legislation."[35]

The controversy and political heat generated by the labor legislation prompted Hughes to make a rare midsession address to the legislature on May 5. No governor in living memory had done so. Hughes said that Iowans' "bias toward unions is so great that it is generally assumed that anything organized labor wants is wrong and should be denied." Yet he did not want to see labor or any special group "become so powerful that it can exert unfair pressure on majority rule." His support for the union shop was designed to enable unions to get rid of "freeloaders," or employees who were not union members but still enjoyed the benefits of the union's collective bargaining. "Either we believe in collective bargaining or we do not. To me, this is the point on which it all hinges." Defending the details of the legislation, he called on lawmakers to grant labor "the dignity of fair partnership in the industrial and business future of Iowa . . . instead of treating them as a distrusted and ill-favored stepchild." He ended by saying, "We have nothing to lose but our prejudice."[36]

The speech accomplished little. Although it was generally well received among labor supporters and Democrats at the capitol, others were not impressed. Senator Warren Krock of Boone, leader of the Democratic opposition, said, "He might have picked up two or three votes from the jellyfish, but if they are men they are not going to be moved." Robert Rigler, Republican senate majority leader, said Hughes was "trying to squirm out of a tight and embarrassing political situation." At a press conference before the speech, even Hughes downplayed his effort, saying the bill had only a fifty-fifty chance of passage and adding, "I don't think management will be happy with the speech, and I don't think labor will be happy with it."[37]

The overwhelming Democratic majority in the Iowa house was enough to pass the labor legislation, 75–46, on May 18, approving a union shop amendment to the Iowa right-to-work law. However, twenty-four Democrats joined nearly all the Republican representatives in opposing the bill. Later that day, the house passed a measure calling for the creation of a state mediation and conciliation commission, by a vote of 92–23.[38]

The labor legislation met its death in the Iowa senate, failing by a vote of 31–27. Seven Democrats joined all twenty-four Republicans in rejecting the measure, and all twenty-seven favorable votes were cast by Democrats. Said Hughes, "I am disappointed. I regret they didn't pass it. I am glad it got a thorough airing and that everyone had a chance to cast his vote." Republican senator David Stanley of Muscatine summed up the attitude of opponents when he called it "a dangerous bill" and said, "It will take away the most precious civil right of a worker—to join or not to join." Democratic majority leader Andrew Frommelt declared this legislation the "most misunderstood, most twisted-out-of-proportion issue to come before the Iowa Legislature since 1949 when labor-haters passed the (right-to-work) bill, hoping to destroy unions."[39]

Despite the historic height of union power in the Iowa legislature, the labor movement failed to pass legislation that would have given unions a leg up in Iowa. Even the compromise pushed by Hughes could not entice all Democrats to his side in the senate, where opposition was strongest. Iowa would continue to be a right-to-work state.

Hughes's victories in the historic 1965 legislature certainly surpassed his defeats. One was especially close to Hughes's heart: abolition of the death penalty in Iowa. The governor's longtime, deeply held moral position was that capital punishment "inflicts severe spiritual damage upon all of our citizens" and "brings out the beast in people." Hughes lamented his failure to prevent the execution of Victor H. Feguer, which had been one of the darkest days of his governorship, and he had commuted the death sentence of Leon Tice Jr. to life in prison. He did not want to face those issues again.[40]

He did not have to. The overwhelming Democratic majority had been elected with a party platform that included repeal of the death penalty. And public opinion was on their side. In 1960, according to a *Des Moines Register* poll, Iowans opposed abolishing the death penalty, 46 to 40 percent. In 1963 they were evenly split, and in 1965 57 percent favored abolishing it. According to the *Register*, "This reversal in sentiment can be credited partly to the influence of Gov. Harold Hughes, who said capital punishment is against his moral beliefs." The path was set for change.[41]

On February 4 the Iowa house voted 89–29 to abolish the death penalty and made life sentences in capital offenses mandatory. Two weeks later, the Iowa senate passed the bill, 35–20, with six Republicans joining twenty-nine Democrats to vote in favor of it. When he signed the bill in late February, Hughes said, "I've always felt capital punishment inflicted damage on our citizens."[42]

For the first time since the 1870s, Iowa was without a death penalty. And this governor would no longer suffer from dark days prompted by an Iowan's execution.[43]

Another victory for Hughes was in the civil rights arena. Nationally, the civil rights movement culminated in passage of the Civil Rights Act of 1964, which abolished Jim Crow laws in the South, and the Voting Rights Act of 1965, which enfranchised Blacks in the region. The question was how northern states would react, especially states like Iowa that had small minority populations.

There was no doubt where Harold Hughes stood, as evidenced by his response to events in the South. On March 7, 1965, civil rights supporters decided to march in Selma, Alabama, to protest legal obstacles to Blacks' voting, hoping to prompt passage of the voting rights bill in Congress. They came face-to-face with Alabama state troopers and county posse men, who brutally attacked the unarmed protesters with billy clubs and tear gas. The assault—known in civil rights lore as "Bloody Sunday"—was broadcast on national TV during a primetime news update.[44]

Like many Americans, Hughes was appalled at the violence used against people marching for the right to vote. Several days later, he sent a telegram to his fellow governor George Wallace of Alabama: "I join with all Iowans and all Americans in objecting to the senseless and un-reasonable use of brutality in any situation, on the part of either the police or private citizens. The recent savage oppression of human rights in Selma is a disgrace to the entire nation." At the same time, Hughes sent a telegram to Dr. Martin Luther King and Mrs. James J. Reeb, widow of a Boston minister who had died after being attacked in Alabama, expressing his condolences. To King, he wrote that it is "incredible that such police state injustice could exist in the name of law in America" and likened it to the way of "Communists and Nazis, not the way of free Americans. . . . We must all share with the white citizens of Alabama, the shame and guilt of this tragic example of man's inhumanity to man." The governor's office made sure that these telegrams were well publi-cized.[45]

Words were one thing; action another. The action taken by Hughes and the Iowa legislature was the Iowa Civil Rights Act of 1965. The Gov-ernor's Commission on Human Rights, a forty-member panel appointed earlier by Hughes, wrote the legislation and released it in January. The measure called for a full-time staff to enforce nondiscrimination laws already on the books. That staff would be monitored by a seven-member board appointed to four-year terms by the governor and ap-proved by the state senate. Preferably, the commission would use concil-iation and persuasion to settle complaints about unfair practices; if that failed, hearings were an option. A final alternative was civil court actions to enforce the commission's mandate.[46]

The bill had bipartisan support and passed both houses unani-mously. It remained to be seen whether this would be enough to keep racial peace in the Hawkeye State in the years ahead.[47]

One of the prime responsibilities of the biennial legislative session was to set the state's budget for the next two years. After debating back and forth for months, legislators finally passed a record budget of $267 million and, according to the *Des Moines Register*, "voted more tax increases than any session since the 1930s." This marked an increase of about $59 million a year over the last approved budget, and the annual budget was $13 million more than Hughes had recommended at the beginning of the session. The lawmakers were responding largely to higher educational needs—expanded funding for state universities and the creation of vocational schools—as well as highway construction and additional state services.[48]

The tax increases came from multiple sources but did not represent fundamental reform. Both income and corporate taxes were moderately raised, along with increases in cigarette, gasoline, inheritance, and other taxes. One significant change was state tax withholding from Iowans' paychecks, similar to the current federal tax withholding, set to begin on January 1, 1966. Under this change, Iowans would be paying two years of taxes in 1966—taxes for the past year, 1965, as they had done regularly twice a year, and withholding taxes for the current year, 1966. Withholding was designed to catch tax evaders; it was estimated that between 100,000 and 150,000 Iowans had been evading state income tax each year. Now, through mandatory withholding, the state estimated that it would collect an extra $2.5 million to $3 million. Hughes said the additional money would be used for buildings at state universities and hospitals and around the capitol grounds in Des Moines. This was almost certainly going to be a hot political issue in the next election.[49]

Legislators did not touch property tax reform. Property taxes were the fundamental source of public school funding, which put the onus on farmers, businesses, and other property owners and resulted in uneven funding for schools around the state. Rather than tackling the issue outright, the legislature appropriated $50,000 for a study of state and local taxes in Iowa. Hughes later chose Purdue University professor James A. Papke for the job. A second study approved by the legislature—and allotted $100,000—was designed to develop concrete plans for the reorganization of Iowa government. Hughes later selected the Public Administration Service of Chicago to spearhead that effort. Both studies would have a significant impact on the modernization of Iowa government in the next session two years later.[50]

The 1965 Iowa legislature changed Iowa government. The session was clearly owned by the Democrats, and they—together with their activist governor Harold Hughes—began the work of transforming the state to meet modern needs. A *Des Moines Register* editorial titled "A Look-Forward Legislature" stated, "The 1965 Legislature approved the first fundamental reform and modernization of state government in this century." The *Des Moines Tribune,* calling 1965 "one of Iowa's most decisive sessions," noted, "It tackled everything the Republicans had skirted warily for years. It brushed away the cobwebs in the legislative chambers." The *Cedar Rapids Gazette* wrote, "The 61st General Assembly tackled one of the most ambitious programs ever presented to an Iowa legislature, and accomplished much of it."[51]

Said Hughes of the lawmakers, "No Iowa Legislature in this century has had the courage to tackle such a broad range of important and difficult public interest problems as you have undertaken." In typical Hughes fashion, he also acknowledged his sometimes tense relationship with legislators. "They fought with each other and everybody else, including me. This was no congregation of rubber stamps. You can accuse them of wrangling and of getting off course at times but nobody can deny that they demonstrated the courage of their convictions."[52]

Through multiple constitutional amendments, Hughes and the Democrats fashioned a more modern government. With the creation of vocational schools, they added a necessary level of education and training for the state's youth, clearly aimed at keeping students in Iowa. And they took another stab at reapportionment to make representation more just. From the perspective of the labor Democrats, there were some disappointments, such as failure to pass laws to enhance justice for workers. The legislature also failed to pass civil service reform, which would be a task for future lawmakers. For many, however, Iowa became a more progressive state with repeal of the death penalty and creation of a civil rights commission. At the helm of these accomplishments was Governor Harold Hughes. By his nature, he sought the center of the debate, wading deeply into discussions with legislators and, when needed, using the bully pulpit to make an impact. The Hawkeye State saw a different sort of governor in 1965—and became a different sort of state.

9 | Where Angels Fear to Tread

Along with a momentous legislative session, 1965 was a significant year for Hughes in other ways—both personally and politically. On the personal side, tragedy struck the Hughes family in early March. Hughes's father, Lewis, had been suffering from heart problems and was scheduled to undergo surgery at University Hospitals in Iowa City. Expecting the surgery to be routine, the governor, an avid hunter, went ahead with a planned hunting trip to the Yucatan rain forest in Mexico. While at the hospital, Lewis suffered a heart attack and died at age seventy-four. Hughes was notified and returned home immediately. After the funeral, Hughes's mother, Etta, moved into the governor's mansion and stayed there for the remainder of Hughes's time in Iowa. After he left for Washington, Etta—"an independent Kentucky mountain woman," according to granddaughter Phyllis—moved to Friendship Haven, a senior care facility in Fort Dodge, where she remained until her death in 1974.[1]

On the political side, Hughes charged directly into two crises with no easy solutions. In both cases, the governor of Iowa risked his prestige, applying his unique style of leadership to resolve these conflicts peacefully.

A labor dispute between the United Packinghouse Workers of America (UPWA) and the Iowa Beef Packers threatened to explode into violence in the west-central Iowa city of Fort Dodge. Meat production (especially hogs) and meatpacking had been part of the Iowa landscape since the mid-nineteenth century, when railroads linked producers with stockyards in Chicago, Kansas City, and Omaha. In Iowa, slaughtering operations were soon established, sourcing animals directly from farmers rather than from stockyards, as was the practice in larger operations outside the state. By the early twentieth century, meatpacking flourished in Cedar Rapids, Ottumwa, Mason City, Fort Dodge, Des Moines, Waterloo, and Dubuque. From 1929 to 1954, employment at Iowa slaughterhouses increased by 132 percent, making it a major industry.[2]

Founded in 1961, Iowa Beef Packers used modern technology and innovative marketing strategies to become one of the fastest growing meat processors in the nation. At its plants in Fort Dodge and Denison,

Iowa Beef introduced cutting-edge processing technology to package meat products in boxes ready to be sold. This marked an improvement over traditional processors, which shipped whole carcasses to customers, who then had to slice and prepare the meat. It also allowed Iowa Beef to ship by truck rather than rail, which meant that it could build plants in smaller communities, closer to where the livestock was raised. In addition, Iowa Beef's innovative freezing techniques allowed its plants to operate far from cities and close to rural beef sources, cutting transportation costs. This advanced technology and greater efficiency reduced the need for skilled workers, which translated to lower wages. By 1965, Iowa Beef was the nation's fourth largest meat processing company, and it had recently joined the Fortune 500.[3]

The UPWA, which represented the 260 workers at Iowa Beef's Fort Dodge plant, took a stand there for higher wages. At a rally before nine hundred people on February 7, 1965, UPWA president Ralph Helstein of Chicago promised all-out "financial and moral" support from the national union for the Iowa workers. He pointed out that the laborers' hourly rate at the Fort Dodge plant was $2.39, compared with $2.64 for the industry. "The Iowa Beef Packers firm has been unwilling to give their employees a share of the fruits of their success," said Helstein in a passionate speech. He announced that contributions from twenty-three thousand laborers throughout the Midwest would be pouring in to support a strike fund for the Fort Dodge workers.[4]

Company officials countered that although the hourly rate at Fort Dodge was lower, the annual wage per worker was the highest in the industry. This was possible because of guaranteed stable employment, compared with unsteady seasonal work elsewhere. Nevertheless, the die was cast for conflict in the Fort Dodge community.[5]

On March 6, after nearly seven months of unsuccessful negotiations, both sides broke off talks and workers declared a strike. More than 250 workers picketed in front of the plant, blocking the entrance and not permitting anyone to enter or leave. Observers called the situation "potentially dangerous." A local district judge issued a restraining order that limited picketing, barred interference with movement into and out of the plant, and prohibited unlawful acts or "breach of the peace." However, as the days passed, violence broke out, including threats with guns. The company charged union members with shooting at boxcars, slashing tires, and starting fires. The situation grew tenser by the day.[6]

While monitoring the situation, Hughes initially maintained a hands-off policy, careful not to show support for either side. He vowed to stay out of it unless it became necessary to send in the state patrol or the National Guard due to violence. Lamenting that there was no official mediation service, he said, "I have many complaints from management that they have no place to go when they have a grievance against labor."[7]

The situation changed dramatically on March 16 when Iowa Beef decided to bring in nonstriking workers. When these workers tried to enter the plant in cars, some of the picketers shattered their windshields with bats and iron clubs. At this point, Hughes entered the fray, calling Arden Walker, Iowa Beef vice president of industrial operations, and asking him to keep the plant closed until negotiations resumed in a few days. Dave Hart, district director of the UPWA, was in the governor's office when he made the call. According to Walker, "The governor asked us in the interest of peace and public safety not to resume operations until after negotiations. . . . We agreed to the governor's suggestion."[8]

By this time, Hughes was fully engaged in the negotiations between Iowa Beef and the UPWA. On March 25 Hughes and three federal mediators, led by Robert Patterson of Washington, DC, met with officials from the company and the union in the governor's office. Hughes had personally asked Iowa Beef president A. D. Anderson and board chairman Currier Holman to represent the company's perspective. UPWA president Helstein headed the union's bargaining unit. After the initial meeting, the group agreed to meet later in Des Moines to continue negotiations.[9]

In the meantime, Iowa Beef muddied the waters by announcing that it was going to reopen the Fort Dodge plant on Monday, April 5, despite the picket lines. The company stated, "It is imperative that we resume operations. We have delayed doing so in deference to two requests by the governor." This announcement—along with the company's appeal for state law enforcement protection to ensure the safety of replacement workers entering the plant—did not sit well with Hughes. According to media reports, the governor was "peeved." Union members had threatened to destroy the plant if Iowa Beef brought in these "scab workers."[10]

Facing this company-imposed deadline and the threat of real violence in Fort Dodge, Iowa Beef and union officials, along with the federal mediators, met in the governor's office over the weekend to try to reach an agreement. The group met on Saturday, April 3, for ten and a half torturous hours, with no resolution, and continued into Sunday.[11]

Given the threat of violence, Hughes had developed a plan with the adjutant general of the National Guard, who was waiting in an unmarked car a few blocks from the statehouse. One option was to call up National Guard troops from outside the area and assemble them, in full combat gear, at Fort Dodge. If an agreement could not be reached by midnight Sunday, Hughes planned to issue an executive order imposing martial law and to send troops into the plant. Hughes desperately wanted to avoid that action because, with tensions and emotions so high, there was a real possibility that people could be injured or even killed.[12]

Likewise, tensions rose in the governor's office as the two sides threatened and denounced each other. At one point, Hughes interjected, "I want to tell you all that I will enforce the law," reminding them that troops were standing by. "The workers have committed themselves to violence and I'm committed to stop it. There is no alternative. So if you fellows go to the wire without a decision, some people might die; certainly many will be injured." This sobering statement seemed to turn the hot back-and-forth threats into an exchange of specific details on wages, insurance, and benefits. On Sunday, Hughes announced that Iowa Beef had agreed not to open the plant on Monday.[13]

The marathon negotiating session continued until Monday morning at 4:20, when Iowa Beef and the union announced they had reached an agreement. Members of Local 1135 of the UPWA in Fort Dodge voted to ratify a new three-year contract that evening. The workers received graduated wage increases that narrowed but did not close the gap between Iowa Beef and other meatpacking firms. The new contract also included an additional holiday, expanded time-and-a-half pay for overtime work, and improved sick leave, hospitalization, and vacation benefits. The company obtained a "no-strike" provision, allowing it to discipline workers who took part in wildcat strikes or production slowdowns.[14]

The Fort Dodge crisis was just one of many clashes between labor and management, but thanks to the governor of Iowa, significant violence was averted. Both sides were enthusiastic in their praise for the part Hughes played. According to union officials, he brought the two sides together three times during the negotiations when it appeared that they were hopelessly deadlocked. UPWA's Helstein said, "Not to my knowledge, in Iowa history or in the history of any state with which I am currently familiar, has any governor given such immediate personal attention to settlement of a labor management dispute than did your Governor Hughes." He called Hughes a "tremendous mediating force" in getting labor and management together.[15]

Hughes would need all the negotiating skills he possessed to meet the next challenge: a showdown between the Amish community and school officials in Buchanan County.

The conflict involving the Iowa Amish became an international news story, vividly captured in a *Des Moines Register* photograph of Amish children racing into a cornfield, fleeing public school authorities. For some, the issue represented a tyrannical state imposing its will on a peaceful religious minority seeking to live a deeply pious, spiritual life. Others saw it as a group of old, iron-willed Amish men denying children a proper education—in defiance of state law—and sentencing them to a life of ignorance. For many Iowans it was a hot emotional issue without a solution—until Harold Hughes entered the controversy.

Old Order Amish settlements in the Hawkeye State predated statehood, with members arriving in Johnson and Washington Counties in eastern Iowa in the early 1840s. Tracing their theological origins to Swiss Anabaptists during the Protestant Reformation, the Amish in Iowa shunned most twentieth-century technology, preferring candlelight over electricity and using the horse and buggy for transportation. All the Amish dressed in stark black clothing; the men wore lengthy beards, and the women wore long dresses. The Amish did not seek converts among outsiders; they passed down their religion and customs in only one way—through their children. In 1914 a small faction broke off from the Johnson County settlement in Kalona and moved to Buchanan County in northeastern Iowa, claiming the Kalona group had grown "too worldly." Residents of Buchanan County tolerated their Amish neighbors but did not fully accept them. Their separateness and their Old World ways created tension and resentment, which only grew with the impassioned school controversy.[16]

In 1947 the Hazleton Consolidated School District was formed in Buchanan County as part of a statewide effort to improve and standardize primary and secondary education and eliminate antiquated one-room schoolhouses. A select group of Amish families in the area decided not to send their children to the Hazleton schools. Instead, they created two private one-room schools and hired state-certified teachers, as mandated by state law. This Amish group wanted to provide their children with school instruction that adhered to their conservative religious beliefs and practices. Although the Amish schools did not specifically teach religion, the curriculum shunned science and shielded Amish children from the "secular influences" of the public school system. The Amish families paid the teachers' salaries—quite low by the standards of the day—out of their own pockets. These teachers were generally older women who adhered to the conservative Amish syllabus.[17]

The situation changed in 1961 with a proposal to consolidate the Hazleton district with the nearby Oelwein district in Fayette County. School consolidation—which was nearly always a hot issue among affected families—enlarged the tax base, providing more money for schools and permitting a broader curriculum. Both school districts were required to approve the move, which had overwhelming support in the Oelwein area but divided Hazleton residents down the middle, with many fearing a loss of local control. Initially, the Hazleton Amish stayed out of the controversy. But Oelwein superintendent A. A. Kaskadden, in an attempt to gain Amish support in the upcoming vote, approached them with an idea that would allow the Amish to keep their schools. Kaskadden proposed bringing the two Amish schools into the public system by leasing the buildings, providing certified teachers, and changing the standard school curriculum to meet Amish standards.[18]

Kaskadden presented the idea to Dan Borntrager, who represented the Amish families even though he had no children in school. Borntrager accepted the arrangement and expected the expanded Oelwein school district to pay the salaries of the certified teachers at the Amish schools. The Amish then voted as a bloc in favor of consolidation on November 8, 1961, becoming the decisive factor in a close election and further alienating their non-Amish neighbors. After the vote, the Oelwein school board pushed back on the Kaskadden-Amish agreement. It declared that any arrangement to lease the school buildings and pay the teachers' salaries was only temporary, and there would be no accommodation of Amish principles in the school curriculum. The Amish claimed they had been lied to.[19]

In September 1962 the Amish opened their rural schools with two teachers who were not certified—in defiance of state law. In effect, the Amish parents were violating truancy laws by sending their children to unapproved schools. This led to weeks of discussions between school officials and Amish leaders, trying to find a solution. This attempt at local diplomacy suffered a setback when Kaskadden died on September 25. He was replaced by Arthur Sensor, who pledged to enforce state law and took a harsher attitude toward the Amish.[20]

The Hazleton Amish objected to sending their children to secular schools that taught science classes and other modern practices and required mixing with non-Amish children. This was considered problematic by the Hazleton Amish, even though nearly 240 other Amish children attended public school in Buchanan County with no difficulty. Also, the Hazleton Amish, believing that Oelwein had promised to cover the teachers' salaries, simply did not want to pay higher wages for certified teachers (even though they had been doing so for more than a decade).[21]

Negotiations and legal action continued for years. The Amish were represented by Cedar Falls attorney William Sindlinger, who argued that his clients should be exempt from hiring certified teachers based on freedom of religion. That argument failed to convince local and state courts, and the Amish parents faced multiple fines, most of which were paid by sympathetic donors and other Amish groups. The conflict attracted national and international publicity. Foreign reporters, particularly from Germany, often sat in on the decisions issued by justice of the peace Minnie Wengert, who held court on her front porch and served coffee, cookies, and donuts to the reporters.[22]

By the fall of 1965, the Hazleton Amish had been operating their schools with noncertified teachers for four years. In the meantime, a new Buchanan County attorney—Harlan Lemon—had been elected, and he promised to end the Amish school dispute. A number of new school board members had also been elected in Oelwein, with the same goal in mind.[23]

By this time, state attorney general Lawrence Scalise had become involved. He worked with local school officials to try to reach a compromise, but to no avail. Scalise, elected in the Democratic wave of 1964, had been updating Hughes on the situation. The governor was staying out of the conflict but was sympathetic to those enforcing the truancy law. "I don't know what the county attorney and attorney general can do except uphold the law," said Hughes. His office was getting fifteen to twenty letters a day, many of which blamed him for persecuting the Amish. "If there is any blame, I wish that they would blame the right people," he complained.[24]

Wave after wave of fines did not move the Amish. By late October 1965, Buchanan County threatened to place liens on property held by the Amish fathers who refused to send their children to state-approved schools. At a meeting with the Amish, Lemon said, "You people must realize that we do not intend to kid. We are very serious about this and we will confiscate properties until assessments are satisfied in full." Borntrager, speaking for the group, responded, "Our beliefs are of more value to us than our personal property." The Amish were saved from having their property confiscated when a northeast Iowa attorney paid the fines out of his own pocket.[25]

The intense media coverage and passionate statewide debate were too much for Hughes to ignore. Also, the Hazleton Amish families petitioned the governor, claiming to be "sorrowfully grieved that we are about to be persecuted for our religious freedom in educating and training our children according to the way we understand the Bible and to the dictates of our conscience." Hughes took to the airwaves in a radio broadcast on November 13, saying, "My heart is with the Amish." But he defended local and state officials, who were only trying to enforce the law, and argued that the issue was not one of religious freedom. "Neither state nor local officials have any thought of persecuting the Amish because of their religion. No one questions their right to educate their children in their own parochial schools. The law that is in question simply protects the right of children to be educated by qualified teachers, whether in public or private schools."[26]

With pressure building for a resolution, county attorney Lemon met with several Amish fathers—without Borntrager in attendance—on the evening of November 18, their twenty-third appearance before Wengert's court. He played Hughes's radio address and, according to a *Cedar Rapids Gazette* reporter, "the fathers were visibly shaken when they heard the recording." After the meeting, Lemon thought he and the fathers had reached an agreement for their children to be picked up by bus and taken to school in Hazleton the next day. Later, the Amish fathers—this time with Borntrager—met long into the night to discuss their actions the next day.[27] Lemon and Oelwein school authorities were not prepared for what happened next.

Bus 8 left the Oelwein Community School at 7:30 a.m. on Friday, November 19, 1965, carrying superintendent Sensor, a school nurse, and a driver. It then picked up Owen Snively, principal of the Hazleton school. Multiple cars of reporters, including *Des Moines Register* photographer Thomas DeFeo, followed the bus. When it stopped at one Amish home, the group on the bus discovered that all the children were at the single-room schoolhouses. The bus proceeded to one of the schools, and the children came out. According to *Register* reporter Gene Raffensperger, who had been covering the issue for years, "Nervous, not sure which way to turn or look, they milled in a tight little knot at the edge of the school yard. The big yellow bus was waiting. Its door was open." Suddenly a woman's voice rang out, "Run!" With that, about fifteen Amish children bolted for a nearby cornfield, and DeFeo snapped the photo that would become world famous. Some of the children did not stop running until they reached their homes. The authorities gave up on pursuing the children that morning, but what is not widely known is that they returned later and picked up twenty-eight Amish children, who spent a pleasant afternoon at school in Hazleton, each with a selected elementary school "host" to guide them through the day. But it was the photo of the fleeing Amish children that received widespread coverage, spanning seven columns on the front page of the next morning's *Register*. In case readers missed it, the photo ran again in the newspaper's widely circulated Sunday edition.[28]

The resistance continued on Monday, and school officials faced an emotional media circus they could not control. Amish fathers blocked the driveway to one school. Once school officials got past the blockade, they found frightened children in the schoolhouse singing "Jesus Loves Me" and weeping mothers holding their children, along with Borntrager carrying a Bible. Principal Snively moved forward and placed his hand on the shoulder of one youngster, who pulled away screaming. Realizing their task was impossible, the officials announced they would not forcibly transport the children. Lemon added, "I want some responsible state official in Des Moines to give me some advice and some help."[29]

Later that morning, Sensor, Lemon, and others flew to Des Moines to meet with members of the Iowa Department of Public Instruction and Governor Hughes. After the meeting, Hughes called for an "all-inclusive moratorium" on efforts to get the Amish children into public schools. Declaring that everyone wanted "a peaceful solution within the confines and structures of the Iowa law," Hughes said, "I'm not going to be critical of people who are trying to uphold the law which they have sworn to protect. But that doesn't keep me from having compassion in my heart for people who believe so strongly in their faith that they are willing to sacrifice everything." With that statement, Hughes assumed control of the crisis, plunging directly into this political minefield.[30]

Days later, Hughes again took to the airwaves to calm tempers and urge compromise. Addressing the families' religious argument, he said, "These Amish people say that God's law, as they see it, transcends all civil law. I cannot argue this point with them for I believe this as devoutly as they do." He also recognized that school authorities "have a sworn duty to uphold the law of the state that protects the right of children to be instructed by qualified teachers." Citing a failure of communication, he asked for a cool-down period and time to devise new approaches.[31]

Hughes's first step was to talk to all the parties in person. On Monday, January 10, 1966, he and aides flew to Oelwein and drove to the Borntrager farm southwest of Hazleton to meet with the Amish elders. Outside the house, an American flag flew upside down—an international sign of distress. During the two-hour meeting, Borntrager did all the talking. Hughes listened and responded that he was trying to find a solution that all sides could accept. After the meeting concluded, Hughes inspected one of the rural schools.[32]

Next, Hughes drove back to Oelwein for a two-and-a-half-hour meeting with the school board. Initially, Hughes received a cool reception, but he broke the ice by acknowledging that school officials were in a tough spot. Said the governor, "I know you have to enforce the law; the law is the law. You're in a very difficult position and I want to be your shock absorber." With that, according to Hughes aide Bill Hedlund, "It just kind of lightened up." The board members knew they had an ally who understood them and could work toward a solution.[33]

Hughes continued to hold meetings with both the Amish and the Oelwein school board in Des Moines. (After one meeting with the board, Hughes said to the media, "I think it is in the public interest that you leave us alone with our misery and let us work it out.") After weeks of discussion, Hughes announced a preliminary plan on February 22. The Danforth Foundation of St. Louis, known for funding religious education, would pay $15,000 for two certified teachers at the Amish schools. The school board agreed to lease the two school buildings. The Amish agreed to follow state education and attendance requirements, with some allowances, consistent with Iowa law, to avoid conflicts with their religious beliefs. All parties signed a document outlining the agreement. Attorney Sindlinger, representing the Amish, said he would not "describe the Amish reaction as happy but they find the solution acceptable."[34]

At the press conference announcing the agreement, Hughes said, "Only those who know these good people personally, and who have the patience to understand their utterly sincere devotion to a way of life prescribed by their religious convictions, can appreciate the delicate communications problems involved." Hughes admitted that he had changed his mind during the discussions. Originally, he had dismissed religion as an issue, since religion was not taught at the Amish schools. Now he understood that religion was involved in everything the Amish did. "I doubt that many people really understand their way or religion." He added, "From the outside it looks like a very simple problem, but when I got into it, it turned out to be one of the most complex situations I've ever gotten into in my life."[35]

The Danforth grant was only a one-year fix. Hughes's long-term solution was for the state legislature to appropriate "supplemental aid" for the Amish schools through the Iowa Department of Public Instruction. Under his plan, funds would be directed to districts with special institutions, such as the Amish schools, that were "deemed to be necessary and in the public interest."[36] This plan went absolutely nowhere with legislators. It was one thing for a private foundation to finance private religious schools; it was quite another to use public money to do so. The concept of separation of church and state was simply too strong in Iowa for Hughes's plan to fly. Democratic senator Adolph Elver of Elkader spoke for most of the legislators: "You can get yourself into the darndest hot water with this kind of thing. . . . You could start a real controversy involving all the private schools." Dozens of Catholic, Lutheran, and other religious schools would demand public funding if an exception were made for the Amish.[37]

Hughes recommended funding for the Amish schools in his inaugural address in 1967, but the opposition was solid. Representative Charles Grassley, chairman of the house subcommittee on school appropriations, flatly said, "Giving public funds to Amish schools is a violation of the principle of church and state under state laws and the state constitution. We cannot give public funds to private schools." Recognizing the futility of pushing this idea, Hughes appointed a blue-ribbon committee to study the issue. The committee was aided by the American Civil Liberties Union (ACLU), which suggested exempting the Amish schools from state standards in exchange for student testing and class monitoring. This is what the committee recommended in its report issued on April 14, 1967.[38]

Legislation was passed in the waning days of the 1967 legislature—34–12 in the senate and 81–35 in the house. It permitted the Amish to keep their two private schools taught by noncertified teachers, with an exemption granted by the state superintendent of public instruction and approval by the State Board of Public Instruction. In return, Amish students had to take tests showing proof of achievement in basic subjects, and a state consultant would be allowed to visit the schools and report back to the board. Republican representative James Klein (Lake Mills), the bill's floor leader in the house, said he changed his "position almost 180 degrees" after meeting with the Amish and studying their history in Iowa. "I am convinced that the greater majority of Amish people in Iowa would migrate out if we do not pass this bill."[39]

The initial exemption was for two years, with subsequent one-year exemptions. This seemed to solve the problem, although there were a few bumps in the road. For instance, in August 1967 Borntrager objected to some of the books the Oelwein board wanted to include in the regular curriculum, a violation of the agreement. When Sensor informed Hughes, the governor sent Hedlund, whose wife had grown up in Oelwein, to Borntrager's farm. Hedlund recalled, "I said to Borntrager that the governor said we've got an agreement and you agreed to it. And he's holding up his side of it and he expects you to hold up yours. We want you to let those books come into the school. So that was that." The books were accepted.[40]

A conflict that had raged for years, commanding national and international media attention and often resulting in emotional disagreements over the very essence of religious freedom, had finally been solved. And Harold Hughes was the source of that solution. His personality and his willingness to risk his political capital contributed to ending the standoff. Said Hedlund, "Hughes took a leadership role where other people would have backed off." His decision to enter this prickly conflict lowered tensions and tamed emotions. By meeting with and listening to both parties, he calmed tempers. In the end, these Amish children obtained a quality education within their unique culture.

10 | Vietnam, State Politics, and Aid to Alcoholics

On October 6, 1962, Charles Griffin of Dubuque, Iowa, a twenty-eight-year-old navy doctor assigned to the marines, was killed when his helicopter crashed in a mountainous region of South Vietnam. Six others died in the crash, including Owen Norton, age twenty-three, of Moulton, Iowa. They were the first Iowans to die in Vietnam. More deaths followed. At this stage, the US mission to keep the fragile South Vietnamese government from falling to the communists was barely known as a war. Americans involved in the conflict were euphemistically known as military advisers. This US commitment would continue to expand through the 1960s and later define the public career of Harold Hughes.[1]

Normally, governors avoid commenting on US foreign policy, typically limiting their remarks to state budgets, sales taxes, local crime, highway safety, and other such issues. This was not Hughes's style. As media coverage of the Vietnam conflict expanded, Hughes was asked questions about the war, and he answered them. Initially, he was completely and unambiguously in favor of the US effort. In late July 1965, as the United States introduced ground troops into Vietnam, Hughes received a two-hour briefing at the White House, led by President Johnson. Afterward he said, "I am more than ever convinced the nation is doing the right thing in Vietnam. . . . I support the president's position without question." In a speech in August to the American Legion in Sioux City, Hughes repeated his support, saying, "Our present national policy in Vietnam—whether we like it or not—is the only way we can go with logic or honor."[2]

At the same time, protests—especially on college campuses—over the expanding US military involvement in Vietnam became more frequent. Students at the University of Iowa, Iowa State University, Drake University, and other smaller colleges demonstrated peacefully in the fall of 1965. In Iowa City, an English major at the University of Iowa, Stephen Smith of Marion, sparked a statewide debate when he publicly burned his draft card before one hundred witnesses on October 20. "There are times when you have to challenge a law to make people decide it fits the kind of law they want," he said. Publicly, Hughes defended the students' right to protest the war. "They have every right to demonstrate, if the demonstrations are conducted properly," he said, but "I totally disagree with their motives."[3]

Privately, Hughes fumed against the protesters. In late 1965 a young Tom Harkin, then a navy pilot and later a congressman and senator from Iowa, visited Hughes's office with E. B. Smith of Ames, who was planning to run for the US Senate the following year. Harkin recalled that Hughes "got off on this tangent about the Vietnam War and 'those sons-of-a-bitches against the war. Where the hell's their patriotism? Why don't they stand up for America?' He just went on and on." When the pair left the governor's office, Smith turned to Harkin and said, "Well, he certainly has fallen in with LBJ. He's just mouthing LBJ's stuff."[4]

In November 1965 Hughes joined nine other governors—six Republicans and four Democrats in all—on a visit to Vietnam. The trip, tacked on to the end of a goodwill trip to Japan arranged by the National Governors Conference, was sponsored by the White House to build support for the war among US political leaders. The result was a polished, well-organized, four-day tour of the country. The trip began with extensive briefings by top military aides, who reported that although the initial situation had been "rather bleak," US and South Vietnamese forces had "stemmed the tide." The governors toured the battle fronts, and on November 6, while flying over the Mekong Delta, Hughes watched in the distance as US fighter-bombers pounded what was described as a "Communist Viet Cong encampment." That same day he spent time at a pacified model hamlet, home to two thousand Vietnamese. Hughes visited the aircraft carrier USS *Ticonderoga* off the southern coast of China as warplanes took off for assaults against the Vietcong. He toured American facilities at Cam Ranh Bay, ninety miles northeast of Saigon, and Nha Trang, twenty miles further northeast. Toward the end of the tour, the governors attended a reception by South Vietnamese prime minister Nguyen Cao Ky. To cap the tour, the governors were greeted at the Saigon airport by US ambassador Henry Cabot Lodge and General William Westmoreland, commander of US forces in Vietnam. Hughes traveled about six hundred miles in Vietnam and talked with an estimated one hundred Iowans stationed there.[5]

From Hughes's perspective, the trip reinforced his support for the Vietnam War—at least as evidenced by his public comments. To reporters he said, "I feel confident not only that the war can be won, but also that the nation can be rebuilt." He added, "I am firmly convinced that this is the commitment of the free world today, and that it not only will be kept but that it is the right thing to do to keep it."[6]

Hughes's private thoughts were different, and at the time, he kept them to himself. Years later, he confessed that he was acting the good soldier for Lyndon Johnson. "I supported the war on the basis of simply supporting my Commander-in-Chief rather than looking at the moral reasons behind the war." Hughes admitted that, after numerous briefings by the administration and the military, "it was obvious that the intelligence was indicating things that were wrong." Hughes's daughter Phyllis later said that, during the November 1965 trip, her father perceived a difference between what the military leaders were saying and what was actually going on in Vietnam. The Iowa governor was not the only one who subsequently expressed doubts about the veracity of the briefings. Michigan governor George Romney, who was also on the 1965 tour, later said he had been "brainwashed" by the American military. Hughes added, "Friends started to impress upon me the fact that what we were doing there in the beginning was wrong."[7]

One such friend was Joseph Rosenfield, head of the Younkers Department Store chain and an early financial backer of Hughes and other prominent Democrats. Hughes relied so much on Rosenfield's support that he called him his "Iowa angel." Rosenfield was an early opponent of the war and kept close counsel with Hughes, expressing his disapproval of US involvement in Vietnam. "Hughes would show up at Joe's office weekly," said Rosenfield biographer George Drake. "Joe was certainly against the Vietnam War. I'm guessing that Joe and Hughes talked about Vietnam a lot." Rosenfield served on the board of trustees of his alma mater, Grinnell College, which was a hotbed of antiwar protest. "Joe would be able to convey to Hughes what was going on on campuses probably better than anybody," said Drake. Hughes later revealed, "Joe said that if I didn't change on the war, he would still contribute but he wouldn't run my campaigns anymore." As Rosenfield was a key fundraiser for Hughes, this gave the Iowa governor significant pause.[8]

Publicly, Hughes continued to support the war throughout 1966. In January he called the antiwar position of the Student Nonviolent Coordinating Committee (SNCC) "horrible" and said its statement against US policy was "bound to have a demoralizing effect on men serving their country." In a Des Moines speech in February he commented, "If anyone thinks the Communists are any less determined to rule the world and destroy our free institutions than the Nazis, then let me only hope that he will enjoy the ventilation from the holes in his head." This attitude was shared by most Americans, who showed strong support in public opinion polls for the battle against communist forces in Vietnam.[9]

Hughes's support for the war helped cement his close relationship with Lyndon Johnson, who continued to call Hughes one of his favorite governors. In early February, while in Washington visiting members of the Iowa congressional delegation, Hughes was invited to the White House to chat with LBJ about the Iowa economy and politics. Vietnam was not part of the discussion.[10]

Vietnam was, however, the main thrust of the president's agenda when he paid a celebrated visit to central Iowa in late June 1966 as part of a political pep rally and fund-raiser. Hughes met the president at the Des Moines airport, along with 4,000 other Iowans. LBJ traveled to Indianola, south of Des Moines, where the turnout was estimated at 7,000. In a swing through Des Moines, the president attracted about 150,000 people along the motorcade route, and the Texan enjoyed every minute of it. At an evening event at Veterans Auditorium in downtown Des Moines, Democrats raised $200,000 from the 2,500 attendees on the floor and the 5,000 in the balcony. Johnson gave a speech that strongly defended his Vietnam policy and lashed out at his critics. "The American people, when they understand what is at stake, have never run from their duty. And we will not run now." As he entered the auditorium, the president had seen several protesters holding signs, and with venom in his voice, Johnson told them, "The thing that you genuinely want most, getting out of Vietnam, is being postponed a little longer by you and your signs." After Johnson's visit, Hughes said that Iowans were solidly behind the president on Vietnam, including the governor.[11] This attitude would change before year's end, but Hughes would first have to deal with an internal state party conflict.

On the state level, Democratic politics was undergoing an upheaval led by the aggressive and charismatic Lex Hawkins, Democratic Party chairman. Smarting from the defeat of labor legislation in the last session at the hands of some Democrats, Hawkins backed a proposal for party endorsement of candidates prior to the primary. He pushed new rules through the party's central committee on July 14, 1965, that would allow party conventions to endorse favorite candidates for county, district, and state offices before the primary. Hawkins freely admitted that party leaders had unofficially sided with certain individuals in the past, and "this move," he said, "will take the power out of the hands of a few and put it into the hands of the entire party." Candidates would need 60 percent convention support for party endorsement.[12]

Hughes openly opposed this proposal. In mid-1965 he was mulling whether to run for a third term as governor, run for the US Senate against Republican incumbent Jack Miller, or retire from politics. At this point, Hughes could get an endorsement from the state party for any state post he wanted. But back in 1958 or 1960, Hawkins's proposal would have shut Hughes out of the process, and it had the potential to end the careers of other able candidates before they even began. At a morning press conference the day after the committee made its recommendation, Hughes blasted the move. "I feel that this was a grave mistake that will take the selection of our candidates for elective office out of the hands of the rank and file of the party membership and put it in the smoke-filled room, if it is approved."[13]

Hughes was not alone. Nearly all the other state elected officials— Gary Cameron, secretary of state; Lorne Worthington, state auditor; Paul Franzenburg, state treasurer; and Kenneth Owen, secretary of agriculture—issued a public letter condemning the action. (Lieutenant Governor Robert Fulton would have signed the letter, but he was out of town. Attorney general Lawrence Scalise, Hawkins's former law partner, declined to sign.) Miffed that they had not been consulted, the group expressed "solid support of the position taken by Governor Harold Hughes." Writing that their goal was to "bring the best possible government to the people of Iowa," they proclaimed that "this can be accomplished only through free competition among highly-qualified candidates who will reflect the hopes and aspirations of all facets of our party."[14]

The conflict between Hawkins and other elements of the Iowa Democratic Party attracted statewide media coverage. Hawkins argued that a political party had to stand for something, and that was accomplished through party endorsement. Hughes and his allies maintained that an open process was key, and a party stood for whatever the broad grass roots said it did. The debate did not go unnoticed by others. Republican state senator Tom Riley of Cedar Rapids taunted, "We will be glad to welcome into the Republican party any Democrat whom Hawkins is trying to read out of his party."[15]

Iowa Democratic congressman Neal Smith proposed a compromise to allow the endorsement of two candidates, which Hughes indicated that he might accept. Hughes and Hawkins met several times through the summer of 1965 and said they would "explore ways to reach a middle ground" before the state convention next summer.[16]

When Democrats met in Des Moines for their mid-1966 convention, they agreed to a compromise whereby two candidates could gain party endorsement if they both got at least one-third of the delegates' votes. If one candidate received two-thirds of the convention vote, he or she would be the endorsed candidate. Iowa Democrats also witnessed what *Register* writer George Mills called a "hammer-and-tongs speech" from Hawkins, who took off his coat and delivered a diatribe on behalf of the endorsement policy. Hawkins, who resigned as party chairman at the end of the convention, said it would be naïve to think party officials had not taken sides in prior primary contests. "I have illegally used the Democratic party machinery in support of candidates whom I wanted. . . . I used my power illegally to get Congressman Neal Smith nominated and elected. In 1962 I used the state chairman's job, the party machinery, and party money to get Harold Hughes nominated over his opponent. I am not embarrassed by this." He described himself as a dictator and warned that his successor might not be as "benevolent as I am."[17]

The endorsement strategy was short-lived. It was used only once at the 1966 convention, and the results were disappointing. If the goal was to build stronger candidates for the November elections, it did not work. E. B. Smith won the convention's endorsement for a second run at a US Senate seat but was thoroughly defeated in the fall by Republican incumbent Jack Miller. In fact, Miller carried all ninety-nine counties, a first in Iowa history. Democrats also lost the Iowa house and most of the state executive races. Iowa Democrats ended the endorsement policy two years later.[18]

More important than politics was the act of governing, and for Hughes, this included helping Iowans obtain long-term employment. Until the community college system was up and running, reasoned Hughes, vocational training programs were insufficient to keep Iowa's youth in the state, contributing to "brain drain." In addition, with the increased mechanization and consolidation of agriculture, displaced rural workers moved to urban areas, where they needed jobs. With no central state planning agency, efforts to address these needs were uncoordinated;

there were some 120 state government agencies, and many were autonomous by law or tradition and difficult to track. Knowing that funds were available through federal Great Society programs to address these challenges, Hughes set out in early 1965 to coordinate efforts from the governor's office.[19]

Hughes first turned to Russell Wilson, his confidant from Ida Grove who was now serving on the Board of Control. Wilson drafted a $35,000 proposal for state coordination and took it to the US Department of Labor's Experimental and Demonstration Manpower Programs in Washington, DC (Wilson's original proposal totaled $75,000, which Hughes thought was too high). To Hughes's surprise, federal officials responded with an eighteen-month, $442,950 grant to help the Iowa governor coordinate the myriad state agencies working on training, education, poverty, and other related fields. These funds, managed from the governor's office, became the foundation for the Iowa Manpower Development Council, charged with coordination, technical assistance, research, and program development.[20]

One of the specific missions of the Manpower Development Council was to "retrain agricultural workers for jobs in urban communities," making it unique among such efforts in the United States. Edward Jakubauskas, a thirty-five-year-old associate professor of economics at Iowa State University, took a year's leave of absence to head the council, proudly claiming, "the whole nation is looking to Iowa for leadership in this area."[21]

With little experience to go on, the council's initial actions were pioneering and strongly supported by Hughes. For instance, a school bus was converted into a mobile manpower information center that toured rural and low-income urban areas and provided information on a range of human resources programs in Iowa. More substantially, in early 1966 the council announced a statewide $100,000 on-the-job training program for more than two hundred Iowans. By May, the project had completed ninety-one contracts to place 186 trainees in about one-third of Iowa's counties. The majority of trainees came from welfare rolls and soldiers' relief offices.[22]

As efforts advanced, Hughes's confidence in the council grew. James Socknat of Iowa State University wrote, "It was a relationship in many respects similar to an arranged marriage where the one partner is somewhat surprised at the looks of the other partner on first inspection, but grows to like the arrangement."[23]

In 1967 the Manpower Development Council sent out thousands of form letters from Hughes to businesses throughout Iowa requesting that they offer summer jobs to youths. Through the council, the governor sent personal letters to every high school dropout, urging them to return to school or, if that was not possible, providing a card of introduction to the employment office, where they could obtain counseling, job placement, or training. The same year, the council established the Neighborhood Youth Corps Program, establishing career-motivation projects for seventy-five mentally challenged young people in conjunction with the Public Health Service. It also worked with the Iowa Conservation Commission to hire thirty-five dependent and neglected youths from foster homes to work in state parks, fish hatcheries, and forest nurseries. Also in 1967, the council helped the Iowa Farmers Union find jobs for 125 former agricultural workers.[24]

Based on this experience, Hughes looked to acquire additional federal funds to aid Iowans. This time, however, his goal was to help fellow alcoholics, using the government to do what he had been doing personally for years.

One of the first Great Society agencies was the Office of Economic Opportunity (OEO), created in 1964 shortly after Johnson became president. It was headed by the hyperenergetic Sargent Shriver, husband of the equally energetic Eunice Kennedy and brother-in-law of the late President Kennedy. OEO's goal was to fight poverty and unemployment through local grants distributed via community action agencies (CAAs). The CAAs' mission was to define local grassroots programs needed to fight poverty and create and manage these programs. This effort had a mixed record, sometimes aiding the unemployed and sometimes not. One problem was that the CAAs were required to seek "maximum feasible participation," meaning that the poor themselves were part of the operation. This often led to CAAs that opposed local politicians, resulting in complaints to the White House. Another difficulty—a common criticism of Great Society programs—was that OEO often issued grants without informing local and state governments. That was one of the criticisms Hughes aimed at OEO: "I barely know what's going on," he said. "And I'm not sure those fellows in Washington do either." Hughes's complaint was that the federal government bypassed state agencies when allotting the $5 million in programs designated for Iowa.[25]

In early January 1966 Shriver was scheduled to address a statewide conference of community antipoverty leaders in Des Moines. Hughes made sure he had a one-on-one breakfast meeting with the OEO head to air his complaints. Speaking to the press afterward, the always optimistic Shriver said the conversation had been highly agreeable and the governor "gave no indication of any dissatisfaction with the program. It is certain to progress rapidly in Iowa." Hughes called it a "frank exchange of ideas." More importantly, Hughes used the meeting to spring an idea on Shriver. The governor pointed out that alcoholism contributes to poverty because a severe alcoholic who has no tools to help him- or herself cannot get a job and contribute to society. Hughes suggested that providing such tools through OEO would be an ideal opportunity to help these individuals. Shriver was open to the idea and asked Hughes to come up with a plan for Iowa.[26]

During one of his earlier visits to the White House, Hughes had proposed the same idea to President Johnson, getting tentative approval for a $1 million program. With a thumbs-up from the president and Shriver, Hughes again approached Russell Wilson and asked him to draw up program specifics to present to Shriver. "How much time do I have?" Wilson asked. "A week," Hughes replied. Said Wilson later, "That's the way Hughes operated at times." Working with staff from the Iowa Manpower Development Council, Wilson consulted a psychologist from the Board of Control and a vocational rehabilitation professional, who in turn conferred with others on how to develop the program. The group pooled their rapidly compiled research, conceptualized the program, developed details, and, together with an accountant, drew up a budget of $1 million.[27]

The focus was not on the treatment of alcoholics. The assumption was that this was best handled by local AA groups and state mental health hospitals, which treated severe cases of alcoholism. This new program was intended to identify gaps in services and concentrate on reentry into society after treatment. Many of these efforts already existed in the state, but they were scattered and unorganized. The goal was to bring them together so recovered alcoholics could get mental and physical health care, social services assistance, and job training. This emphasis on introducing alcoholics into the job market was in sync with OEO's mission. Most important, the program countered the overwhelmingly negative stigma of being an alcoholic with the concept that alcoholism is a sickness and that sufferers need understanding and support. It facilitated sobriety by helping alcoholics become functioning members of society.[28]

Wilson and his group met the deadline, flew to Washington in early March, and presented the plan to Shriver. In a letter to Shriver urging his approval, Hughes pointed out that there were an estimated fifty thousand alcoholics in the state and some eighty thousand children who had at least one alcoholic parent. A quarter of the patients in Iowa's mental health institutes were alcoholics. The proposed plan's mission, wrote the governor, was to carry out "a total assault on alcoholism" by completing the cycle in recovery. Shriver enthusiastically approved the Iowa Comprehensive Alcoholism Project (ICAP) as a pilot project, calling it one of the best proposals he had ever received. Shriver shared Hughes's belief in the link between poverty and alcoholism, but he had neither the experience nor adequate research to clearly define the relationships and ramifications. Shriver gambled that Iowa's program could provide valuable information for future alcoholism programs.[29]

The effort to aid alcoholics clearly blossomed from Hughes's heart. In April he spoke at a two-day workshop on alcoholism held in Iowa City for educators, ministers, judges, law enforcement officials, doctors, social workers, and others, continuing his rhetoric urging an all-out assault on alcoholism. Citing his personal history, Hughes pointed out that others needed help and said the problems caused by alcoholism "require the dedication of the people involved—and that includes all the social agencies and their families." By midsummer, his office announced the receipt of a fifteen-month OEO grant for $579,958, together with $145,701 from the state Vocational Rehabilitation Administration (VRA). In addition, the VRA would contribute $75,000 annually for three years to provide direct services to alcoholics. Though not quite $1 million, it marked one of the nation's most significant state efforts to aid alcoholics.[30]

In late August Hughes and Wilson jointly announced plans to create ICAP centers in eight major Iowa cities. These halfway houses would provide places where alcoholics could live following treatment at institutions or medical facilities or outpatient services for those living at home. Hughes emphasized that, if successful, these centers could serve as models for other states.[31]

By early 1967, six of these centers were staffed, and multiple links had been established with state agencies and private organizations to aid alcoholics. Negotiations were ongoing to set up the two other centers. By this time, ICAP had reportedly helped about two hundred alcoholics. By midsummer, the number was more than seven hundred, and by the end of 1967, it was nearly two thousand. That year, ICAP funding also contributed to the creation of the Harrison Treatment and Rehabilitation Center in Des Moines, which functioned as a detoxification center for alcoholics. Patients could also get additional treatment and follow-up care.[32]

After Wilson left the program, ICAP was headed by two directors—John MacKey and Ken Eaton—who implemented a three-step process to aid alcoholics in Iowa. First, ICAP staff members aggressively sought out those in need in hospitals, police stations, welfare offices, and other sites, directing them to ICAP centers. Second, they directed clients to "rehabilitation resources," such as AA units, mental health professionals, and employment opportunities. Third, ICAP administrators followed clients through the process, with the goal of returning recovered alcoholics "to family and to job."[33]

Ultimately, the results of the program were mixed. In a letter to Shriver in early 1968, Hughes reported that about 40 percent of ICAP clients have remained sober "for a significant period of time, thus permitting rehabilitation to be effective." He also stated that the number of alcoholics admitted to mental health institutes close to where the ICAP centers were located was down 50 percent. On the link between alcoholism and poverty—justifying the OEO budget—Hughes admitted there was no way to establish cause and effect between the two but added, "Our experiences thus far indicate that it is possible to disrupt this pattern and the apparent chain-reaction between poverty and alcoholism."[34]

ICAP received kudos from several sources. Hugh P. Finerty, city attorney for Council Bluffs, told Hughes that ICAP had helped the local police department treat alcoholics who were arrested. "I feel that the ICAP is doing a most worthwhile job and hope for its continued success," he wrote. Mac Leaming, a businessman from Fort Dodge and a recovered alcoholic, noted that he had seen a 75 percent increase in local AA membership, contributing to sobriety for "a lot of former drinkers . . . through the direct efforts of ICAP." P. Keith Simpson, director of the Harrison Center, had been working with alcoholics in Iowa for eight years and wrote to Hughes that ICAP placed a wedge into a prior revolving door for alcoholics, lauding it as a national model. "Agencies who previously gave the alcoholic only directions to another agency suddenly became involved performing duties for the alcoholic, previously available only to the 'normal client.'"[35]

While ICAP helped individuals on the local level, the statewide organization was less successful. After Wilson returned to the Board of Control, ICAP suffered from poor management and infighting. ICAP employee Leo E. Chester wrote in a slashing letter to Hedlund that ICAP was "the most screwed up mess I have ever seen" in eleven years in government work. He charged that ICAP did not fulfill the terms of the contract with OEO, operated without a statewide advisory committee, and did not have guidelines for local offices. In many cases, he said, the office only referred clients to AA, which "could be accomplished by a telephone answering service." He charged that, through "sheer stupidity and ineptitude," ICAP management "dumped a good program down the drain and failed not only the alcoholic in Iowa but all people across the country." Wayne Shoemaker, Hughes's confidant from Ida Grove, wrote to the governor about one ICAP center head who had "received practically no tangible help of real value from the state office staff." He accused critic Chester of being "the chief sore spot—no compassion or concern—no understanding or consideration for the alcoholic."[36]

ICAP was eventually integrated into the Iowa Department of Social Services, created in 1967. That year, Great Society budget cuts dramatically impacted OEO. In a February 1968 letter to Hughes, Shriver lamented slashing the budget by more than a third. In a personal handwritten note he added, "I'm really sorry about his—but we're having to cut back everywhere. Sarge."[37]

Hughes chalked up the experience with ICAP as a lesson learned. He would later take this real-world schooling on government aid to alcoholics onto the national stage, where he would leave his permanent mark.

11 | Third-Term Reelection

In early 1966 Hughes faced three career choices. He could run for reelection as governor, run for the US Senate against Jack Miller, or leave politics and enter private business. Running against the popular Miller was not out of the question. Hughes had a 3–2 advantage over the incumbent senator in a *Des Moines Register* poll taken in late 1965. Another poll showed that 55 percent of Iowans would support him for another term as governor. Only four Iowa governors had ever been elected to a third term—none of them Democrats.[1]

Hughes removed all doubt in early January by announcing his intention to run for reelection. He would run on his record and continue his efforts to move ahead. "Much has been accomplished but much remains to be done," he declared, pledging to "consolidate our gains and to move on to new plateaus of growth and development." Another factor in his decision was that he had recruited many of those elected to statewide executive offices and felt obliged to run for another term with them. Also, he felt that the government reform he had initiated was only partially complete, with studies on government reorganization and tax reform yet to be reviewed by the 1967 legislature.[2]

Iowa's economy was building on the postwar boom in both industrial and agricultural areas, and this boded well for the incumbent governor. The state's industrial production had surpassed $8 billion, a new record, and higher crop and livestock prices had made farming profitable again. This boom reflected the way Iowans felt about their governor and Iowa Democrats in general. With a 73 percent approval rating in May, Hughes had a significant lead over his Republican opponents.[3]

When asked what he considered the major issue of the 1966 campaign, Hughes said with a wry grin, "Me." But he could have added state taxes. In making the transition to the new method of withholding state income taxes from paychecks, Iowans were paying their 1965 taxes through the old method of twice-a-year direct payments plus their 1966 taxes through withholding. Calling this "double taxation," some critics—which included a significant number of Democrats—called for a special session of the legislature to forgive either 1965 or 1966 state taxes.[4]

The political problem was one of the Democrats' own making. Recognizing in 1965 that this would become an issue, Hughes had originally asked that the new tax law forgive the first half of Iowans' 1966 taxes. This would have eliminated most of the windfall through the so-called double taxation. As the 1965 legislative session was ending, Hughes confirmed with experts that this plan would balance taxes and revenue for the coming year. However, senate majority leader Andrew Frommelt objected because, to get the votes needed to pass the tax withholding change, he had promised additional revenue for state capital improvements, such as new buildings and repairs. Hughes and other legislative leaders reluctantly agreed and removed the tax forgiveness portion of the legislation. Because this "extra" money could not be spent until it was allocated by the 1967 legislature, the taxes collected would become a massive state surplus of more than $30 million—and Iowans were still complaining about paying two years of taxes at once.[5]

Democrats argued that there was no double taxation; the tax bills were for two different years—1965 and 1966. But because they were being paid in the same year, criticism was inevitable. Republican state chairman Robert Ray blared, "It took no genius during the last legislative session to forecast an unneeded surplus when the Democrat legislature under Hughes's leadership insisted on making Iowans pay two years' taxes in one year, and at the same time increased eight major areas of taxation." He cited growing household expenses as paychecks were being "sliced by the Democrats in Iowa through this double taxation."[6]

Hughes struck back in a Saturday afternoon press conference in late March 1966 with state treasurer Paul Franzenburg and state auditor Loren Worthington, both Democrats, and state comptroller Marvin Selden Jr., a Republican, at this side. Yes, Hughes admitted, there would be a $30 million surplus at the end of the biennium, but the state needed an "absolute minimum" of $12 million to $15 million in surplus funds to cover emergencies. Hughes denied that Iowans were "overtaxed" and brushed off demands for a special session to deal with the issue.[7]

In a mid-April press conference, Hughes said he would be in favor of forgiving a portion of state income tax if the state did not need funds for essential programs. "But," he added, "this simply won't happen" because the expected surplus would be needed for "absolutely necessary" programs, such as aid to schools. Also, Iowa's penal and mental health institutions were in a "rundown condition" and needed improvements.[8]

At the end of the 1966 fiscal year on June 30, the total tax collected by the state of Iowa amounted to $419.6 million, an increase of $93 million over fiscal year 1965. About one-third of this total was attributable to withholding income taxes from paychecks. The rest, experts estimated, stemmed from the better state economy and from Iowans who had previously evaded paying state income tax. More than forty-one thousand additional state tax returns had been received that year, an increase of 6.5 percent. The increase in tax revenue also included new taxes on gas, cigarettes, new auto purchases, and other items. Instead of a $30 million surplus, the state was expecting a balance closer to $80 million. The stage was set for the fall debate.[9]

Hughes had no problem winning his party's nomination. He was endorsed by the convention—the first and last time a gubernatorial candidate was endorsed by an Iowa Democratic convention—and was unopposed in the September primary.[10]

The race for the Republican nomination was a more lively affair, pitting William Murray, an economics professor at Iowa State University in Ames, against Centerville newspaper publisher Robert Beck. For Murray, this was his second run at the governorship. In 1958 he had won the Republican nomination to oppose incumbent governor Herschel Loveless and lost. Beck was running for the first time, building on a successful newspaper career; he had recently been named Iowa master editor-publisher. Naturally, both candidates railed against Hughes and the Iowa Democrats on the "double taxation" issue but differed on the solution. Murray campaigned for a special session to cancel the paycheck deductions for the second half of the year; alternatively, if that could not be done, he urged refunding taxes to Iowans from the "enormous surplus." Beck called that "a gimmick to buy votes"; instead, he wanted the money directed toward local schools and property tax relief.[11]

The campaign between the two Republicans resulted in the closest statewide primary fight since 1920, with Murray defeating Beck by a vote of 87,371 to 85,733. The September 6 primary also marked the lowest voter turnout since 1930. The battle was on to deny a third term to Harold Hughes.[12]

Hughes was ready—armed with the strategic thinking of Park Rinard. In August the soft-spoken adviser prepared a confidential memo for Hughes about the November election. With a commanding lead in the polls, it would have been easy for Hughes to play it safe, but Rinard rejected that idea because "it is uncharacteristic and unworthy of the candidate" and would "bore all of us to death—particularly HEH." Instead, he recommended conducting "the daring, keep-them-off-balance, moving target Hughes type of campaign, as in the past." This included "an all-out campaign on behalf of state candidates" to show "a chief executive who is willing to risk his own popularity to fight for the team." Rinard proposed talking continually about the economic health of Iowa and emphasizing that "not everyone is getting an adequate share and some groups are suffering from inequities in the tax system." The Republicans, he said, would probably focus on "the narrowness of . . . governmental problems. By the time the campaign is well along it should seep through to the electorate that HEH is dealing with the whole big structure of the government while these people are throwing darts at a few selected issues." Rinard was recommending the only type of campaigning with which Hughes was comfortable.[13]

Charging out of the gate in early September, Hughes cast the contest between Murray and himself as a "give-back program" versus a proposal to "invest . . . in the urgent needs of the state." In a speech at the Hotel Savery in Des Moines, Hughes said, "We will have to show a fortitude and staying power to forgo some immediate personal advantage to gain longer-range objectives for the public good." To do otherwise would be a "retreat into the dead-end streets of the past."[14]

For most Iowans, their state tax bill averaged $110 a year. Under the Murray plan, the average refund would be $55 for half a year—not an insignificant amount in the mid-1960s, but hardly a fortune. Some would get more, some less. The problem for Murray—in addition to Hughes's relentless emphasis on the need to pay for essential state services—was division within his own Republican Party. Many still agreed with the defeated Beck that property tax relief was the best use of the extra money; others frankly agreed with Hughes that increased state spending was necessary. In an affront to Murray, four GOP candidates for state senate seats in Polk County refused to support the rebate plan during a televised debate in Des Moines. Republican chairman Ray was caught in the middle and said it was "premature" to specify what Republicans would do. Even Murray admitted that many fellow Republicans were "cool" to the idea, and his candidate for lieutenant governor outright opposed the refund.[15]

By late September, Murray was "phasing out" the refund plan from his campaign rhetoric and emphasizing other issues such as property tax relief, education, and simplifying tax forms. But Hughes would have none of it. He charged that "Murray wants to divide up the pot and go home instead of investing in Iowa's future." He had no intention of letting the Republican candidate avoid the issue.[16]

By early October, Hughes seemed poised for reelection. One poll had him ahead of Murray 50 percent to 36 percent. A poll later in the month showed that 74 percent of Iowans wanted to use the surplus funds for state expenses, rather than receive a refund or lower their taxes. This was a dramatic reversal from an early summer poll in which 54 percent had wanted a refund of all or part of the surplus. It looked like Hughes's campaigning and oratory had succeeded in changing public opinion.[17]

With his own reelection chances looking good, Hughes used his political capital to press for the rest of the statewide Democratic ticket, bringing them along on his campaign and touting their importance to him. He introduced the other candidates by saying, "These men are my cabinet. You wouldn't think of electing the President of the United States and giving him a cabinet of members of the opposite party." Hughes also used his campaign appearances to boost local Democrats running for the state legislature, hoping to keep majorities in both houses. He announced that this would be his last race for governor. As to the future, he said, "The alternatives are retiring from public office or running for the Senate and I don't know which at this time at all."[18]

In the last days of the campaign, Hughes visited the twelve largest cities in Iowa via helicopter, which never failed to attract crowds. Despite his lead in the polls, Hughes aggressively lashed out at his opponent during every appearance. The *Des Moines Tribune*'s Drake Mabry wrote that Hughes's rhetoric "sharpened a campaign that otherwise has been something less than exciting." He continued, "The direction and force of the Hughes attack was unexpected, because in past campaigns he usually has steered clear of the more emotional political charges." Now, wrote Mabry, Hughes was accusing Murray of being "ludicrous," "nit-picking," "carping," and "desperate for an issue in this election." In the final *Des Moines Register* poll, Hughes led Murray 58 percent to 42 percent. The irony is that, once again, the small-town native's strongest support came from Iowa's large cities, by a margin of 71 to 29 percent.[19]

Hughes's reelection on November 6 was no surprise. He received 55 percent of the vote to Murray's 44 percent, winning by 100,000 votes out of nearly 900,000 cast. Mills of the *Register* called Hughes "the greatest Democratic vote-getter in Iowa history." But overall, the results were a mixed bag for the rest of the Iowa Democrats. Lieutenant Governor Fulton narrowly won reelection, largely on Hughes's coattails, and state treasurer Paul Franzenburg also won another term. Otherwise, the statewide slate of Republican candidates was victorious, including conservative Richard Turner of Council Bluffs, who, as attorney general, would become a thorn in Hughes's side over the next two years. Republicans also retained the US Senate seat, with Jack Miller's overwhelming win, and won back most of the congressional seats they had lost in 1964, with the exception of John Culver in the east and Neal Smith in central Iowa. More importantly for Hughes, the Republicans regained control of the Iowa house, 89–35, while the Democrats narrowly retained control of the senate, 32–29.[20]

These mixed political results were very much on the governor's mind when he pledged his full cooperation with Republicans in the coming year. "There is no time for post-mortems and no room for bitterness. . . . We are all Iowans before we are partisans." Many saw the win by Hughes as a personal victory for the governor, representing his widespread popularity among Iowans.[21]

The Republican wins were due, in part, to the natural cycle of American politics, whereby voters turn against the party in the White House—in this case, Democrat Lyndon Johnson—in midterm elections. That trend was evident throughout the rest of the country, as the GOP gained forty-seven House seats, three Senate seats, and eight governorships. This year, however, Democrats felt a special resentment toward the president, who had promised to campaign for Democrats and then failed to do so. There were also grumblings among Democrats that some of the Great Society programs tossed out of Washington had failed to live up to expectations. Also, some were starting to criticize the growing commitment of American troops to the open-ended war in Vietnam.[22]

These complaints by Democrats would soon place the governor of Iowa in direct conflict with the powerful politician in the White House and forever change the career of Harold Hughes.

12 | Presidential Confrontation and State Reform

Harold Hughes entered the White House for a scheduled fifteen-minute meeting with President Johnson in mid-December 1966. Elected chairman of the National Democratic Governors Conference the prior July, Hughes had been summoned to confer with LBJ ahead of the governors' meeting at the Greenbrier Hotel in White Sulphur Springs, West Virginia. He was prepared to give Johnson his honest assessment of the negative political climate, but that did not happen. Instead, the Iowa governor received a one-sided presidential rant for more than an hour—as only Lyndon Johnson could do. The president paced back and forth in the Oval Office, raging about the Vietnam War—roaring about "my tanks, my airplanes, my bombings"—and thundering about other complaints as well. Hughes never got a chance to talk and departed the White House stunned. He later wrote, "When I left, I wondered if Lyndon Johnson had begun to lose touch with reality."[1]

The mood was somber among the eighteen Democratic governors who sat around a large oval table at the Greenbrier Hotel late on the evening of Thursday, December 15. In the words of Hughes aide Dwight Jensen, who was present, "This was a meeting when the Democratic governors really let their hair down." Virtually all of them had significant complaints about the president, his policies, and his personal activities. Some of the complaints involved the escalating Vietnam War and the ongoing bombing, while others complained about federal Great Society programs being thrown into their states with no consultation. Others complained about LBJ's imperious manner and his broken promise to campaign for Democrats in the November election. After all the governors had had their say, Hughes spoke up. Said Jensen, "My recollection of that meeting is that Hughes really did unload and Roger Branigin, governor of Indiana, said, 'Give 'em hell, Harold!'"[2]

The meeting broke up around midnight. As the tall double doors opened and the governors rushed out, reporters were waiting for statements. As chairman, Hughes knew he was the primary spokesman, and he yelled at the departing chief executives, "What do you want me to say?" Said one fleeing governor, "Tell them the truth." So, Harold Hughes being Harold Hughes, that is what he did.[3]

Hughes bluntly told reporters that the governors believed the sweeping Democratic losses in 1966 stemmed from an anti-Johnson trend throughout the country. He said the governors felt sidelined by the administration. "We feel that we should have a broader role in expressing opinion from the state to the national level. . . . The governors want a greater voice before the fact, rather than after the fact of proposed administration legislation." Although the governors were not critical of the Great Society legislation itself, it "was moving too fast" and was not being implemented well. About Johnson himself, the governor cryptically said, "The problem of the President's personality was discussed." On the upcoming presidential race in 1968, Hughes said it would be "a tough race" if the Republicans presented a "respectable opponent" two years from now. He added that most of the Democratic governors felt they had no real communication with the administration.[4]

The next day, when Hughes's comments hit the front pages of the nation's newspapers and the morning TV news shows, the president of the United States was not pleased. (The *Des Moines Register*'s banner headline was "Hughes Blames Johnson.") LBJ's first call was to White House staffer Sherwin Markman of Des Moines, who had arranged the meeting between Hughes and Johnson. "It was a ten-minute rant," recalled Markman. "And if you cut through all the profanity of the President, he said, 'How the hell can that man say that he never speaks with me when he just spent a day with me. . . . You get that goddamn son-of-a-bitch on the line and take back every word he said.' And that's the short-hand version." Reeling from the call, Markman phoned Hughes and conveyed the president's red-hot words—"with basically no profanity"—and listened to the governor's reply: "Well, yeah, I did go to the White House and I did sit with him for an hour, and, for that hour, he talked, I listened, and I couldn't get a word in edgewise. So what I said is absolutely accurate. We never get a chance to talk to the President. And you tell him that."[5]

The controversy thrust Hughes onto the national stage as, in the words of *Des Moines Register* reporter Nick Kotz, "the man who stood up to the President of the United States." Said one governor to Hughes, "Nobody could accuse you of being diplomatic. By God, I've always heard you were candid, honest, and blunt—and all three adjectives fit." Another said Hughes and his wife "can count on never being invited back to the White House as long as Lyndon Johnson is President." As the days passed, several governors publicly denied voicing the criticisms they had privately expressed at the West Virginia meeting, and one said that Hughes spoke only for himself. In an attempt to defuse the tension, Hughes arranged a meeting with the president and several governors at LBJ's ranch in Texas.[6]

A few days before Christmas, nine Democratic governors traveled to Johnson's Texas home to confer with the commander in chief. There are conflicting reports about the tenor of the three-hour meeting. According to Hughes's memoir, the president asked each politician to speak his mind, and Johnson "retained his calmness" and allowed each governor to have his say. Other outsiders reported that they could hear raised voices and arguing back and forth, particularly between Johnson and Hughes. Ernie Olsen, a member of the Secret Service from Iowa, later told Hughes aide Bill Hedlund, "Hughes and LBJ were going at it. Nobody ever really stood up to LBJ, but Hughes did and he was imposing." After the meeting ended, Johnson invited Hughes into his bedroom. Alone with the Iowa governor, the president turned on him—"eyes blazing," according to Hughes—and accused him of hurting the party and the president himself by his statements. Jabbing Hughes in the chest with his forefinger, Johnson blared, "You had damn well better back off before you get yourself in a pot of trouble." As Hughes struggled to stay calm, he said he was sorry the president felt that way but replied, "I'm not going to change what I said. I told the truth and if that's wrong, then it's wrong." The two men then joined the other governors for lunch.[7]

The heat expressed in Johnson's bedroom was not apparent during the joint press conference later held by Johnson and Hughes. In summarizing the meeting, the governor was careful to use diplomatic language. Hughes called the meeting "very open and frank" and reported that "all factors were discussed." He added, "There were no words minced in the meeting" and characterized it as "a dialogue, not a monologue" that "went directly to the nub of the issues concerning us." He refused to go into detail about content. After the press conference, Hughes and Johnson, according to those attending, "shook hands warmly."[8]

In reality, the relationship between Johnson and Hughes was anything but warm. It was irrevocably broken. Never again would Hughes be invited to the White House as Johnson's "favorite governor." Although the break was primarily over domestic policies and politics, another issue that split the two was the escalating war in Vietnam. Hughes, by this time, was having doubts about the conflict, holding his tongue in public but privately opposing the buildup. Soon, this would lead to an open break with the Johnson administration and the Iowan's rise as one of the significant national voices against the Vietnam War.

Next, Hughes turned to Iowa government and the upcoming 1967 legislative session. Hughes and others had been doing a substantial amount of legwork on government reorganization, stemming from the detailed review and recommendations by the Public Administration Service (PAS) of Chicago. Reports about reforming Iowa government were nothing new. The Iowa legislature had commissioned a Brookings Institution study in 1933, in the midst of the Great Depression; another report by a group known as the Little Hoover Commission in 1950; and still another report in 1958. Very few of the recommendations in these reports were ever transformed into law, largely due to a lack of support from the governors at the time.[9]

This time, it would be different. When the Hughes-appointed Advisory Commission on Governmental Reorganization met in June 1966 to hear a preliminary report from PAS, the governor attended to show his support. "I think today is entirely a different ball game," he said. "We are just absolutely playing in a different realm than we have played in the past with these various other committees."[10]

One problem was that the myriad administrative commissions throughout the state were headed by three commissioners appointed by the governor and approved by the legislature. Management by three individuals is fraught with problems in the best of circumstances. Adding to the difficulties, few commissioners were expert managers or even experts in the fields they supervised, and because these commissioners were independent, it was difficult if not impossible to coordinate policy statewide. Most citizens held the governor responsible for the executive branch, but in this situation, responsible management was nearly impossible. Commissioners were usually appointed to staggered six-year terms, which meant that a governor could appoint all members only if he were elected to three terms. Hughes intended to change that.[11]

To guide these efforts, Hughes hired Frank Covington as director of planning for the state of Iowa. Covington, a native of Ottumwa, had previously worked for PAS and played a major role in developing the recommendations for Iowa. He was charged with preparing and maintaining long-range development plans—on both a two-year and six-year basis—and working with the newly reorganized state boards, commissions, and departments to implement those plans. The goal was to move beyond reactive efforts and push for proactive planning and initiatives within the redesigned state government.[12]

Covington's hiring coincided with release of the PAS report in November 1966, which recommended wholesale changes in the Iowa government. For instance, it called for consolidating Iowa's approximately 120 departments, commissions, boards, and agencies into thirteen administrative departments. One of the more significant changes was the creation of a new Department of Social Services, fusing the State Board of Social Welfare, Department of Social Welfare, Board of Control of State Institutions, Board of Parole, and Commission for the Blind into a single department under an appointed commissioner.[13]

Hughes's attitude was that the reorganization should be accomplished "wholesale." "Doing it piecemeal, as we have done in the past just compounds the problem," he said. In presenting the plan to Iowans, he emphasized that the changes would offer $10 million in additional state services by eliminating overlapping agencies and duplication of effort. The challenge was how to convince a divided legislature. With Republican majorities in both houses in his first term and Democratic majorities in his second, Hughes now faced the challenge of a sizable Republican majority in the house and a slim three-vote Democratic majority in the senate. To push these reforms through the legislature, Hughes had to rise above partisanship and plot a course that would benefit all Iowans.[14]

In his State of the State address on January 10, 1967, and his inaugural address two days later, Hughes pushed these reforms and linked them with a state economy that was expanding dramatically and needed a modernized government to match it. Hughes called the business expansion "Iowa's economic awakening" and cited both agricultural and industrial growth. Net farm income was 46 percent higher in 1965 than in 1964; on the industrial side, six hundred new businesses were created in 1965–66, offering nearly twenty-seven thousand new job opportunities, a total investment of more than $446 million, and new payrolls exceeding $162 million. In his inaugural address, Hughes advocated more than twenty significant recommendations, including implementation of PAS's government reorganization plan and tax and civil service reforms. An editorial in the *Des Moines Register* called Hughes's inaugural address "one of the most comprehensive designs for the future of the state which any governor has presented."[15]

The lawmakers' first task was reaching bipartisan agreement on the recurring issue of reapportionment, clearing that item off the table to make way for other measures. In April 1966 the Iowa Supreme Court had provided further guidance on this issue by ruling, 5–4, in favor of single-member districts rather than multiple-member, at-large representation. The majority of justices ruled that it was unconstitutional for rural residents to vote for only one representative while urban residents voted for several.[16]

After an early January meeting between Hughes and legislative leaders—which participants called a "harmony session"—the legislature created a fourteen-member commission, with seven members appointed by each state party chairman, to draw up another temporary apportionment plan. The commission, composed of representatives from each of Iowa's congressional districts, assembled for the hard and detailed work of drawing up Iowa house and senate districts for the 1968 elections. The commission submitted its proposal to the legislature, and it easily passed both chambers.[17]

The second redistricting task was approving a permanent plan, which currently consisted of a constitutional amendment passed by the Democrat-controlled 1965 legislature. The bipartisan strategy was to pass the amendment a second time and submit it to the voters. In addition, both the house and the senate created another amendment that made single-member districts mandatory in future reapportionment arrangements, in line with the recent Iowa Supreme Court ruling. The first amendment was approved by voters in the 1968 election, creating two houses based on population and allowing districts to cross county lines. This, however, was not the end of the debate. Legislative debates and court actions would continue into the next decade.[18]

Passage of the reapportionment compromise by late March opened the floodgates for other legislation, the most significant of which was long-term tax reform. In June 1966 Hughes had received the in-depth tax study carried out by respected Purdue University economist James Papke, who criticized the state's tax system as "deeply regressive." Due to high property taxes dedicated to local school funding—accounting for half of all taxes collected—lower-income Iowans paid a higher percentage of their income than families in higher income brackets. The average family with an income of $5,000 had a state and local tax burden that was 60 percent higher, relative to income, than that of the average family with an income above $10,000. The solution, according to Papke, was to expand state aid to schools and lower property taxes by increasing personal and corporate income taxes, as well as retail and sales taxes, to make taxation more equitable.[19]

Long a complaint of Iowa taxpayers, high property taxes had now become an issue too big to ignore. In August 1966 the Iowa Taxpayers Association estimated that in the following year, property taxes would rise a record $55 million or more, based on budget estimates from school districts, cities, towns, and counties. George Mills of the *Register* wrote that, compared with the $30 million property tax increase in 1960, this one would "smash that old record to smithereens."[20]

To address this issue, Hughes appointed a twenty-nine-member committee headed by former Des Moines mayor Charles F. Iles to review the Papke study and make recommendations. Releasing its report ahead of the 1967 legislative session in early January, the committee not unexpectedly recommended more progressive personal and corporate income taxes and a 2 percent sales tax increase, as well as the extension of sales tax to the purchase of consumer services. It also decried the current heavy reliance on property taxes, noting that there was "relatively limited revenue elasticity" and pointing out that property taxes do "not respond effectively to growth in the State's population and economy."[21]

Before Hughes could push for fundamental tax reform, he had to deal with annual budgets. He announced in January that the state treasury would probably collect some $90 million in surplus taxes, resulting from the expanding Iowa economy and the windfall from collecting two years' worth of state income taxes in one year. Hughes's preference was to dedicate these funds to badly needed building projects. In an address to the legislature on budget and taxation issues, Hughes recommended $376.3 million in state spending, marking a 38 percent increase over the previous year's budget but far short of the amounts various state departments and agencies claimed they needed. Given the surplus, Hughes recommended no significant tax increases "at this time" and turned to tax reform as the main priority.[22]

As summer loomed and the legislative session anticipated adjournment, budget and tax bills moved back and forth between the Republican house and the Democratic senate with seemingly no agreements on the table. Said Hughes in late June, "There is a conglomeration of bills up there that defy me to know which direction the Legislature is going . . . I can't calculate what it all means." By now, overall tax reform and increased state aid to schools were getting serious attention, so the time to attack seemed to be at hand.[23]

By the third week in June, Hughes let legislators know that he was willing to take a personal role in negotiations between the two chambers. After several preliminary meetings, Hughes and legislative leaders, along with Hedlund and state comptroller Marv Sellers, gathered for a closed meeting on Friday, June 23. According to Hedlund, Hughes spoke up and said, "Here we are, guys. We need to get something done. What do you think? Let's go around the room and say what you think." Some wanted higher taxes on services. Others demanded state aid to schools to equalize per student spending. Once everyone had spoken and the discussion continued, a consensus started to take shape. Then Hughes said, "OK, we've kind of agreed on the basic things. You guys put it together. Now, we've agreed that this has to be done and we're gonna do it."[24]

As the politicians left the meeting, the only response to the anxious media was "no comment." (Hedlund recalled, "Jim Flansburg [reporter for the *Des Moines Register*] just went ape over that.") In a controversial move, lawmakers decided to forgo the committee system, develop legislation on their own, and send bills directly to the two chambers. On Tuesday morning, June 27, Hughes and legislative leaders announced at a press conference that they had reached a major agreement on school aid and property tax relief, but they refused to disclose the details until other legislators had been briefed. The *Cedar Rapids Gazette*'s Frank Nye wrote, "This is believed to be the first time in Iowa history when the leaders of both political parties in both houses have met at such length in secret with the state's chief executive in an earnest and dedicated effort to solve a major state problem—property tax relief."[25]

The result was the most expensive state tax increase in Iowa history, raising state revenue by $100 million a year through higher sales, income, corporate, cigarette, beer, and other taxes. On the spending side of the agreement, the plan included more than $100 million a year in school aid, $18 million in personal property tax replacement, a $3 million increase in agricultural land tax credits, and a $4 million increase in homestead tax benefits for elderly, low-income homeowners. The plan also contained a complicated formula for distributing state aid to high school districts, designed to take the financial pressure off property owners. The state would pick up 36 percent of the total cost of running Iowa's public elementary and secondary schools, a substantial increase over the 13 percent it currently paid. The agreement landed on the floors of the Iowa house and senate in two pieces: a tax bill and a property tax bill.[26]

Over a number of days in late June, the Iowa house and senate briefly debated the bills and passed them—with plenty of grumbling from both parties in both chambers. In the senate, Democratic majority leader Andrew Frommelt and Republican minority leader Robert Rigler said the package was "far from perfect" but insisted that it must be accepted without change to ensure passage in the house. A Council Bluffs senator said he would vote for the bill and "go back home and take the heat. Believe me, there'll be plenty of it." On the house side, a Des Moines representative said, "We have been here 170 days and now have been thrown a package we have to vote on in eight to 10 hours." Nevertheless, a sufficient number of legislators agreed to pass the overall package, with Hughes's signature guaranteed at the end.[27]

According to Papke of Purdue, the package was "jam-packed with equity," ensuring the taxation of all parties in a fair manner. He added, "This really is to me a payoff to see something I have worked so hard [on] become an actual tax policy." Said Hughes in a radio broadcast on July 1, "This is the first time within my memory that the legislative leadership of both political parties and the chief executive have worked out, together, a major tax revision program." To the criticism that the legislation had been put together hastily, Hughes dismissed that charge, noting that the issue had been discussed throughout the session with legislators "devoted to studying and debating the many complicated problems of property tax relief and raising the revenue to support it."[28]

There was plenty to complain about in the tax and property tax package, especially among those whose taxes increased. The criticism was especially sharp from the business community, which saw a rise in corporate taxes. To that complaint, Papke responded at a July media briefing: "Economic growth is much broader than just the expansion of industry, and industry requires good recreational facilities for its employees, good schools, good roads. All these things benefit industry."[29]

The school funding–tax bill was not the only important piece of legislation completed by the 1967 legislature—at the time, the longest serving

in Iowa history. Under Hughes's leadership, lawmakers significantly reformed Iowa government by abolishing the three-member boards that
managed tax collection and social services and replaced them with professional managers and advisory boards. Based on recommendations
from the PAS study, legislators replaced the three-member Tax Commission with the Department of Revenue, with a single administrator
appointed by the governor and subject to state senate approval. A much
more significant change was the creation of the Department of Social
Services, fusing the former Department of Social Welfare, Board of
Control of State Institutions, and Board of Parole. It, too, was managed
by a single administrator appointed by the governor. The new Department of Social Services was divided into five operating divisions: Child
and Family Services, Mental Health, Corrections, Administration and
Planning, and Research and Statistics. The three-member boards that
had administered the Department of Social Welfare and Board of Control were abolished, while the three-member Board of Parole continued
under the Division of Corrections. The goal was more efficient operation through an entity that reported to the governor.[30]

Also, the legislature finally passed civil service reform in Iowa, a move
Hughes had been advocating since 1965. The goal, he said, was to transform employment in Iowa government from pure politics into a more
professional operation. At a January press conference, he stated, "Let's
don't kid the people of the state. Let's either make it a political patron-
age system or provide for job protection, fringe benefits, and make it
possible for people to plan careers in government work." The result
was the creation of the Iowa Merit Employment Department, which ensured that fourteen thousand state government employees would be
hired, fired, and promoted on the basis of tests and merit, rather than
which political party was in power. When Hughes signed the bill on
June 20, he declared it a "constructive step toward enabling us to attract
and retain the conscientious and competent type of people required for
efficient government."[31]

Lawmakers passed for a second time the constitutional amendment
to reapportion the legislature, as well as amendments to give the governor a line-item veto on appropriation bills, establish annual sessions of
the legislature, and grant home rule for Iowa cities. This set the stage
for an up-or-down vote by Iowans in the next election.[32]

At the end of the third session of the Iowa legislature under his administration, Harold Hughes could say that Iowa was a more modern

state that more closely met the standards of mid-twentieth-century government. Through the force of his will and his deft political alliances, Hughes played a major role in streamlining Iowa government and abandoning many of the antiquated systems of the nineteenth and early twentieth centuries. The result was not perfect, nor was the task completed; more reforms would be accomplished under Hughes's successor, Robert Ray. But Hughes was the instigator who said these obsolete systems must not stand and the state must move on. He persuaded many to make that move with him. On these results alone, Hughes stands out as one of the most impactful governors in Iowa history.

It was not only across state government that Hughes initiated reform; it was also within the governorship itself. Hughes expanded his staff to both modernize the office and achieve his goal of being a more activist governor. Dwight Jensen managed the staff as Hughes's executive assistant during his three terms. Les Holland was hired in 1963 to replace the departed Kirk Boyd; Holland had worked for three years in the Iowa League of Municipalities and had no doubt been recommended by Park Rinard. In March 1964 Bill Hedlund, a veteran of the Iowa Legislative Research Bureau, was recruited to join the staff.[33]

In July 1965 Ed Campbell joined the expanded staff. A native of Fort Dodge, Campbell had been manager of the Charles City Chamber of Commerce. In contrast to other staffers who worked primarily within the state bureaucracy, Campbell concentrated on political affairs and often traveled with Hughes. Attorney Wade Clarke Jr. was added as legal assistant to the governor in December 1966.[34]

In 1967 reporter Martin Jensen of WMT News joined Hughes's staff, concentrating on media relations and speechwriting. When Holland left in mid-1967, he was replaced by Allen Jensen, formerly a senior planner in the Office of Planning and Programming. This created the unique situation of having three Jensens on the governor's staff. According to Dwight Jensen, this meant that people contacting the office had to know which Jensen to ask for, which seemed to sharpen callers' skills.[35]

When Hughes took office, he had only two staff members and secretarial help. By the time he left, he had six aides. The result was a more professional, skilled staff with specific responsibilities that could better serve the governor and the people of Iowa.

Hughes throwing the shot put. He excelled in athletics at Ida Grove High School, earning all-state honors in football and winning the state discus championship. (Courtesy of Phyllis Hughes Ewing)

Hughes in his military uniform. He served during World War II, participating in the invasions of both Sicily and Italy. (Courtesy of Phyllis Hughes Ewing)

Hughes poses with his family shortly before being elected governor in
1962. Front row (*left to right*): wife Eva, father Lewis, mother Etta, and
Hughes. Back row (*left to right*): daughters Carol, Phyllis, and Connie.
(Courtesy of Phyllis Hughes Ewing)

←

Hughes and Eva pose in front of their new house holding daughters Carol
and Connie and flanked by representatives from the local bank and loan
agency. Hughes was the first in Ida County, Iowa, to obtain a GI loan.
(Courtesy of Phyllis Hughes Ewing)

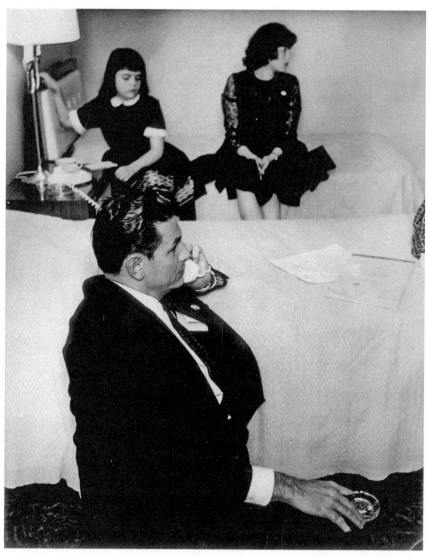

Hughes on election evening, November 1962, receiving word of his election as governor of Iowa. Sitting on the bed are daughters Phyllis and Carol. (Courtesy of Phyllis Hughes Ewing)

Hughes (*seated*) meets with Governor Norman Erbe (*center*) shortly after soundly defeating him in 1962. (Courtesy of Phyllis Hughes Ewing)

Hughes engages with students at Grinnell College during his governorship. (Papers of Harold E. Hughes, Special Collections and Archives, University of Iowa Libraries)

Democrats were elected across the board to statewide office in Iowa in 1964, many of whom were recruited by Hughes. *Left to right*: Paul Franzenburg, state treasurer; Gary Cameron, secretary of state; Robert Fulton, lieutenant governor; Hughes; Lawrence Scalise, attorney general; Loren Worthington, state auditor; and Kenneth Owen, secretary of agriculture. (Courtesy of the State Historical Society of Iowa, Iowa City)

←

Meeting in the Oval Office of the White House are (*left to right*) former Iowa governor Herschel Loveless, aide Dwight Jensen, Hughes, and President Lyndon Johnson. Hughes was frequently referred to as Johnson's "favorite governor" until their falling out in late 1966. (Courtesy of Dwight Jensen)

Hughes in Vietnam, where he got an extensive tour of US military operations there. Although he expressed firm support for US involvement at the time, doubts emerged as a result of this trip. (Papers of Harold E. Hughes, Special Collections and Archives, University of Iowa Libraries)

Hughes and an Amish father in Hazleton, Iowa. The governor was there to resolve a dispute between the Amish and the Oelwein school board. Issues included the hiring of uncertified teachers and the annual testing of Amish students. (Papers of Harold E. Hughes, Special Collections and Archives, University of Iowa Libraries)

Hughes and his wife, Eva, during his governor years. (Papers of Harold E. Hughes, Special Collections and Archives, University of Iowa Libraries)

Hughes meets with businessmen in Japan. He initiated trips abroad to promote Iowa industries in other countries. (Papers of Harold E. Hughes, Special Collections and Archives, University of Iowa Libraries)

Hughes's staff during his third term as governor. First row (*left to right*):
Marilyn Osborn, Fran Miller, and Fran Frazier. Second row: Helen Boyce,
Ruth Yauk, Mary Cullison, unidentified, Elva Pittman, and Mildred
Galenbeck. Third row: Bill Hedlund, Dwight Jensen, Wade Clarke Jr.,
Hughes, Les Holland, Martin Jensen, Ed Campbell, and Chief Warrant
Officer Dick Nehring. (Courtesy of Dwight Jensen)

Hughes and Senator Robert Kennedy on a private plane. Kennedy played a decisive role in persuading Hughes to run for the Senate in 1968. (Courtesy of Dwight Jensen)

Hughes campaigns among Iowans. (Papers of Harold E. Hughes, Special Collections and Archives, University of Iowa Libraries)

Hughes and Senator Eugene McCarthy (*left*) during a stop in Iowa prior to the 1968 Democratic convention. Hughes supported the Minnesotan for the Democratic presidential nomination. (Papers of Harold E. Hughes, Special Collections and Archives, University of Iowa Libraries)

Senator Edward Kennedy of Massachusetts (*left*) supported Hughes's
effort to create a special Senate subcommittee on alcoholism and drug
abuse. This resulted in the Comprehensive Alcoholism Prevention and
Treatment Act of 1970, known as the Hughes Act, which transformed
alcoholism treatment in the United States. (Papers of Harold E. Hughes,
Special Collections and Archives, University of Iowa Libraries)

Hughes with Robert Goralski of NBC News, discussing the covert US bombing of Cambodia. The senator frequently appeared on national television to discuss alcoholism and his opposition to the Vietnam War. (Papers of Harold E. Hughes, Special Collections and Archives, University of Iowa Libraries)

Harold Hughes and his second wife, Julie Holm Hughes. (Courtesy of Jacquie Holm-Smith)

13 | Civil Rights, Crisis Conferences, and a Senate Candidacy

In early August 1965 Lyndon Johnson had no sooner signed the Voting Rights Act—one of the crowning glories of his Great Society programs—when the US civil rights struggle shifted to a new phase, with race riots in the Watts neighborhood of Los Angeles. Stemming from a clash between police and Black youths, the confrontation lasted six days and resulted in thirty-four people killed, nearly nine hundred hospitalized, and more than four thousand arrested. With entire city blocks destroyed, property damage surpassed $45 million. This event symbolized the shift from the integrationist dream of Martin Luther King to the more confrontational cry of "Black Power" championed by Stokely Carmichael and other young Black leaders. No longer was the civil rights movement simply a moral crusade to eliminate Jim Crow laws and ensure Black voting rights in the South. Amid rising expectations, Blacks in the North had faced raw discrimination for decades, and protests against racism and police brutality launched a much more difficult and ambiguous stage of the civil rights struggle—combating economic inequality—which often manifested as inner-city violence.[1]

These urban upheavals continued the next summer. In 1966 there were eleven major riots—defined as civil conflict lasting two days or more—and thirty-two minor riots. The next summer, this increased to twenty-five major and thirty minor disturbances. One substantial conflict took place in Detroit, where forty-three people died in July 1967. Long denied the riches of the American dream, African Americans were now making their voices heard loud and clear in urban centers across the land.[2]

Despite its small African American population, this unrest found a home in mid-1960s Iowa, perpetuating an uneasy and ambivalent relationship between Black and white Iowans. Race relations were embedded in Iowa law even before statehood. As early as 1839, the Iowa territorial legislature passed a series of "black codes" restricting civil liberties among the few Blacks in the state, denying them the right to serve on juries, give court testimony, and attend public school. Later, legislators outlawed interracial marriage in the Iowa territory, and these laws carried over into statehood in 1846. In 1851 the legislature prohibited Blacks from moving into Iowa, although those already present in the state were allowed to stay.[3]

This attitude started to change in the 1850s when abolitionists migrated to Iowa and joined the new Republican Party coalition. Whig (later Republican) James Grimes's 1854 campaign for governor was based largely on opposition to the Kansas-Nebraska Act, which offered states the right to vote on slavery and threatened that Nebraska might join Missouri as a neighboring slave state. Although Grimes and Iowa Republicans opposed the extension of slavery—and the state voted in 1856 for Republican presidential candidate John C. Fremont, who also opposed the growth of slavery—that did not mean Iowans were pro-Black. In 1857 Iowans decisively voted down a public referendum granting African Americans the right to vote.[4]

That changed with the Civil War and the Republican Party's shift toward emancipation and civil rights. In 1864 the Iowa legislature voted to allow Blacks to settle in the state, and in 1868 Iowans approved a state constitutional amendment via a public referendum granting Blacks civil rights, including the right to vote. Iowa and Minnesota were the only states to grant these rights prior to passage of the Fifteenth Amendment to the US Constitution, removing race as a condition for suffrage. In the mid-1880s Republicans in the Iowa legislature approved a state civil rights act outlawing racial discrimination, although its scope and enforcement were limited.[5]

The state's legal system also supported racial inclusion. In 1868 and again in 1875 the Iowa Supreme Court ruled against racial discrimination in schools, outlawing segregation. In 1873 the court declared segregation in public accommodations unconstitutional. According to both statute and common law, Iowa provided a welcoming home to its Black citizens. However, everyday life was another matter.[6]

As agricultural mechanization and regional racism made farming untenable for southern Blacks, they were attracted to new opportunities in the North, including Iowa. In 1870 Iowa's Black population stood at 5,762; it was 9,516 in 1880 and had increased to 19,005 by 1920. By 1940, more than 60 percent of the state's Black population lived in Iowa's four most populous counties, home of industrial jobs. Sometimes, however, factory managers hired these Blacks as strikebreakers to crush unions, exacerbating racism among whites. This was the case in Waterloo in Black Hawk County, where the Illinois Central Railroad shipped Blacks from the South to replace unskilled workers seeking to unionize. This helped increase Waterloo's African American population from twenty-nine in 1910 to nearly nine hundred ten years later. Racist property covenants in Waterloo forced Blacks into a twenty-block area on the city's east side, where 94 percent of them lived, isolating them from white residents. Other businesses, such as Rath Packing Company and John Deere Tractor Works, attracted additional Black migrants to Waterloo.[7]

Racial prejudice remained a dominant attitude in Iowa, perhaps contributing to its small Black population. Waterloo native Nikole Hannah-Jones, author of *The 1619 Project*, notes that when her mother arrived from Mississippi with her three children in the 1940s, she had "her hopes of the mythical Promised Land shattered when she learned that Jim Crow did not end at the Mason-Dixon Line."[8]

Throughout the first half of the twentieth century, it was clear that racism impacted the livelihoods of Black Iowans. During this period, according to author Charles Connerly, white Iowans treated Black Iowans "as second-class citizens, isolating them from the state's predominately white residents and denying them access to the public accommodations and employment opportunities routinely available to whites." Post–World War II surveys and studies showed widespread racism among Iowans, revealing physicians and dentists who refused to treat Blacks, barbers who declined to cut the hair of Blacks, and even cemeteries that rejected African Americans for burial or segregated their plots.[9]

In the 1960s only 1 percent of Iowa's population of 2.7 million, or about 27,000 people, was Black. In the summers of 1966 and 1967—particularly in Des Moines and Waterloo—tensions rose as Black Iowans protested the racism that led to unemployment and unfair treatment by local police. Much of the unrest surfaced on hot summer evenings, when young African Americans without jobs gathered; they needed little incentive to strike out against local authorities. In Des Moines in July 1966, Black youths clashed with police in violent confrontations caused by boredom, bad housing, heat, and other factors "intensified by poor police handling," according to reports. Some two hundred to three hundred Blacks pelted police with rocks and bottles, damaging five squad cars and wrecking streetlights before local Black leaders managed to cool down the crowd. Another incident took place in Des Moines in September following a football game; authorities arrested more than two dozen Blacks near Drake University during a window-breaking spree.[10]

Governor Hughes's initial reaction to these events was only rhetorical, since the mayhem had been quelled locally. He condemned the violence and blamed the young people. When asked about the September incident at a press conference, he said, "I am neither antiblack nor antiwhite, but I am sure as hell antiriot. . . . I think the parents of these people ought to keep them at home and teach them what they are doing. They are hurting their own race and their own people and their own cause." He called the disturbance "an irresponsible act by a group of delinquents."[11]

The conflicts continued during the summer of 1967, especially in Waterloo. The city's Black population, concentrated on the east side, was the largest in the state in proportion to its total population of 75,000. Several nights of racial conflict and violence began on July 7 when police accused a Black youth of stealing hubcaps. Clashes between Black crowds and local police continued until, on the third night, gangs of youths ran through downtown Waterloo starting fires, smashing windows, looting stores, and pelting cars with stones. Police arrested seventy-five people. The all-white police force, resorting to racial slurs and billy clubs, only contributed to the problem.[12]

Hughes sent Father Cyril Engler of the Manpower Development Council, a former prison chaplain, to Waterloo. He spent eleven days evaluating the situation and talking to several hundred people. Engler reported that the "bigger issue was overall jobs, racial discrimination and housing." He explained that promises made to the Black community years ago for more open housing and on-the-job training programs had never materialized. In a deeply divided city, there was "no feeling of community between the two sides. . . . Residents of the white community on the West Side speak in terms of 'their problem' and refer to the East Side as if it were a thousand miles away." The chief of police and mayor spoke only in terms of "rigid police control" and "nothing in the way of long-term solutions." "In my opinion," Engler concluded, "the problems . . . can never be solved unless there is an obvious sincere desire on the part of residents of both the east (Negro) and west (white) sides . . . to do something."[13]

Several days before Engler's report landed on his desk, the governor of Iowa pondered the unrest and, after conversations with aides and friends, decided "to do something." Hughes ventured outside his white comfort zone and visited Black neighborhoods in person, determined to see firsthand how Black Iowans were living. The first visit, arranged through a federal worker who lived in the area, took place on Friday night, July 21, when Hughes, accompanied by aides Ed Campbell and Bill Hedlund, toured the Southeast Bottoms area of Des Moines, within sight of the state capitol. They visited a house on Raccoon Street, where three women lived with no indoor toilet. Hughes then walked past ramshackle homes on unpaved streets and paths filled with broken glass until he reached the Southeast Side Project House, where he spoke to about one hundred residents. They told him about medical and dental bills they were unable to pay, unlit streets that led to crime, and widespread hepatitis from poor plumbing and sewage. The conversation lasted until 2:00 a.m.[14]

During this discussion, Hughes said, "It is a shame on our nation that for so many years we have not attacked these problems." He called for "mutual understanding" between Black residents and "people in high places who have responsibilities for correcting these conditions." On the fundamental issue of racism, Hughes added, "We must turn within ourselves and rid ourselves of feelings that may lie there in regard to people of other races, religion, and nationalities." His visit was "well-received," according to the *Des Moines Register*'s James Risser, who quoted one resident's impression of Hughes: "He meant it where a lot of them [politicians] wouldn't."[15]

Hughes continued to make these visits around the state. On July 31 he conducted a secret "look-and-listen" tour of Waterloo, viewing, in his words, "the tragic signs of what they are up against—poor housing, lack of recreational facilities and economic opportunities and the like." When he talked to residents, he discussed problems, not solutions. "I listened," he said at a press conference the next morning. "I didn't go there to make a speech."[16]

In the coming weeks, Hughes visited Black neighborhoods in Sioux City, Davenport, and Cedar Rapids. When the mayor of Clinton invited officials from twenty-two Iowa cities to attend a meeting in Des Moines to discuss civil disorder and how to prevent it, Hughes attended—and listened. At a meeting in Davenport with thirty members of the NAACP, Hughes said, "I'm here—and I say it with some feeling of guilt—because I didn't know about the problems of minorities in Iowa. I'm no expert now, but I know of no other way to find these problems than to talk with the people in their homes." Noting that Hughes was "genuinely interested in the problems," Davenport NAACP president William Cribbs commented, "I don't think you'll find many governors who are doing this."[17]

These listening sessions prompted Hughes to call for a mix of public and private investment in minority communities, tempered by the realization that this would never be enough. Looking at prior government programs that had failed, Hughes admitted that solutions "would require not a single attack by government at all; that won't be a solution." It would also require "a greater examination by industry and business to really examine themselves." Hughes suggested "backward discrimination"—or affirmative action, as it would later be called—to make up for past discrimination by proactively promoting minorities in business and government to "correct the imbalance that already exists, to make an all-out effort to equalize where people are equal in talent." Ultimately, said Hughes, "the final solution lies in the hearts of men."[18]

Hughes addressed top officials from Iowa's twenty largest cities at a League of Iowa Municipalities gathering arranged by Park Rinard at the Hotel Fort Des Moines on August 12. There, he discussed his inner-city visits. "I was appalled by my own ignorance," said Hughes, "and I could feel only shame that I hadn't done this before." Delivering part policy directive and part sermon, he urged the municipal leaders to do what he had done and talk with their urban constituents. "Don't hold a meeting and make a cotton-picking speech. If I'd done that, in about the third town, I'd have been run out on a rail. Talk with the underprivileged—not one group but all groups. Go into their homes, discuss their neighborhoods, and their problems. Get into these areas after the sun goes down and the problems come out onto the street." He brought up programs that had failed in the past, such as job training for jobs that did not exist. "We failed. I'm not denying that. All of us have failed."[19]

Hughes urged action on the local level and promised help on the state level, where he could provide it. The most aggressive action was taken in Des Moines, led by Joe Rosenfield, who raised $75,000 at a businessmen's luncheon to form a corporation called Community Improvement Inc. Within days, another $50,000 was raised among seventy businesses and industries. By early August, several hundred minority youths, ranging in age from fourteen to twenty-one, were employed by public works departments, performing jobs such as tree removal and park cleanup under the supervision of city and state employees. For many, this was their first job. Said Hughes, this action "explodes the common allegation that the business community is too busy making money to care about human needs in the community."[20]

In August four other cities—Waterloo, Cedar Rapids, Sioux City, and Davenport—joined Des Moines in forming private nonprofit corporations with contributions by business leaders in each community. In all, they raised more than $350,000 for public works programs for young people from low-income families—about one thousand in the late summer of 1967—providing jobs through the state, the cities, and private social welfare organizations. However, these investments and community actions were only an ad hoc reaction and a temporary fix. A 1968 report to Des Moines mayor Tom Urban referred to that city's efforts as "a crash program" and noted "a long-term need to have a more sustainable program." The result was no doubt similar in the other cities.[21]

Jobs were important, but Hughes knew the larger issue was racial discrimination itself, simmering under the surface in 1960s Iowa. He said so directly in his speeches. This challenge—a moral one—involved changing Iowans' attitude toward race, and it called for one of Hughes's key strengths: using the bully pulpit to transform public concerns into principled, ethical questions, as he had done with liquor by the drink, the Shaff Plan, and the death penalty. This was on Hughes's mind when he asked his friend Russell Wilson to arrange a meeting with Bishop James Thomas of Des Moines. Appointed in 1964, Thomas was the first Black bishop of the north-central jurisdiction of the Methodist Church and, like Hughes, was a persuasive speaker and a natural leader. When Thomas first came to Des Moines, Hughes had helped him find a house—a challenge for a Black man at the time—and introduced him to influential people in the city. Hughes, Thomas, Wilson, and Wayne Shoemaker, Hughes's Methodist minister from Ida Grove, met on November 20, 1967, around Wilson's kitchen table. Recognizing the need to break through the racial barrier among Iowans, the group hatched an idea that became known as the Crisis Conferences. The following day, Hughes addressed a meeting of fifteen Protestant, Catholic, and Jewish leaders and, in Wilson's words, "laid his heart right out on the table" as he made a passionate plea for racial harmony. Agreeing that all Iowans should hear the governor's words, the clergymen said, "We can provide you a pulpit."[22]

The Crisis Conferences were a series of assemblies held throughout

January 1968 and organized by religious leaders of Iowa's six largest cities—Des Moines, Cedar Rapids, Davenport, Sioux City, Waterloo, and Council Bluffs—to rally Iowans against racism. In all, more than twelve thousand Iowans attended. Each gathering opened with a prayer, a Bible reading, and a patriotic song, but the centerpiece was an address by Hughes. In his commanding voice, he called on citizens to empathize with the immense burden of bigotry suffered by their African American neighbors, pleading with white Iowans to put themselves in the shoes of their Black brethren. Hughes recapped his extensive conversations with Black Iowans in their homes, offering startling revelations of their poverty and despair and referring to "islands of hopelessness within a few blocks of our homes." Although he suggested how church groups could help their Black neighbors, these addresses were more inspirational than practical. He offered no hope that anything they did would render racism obsolete. "The eye of the hurricane is the racial issue," he said in his first address in Des Moines. "The problem is not going to go away. We have a job, an incredibly massive job. It is a complex matter of rebuilding our present society." It was a call, to paraphrase Abraham Lincoln, to the better angels of Iowans' nature.[23]

Hughes clearly saw this as a moral calling based on his deep Christian beliefs, which were shared by the majority of those listening. He delivered his message, however, in his typical blunt style, not often heard from the pulpit. In Council Bluffs, for instance, he orated, "If a man says he loves God and loves not his brother, then he is a liar." In Cedar Rapids, he referred to the "100 years of the white power structure depriving minorities of their rights." To those who said people should pull themselves up by their bootstraps, Hughes responded, "They can't pull themselves up if they haven't any boots."[24]

Did these Crisis Conferences make a difference? Most of those in attendance were probably open to Hughes's plea for racial understanding, but for many, this was an added call to action in their communities. Paul H. King, executive secretary of the Iowa Council of Churches, wrote to Hughes that many religious leaders had expressed thanks to him for the governor's speech. Of those joining the Crisis Conferences, King wrote, "Many of them have identified the series of meetings as a high moment in their lives. I have never been involved in a project that brought forth so much creative leadership and cooperation on the part of so many people." However, among the majority of Iowans, Hughes's plea made little difference. In a private poll conducted for the governor, only 10 percent of Iowans thought Blacks had been oppressed for many years. In a general Gallup poll in the Midwest, 75 percent believed African Americans were treated the same as whites in their communities, and half thought Blacks were responsible for their own distressing circumstances.[25]

Hughes himself was ambivalent about the results. A year later, he said:

> I felt that I was not only swimming upstream, but that I was taking a major step to destroy whatever political future I might have had. . . . But it really didn't matter to me. I felt that a message had to be brought to the people of Iowa and America and that for a man to shirk his responsibility in bringing the message would be the worst thing he could ever do. Maybe that's the reason I'm here—to bring that message. If that was my purpose I didn't want to be guilty of not bringing it. It had to be brought. It had to be understood and we had to start down the road.[26]

Hughes and others knew that the few activities undertaken in the late summer of 1967 would not be enough. To quell anticipated unrest in the summer of 1968, direct organized action would be needed throughout the state. In early January Hughes asked the US Department of Labor for additional federal aid to build on the employment programs instituted the prior year, but he realized that most of the effort would have to come from private businesses. Calling the problem of the urban poor "a malignancy which will spread and explode unless we do something about it," the governor initiated a program to create more permanent jobs and expand the temporary remedies implemented earlier. On the state level, Hughes pooled resources from a wide variety of state agencies involved with employment, education, social welfare, state planning, and other areas to help cities and local communities create programs.[27]

On March 6, 1968, in a gathering at the Hotel Kirkwood in Des Moines, Hughes announced that he would lead a task force of state officials into sixteen cities to help local leaders plan programs to avert a social crisis that summer. Speaking to a group of mayors, city managers, chiefs of police, city council members, and clergy, Hughes said the state group "would not tell you how to do anything" but would "be there to tell you and your leaders that we will stand ready to help you do what you want to do." He wanted these local programs to be in place by the end of the school year that spring. Warning that summer violence would not be tolerated, he added, "Neither are we going to be found guilty of sitting by and not alleviating the problems that we know damn well we have." He offered little hope that the state could provide funds, saying, "the state won't have very damn much money." As an example of the type of fund-raising needed, he cited the successful efforts by five cities that had raised money through private sources last summer. "I think we should try to raise $1 million locally this summer to meet these needs."[28]

Beginning on March 14, the task force blanketed the state, conducting a morning meeting in Des Moines and an afternoon one in Marshalltown; the statewide effort ended on March 29 in Council Bluffs and Sioux City. Typically, Hughes began each session with a short speech—"I call on you to answer the challenge to be involved—to be concerned about your neighbors and to do something about it"—and then turned the proceedings over to local officials, who had gathered a cross section of leaders in city and county government, schools, churches, labor, and service organizations. After the chairmen of the state committees laid out the opportunities for local activities, city residents broke into working groups to plan for the summer, targeting youth employment, vocational training, adult employment services, low-cost housing, camping, and recreational and cultural activities.[29]

Responses from the cities varied. According to one report, Waterloo exerted "every effort to implement the plan of action," whereas Council Bluffs and Fort Dodge did "absolutely nothing." The rest of the Iowa cities fell somewhere in between. In a 1969 report prepared by Dr. W. H. Stacy of Iowa State University, 19,987 youths were employed through various programs from May to July 1968. The report noted that the "private sector seemed well satisfied that their dollars were well invested." More importantly, it concluded, "The programs had been effective in curbing riots and providing a 'back to school' incentive for youth." Another follow-up study conducted by James Socknat, also of Iowa State, concluded that the entire effort "had a calming effect on tensions," adding that it might have been "the establishment's efforts to cure problems rather than the accomplishments themselves that produced the calming effect."[30]

Although these programs involved the work of thousands of Iowans, the person at the center of these efforts was the governor. Harold Hughes rose from his comfortable chair to talk with African Americans in their homes and walk with them through their neighborhoods. He directed white Iowa businessmen to invest in jobs and programs. More important, Hughes crusaded throughout the state, spreading a clear moral message against racism. Such action is the very definition of bold, progressive leadership.

On Iowa's college campuses, protests against the Vietnam War began in 1965 and rose to full intensity by 1967. Nowhere were the protests hotter than at the University of Iowa in Iowa City. In January thirty-five students chased a CIA recruiter from his campus office in Gilmore Hall. When he took refuge in another office across the street, protesters staged a sit-down, blocking potential recruits and issuing an open letter charging the CIA with "suppression of democracy" in Vietnam. Later that month, students picketing against the war clashed with campus police in subzero temperatures.[31]

Protests continued in early 1967 on large campuses and small. In January Parsons College students in Fairfield picketed a Marine Corps recruiter on campus. In April more than four hundred people, many from Drake University, marched to the statehouse in Des Moines to protest the Vietnam War. In May about twenty demonstrators in Ames, home of Iowa State University, sat down in front of a bus carrying four inductees into the armed forces and delayed its departure for about an hour.[32]

After the summer break, the protests continued. In October 1967 more than three hundred students in Iowa City took part in an antiwar march and rally at the Old Capitol; this was countered by a prowar rally, with shouts traded back and forth. At the newly renamed University of Northern Iowa in Cedar Falls (formerly the State College of Iowa), English instructor Edward Hoffmans openly urged students to defy the draft in an article published in the university newspaper. The largest protest of the year erupted into violence at the University of Iowa on November 1, 1967, when more than one hundred students blocked others from talking to Marine Corps recruiters at the campus's Memorial Union, with a crowd of fifteen hundred supporting them. They faced at least one hundred helmeted policemen carrying riot sticks, leading to, in the words of one reporter, "a morning of cursing, pushing, scuffing, kicking and slugging." In all, 108 students were arrested. A month later, another demonstration resulted in multiple arrests when students in Iowa City protested an appearance by a recruiter for Dow Chemical, which supplied the ingredients for Agent Orange, a cancer-causing defoliant used in Vietnam.[33]

Of course, activities on college campuses gained headlines, but what did average Iowans think about the escalation of US involvement in the far-off nation of Vietnam? In early 1966 a *Des Moines Register* poll found that 56 percent of Iowans approved of President Johnson's handling of the war, with 25 percent disapproving. By October of that year, only 31 percent still supported Johnson's Vietnam policy, and by August 1967, that had fallen to 25 percent approving and 61 percent disapproving. On the question of sending additional troops to Vietnam, Iowans opposed that action 46 to 40 percent in late 1967.[34]

It was against this backdrop that Harold Hughes pondered running for the US Senate in the fall of 1967. Vietnam would clearly be the most significant issue in what would be one of the most tumultuous years in US politics.

Speculation about Hughes's political future had become a cottage industry in Iowa and in national political circles. During his last campaign, Hughes had ruled out running for a fourth term as governor. "With this job, you just pile up enemies," he reiterated in late 1967. Several national publications, including *U.S. News & World Report*, reported that Hughes would retire from politics and take a job in private industry; one speculated that he would work for "a major farm implement firm." To that, Hughes responded, "If anyone is going to offer me something in private business, I wish they'd let me know about it. I really don't know what I may or may not do."[35]

In Iowa, the US Senate seat up for grabs in 1968 was held by longtime Republican senator Bourke Hickenlooper of Cedar Rapids. A one-term governor during World War II, Hickenlooper had been elected to the Senate in 1944 and handily reelected three times. Now in his early seventies, Hickenlooper was a staunch conservative, favoring forceful US military action abroad and limited government at home. He would be a clear ideological contrast to Hughes if they opposed each other in 1968. As the ranking Republican on the Senate Foreign Relations Committee, Hickenlooper held a powerful position in Washington. However, many thought he would retire at the end of his current term, especially since his wife was suffering from heart trouble.[36]

That was the thinking of Republican state senator David Stanley when he declared his candidacy for the US Senate on June 26, 1967. The thirty-eight-year-old Stanley was the scion of a prominent Muscatine family, graduating first in his class at the University of Iowa Law School. Elected to three terms in the Iowa house, he was now in his second term in the Iowa senate. At his announcement in Des Moines, he said he had had two "cordial" meetings with Hickenlooper and had decided to announce his candidacy prior to the senator's decision on running for reelection. If Hickenlooper chose to run, Stanley would challenge him. Less conservative than Hickenlooper, Stanley ran the risk of seeming to be an opportunist. Exuding energy, Stanley said he would "start earlier, work longer, meet more citizens directly, organize more intensively and enlist more volunteer workers than in any previous Iowa campaign." He also said he expected Harold Hughes to be the Democratic nominee.[37]

If that happened, Stanley would face a formidable foe. In an October 1967 poll, Hughes led Stanley 51 to 28 percent, with 21 percent undecided. Against Hickenlooper, Hughes led 47 to 40 percent.[38]

Despite these opinion polls, Hughes had decided to leave public life after three terms as governor. He later recalled, "I was very tired. We had been successful to a modest extent, and it's nice to quit a winner. The future looked very tough," he said, referring to the higher state taxes that some Iowans were grumbling about and the mixed reception of the 1967 revenue law Hughes had been forced to defend. As he moved into middle age, a higher salary in private business looked good to someone who had never made much money in the past.[39]

Harold Hughes, however, had not counted on the persuasive power of Robert F. Kennedy.

By 1967, the brother of the slain president had emerged as a prominent critic of President Johnson's Vietnam policy. Though the former attorney general had supported the introduction of "military advisers" into Vietnam during his brother's administration, Kennedy—now a US senator from New York—believed that Johnson's bombing policies and accelerated troop buildup were counterproductive and, more importantly, were dividing the nation. On a personal level, the two men clearly hated each other. Their mutual revulsion stemmed from Kennedy's opposition to Johnson's selection as the Democratic vice-presidential candidate in 1960, and it had only grown since then. To Kennedy, Johnson was the vulgar usurper of his brother's legacy; to Johnson, Kennedy was the ruthless, ambitious striver who coveted the lost presidential throne. Under pressure from other Senate liberals to take a stand, Kennedy demurred at first, hesitant to challenge a president from his own party.

However, in a February 1967 White House meeting with the president, the two brawled in an emotionally charged exchange. Displaying his pure hatred of Kennedy and perhaps expressing years of pent-up frustration, Johnson lashed out at the senator, saying that he and other liberals had the blood of American soldiers on their hands and were giving aid to the enemy. A month later, Kennedy publicly outlined his opposition to Johnson's policies on the floor of the Senate, urging a halt to the bombing and proposing steps toward negotiation. Accepting part of the blame for the war, Kennedy said, "It is we who live in abundance and send our young men out to die. It is our chemicals that scorch the children and our bombs that level the villages. We are all participants." Kennedy was looking for Senate allies in his effort to change US policy in Vietnam, and he saw the governor of Iowa as a potential partner on the national stage.[40]

Hughes had first met Robert Kennedy in 1962 and, like many, considered him a "hatchet man" for his brother. Since Kennedy's election to the Senate in 1964, however, he had focused on liberal positions, and Hughes now saw that Kennedy was "motivated by a genuine compassion for the poor and underprivileged." Hughes sought Kennedy's opinion on public issues, which they often discussed for hours at a time, and the two grew close. "I found him to be a very warm, compassionate human being," recalled Hughes. "I knew that in his heart and in his soul, here was a man seeking freedom for his brother [i.e., his fellow man] by whatever means was necessary, to do it regardless of the odds and consequences. I couldn't help but be attracted to a man like that."[41]

The feeling was mutual. According to one of Hughes's aides, "Robert Kennedy once said, 'There's only one man I hold in awe in politics and that's Harold Hughes.'"[42]

As word spread that Hughes was seriously considering retiring from politics, Kennedy called him in the fall of 1967 and got right to the point: "I think you should run for the Senate," he said. When Hughes protested, Kennedy shot back, "Governor, one more vote here might make a difference on this war," and "the country needs you." Hughes still resisted, but sensing that he could be persuaded, Kennedy invited Hughes to New York for a personal conversation in conjunction with the Empire State Dinner, a large Democratic fund-raiser. Arriving a day before the event, Hughes spent several hours with Kennedy in his Plaza Hotel suite, listening to the senator berate Johnson and his Vietnam policy and receiving intense pressure to run for the Senate. Hughes, in turn, urged Kennedy to oppose Johnson for the Democratic nomination, an action the senator was considering, despite his misgivings about challenging a sitting president. Hughes felt uneasy about a Senate candidacy, pointing out that he was not knowledgeable about foreign policy and certain national problems, not to mention his political challenges in Iowa, given the recent tax increases he had approved. Besides, said Hughes, he was in poor shape financially after five years on a governor's salary and estimated it would take nearly $400,000 to run a campaign. Kennedy pledged to help Hughes financially. At the end of the meeting, Kennedy looked the Iowan in the eye and said, "Think it over, Governor." Hughes agreed, saying, "OK, Senator. I'll seriously consider it."[43]

Hughes returned to Iowa and consulted Eva, who said, "If this is what you want, I think you should run." Then he consulted his mentor Park Rinard. As they discussed the pros and cons of running, Rinard became more enthusiastic about the idea. As a follow-up to the discussion, Rinard took the extraordinary step of flying to Washington, DC, to consult with Senator Gaylord Nelson of Wisconsin, a former governor. Nelson told Rinard that although his current job lacked the command of being governor, he very much enjoyed being a senator and dealing with important national issues. After Rinard relayed this information to Hughes, the Iowa governor decided to take the plunge, but only if Rinard agreed to come to Washington and work on his staff, which he did.[44]

Hughes announced his candidacy for the US Senate on Saturday, December 16, saying that he had "serious reservations" about the direction of Johnson's Vietnam policy and urging "restraint rather than escalation of the war." Acknowledging that the Vietnam War involved "torturing questions of morality and national security," he advocated a "negotiated peace" and warned, "I believe abrupt withdrawal is not realistic, however desirable." Hughes also said he supported President Johnson for reelection. But with typical Hughes candor, he added, "My disagreement with President Johnson on Vietnam and other issues could grow deeper. I will speak my mind freely as have other members of my party."[45]

According to George Mills of the *Register*, many Iowa Republicans were secretly delighted that Hughes, the perennial Democratic vote-getter, was running for the Senate rather than for a fourth term as governor (although he had never seriously considered the latter). Many Republicans believed that Hughes would be easier to beat in a Senate contest. Wrote Mills, "The Republican hope is that the past Hughes magic will not carry over into a Senate race."[46]

If the Republicans hoped to defeat Hughes, they would have to do it without the incumbent. Days after Hughes's announcement, Hickenlooper declared at a Des Moines press conference that he would not run for reelection. "There comes a time when a person should bow out," he said. When asked, Hickenlooper said that Hughes would not be easy to defeat, calling him "the most powerful vote-getter the Iowa Democrats have had, in modern times at least." He cautioned his fellow Republicans that they could beat Hughes only "with a vigorous campaign." Immediately following Hickenlooper's announcement, former US congressman James Bromwell of Cedar Rapids declared that he would seek the Republican nomination for Senate; he was widely seen as Hickenlooper's choice as his successor. This set up a battle in the Republican primary between the moderate Stanley and the more conservative Bromwell.[47]

As the calendar turned to 1968, the American people faced a year like no other—a year that would bring tragedy and heartache in one of the most tumultuous twelve months in US history.

14 | Political Upheaval in Iowa and the Nation

The upcoming presidential campaign was well under way in 1967 when Hughes, attending a governors' conference aboard an ocean liner in the Atlantic, took note of one potential candidate. As the meeting began, the Iowa governor was seated next to newly elected governor of California and emerging presidential contender Ronald Reagan. Photographers' flashbulbs lit the room continually for several minutes, snapping shots of Reagan and interrupting the proceedings. Finally, fed up with the delay, Hughes said in his booming voice, "Mr. Chairman, could we get this meeting under way? Not every one of us is running for the goddamn presidency!" Amidst applause from the other governors, the meeting commenced immediately.[1]

One candidate who received less intense notice in late 1967 was US senator Eugene McCarthy of Minnesota, who began a seemingly quixotic campaign to challenge Lyndon Johnson for the Democratic presidential nomination over the Vietnam War. He did, however, receive significant attention from Iowa Democrats. Sixty of them, along with 450 others, traveled to Chicago in December for an event dubbed "Concerned Democrats," a well-publicized effort to oppose Johnson's reelection. Iowa's delegation tied with New York's for the largest at the gathering. Headed by state representative Harry Beardsley of West Des Moines and including several other Iowa legislators and Democratic leaders, the Iowa delegation voted overwhelmingly in caucus to support McCarthy for president and "work for his nomination and election." The group followed up with an organizing meeting in Des Moines in mid-December, attracting more than forty activist Democrats.[2]

In late January 1968 Vietcong and North Vietnamese forces initiated the Tet offensive throughout South Vietnam, upending the confident assurances of the White House and US military leaders that there was "a light at the end of the tunnel." No such light appeared as American troops engaged in bloody combat for weeks in an effort to quell the uprising, which was broadcast night after night on national TV and blazed across newspaper headlines. Having been assured by Pentagon and White House sources that the United States was winning the war, Americans were stunned as communist forces launched a broad attack on US and South Vietnamese positions. One result was Senator McCarthy's surprisingly strong finish against Johnson in the New Hampshire primary in March 1968, transforming the political landscape by showing the president's electoral vulnerability.[3]

Despite his split with LBJ and his private plea to Robert Kennedy to run against the president, Hughes publicly supported Johnson in early 1968 and fully expected to lead the Iowa delegation in support of him at the Democratic convention in Chicago. On March 13, however, in a break with LBJ's Vietnam policy, Hughes called for a complete halt to all US bombing in North Vietnam. He argued that this move would show the Vietnamese communists that the United States was serious about negotiations to end the war.[4]

The matrix of the presidential campaign changed on March 16 when Kennedy, sensing Johnson's weakness after the New Hampshire primary, announced his own bid for the presidential nomination, further dividing the Democrats. Hughes claimed he did not know about Kennedy's announcement in advance but was not surprised by it. Walking a fine line in mid-March, Hughes said his position "for changing the course of events in Southeast Asia probably is equal to that of Kennedy and McCarthy," but he also attributed to "the President an equal desire to procure peace for the people of Southeast Asia and for the world."[5]

The 1968 race for the Democratic nomination took another dramatic turn on the evening of March 31 when Lyndon Johnson addressed the nation and announced a partial reduction in the bombing over North Vietnam to encourage the parties to come to the peace table. The speech is best remembered, however, for the political bombshell at the end, when Johnson announced that he would neither seek nor accept the Democratic presidential nomination. The next morning, Hughes admitted being "in a state of shock, like everyone else"; regarding the other candidates, he said, "I just want to re-assess the game." Soon, Vice President Hubert Humphrey joined the lineup of Democratic hopefuls.[6]

These events initiated a rancorous fight in Iowa at the grassroots level. There had been record attendance at the Iowa caucuses—not yet the national phenomenon they would later become—held in late March 1968, prior to the president's withdrawal from the race. The caucuses witnessed heavy anti-Johnson voting for either McCarthy or Kennedy in

Dubuque, Scott, Johnson, Story, and Woodbury Counties and in some parts of Polk County. Overwhelmed by the unexpectedly high turnout, confusion reigned in many of the caucuses, and party regulars decried the chaos caused by these so-called outsiders. One Des Moines Democrat described an initial turnout of party regulars at his caucus, noting that everything was under control until the start time at 8:00 p.m. "Then they came in like a swarm of locusts and took over." Hughes avoided his caucus in Ida Grove by saying he had a heavy day of work at the statehouse.[7]

Days after the caucuses, Iowa Democratic Party chairman Clark Rasmussen issued a letter to party members outlining "irregularities" in some caucuses and laying the groundwork for the possible disqualification of some precinct delegates. He argued that if one ineligible person had taken part in a caucus, the entire delegation "should be challenged." He wrote, "The fact remains, precinct caucuses are a party function and open only to Democrats." He cited examples of some participants who were not old enough to vote or who lived outside the district. Rasmussen suggested that county party officials review the names and registration declarations of all participants.[8]

Hughes opposed Rasmussen's statements and was surprised by the chairman's letter. The governor said, "I welcome anybody into the Iowa Democratic Party. I came into the party as a convert myself and I hope the young people and others take hold and work for the party." He added that the party needed to face the challenges that had brought these new attendees to the caucuses and "also see to it that all the needs of a political party are met." The contest between the upstarts and the party regulars played out over the next several months as supporters of Kennedy, McCarthy, and Humphrey fought on the county and state levels for delegates. In many counties, the more experienced party members were able to outflank McCarthy supporters and build delegate support for either Kennedy or Humphrey.[9]

Hughes remained publicly neutral during the hotly contested fight for delegates, but it was an open secret that he supported Kennedy. Those around him were clearly Kennedy supporters. Bill Sueppel of Iowa City, a longtime Hughes confidant, was chairman of the Kennedy campaign in Iowa. Lieutenant Governor Bob Fulton endorsed Kennedy during the senator's visits to Davenport and Des Moines in May and traveled with him at both stops. When Kennedy spoke at the Des Moines airport, Hughes introduced him to the crowd of one thousand but told reporters this did not mean an endorsement. Hughes later admitted he had seriously considered announcing his support for Kennedy after the New York senator lost the Oregon primary in late May, but he believed Kennedy would do well in California, and Hughes wanted to preserve his neutrality among Iowans as long as possible.[10]

At the Iowa Democratic convention in late May, the Kennedy organization proved superior, winning 26½ delegates, compared to 11½ for Humphrey and 5 for McCarthy. According to Sueppel, this was the first state convention where Kennedy won a major victory. McCarthy organizer Beardsley took the disappointing results philosophically. "We have had here a typical Democratic bloodletting, after which, in accord with the medieval practice, we should all come out much healthier." At the same time, several convention delegates expressed support for Hughes as a favorite-son candidate for president. Named an at-large delegate, Hughes said, "Many changes may take place within the party between now and the Democratic national convention."[11]

Little did he know how prophetic that statement would be.

Presidential politics was not the only activity on Hughes's agenda in early 1968. After completing the Crisis Conferences in January and a statewide tour of cities to initiate summer programs for minorities, the governor continued to meet with African American leaders to discuss racial issues. On the evening of April 4, Hughes was attending a meeting of about twenty Black ministers on the east side of Des Moines. As the clergymen discussed the challenges of housing, education, and good jobs for Blacks, the governor listened and promised his support. At one point, Hughes was called to the phone, and a reporter informed him that civil rights leader Martin Luther King had been murdered and asked him for a comment. Hughes responded with words about the "horrible tragedy" and "great loss" for the nation and then hung up the phone and stood silently, thinking about the roomful of ministers he had just left. Moving slowly, Hughes returned to the group and told them the news. "What happened in that church basement is something I'll never forget," he recalled. A Black bishop dropped to his knees and prayed for forgiveness for the assassin. Only afterward did he pray for King and start singing "Come by Here, Lord," a Negro spiritual, with Hughes joining in. Then, recalled Hughes, "We headed for our homes in the darkening evening."[12]

The next day, Hughes issued a proclamation of mourning for King.

That evening, speaking at a Polk County Democratic fund-raising dinner, he decried the "malignancy eating away at our nation today" but declared that it "is not terminal—it can be cured." He emphasized the same theme articulated during the Crisis Conferences, "We live in turbulent times. Millions of citizens are unaware of the conditions other millions of Americans live under. If they knew, they wouldn't tolerate it. I appeal to all of you—look and see your brother's problems."[13]

In the wake of the King assassination, there were sporadic outbursts of violence in some Iowa cities, but nothing like the upheavals in San Francisco, Baltimore, Chicago, and other places. The most destructive violence occurred in Washington, DC, resulting in twelve Black citizens killed and more than $25 million in property damage. Soldiers armed with machine guns stood guard over the Capitol while other buildings burned within sight of the White House. In downtown Des Moines, Black youths broke windows and scuffled with city police. In downtown Waterloo, two carloads of Black men threw rocks through windows. Hughes activated the Iowa National Guard "for an indefinite period" in case the troops were needed. They were not.[14]

In Iowa, the far larger response to the King assassination was an outpouring of unity and reverence, especially in the larger cities. On April 7 a crowd estimated at between three thousand and five thousand marched in Des Moines from Good Park to the statehouse, taking an hour to wind through the streets. This was followed by another hour of speeches and songs, despite threatening weather and strong winds.[15]

Despite racial conflict, the Vietnam War, and his own senatorial campaign, Hughes was still the governor of Iowa, and he had a state to run. One challenge he faced was the divided government within the executive branch presented to him by Iowa voters after the 1966 elections. A singular test came from Iowa attorney general Richard Turner. A former state senator from Council Bluffs, Turner was a staunch conservative and a frequent maverick when interpreting state statutes and issuing legal opinions as Iowa's top elected lawyer. Critics frequently accused him of narrowly interpreting the law—not seeing the forest for the trees—often in defiance of the expressed intent of legislators. This often set him at odds with Hughes.

One of the first clashes between the governor and the attorney general happened in April 1967, when Turner issued an opinion that the Iowa Comprehensive Alcoholism Project (ICAP)—a program close to

Hughes's heart—had allocated funds illegally. Although the funds originated from the federal government, Turner decreed that the money
became state money once it arrived in Iowa; therefore, state legislators
were required to appropriate it. When state comptroller Marvin Selden
hesitated to issue paychecks to ICAP employees, Hughes shot back, "I'm
Selden's superior and I'm telling Selden to pay them." Hughes said that
Turner's opinion was just that—one man's opinion. "I have the opinions of several lawyers who tell me that I have complete authority to run
the programs under the direction of my office and that's precisely what
I'm doing." Hughes cited a 1965 law giving his office broad authority
to accept federal funds and set up agencies to administer those funds.
Eventually, in 1967, both the Iowa house and senate passed a bill giving
Hughes the right to set up and operate ICAP, even though, according
to the governor, he did not need it.[16]

For his legal opinions, Hughes often relied on a brain trust of lawyers from public and private sources. They included Arthur Bonfield, a
recognized expert in constitutional law, and Allan Vestal, both University of Iowa law professors; Bill Sueppel of Iowa City; and Val Schoenthal
of Des Moines. He also sought legal advice from Lieutenant Governor
Fulton and state senator George O'Malley of Des Moines. This group
often dismissed the attorney general's opinions as being out of the legal
mainstream. In a private letter to Hughes's office regarding the state's
acceptance of federal highway funds, Vestal wrote, "I'm afraid that the
Attorney General has turned out another of his opinions which reflect
his political point of view which is not a very realistic one in the 1960s.
He still is adhering to a position which has not been a viable alternative
for more than a quarter of a century."[17]

In the latter half of 1967, conflict arose over Turner's interpretation of the new tax law. The attorney general ruled that the 3 percent
sales tax applied to new construction in the state, rather than to repairs
on existing structures only. This prompted the circulation of a petition
signed by eighty-one state representatives and twenty-eight state senators declaring that, in passing the law, they had no intention of taxing new construction, which would hinder building projects in Iowa.
Hughes responded that Turner's ruling was "one man's opinion" and
"has no force or effect in my humble opinion." The Iowa Tax Commission disregarded the attorney general's opinion.[18]

Turner's response was a caustic letter to Hughes decrying the "one
man's opinion" remark. He wrote, "Yet, you have failed to disclose to

me a single instance where you, or any lawyer advising you, has found a defect in any of my legal opinions." Turner cited a number of Hughes's public comments that he said were untrue and ended by stating, "If you have any further criticism, I would appreciate your telling me directly instead of running to the newspapers."[19]

The conflict continued within the Executive Council in late 1967, when it voted 5–0 to allocate $202,000 to purchase a new plane for the governor's use. At the meeting, Turner informed the council that the amount it could spend on a plane was limited by the legislature to $150,000; the extra $52,000 the council had allocated was to be used only for emergencies. And, Turner declared, this was not an emergency. According to later reports, Hughes and Turner faced off in a "tense confrontation." Later, the Republican council members voted to rescind their approval. Hughes, recognizing that this was a political move, dropped the issue.[20]

Few were surprised when, at year's end, Turner gave a speech in Cedar Rapids criticizing Hughes in everything but name. Citing "the new legality" of "the end justifying the means," Turner said that "some seem to think that the law is our servant rather than our master." He defended his office's interpretation of the law, charging, "There is a foot in the door, here and elsewhere, that the law is not so important as the desired goals. This idea will shatter our system."[21]

Turner's attack on Hughes stemmed largely from differing interpretations of the 1967 tax law. In addition to his declaration about the tax on new construction, the attorney general claimed the 3 percent sales tax on advertising was unconstitutional, arguing that it was applied unequally within Iowa and made no provision for the taxing of interstate advertising. The larger issue was that sections of the 1967 tax law were sloppily written and vague. During his review of the law, the attorney general found much to criticize. Hughes, as one of its prime backers, felt bound to defend it. Some pressured Hughes to call a special session of the legislature to fix and clarify the new service taxes—a move the governor rejected. In an address to the Iowa Council of School Boards, Hughes admitted that the law was not flawless and contained ambiguities, but he defended it against "special interests" that were trying to torpedo the new 3 percent service tax that would benefit Iowans. "It is my feeling at this time that we should live with the great benefits of this bill and with its minor shortcomings until the next regular session of the legislature [in 1969]. If this be political suicide for me, then I can only say that I am expendable but the future of this state is not." He strongly defended the increased and more equitable investment in education, asking educators and school board members to "wake up and fight for what has been won against those who would now take it away." Attacking Turner, he declared that the attorney general has "departed from the objectivity traditionally cherished by most departments of justice to enter the fray on the side of those who would damage or destroy the tax bill by an interpretation that exceeds the legislative intent."[22]

It did not help matters when the three-member Tax Commission, set to transition into the single-administrator Department of Revenue in the new year, reversed a decision in early November and declared that the tax on new construction was legal. In addition, it ruled that a tax credit designed for low-income individuals and families also applied to middle-income earners. This meant that if all those eligible to do so claimed the tax credit, it would cost the state nearly $17 million in lost revenue. Hughes appealed to Iowans to ignore what he called a "technical flaw" in the law and not apply for the tax credit, saying that Iowans had a "moral responsibility" not to take advantage of the tax break if they did not deserve it. Republican Party chairman Robert Ray called Hughes's plea "arbitrary" and said, "I hardly think people should be made to feel immoral by merely abiding by the law." Turner was less guarded. "It is incredible that anyone would suggest that the people may morally disregard a part of the law . . . and persuade them that they have a moral obligation to refrain from claiming exemptions to which they may be legally entitled."[23]

The tax legislation was a particular burden for Hughes as he headed into his final year as governor and became a candidate for the US Senate. Critics reminded voters that the law had been designed in private sessions without committee hearings, and many legislators had simply been told to vote for it because the governor and legislative leaders had agreed on it. Despite passage by both houses of the Iowa legislature, Hughes was the one holding the bag and facing the criticism when the law's flaws emerged later in the year. He was clearly on the defensive on the issue, and by the end of the year, Hughes acknowledged that confusion over the tax law would have to be settled by the courts and eventually reconciled by a future legislature elected after he left office.[24]

This was proving to be a liability at a time when Hughes was asking Iowans to elect him to national office.

15 | The 1968 Democratic Convention and Senate Race

As promised, Robert Kennedy came to Des Moines to raise money for Hughes's 1968 Senate campaign. On Saturday evening, March 9, the New York senator spoke at Veterans Auditorium before a crowd of eighteen hundred on the floor and another twenty-five hundred crowded into the balcony. He cited "the brilliant leadership of Governor Hughes" and then launched into an attack on President Johnson, who was still in the race at the time. Over the next few months, Kennedy defeated McCarthy in the primaries in two midwestern states, Indiana and Nebraska, only to lose in Oregon, a first for a Kennedy. The final contest between them was the California primary on June 4, which Kennedy won.[1]

Like many Americans, Hughes went to bed late that night after watching the returns from California. With Kennedy's win, Hughes believed the contest was close to being settled, and he planned to publicly announce his support for Kennedy. Soon after resting his head on the pillow, Hughes was awakened by a phone call from a friend. Kennedy had been shot. Hughes and Eva raced to the television to view the chaos in the California ballroom. Over the next few days, Hughes was in shock—calling the assassination "one of the unspeakable tragedies of American history"—and he joined the rest of the nation in mourning the second Kennedy assassination that decade. Bill Sueppel joined Hughes to represent Iowa at the funeral.[2]

After a short time for grieving, the Democratic presidential campaign commenced in late June with McCarthy and Humphrey the only significant candidates remaining. McCarthy was hoping to inherit the antiwar Kennedy supporters and clinch the nomination. Humphrey had won no significant presidential primaries that year, but he was working behind the scenes, collecting substantial numbers of convention delegates as the summer wore on. Both men targeted the Iowa Democratic convention in Des Moines on Saturday, June 29, where they would battle for the twenty-eight Kennedy delegates.[3]

The two candidates arrived separately at the Des Moines airport. McCarthy's enthusiastic crowd was estimated at three thousand, Humphrey's at six hundred. Both attended the annual wild-game dinner hosted by Hughes at the farm owned by Bill Knapp, a real estate developer and Hughes fund-raiser, west of Des Moines. But when McCarthy's party heard that the vice president was on his way, they left the gathering. At the convention downtown, McCarthy spoke first. He was introduced by Hughes, who called him "one of the extraordinary figures in American public life." Acknowledging the growing forces coalescing around Humphrey, McCarthy declared that the Democratic Party "is not a private club nor is it the possession of a privileged group of office holders," and he reemphasized his more dovish policy on Vietnam. After McCarthy left, the delegates applauded the empty stage for five minutes. Humphrey followed with a fifty-minute oration, including a rebuke of McCarthy's position on ending the Vietnam War. To both cheers and boos, the vice president said, "The business of peace talking is easy business. The business of peace making is delicate business. The business of peace booing is ridiculous business." In a straw poll among convention attendees, Humphrey defeated McCarthy 756 to 530, with 67 votes for Edward Kennedy and 27 for Hughes.[4]

Hughes met with McCarthy privately in a room at the Hotel Savery for about forty minutes that afternoon. The Minnesota senator did not ask for his support. Said the governor later, "I'm sure, the senator being a sensitive man, he wouldn't want to embarrass me [by having to refuse him]." The conversation, according to Hughes, concentrated on Iowa issues and Hughes's senatorial campaign. But the meeting set the stage for a relationship that would grow in the coming months.[5]

In the meantime, the bulk of Iowa's now uncommitted Kennedy delegates decided to support Hughes as a favorite son going into the convention. "Individually and collectively," said former Kennedy campaign chairman Sueppel, "we have not decided which of the presidential aspirants best represents the ideas for which Senator Kennedy lived and died." Many were torn. Although they opposed Humphrey's support of Johnson's Vietnam policy and admired McCarthy's antiwar stance, some feared the latter would be a weak candidate against the Republican nominee in the fall. Hughes reluctantly agreed to the favorite-son candidacy but considered it little more than an ego trip; he eventually urged all Kennedy delegates to vote their consciences.[6]

For Hughes, the period between Kennedy's assassination and the Chicago Democratic convention was a time of soul-searching. In a mid-July interview with political reporter Drake Mabry of the *Des Moines Tribune*, Hughes described the mood of many Democrats as a "vast uneasiness . . . a feeling of emptiness . . . a void." Hughes refused to concede the nomination to Humphrey and thought McCarthy had "an outside chance to win." He dismissed the call for his own candidacy, saying that it "can't be taken seriously . . . they're just hunting for some place to go." At that point, Hughes was "genuinely uncommitted" and said, "I'll base my choice for president on a man's abilities and his feeling on the issues—not on any popularity poll." In late July Hughes speculated about the candidacy of Edward Kennedy, a US senator from Massachusetts and the remaining Kennedy brother. "I don't concede that the Democratic nomination is locked up. If the Kennedy organization or Ted Kennedy were to become a rallying point for Kennedy supporters, some interesting things might happen."[7]

At a closed-door meeting at Chicago's O'Hare airport on Sunday morning, August 4, Hughes and seventeen other former Kennedy supporters met to discuss working as a bloc to further the late senator's Vietnam and domestic policies. Organized by Senator George McGovern of South Dakota, the meeting turned into an attempt to gauge support for his own candidacy, which surprised most of the people attending. Recalled Hughes aide Martin Jensen, "What the hell? We didn't come here to pick a presidential candidate." The response was mostly negative, and Hughes boomed, "Look, George, I love you, but you can't do anything for me." Despite this reaction, McGovern later declared his candidacy at the convention but failed to get much support.[8]

Later that afternoon, Hughes decided to support McCarthy. He had refused an earlier request to endorse the Minnesota senator, knowing that McCarthy had only an outside chance of winning the nomination. Nevertheless, on the most important issue of the campaign—the Vietnam War—Hughes's position was close to McCarthy's, and unless someone stood with McCarthy, the practical Iowan reasoned, he had absolutely no chance at all. Hughes phoned the Minnesota senator and said he would endorse him at the convention. A pleased McCarthy then surprised Hughes by asking him to give the nominating speech, a task Hughes accepted.[9]

Prior to the Democratic convention, Hughes announced at a press conference that he was supporting McCarthy for president. Calling the Minnesotan a "different kind of evangelist—an evangelist of reason,"

Hughes said McCarthy "has caused a clean wind of hope to blow across this land." Although Hughes disagreed with some aspects of McCarthy's position on Vietnam—for instance, Hughes favored a coalition government but rejected McCarthy's position that the United States should withdraw from Vietnam if the current South Vietnamese government refused to accept this option—his support stemmed from McCarthy's willingness to try something dramatically different. "Something must give. Something must change from the status quo. . . . At a time when it seems that every honest difference of opinion in America degenerates into a shouting match, Gene McCarthy has spoken with strength and logic, shunning the emotional appeal." Hughes added that he would encourage other Iowa delegates to follow him but would not pressure them to do so.[10]

The decision to support McCarthy was heartfelt, reflecting the Iowa governor's deep feelings about the Vietnam War; it certainly was not an act of political expediency. As a candidate for the US Senate that fall, Hughes had to know that his support for McCarthy would generate controversy in Iowa. One opinion poll showed that Iowans favored Richard Nixon over McCarthy, 49 to 26 percent, when asked who "could best handle the war." The same poll found that, in a presidential race between the two, Nixon would win, 50 to 34 percent. The conservative *Waterloo Courier* editorialized that the endorsement of McCarthy showed that Hughes had moved "to the far left of American politics." Hughes was clearly facing a strong headwind, which was not unusual for this particular politician.[11]

As the fifty-two members of the Iowa delegation gathered at the Drake Hotel in Chicago for the 1968 Democratic convention, they entered an armed camp. Chicago mayor Richard Daley, knowing that thousands of protesters planned to descend on the city and disrupt the convention, had suspended all leaves for the city's police force and equipped the officers with riot gear and clubs. Most of the demonstrators simply wanted to peacefully protest the Vietnam War. Others aimed to provoke confrontations. The stage was set for a level of violence unprecedented in the history of US political conventions.[12]

By the opening weekend of the convention, the McCarthy campaign had announced that Hughes would deliver the nominating speech. Representing the candidate, Hughes appeared on *Meet the Press*, NBC's Sunday morning news show, along with Senator Edmund Muskie of Maine, who supported Humphrey. The governor said he backed

McCarthy because of a "basic anti-Vietnam feeling" among Americans; he called the war a "primary issue" in the 1968 campaign with a "direct tie-in to all our social problems." Like McCarthy, Hughes supported an end to all bombing in Vietnam as a way to advance peace talks, which he believed could be accomplished "without lessening our effectiveness in South Vietnam."[13]

For many people—certainly for President Johnson, watching the convention in Washington, DC—the most important battle was over the Democrats' platform on the Vietnam War. The Iowa delegation voted 38–11 to support an unconditional halt to all bombing, the position taken in the minority report from the platform committee. The alternative, the majority plank, called for certain conditions to be met by the Vietnamese communists prior to a bombing halt. Hughes urged support for the minority plank, whereas Iowa congressman Neal Smith warned it would be impossible to protect American troops without bombing. To that, Hughes responded, "We've dropped more bombs on North Vietnam than we did in World War II on all countries of the world and the infiltration of troops into the South has not stopped." Said one Iowa delegate who was a Humphrey supporter, "The only reason in God's world that so many Iowans voted for [the minority plank] was simply out of deference to Harold Hughes." On the convention floor, under immense pressure from the White House, the majority plank carried by a vote of 1,567¾ to 1,041¼.[14]

With Hughes now firmly in the McCarthy camp, he spoke on the candidate's behalf before six delegations in two days. After spending all of Monday night at the convention, he went to bed at 4:00 a.m. and was up three hours later. According to the *Register*'s George Mills, "Hughes was well received in all his appearances before state delegations. He was frequently applauded." The pace was exhausting, however. Daughter Phyllis, watching events from Des Moines, told Hughes, "You looked all right on TV until 1:30 a.m. After that you drooped pretty badly."[15]

Park Rinard, as usual, wrote Hughes's convention speech, finishing it at the last possible minute. As the deadline for the national prime-time address approached on Wednesday, Hughes aide Ed Campbell called Rinard in Des Moines and urged him to put the speech on a plane to Chicago to make sure it got there in time. But Rinard continued his wordsmithery into the early evening. As the deadline neared, Rinard phoned Campbell to say he was sending the speech to the convention hall via Western Union. Campbell frantically sought the help of a technician and arranged to have the speech placed on the teleprompter as soon as it arrived over the wire. Meanwhile, Hughes took the podium before a national television audience with no text before him. Ad-libbing, he immediately announced that he was nominating Eugene McCarthy for president. Traditionally, a nominating speech praises the aspirant without mentioning him, saving the name for the end, after which wild and boisterous applause erupts from the floor. Most listeners who knew the Iowa governor simply chalked up his nontraditional approach to his unconventional manner. Shortly thereafter the speech appeared on the teleprompter, and Hughes began to read it. As he neared what appeared to be the end, Hughes turned to Campbell, standing behind him, and loudly whispered, "Is that it?" "Yes," replied Campbell, and Hughes concluded by mentioning McCarthy's name again, to sustained applause.[16]

With this prime-time speech, Hughes played the most prominent role by an Iowan in a Democratic national convention since Henry A. Wallace was nominated for vice president in 1940 and fought unsuccessfully for renomination in 1944. Hughes was certainly the most prominent Iowan at any convention in the age of television. In his oration—through Rinard's prose—he called McCarthy "a man with the wisdom and the courage to change the direction of our foreign policy before it commits us for eternity to a maze of foreign involvements without clear purpose or moral justifications." In a direct crack at President Johnson, Hughes said, "The political world of Gene McCarthy is lean, spare, streamlined—strangely unlike the wheeler-dealer political world to which we are accustomed." On the Vietnam War, the Iowa governor praised McCarthy's policy of "disengagement from this jungle war and a rejection, in fact, of the erroneous concept that there can be a military victory in such a conflict." By nominating the Minnesota senator for president in this national forum, Harold Hughes firmly established himself as an antiwar leader.[17]

As Hughes spoke—indeed, throughout the evening—the Chicago police and the Illinois National Guard were savagely beating and arresting antiwar demonstrators outside the convention center. In what was later called a "police riot," working-class police clashed with middle-class students in a violent display broadcast across the nation and throughout the world. Tear gas rose from the streets and seeped into the hotel rooms above the bloody conflict. McCarthy watched helplessly from his suite at the Conrad Hilton Hotel and, extremely upset, called Hughes on the floor of the convention forty-five minutes before the balloting began. The two debated whether withdrawing McCarthy's name would stop the violence. Hughes opposed this move, arguing that the violence had nothing to do with the senator's candidacy. He told McCarthy, "To withdraw would mean that millions of your followers who have devoted a lot of time, effort, and money to your cause and campaign would be tremendously let down and disappointed."[18]

That seemed to satisfy McCarthy at the time. Soon after the balloting started, however, he called Hughes again and dictated a withdrawal statement that the Iowan wrote down. McCarthy left it up to Hughes whether to issue it. Hughes chose to do nothing. "All he had in mind was to calm things down," Hughes later recalled. "But his withdrawal might have made it worse because his people might have reacted and contributed to the disorder." The balloting continued, and Humphrey overwhelmed McCarthy to become the Democratic nominee for president.[19]

The Iowa delegation gave 19½ votes to McCarthy, 18½ to Humphrey, 5 to McGovern, and 3 to Ted Kennedy. With Humphrey's nomination, most of the Iowa Democrats left the convention in despair. Said delegate Esther Mallon of Des Moines, "I think we will go down the drain. I think we are going to have to work like dogs even to get Hughes elected." Loren Modt, a delegate from Boone, lamented, "Around my hometown they tell me Humphrey cannot win. The Democrats as well as the Republicans say that." Before driving home, Hughes told a reporter, "There was an awful lot wrong with the convention," referring to both party regulars' tight control and the violence in the streets.[20]

As Hughes and the rest of the Iowa delegation crossed the Mississippi River into their home state, it looked like it might be a long autumn for Democrats there.

When Hughes resumed his Senate campaign, his lead over Republican David Stanley had narrowed, 52 to 43 percent, based on the *Register's* September 1 poll. There were plenty of reasons for the tightening race. One was the tenacious campaigning by the Republican state senator from Muscatine. Since beginning his effort in mid-1967, Stanley claimed he had shaken hands with more than 220,000 Iowans and traveled 87,000 miles throughout the state. Stanley overwhelmed former congressman

James Bromwell and two other candidates in the Republican primary in September, winning nearly 60 percent of the vote and carrying eighty-seven of Iowa's ninety-nine counties. The young, energetic Republican was racing into the fall campaign with a relatively united party and a full head of steam.[21]

Another reason for the closeness of the race was the central issue of the campaign: the Vietnam War. Hughes's call to end the bombing of Vietnam to aid peace negotiations was not popular among Iowans. In a poll that fall, 53 percent of Iowans opposed an end to the bombing of North Vietnam, while only 28 percent supported a halt to the bombing. Hughes was clearly swimming upstream against public opinion in one of the most salient issues of the campaign.[22]

Also, the violent and divisive images from the recent Chicago convention hurt Humphrey's candidacy and acted as a drag on other Democratic candidates as well. In a poll conducted in the fall by the *Register*, Nixon led Humphrey in Iowa 56 to 27 percent, with third-party candidate George Wallace of Alabama at 11 percent. Nixon was clearly on his way to winning the state. According to an analysis by Hughes aide Martin Jensen, Hughes would have a problem winning his race if Nixon won Iowa by more than 150,000 votes, a definite possibility. Against these odds, Hughes would need every bit of his personal charisma and popularity to win the US Senate seat.[23]

It did not help that the candidate intentionally removed himself from the campaign for three days in August, just as it was starting to heat up. Hughes had been asked to speak at the International Congress on Alcoholism, a conference of sixty-two nations in Washington, DC. The invitation had been extended by a representative of the Christopher Smithers Foundation, dedicated to eliminating the stigma associated with alcoholism and educating the public on alcoholism as a disease. Hughes called his campaign staff together, along with others he trusted, and told them about the opportunity. He later said, "They voted 100 per cent that I shouldn't do it." They argued that he should not leave Iowa at this important time and worried that raising the issue of his past alcoholism would hurt his campaign. "Who cares?" some said. "Well," replied Hughes, "I care, and I'm the person that's got to deal with it the rest of my life." So Hughes agreed to speak at the conference.[24]

The 1964 article in *Look* magazine had established Hughes as a recovered alcoholic, but his presence at the Smithers event in the nation's capital would be the first time a governor or a Senate candidate declared himself an alcoholic at an event covered around the world. In his speech, he declared that Iowans had long known about his alcoholism. "And the people have affirmed and reaffirmed in election after election that that is no longer an issue in Iowa," he said. "So I want to say to every politician in the United States that alcoholism in your life should never be an issue in your political campaign if you've got guts enough to face it." Hughes boldly declared that he was not ashamed of his alcoholism and not ashamed to talk about it. "I'm as competent as I've ever been, probably more so, stronger now than I've ever been. And I believe that if everybody came out of the weeds and discussed what they had then we wouldn't be having the problems we have. The cause of one of the major problems is that we're all scared to death of our shadows."[25]

After spending three days at the conference, speaking in a similar vein with participants and representatives of the worldwide media, Hughes returned to Iowa to face Republican David Stanley in one of the closest political battles of his career.

The first personal clash between the two Senate candidates took place in Waterloo on September 8 at a debate sponsored by the Iowa Daily Press Association. Not surprisingly, the Vietnam War was the central issue. Hughes defended his position on the bombing halt and then called for the withdrawal of some Americans from around the demilitarized zone (DMZ) on the North Vietnam–South Vietnam border "so they would not be subjected to fire across the DMZ or North Vietnam." Stanley ripped into his opponent's position. "I very strongly oppose the unilateral, unconditional halt to the bombing, which Governor Hughes has proposed. I think the result would be needless deaths of many more thousands of American fighting men." He quoted General Creighton Abrams, who said a bombing halt would allow the enemy to throw five times as much strength against American soldiers. "I think the result would be a bigger war, not peace," said Stanley. Hughes countered that the flow of supplies from North Vietnam into South Vietnam had increased over the past several years, despite the bombing. He also stressed the need for free elections in South Vietnam, including communist participation. If the communists won such elections, he added, we should respect that. After all, he said, the United States does business with "dozens of countries around the world which have elected Communists." Actually, Hughes and Stanley held very similar positions on the war. Both stressed negotiations and the need for free elections in South Vietnam. Both believed the war should be fought by the South Vietnamese, not Americans, and that the overall goal was US withdrawal as quickly as possible. Both were skeptical of the possibility of a US military victory. The major difference was over tactics and, specifically, a bombing halt. Hughes was for it and Stanley against.[26]

On September 30 Hubert Humphrey shifted his position on the bombing policy, hoping to ignite his campaign. In a well-publicized speech in Salt Lake City, the Democratic presidential candidate broke with the Johnson administration and supported the halt of all bombing of North Vietnam, characterizing it "as an acceptable risk for peace." Hughes said in a campaign speech in Grinnell, "This is a position that I can endorse and that I believe in. . . . He said many of the things I've been saying all along." Hughes had previously expressed his support for Humphrey, but this new position freed him to embrace the Democratic candidate more warmly.[27]

Hughes's position on Vietnam and, in particular, his endorsement of McCarthy had attracted young volunteers to Iowa to help him get elected to the US Senate. Hughes later said, "You can't believe the offers I had of volunteer help . . . from young people all over the country who just simply wanted to come here if there was somewhere they could eat, sleep, and some way they could get their laundry done. Some even took a sabbatical from college of six months to work in my campaign. They didn't want anything in return. They simply wanted a better world." These youthful, energetic volunteers provided a massive boost to the practical side of campaigning, such as making phone calls, coordinating get-out-the-vote efforts, and distributing literature.[28]

The young volunteers, numbering more than two hundred, were led by Sam Brown, an antiwar activist from Council Bluffs. Brown managed the effort in a separate office at the insistence of campaign manager Ed Campbell. He wanted to keep these volunteers "under the radar" and unconnected from the campaign itself, fearing that Stanley would use the out-of-state antiwar campaign workers to turn conservative Iowans against Hughes. It worked. Stanley never raised the issue.[29]

Hughes needed campaign assistance in early October when he came down with bronchitis, robbing him of the ability to speak. His doctor ordered complete bed rest for ten days, right at the height of the campaign. To fill in for Hughes, the operation relied on surrogates such as state senator Frommelt and Lieutenant Governor Fulton, who took to the road, articulating the candidate's positions and responding to Stanley.[30]

Hughes's absence gave Stanley an opportunity to travel the state and fill the airwaves with an intense media blitz against Hughes. Citing the expanded state budget during the Hughes years, Stanley's ads positioned Hughes as the man who was "spending the state into bankruptcy." Linking the governor with the urban unrest during the Johnson administration—particularly the racial violence in Waterloo in early September—the Stanley campaign ran ads with quotes from Hughes that implied he condoned the violence, followed by the question: "Do you want a man like this representing you in the United States Senate?" Given Nixon's strong lead in Iowa, Stanley's ads featured the two candidates together with the slogan "Nixon Needs Stanley"—next to which one graffiti artist in Cedar Rapids wrote, "But America Needs Hughes."[31]

According to Hughes's media consultant Gene Kieffer of Des Moines, "When I heard those commercials, I knew we were in trouble. . . . I didn't give Stanley the credit early in the campaign for being as smart as he really was. I knew he'd spend the money in mass media, but I didn't know he knew how to use it. It soon became apparent to me he knew exactly how to use it." Estimates were that Stanley outspent Hughes five to one in media ads.[32]

While Hughes was convalescing, the campaign broadcast an ad showing Hughes holding a gun, reflecting his avid interest in hunting. According to campaign worker Pat Deluhery, "There was a constituency that loved that. It had a huge impact that kept the campaign from collapsing when Hughes was out." The Stanley operation initiated a whispering campaign that Hughes was not ill but had started drinking again. Hughes aides vigorously denied this.[33]

By mid-October, the race was tightening. A *Register* poll showed Hughes leading by only four points, 50 to 46 percent. Stanley clearly had the momentum, and Hughes was in the race of his political life. He returned to the campaign trail in Sioux City after twelve days of rest; he was still ill but knew he had to campaign energetically if he hoped to win the seat. His first speech back centered on the Vietnam War, clearly emphasizing his dovish credentials. "Basically, isn't the question this? Do we end war by making more war? By continuing in the same hardline policy we have followed in the past? Or do we seek new approaches, new options, new initiatives for peace? . . . I believe this is the way we must go."[34]

Stanley accused Hughes of changing his mind about the war, moving from an unabashed supporter to a critic, which was certainly true. In a radio broadcast on October 13, Hughes addressed that criticism directly. Referring to his days of brutal combat in Sicily and Italy, he said he had "learned about war not out of books, but at point blank range in the fighting." He claimed that his "hatred of war as a means of settling disputes among nations has not changed. But my view of what needs to be done in Vietnam has changed, as the present policies have proven ineffective in moving toward peace." Declaring that many others had changed their opinions about the war, he said, "I would hate to be so rigid and dogmatic that I didn't have the courage to take a new position when new needs and new conditions demand it."[35]

Weeks before the election, Stanley made a statement that left him open to widespread criticism. In January 1968 North Korea had captured the USS *Pueblo*, an American spy ship, off its coast and had been holding the ship and its crew. While campaigning in northwestern Iowa on October 15, Stanley was asked what he would do about the ongoing issue. He replied, "If we can't win the *Pueblo* back any other way, then we should consider capturing a couple of North Korean ships . . . on the seas." Further, he said, the United States should "make it plain" that those captured "would be given back when the *Pueblo* and its crew is released." Hughes immediately responded that "this is exactly the kind of impetuous and unilateral action that could trigger World War III," claiming that Stanley lacked the "maturity and judgment" to be a US senator. He added that Americans are "living in the nuclear age—not in the era of the Barbary pirates." Hughes continued to raise this issue until Election Day. Even Senator Hickenlooper disagreed with Stanley on this issue, although he endorsed the Republican candidate late in the campaign.[36]

The central issue in the race, however, continued to be the Vietnam War. But as the campaign reached its conclusion, Hughes's rhetoric moved beyond Vietnam and into the more general framework of peace. James Flansburg of the *Register* described Hughes's speeches as "The Campaign of the Angry Dove." Hughes claimed, "We have become so oriented to war and the building of destructive machinery that there are few who raise their voice and question how long we can continue in this capacity. How long must we build toward destruction?" Often, these words were met with reverent silence rather than cheers and applause. "And I want to say to you: I am a man of peace. I believe that peace is the only hope of mankind."[37]

Louis Milton Thompson, who wrote his master's thesis on the 1968 Senate campaign, observed that Hughes's standard speeches were, "in essence, a sermon." Overall, they were not pleasant messages. "The general theme told of foreboding consequences unless men put themselves to the task of making this a better world. The message, which provided little cause for a joyous response, was in marked contrast to the 'cheer-leading' speeches so commonly delivered at political rallies." According to Thompson, Hughes "presented his speech with the demeanor of a man of destiny, a man of purpose," and he called the audience "to a higher plane of understanding on the 'great issues of the day.'" This was the overall approach Hughes took into the last days of the campaign, and it defined his Senate career.[38]

On October 31 President Johnson shifted the political landscape by announcing the end of all bombing of North Vietnam in a desperate attempt to reach a peace agreement—and to aid Humphrey's presidential prospects. Both efforts failed. When Hughes heard the news, he said he was "highly pleased" and had "no interest in the politics involved." He added, "For my part, I would rather see the peace negotiations move on swiftly and successfully than to be elected to any office in the land."[39]

The two Senate candidates met in a final televised debate on Saturday evening, November 2, broadcast over stations in Des Moines, Cedar Rapids, and Mason City. They rehashed many of their disagreements from the past several months. Responding to the president's decision to stop the bombing, Stanley argued that the bombing had actually helped negotiations. "Isn't it fortunate that we didn't agree to a dangerous, unconditional bombing halt last summer that would have thrown away our bargaining power?" To that, Hughes responded, "We could have saved more lives" if the bombing halt had come earlier, and events have "proved the correctness of my position." With the final poll showing Hughes with a narrow 51 to 46 percent lead, it was now up to the Iowa voters.[40]

As he watched the election returns at the governor's mansion, Hughes called it "worse than an all-night poker game," and he smoked an entire pack of cigarettes. It remained a close race all evening. Hughes was somewhat confident at around 1:30 a.m. when he went to the Hotel Savery to greet supporters, but when he eventually went to bed at 4:00 a.m. with a narrow lead, he was still unsure of the final outcome. Once all the votes were counted, the former truck driver from Ida Grove had been elected to the US Senate by one of the narrowest margins in Iowa history. A total of 1,143,353 ballots were cast, and Hughes beat Stanley by 6,415 votes—574,884 to 568,469—or 0.006 percent. Martin Jensen's prediction that Hughes could win if Nixon carried Iowa by 150,000 or fewer votes proved correct; Nixon beat Humphrey by 142,407 votes.[41]

Said Hughes the next day, "I guess the voters have liked the way I've faced up to the tough issues the last six years. They may not always agree with me, but they know I've got the courage to make decisions." He knew his stand on Vietnam was not popular—admitting it had probably been "a minus instead of a plus," dramatically reducing his normally strong vote totals. Essentially, Hughes won the election by carrying the most populous counties; he won in Polk County and also did well in Story and Johnson Counties, home of Iowa State University and the University of Iowa, respectively. These results more than made up for the lopsided margin of Iowa counties carried by Stanley, 65–34.[42]

According to Thomas Smith, who studied the impact of the Vietnam War on Iowa politics, "Hughes' great advantage was his enormous personal stature." A Des Moines Register poll conducted shortly before the election showed that 36 percent of Iowans thought Hughes "would make the best impression for the State of Iowa," compared to 30 percent who chose Stanley. The same poll revealed that Iowans thought Hughes was better equipped than Stanley to handle the war, 43 to 32 percent. This figure, Smith concluded, showed that "Hughes' educational campaign succeeded to a certain extent." Although Iowans confirmed their faith in Nixon's ability to find a solution to Vietnam, Smith wrote, "Clearly, the force of Hughes' personality managed to draw voters who were either ambivalent or even supportive of the war."[43]

The age of Harold Hughes in Iowa state politics was ending. One sign of this was the Republican sweep of all statewide offices, including the governorship, won by Robert Ray. Iowa Republicans also regained majorities in both houses of the state legislature.

At the same time, all five constitutional amendments on the ballot passed, making this the greatest number of changes in the Iowa Constitution in a century. The amendments included annual legislative sessions; home rule for Iowa cities and towns; legislative reapportionment every ten years on a one-man, one-vote basis; and a line-item veto for the governor. Both Hughes and Ray supported all of them.[44]

In the waning days of his third term, Hughes still had to deal with the state budget and the complicated tax issues facing his administration. As the governor found out, there was some validity in Stanley's harsh criticism of Hughes's handling of the state budget. The hefty budget surplus of $112.9 million in the state treasury in 1967 had dwindled to an anticipated $10 million to $15 million by the end of the fiscal year on June 30, 1969, and the state government faced a financial squeeze. The problem was that, despite higher rates, state taxes had not brought in as much revenue as expected. By October, it was clear that the state did not have enough money in the general fund to pay state aid to schools. The Hughes administration would leave this challenge to the incoming Ray administration and the Republican legislature.[45]

The Iowa Supreme Court unanimously upheld the 3 percent sales tax on services, including advertising. In the next legislative session in 1969, lawmakers would repeal it.[46]

In late 1968, Hughes reflected on his years as governor. His greatest accomplishment, in his opinion, was changing attitudes in Iowa, building on the "we can" rather than "we can't" approach. "The greatest personal satisfactions to me," he said, "have been in the lines of things like eliminating capital punishment in Iowa, the solution to the Amish problem . . . and working toward goals in solutions between the races and minorities in Iowa." He may have been best known for liquor-by-the-drink reform, but Hughes called that "a great big zero" because it would have happened anyway. He also cited the creation of the Iowa Comprehensive Alcoholism Project, the state planning program, and the Civil Rights Commission as "tremendous accomplishments, in my opinion."[47]

Harold Hughes submitted his resignation as governor of Iowa on Thursday, January 2, 1969, two weeks before his term was over. He wanted to be able to take the oath of office as a US senator to avoid losing seniority to other senators, an important consideration in committee assignments. This meant that Lieutenant Governor Robert Fulton served as governor for two weeks prior to the swearing in of Robert Ray.[48]

Hughes was on his way to Washington, DC, for another six years of political activity, this time on the national stage.

16 | The Hughes Act and Federal Aid to Alcoholics

On his first day in the US Senate, the former truck driver from Iowa stood in awe of the pomp and pageantry surrounding his swearing-in ceremony amidst senators of national renown and reputation. On the Senate floor, Hughes walked up to a fellow senator, introduced himself, and was abruptly greeted with a venom-filled tongue-lashing. This senator castigated the Iowan for supporting and nominating Eugene McCarthy, letting him know that he thought little of Hughes or his Minnesota colleague. Taken aback, Hughes smelled alcohol on the breath of his fellow senator, reminding him of his own personal struggle with alcoholism.[1]

Hughes wrote about this episode at the beginning of his memoir, *The Man from Ida Grove,* but he did not name the senator. It was Thomas Dodd, a conservative Democrat from Connecticut. The two-term senator had recently been censured by the Senate—the first since red-baiting Joseph McCarthy in 1954—for appropriating campaign funds for his personal use. Dodd was devastated, but he served out his Senate term. On the day of Hughes's swearing in, Dodd was a shattered man, bitter at the condemnation of his colleagues and overwhelmed by alcoholism. That night, a Dodd aide—knowing Hughes's reputation for helping alcoholics—called the Iowan at his home at midnight and put the obviously inebriated senator on the line. He reluctantly talked to Hughes and strongly intimated that he was going to commit suicide. As he had with so many others in the past, Hughes talked with Dodd about his alcoholism, understanding firsthand what he was going through. Hughes then got out of bed, drove to Dodd's office, and talked to the depressed man until 3:00 a.m. Eventually, Dodd was hospitalized. He ran for reelection in 1970, lost, and died the next year. During their time in the Senate, Hughes and Dodd developed a close relationship, despite their tense introduction. Later, Dodd's son Christopher, also a senator from Connecticut, said that Hughes saved his father's life that night.[2]

No one knows how many alcoholics Hughes personally counseled, both inside and outside the Senate, but the numbers are vast. Individuals with drinking problems sought him out because it was well known that Hughes understood the dark side of alcoholic despair and had overcome it. He was willing to listen to sufferers and direct them to appropriate treatment. Hughes made a dramatic difference in countless individuals' lives.[3]

A more public effort to help alcoholics involved a unique path through the Senate committee system, resulting in legislation that would be Hughes's lasting legacy on the national scene.

When Hughes took his seat in the Senate in January 1969, he was ninety-fourth out of one hundred in terms of seniority. Because of his stand on the Vietnam War, he sought a seat on either the Foreign Relations Committee or the Armed Services Committee, but that was not to be—at least not right away. Instead, he was given seats on Labor and Public Welfare, Banking and Currency, and Veterans Affairs. That seemed to satisfy him, as he had been "assigned to three [committees] which served the needs of the people." Labor and Public Welfare was considered the best committee in Congress by proponents of social legislation because it was dominated by a bipartisan coalition of liberal senators who favored such efforts. It was here that Hughes navigated outside the traditional committee system with his singular drive to pass national legislation to aid alcoholics, continuing his innovative use of government tools such as the Iowa Comprehensive Alcoholism Project (ICAP). In doing so, he dramatically altered the federal effort against alcoholism.[4]

Alcoholism as a disease had only recently gotten the attention of Congress. The first congressional hearings on alcoholism were held in 1965, leading to the establishment of the Center for the Prevention and Control of Alcohol Problems within the National Institute of Mental Health (NIMH) under the Department of Health, Education, and Welfare (HEW). This effort marked a breakthrough by characterizing alcoholism as a disease and a public health problem, rather than a moral failure, but it had a limited budget and limited authority. President Johnson stressed the need to treat alcoholism as a disease during an address to Congress in 1966, the first time a president raised this issue on the national level. All these efforts led to the involvement of more than thirty federal agencies and subagencies in some aspect of addiction treatment, but they were scattered throughout the federal bureaucracy, with no central focus. HEW allocated only $4 million to local community assistance for alcoholics across the entire nation.[5]

Calling this a "drop in the bucket," Hughes was determined to forge a greater national effort. He got approval from liberal Democratic senator Ralph Yarborough of Texas, chairman of the Labor and Public Welfare Committee, to create a new subcommittee—the Special Subcommittee on Alcoholism and Narcotics (SSAN)—with the freshman senator from Iowa as its chairman. Hughes agreed to add the more high-profile issue of drug abuse to the subcommittee's mission to give his effort more political backing or, as staffer Nancy Olsen put it, to "piggyback on the drug issue to pass legislation to help alcoholics." The idea for this subcommittee dated back to Hughes's initial conversations with Robert Kennedy in late 1967, when the New York senator was pressing the Iowa governor to run for the Senate. To get the Iowan in the race, Kennedy had promised to ask his brother Ted, a Democratic senator from Massachusetts and chairman of Labor and Public Welfare's health subcommittee, to support Hughes's effort to chair a special subcommittee on alcoholism. Now, Hughes took this promise to the younger Kennedy, who made good on his brother's vow. "If Ted Kennedy hadn't had the interest or authority, I could never have set up the subcommittee," Hughes later said. When Hughes approached Yarborough about the subcommittee idea, they both telephoned Kennedy, who readily approved.[6]

One problem was the lack of a budget, so Hughes initially used members of his own Senate staff to do the subcommittee's work. He also told Yarborough he could staff the subcommittee with volunteers. ("Are you sure you can do that?" asked Yarborough. "I'm absolutely 100 per cent sure," replied Hughes. He later admitted, "I wasn't, but I told him that.") Hughes also donated his personal speaking fees—about $15,000 in 1969—to provide SSAN's initial funding. The Iowa senator joined two other freshmen who directed subcommittees under the Labor and Public Welfare Committee. This was unusual for such junior senators, but Yarborough claimed he wanted to spread the workload and fill newly created vacancies due to the defeat, retirement, or death of senior Democrats on the committee.[7]

Hughes's ambitious first task was to gather information on what was being done in the areas of prevention, education, treatment, and medical training on the federal, state, and local levels. A prominent legislator who joined the SSAN was Republican senator Jacob Javits of New York, who had been working for years to get alcoholism legislation passed. Others included Yarborough, Kennedy, Jennings Randolph of West Virginia, Henry Bellman of Oklahoma, William Saxbe of Ohio, Pete Dominick of Colorado, Walter Mondale of Minnesota, and Harrison Williams of New Jersey.[8]

Hughes assigned Senate aide Wade Clarke Jr., who had also served on the governor's staff in Des Moines, and legislative assistant Mary Ellen Miller to staff the subcommittee. One of the key volunteers was Nancy Olsen, herself a recovered alcoholic, who later became a full-time staff member. Other subcommittee members contributed staffers to the task.[9]

They still faced the challenge of getting skeptics to accept alcoholism as a disease rather than a moral failure. Hughes realized he needed to shift public opinion in this direction if he hoped to gain support for government action, so he initiated his own public relations and education campaign. The Iowa senator appeared on NBC's *Today Show* on March 4, 1969, and told host Hugh Downs his own personal story and discussed the disease of alcoholism. A year later he appeared on NBC's *Tonight Show* with Iowa native Johnny Carson. In a lengthy discussion with the late-night host, Hughes talked freely about his own battle with alcohol. He claimed there were thirteen million Americans who were either alcoholics or had serious drinking problems bordering on alcoholism, costing the nation $7.5 billion a year. In an age when drug use was a concern of many parents, Hughes said, "The drug most young people start with is alcohol." He repeated his message in speeches around the country.[10]

The full force of this education campaign began with SSAN hearings in Washington, DC, on July 23, 1969, and continued around the country. In his opening statement, Hughes said, "This is a new kind of subcommittee. It is, to the best of my knowledge, the first congressional committee exclusively devoted to the cause of helping individual citizens and society gain relief from the human blights of drug and alcohol abuse." Calling the $4 million HEW allocated for alcoholism programs "the puniest type of tokenism," Hughes exclaimed, "If, at times, I sound like an angry and frustrated man, it is because I am." He continued, "We have been too polite and restrained about the subject, as I see it. It is time we got angry and blunt. Alcoholism is a dirty, vicious illness that destroys human life and happiness, and causes staggering economic waste. It is disgraceful that we have done so little about it thus far."[11]

Over three days, nineteen experts and recovered alcoholics testified, beginning with Des Moines municipal judge Ray Harrison, an alcoholic who had been sober for twenty-six years. Also testifying were Marty Mann, cofounder of the National Council on Alcoholism, and AA cofounder Bill Wilson. To prompt national media coverage, the hearings also included testimony from Academy Award–winning actress Mercedes McCambridge, who revealed she had been sober since earlier that year. The hearing room was packed not with reporters and congressional aides but with AA members, many of whom were hearing their problems discussed in a public forum for the first time.[12]

On the final day of the Washington hearings, Hughes and his subcommittee faced Dr. Roger Egeberg, HEW's assistant secretary for health, who was representing the Nixon administration. Although Egeberg was generally supportive of Hughes's effort, he argued that the 375 community health centers around the country were the best places to start an ambitious rehabilitation program. Hughes disagreed, based on his own experience and distrust of medical doctors. "I'm not sure this is the best approach," he said. "The history of the medical profession indicates damn little concern for the alcoholics—and this goes for psychiatrists, too. I'm not inclined to put a patient in the hands of a man who doesn't believe he can heal him." Using a farm metaphor, he added, "When a mother pig has 18 little pigs, you know where the littlest one winds up. Well, that's where alcoholics have been all of these years."[13]

Egeberg's stance reflected that of the conservative Nixon administration, which opposed new government programs and emphasized law enforcement, especially related to drug use. Under intense questioning from Hughes, however, HEW's assistant secretary vowed to let science determine the best means of enforcement and treatment. To Egeberg, Hughes said, "I'm saying that if they [alcoholics] do commit a crime and the reason they committed a crime is that they're a victim of a disease that we know is a disease called alcoholism, then we should have the responsibility of treating the disease that caused them to commit the crime. And if they can then be healed of that disease, that should be considered by the legal structure." Egeberg replied, "I can't disagree with that." The exchange blossomed into a friendship between the two.[14]

With these hearings, Hughes launched a new federal effort to create alcoholic rehabilitation and research programs. The hearings got a ringing endorsement from committee chair Yarborough, who wrote to Hughes, "My belief that you could do the job has been more than justified. Your initial hearings on our Nation's alcoholism problem are a model of deep exploration of a difficult subject. . . . You have made a great beginning."[15]

By this time, Hughes's Senate office had been inundated with hundreds of letters from alcoholics and their families, praising the hearings and Hughes's effort to focus a federal spotlight on alcoholism. Many of these letters were long, heartfelt descriptions of their own suffering and that of family members.[16]

The next stage was to take the subcommittee hearings on the road, continuing to raise public awareness of alcoholism as a disease. After hearings were held in the Los Angeles area in early October, James I. Davidson, executive director of the Alcoholism Council of Greater Los Angeles, wrote to Hughes and exclaimed, "You did it. The publicity on television and radio was as good as any I have seen, for any other event other than moonshots, assassinations, et al." At fourteen hearings held around the country in 1969, the subcommittee listened to testimony from treatment providers, recovered alcoholics, politicians, researchers, and religious leaders—all of whom told Americans it was finally time to take action on alcoholism.[17]

The result of this effort was the Comprehensive Alcoholism Prevention and Treatment Act of 1970, known as the Hughes Act. It marked the high point of the Iowa senator's legislative career. The legislation granted $320 million over the next three years to state and local agencies, both public and private, to finance specific projects, including treatment and rehabilitation facilities, community centers, research projects, counseling, and personal health training. Another $75 million was directed to state grants for alcoholism prevention, treatment, and rehabilitation. The law mandated that federal agencies create programs to deal with alcohol abuse among employees, providing opportunities for treatment and rehabilitation. Modeled in part on ICAP, it provided individual states with funds to create comprehensive alcoholism programs, such as enhanced hospital programs, halfway houses, detoxification programs, and other local initiatives. The legislation also created the National Institute of Alcohol Abuse and Alcoholism (NIAAA), serving as a central source of information and resources based on the latest treatment and rehabilitation techniques. The overall approach was to classify alcoholism as a disease and to emphasize health and rehabilitation, rather than legal action or punishment. The legislation went so far as to deny funding to hospitals that refused to treat alcoholic patients. For the first time in history, the government became a permanent part of the effort to aid alcoholics.[18]

On August 10, 1970, Hughes took to the Senate floor to introduce the bill. He called it "a realistic, practical design at the federal level for setting in motion throughout the nation the mechanism to deal with a deadly, costly disease that has become epidemic in our time" and "has long been neglected at all levels of government." The next day, it passed unanimously in the Senate by voice vote. The bill passed the House later in the year, but that version located the NIAAA within NIMH instead of granting it independent status. Hughes conceded the change in the interest of time. It needed only a presidential signature to become law. President Nixon thought the legislation was unnecessary and threatened to veto the bill, but intense lobbying in the White House—especially by businessman Thomas P. Pike, a prominent Republican and recovered alcoholic—convinced him otherwise. Nixon signed the bill on December 31, 1970.[19]

The act's passage did not lead to immediate action, however. The Nixon administration dragged its feet on implementing the law, much to the ire of the Iowa senator. Three months later, Hughes publicly complained in an open letter to Nixon: "Mr. President, to date, no Institute has been created; no director for the Institute has yet been appointed; and no National Advisory Council has yet been administratively established or selected." In the same document, he complained that the administration was cutting congressionally mandated funding for alcoholism programs from $15 million to $2 million in its proposed 1972 budget.[20]

On the floor of the Senate, Hughes charged that administration officials had informed him "there is no intention on the part of the Administration . . . to implement this new law." In other words, he said, "it would appear that the thrust of the executive budget is to repeal, for all practical effects, the law that was passed without dissent by the two houses of the Congress and signed by the President." At a subcommittee hearing on March 18, Hughes directed his anger at a group of HEW officials who acknowledged that they had no plans either this year or the next to set up the kind of alcoholism program outlined in the law. The main reason, they claimed, was a shortage of trained personnel and the department's belief that the money could not be "usefully" spent without more preparation and groundwork. Moreover, they contended, existing federal efforts to fight alcoholism and drug abuse were sufficient. Hughes did not like the answers he was getting.[21]

On March 25 he again lambasted the administration on the Senate floor, charging that addiction programs were being "derailed, cut back and underfunded." Despite the administration's argument that plenty of funds and programs were available to aid both drug addicts and alcoholics, Hughes cited underfunding or a complete lack of funding in both areas. He said he was "deeply embarrassed and shamed" that the nation had been led to believe in the existence of a massive government commitment to fight both problems "when the job is not being done." He added that the government spent nearly $1 million more on antismoking campaigns in 1970 than it did on "dissuading people from using heroin and LSD." Hughes would continue this battle for the remainder of the year.[22]

Federal funding did not meet Hughes's expectations for several years. In March 1973 he introduced new legislation to extend funding grants for three years under the Comprehensive Alcoholism Prevention and Treatment Act, amounting to $180 million in fiscal year 1974 and $220 million in each of the next two years. In doing so, he pointed out that the administration's budget for 1974 had eliminated new project grants to community groups for treatment and rehabilitation programs, the major thrust of the federal effort to combat alcoholism. "We have made a good start," said Hughes. "But it would be tragic to become complacent, or to cut the already limited grant funds in the name of economy."[23]

The problem was not getting Congress to approve the funding but overcoming the Nixon administration's practice of impounding funds or refusing to spend money allocated by legislators. The administration had allowed no funding of new project grants since the end of fiscal year 1972. In 1972 Nixon had twice vetoed an appropriations act that included funds for the alcoholism program and refused to release more than $80 million for the effort. Nixon adopted this tactic across a number of funding programs during his battle with congressional Democrats over spending.[24]

Slashing the budget and impounding funds for the program meant that the 1970 act "will be shattered into a thousand pieces," according to Hughes. Furthermore, as he frequently pointed out, the amount at stake "over the next three years wouldn't begin to finance a single Trident submarine." Citing calls for multibillion-dollar increases in military spending, Hughes asked, "What does this tell you about the focus of our national priorities?"[25]

Hughes continued to push and, with overwhelming support from his fellow legislators, finally succeeded in 1974 in passing a series of amendments to the Hughes Act. With these amendments, NIAAA became an independent institute within the federal Alcohol, Drug Abuse, and Mental Health Administration, alongside NIMH and the National Institute on Drug Abuse. Nixon accepted these changes, and Hughes was invited to the White House for the bill's signing, but he "couldn't bring myself to attend, since his administration had fought it every inch of the way."[26]

According to William H. White in *Slaying the Dragon: The History of Addiction Treatment and Recovery in America*, the Hughes Act marked "the political recognition of alcoholism as a disease and public-health problem in its own right." Wrote White, "The passage of the Hughes Act marked the political coming-of-age of the invisible army of recovering and non-recovering people who had toiled as the foot soldiers of the 'modern alcoholism movement,'" transforming "this social movement into a new industry" and giving force to "an invisible network of recovered alcoholics who worked in tandem across political parties, branches of government, and government agencies to forge a new national response to alcoholism."[27]

In addition to providing local grants to communities to aid alcoholics, NIAAA became a powerful force for groundbreaking research that dramatically transformed how the health profession looked at alcoholism. Among its many contributions were studying the genetics of alcoholism within individuals and families, helping to identify those at risk for the disease; conducting the largest and most extensive survey on alcohol-associated psychiatric and medical conditions; researching the impact of alcohol on fetal development; nurturing the development of medications to aid alcoholics; and investigating and improving community programs designed to prevent alcohol-related problems. All this was supported by extensive communication and training programs to incorporate these findings into everyday practice on the local level. According to a review written forty years after its founding, NIAAA "still embodies the strong hopes and dedication of those who fought for the Institute's founding."[28]

Among those who fought was recovered alcoholic Harold Hughes, who used his considerable energy and talents to apply the force of the federal government to helping alcoholics. Scholar Kelsey Ensign links that effort to the rhetoric used by the larger civil rights movement to demand rights—in this case, the right to medical treatment for alcoholics through state aid. She wrote, "It was primarily Hughes who ensured alcoholics were added to the expanding group of individuals who were newly designed as entitled to government assistance." The NIAAA and the related provisions of the Hughes Act are a living, active tribute to this man.[29]

Hughes's subcommittee also dealt with drug addiction, a growing concern in the country. The response of the Nixon administration and Congress was largely a law enforcement crackdown through the Controlled Substances Act, Title II of the Comprehensive Drug Abuse Prevention and Control Act of 1970. Hughes tried to create a drug treatment and rehabilitation institute similar to the NIAAA and got strong support in the Senate, but the bill was dropped in the final House-Senate conference committee. Based on the amount of money allocated, drug abuse treatment took a backseat to law enforcement.[30]

A more successful mission of the SSAN was its investigation of federal programs designed to respond to alcoholism and drug abuse, particularly in the US military. This was spawned by tales of servicemen returning from Vietnam with drug and alcohol problems and claims that the military was simply tossing these addicts back into civilian life without professional aid or follow-up. Hughes coordinated his staff's investigative work with Senators John Stennis (D-MS), chairman of the Armed Services Committee, and Alan Cranston (D-CA), chairman of the Veterans Subcommittee on Armed Services, who had jurisdiction over these areas.[31]

Two intrepid investigators—Wade Clarke and Julian Granger, who worked for the Hughes subcommittee—toured military bases around the world and interviewed sources in South Vietnam, Thailand, Hong Kong, South Korea, and Hawaii in mid-1970. Among other problems, they found significant heroin use among American troops. In a September 18 memo to Hughes, Granger recommended that the subcommittee press for funds to enlarge the military's pool of psychiatrists, psychologists, and social workers to treat addicts. He wrote optimistically, "I believe the military has been convinced of our sincerity and our willingness to help solve whatever problem may exist in the drug and alcoholism areas, and now is the time to capitalize on this reaction."[32]

Hughes held public hearings on alcohol and drug problems in the military in the second half of 1970, shining a spotlight on the crisis. In early 1971 he noted that these hearings had uncovered problems previously ignored by military management. "The top level leadership, both civilian and military, in the Pentagon, were unaware of the extent and nature of the problem. They did not realize that some of these drug problems in the services existed until our Senate Subcommittee identified them."[33]

In April 1971 the subcommittee released a report showing that drug use among military personnel—particularly among eighteen- to twenty-five-year-olds—had been growing both in the United States and over-seas. It concluded that the military was "understandably not equipped to handle" this problem. Hughes reported that, with the agreement of Senator Stennis, he had directed the subcommittee staff to meet with military officers and discuss how to deal with the problem.[34]

As Hughes continued to investigate the military drug problem through 1971, he became more critical of the military's response. In mid-June his findings showed that, in the past two years, sixteen thousand servicemen had been discharged for drug abuse, eleven thousand of them dishonorably, which made them ineligible for treatment at Veterans Administration (VA) hospitals. Even for those who were eligible for treatment, the VA had fewer than three hundred beds. Army officials in Saigon publicly admitted that up to forty thousand American servicemen in Vietnam—15 percent of the total force remaining—were using hard drugs. Hughes said, "We have received no evidence that either the Department of Defense or the various services have responded realistically to the urgency of the problem or have charted the kind of treatment-oriented control programs that we consider imperative."[35]

At the same time, at Hughes's urging, the Senate voted unanimously to order Secretary of Defense Melvin Laird to take immediate action to stem the narcotics "epidemic" among American troops in Vietnam. Senators also approved a bill generated by Hughes requiring President Nixon to increase efforts to shut off sources of heroin and report to Congress every ninety days on his progress. According to the *Des Moines Register*'s James Risser, Hughes "is almost solely responsible for the quick Senate action." Senators showed "in a unanimous bipartisan voice . . . that they do not believe the Pentagon has recognized the seriousness of the military drug problem and that they are not willing to wait for the White House to act."[36]

Hughes continued to hold hearings through the summer, publicizing the problem. Testimony from veterans serving from 1966 to 1971 showed that many had started taking narcotics to relieve combat-related tension or boredom from noncombat assignments. Some testified that addicted servicemen stole government property to support their habits. Several estimated that at least 20 percent of the men in their units were using heroin, which was easily accessible in Southeast Asia. Said one, "Heroin becomes your god, your all, and you don't give a goddamn about the military, or going home, or your parents, or your brothers or sisters." Reported another, "You know you're not bulletproof, but you don't care."[37]

The publicity generated by Hughes and the Senate's action prompted the Nixon administration to act. The president ordered servicemen to take compulsory urine exams before they returned home, made possible by new technology enabling some one thousand tests a day. Although Hughes praised Nixon for his attempt to tackle the problem, he cited "fatal flaws" with the military plan, which showed "discouraging rigidity" rather than "flexibility and human understanding," and he criticized the failure to detect addicts earlier.[38]

Hughes would continue to criticize the Pentagon for its treatment of drug addicts. In early 1972 he charged that many drug-using servicemen were being given "undesirable discharges," in violation of Defense Department policy, and were being denied VA hospital treatment. Pentagon representatives testifying before the subcommittee claimed that positive urine tests for heroin had decreased from 4.4 percent to 2 percent. Hughes countered that surprise urine tests for men who were not slated to leave Vietnam showed that 5.7 percent were using heroin. "The question thus arises: Has the heroin epidemic really been turned around in Vietnam?"[39]

The military drug problem seemed like a never-ending battle. For Hughes, the problem would continue as long as American servicemen were in Vietnam. In a speech in Iowa City in the midst of his investigations, Hughes said the best way to solve the drug addiction problem in Vietnam "is to get the hell out of there."[40]

17 | Angry Dove on the National Stage

During his Senate campaign, Hughes established himself as a moderate critic of the Vietnam War. He repeatedly said he was against an immediate withdrawal from Vietnam, and his stance on ending the bombing of North Vietnam was designed to advance negotiations to end US involvement. But after taking his Senate seat and giving the Nixon administration time to set its foreign policy, Hughes became increasingly critical of the US commitment to the South Vietnamese government. He soon moved into the ranks of the vocal doves in the US Senate.

Appearing on the ABC news show *Issues and Answers* in his first month as senator, Hughes declared, "I believe we can begin a withdrawal without any reciprocation . . . because I believe we can couple that with an increased military capability of the South Vietnamese Government which would more than offset our withdrawal." In letters to his constituents in Iowa he wrote, "I am one of the growing number of Senators who are convinced that there can be no military solution to the war and that we must make a determined effort to negotiate a settlement and remove American forces as quickly as possible."[1]

On June 20, 1969, the freshman senator spoke on the floor of the Senate to make his position clear. The speech was a summary of his thoughts and emotions about the Vietnam War that "have too long been bottled up." He recalled his strong support for LBJ from 1963 to mid-1967, despite his 1965 trip to Vietnam, when "questions began to rise and haunt me." By 1967, "these questions became too intense to live with"; seeking counsel from others, he found that "there were no rational answers" and concluded "that the premises on which our involvement was founded were wrong, that we had no business on the basis of moral imperative and national interest to be there." By this time, he said, his thinking had evolved to the point "where I think it would be criminally irresponsible on my part to remain silent." Hughes offered a five-point plan to end the war: a cease-fire on all sides, an international peacekeeping force, free elections in South Vietnam, land reform, and economic aid. He urged President Nixon to take actions along these lines "toward the common objectives of ending the war."[2]

Nixon's campaign promise in 1968 had been that, with his vast foreign policy experience, he would "honorably" end US involvement in Vietnam. However, he refused to provide details on how he was going to accomplish this, claiming that to do so would interfere with the Johnson administration's conduct of the war and the ongoing peace negotiations in Paris. In fact, Nixon had no firm plan; he believed that, once he took office, he and his aides would be able to fashion a viable policy based on the information and tools available. The policy he developed—known as Vietnamization—was a combination of well-publicized withdrawals of US troops from Vietnam and attempts to train and improve the South Vietnamese army to replace the departing Americans. He also continued to apply military pressure to the North Vietnamese and their Vietcong allies to drive them toward concessions through public and private negotiations.[3]

As the president's honeymoon period faded, Hughes became less patient. At a Democratic fund-raiser in Tennessee in January 1970, Hughes said, "We have withdrawn some troops from Vietnam, for which we are all grateful. But the killing still goes on; we are still pouring three-quarters of our expenditures into over-kill capabilities for our military; and we have apparently given up on negotiating a settlement that will win the peace." A few weeks later, speaking in Washington, Hughes noted there are "deep and searching fears about the direction our national policy is taking and the excessive dependence on Vietnamization." For himself, "because of the high stakes, I find it necessary to speak my convictions wherever possible whether this be leadership or folly." Hughes clearly intended to speak out for a quicker end to US involvement in Vietnam.[4]

Hughes's criticism was directed at the South Vietnamese government, the very institution US forces were fighting to preserve. Hughes called it "a military junta-type government" that was anything but a democracy. In October Hughes joined with Senator Thomas Eagleton of Missouri to introduce a resolution calling for the South Vietnamese government to reform itself or lose US support. Speaking in favor of the effort—dubbed the Hughes-Eagleton resolution—before the Senate Foreign Relations Committee in February 1970, Hughes explained that it called for the South Vietnamese government to "end censorship, release political prisoners, allow political organizations to operate without interference, and create a new cabinet broadly representative of the main non-communist political ethnic and religious groups of South Vietnam." If these conditions were not met, the resolution called for the president to "declare officially that our commitment to the present government of South Vietnam is ended, and that we should terminate, with all reasonable haste, our military, political, and economic assistance to that government." The resolution stood little chance of passing in the Senate, and Hughes knew it. But it forced other senators to take a stand and highlighted the corrupt South Vietnamese government that US forces were defending.[5]

Outside the Senate, Hughes took his oratory to high-profile antiwar rallies, establishing himself as one of the leading critics of the war. One such event was a star-studded fund-raiser in March 1970 at Madison Square Garden in New York City that included Dustin Hoffman, Shirley MacLaine, I. F. Stone, and Andrew Young. Introduced by actor Henry Fonda, Hughes called for a nationwide revival of the antiwar movement and urged the election of congressmen who stand for "peace and new priorities." He decried Nixon's Vietnamization policy as a "myth" that "locks us ever more rigidly into our costly propping up of the corrupt and unrepresentative Thieu-Ky regime [president and vice president of South Vietnam]." Interrupted by applause about thirty-five times during the thirty-minute speech, Hughes received a standing ovation from the crowd at its conclusion.[6]

When Nixon ordered US troops to invade Cambodia on April 30, 1970, it was no surprise that Hughes declared himself "shocked" and "saddened" at the president's "tragic mistake," lamenting, "We have come so far and learned so little over the past 10 years." Nixon justified the invasion by characterizing it as an attack against North Vietnamese bases across the border. Calling it "an incredible replay of past mistakes," Hughes declared it "a violation of the principles and policies that halted the bombing of North Vietnam in 1968 and led to the opening of peace negotiations in Paris. It is now apparent that negotiations are not our goal."[7]

Nixon's invasion of Cambodia led to an eruption of protests on US college campuses, including at the University of Iowa, which canceled classes and ended the spring semester early. Domestically, the most violent outcome was the killing of four students by Ohio National Guard troops on the Kent State campus. On the floor of the Senate, Hughes called these shootings "a product of the war, just as surely as deaths in combat." During the widespread protests, the senator sent telegrams to twenty student peace groups at Iowa colleges and universities, advising against violent demonstrations. "The most appropriate memorial for the students at Kent State, and other casualties of this war, will come in a mighty, unprecedented drive for peace that cannot be denied," he wrote to the students.[8]

To this end, Hughes joined a bipartisan group of antiwar senators to sponsor what became known as the End the War Amendment. Joining him were Democrats George McGovern of South Dakota, Frank Church of Idaho, Gaylord Nelson of Wisconsin, and Alan Cranston of California and Republicans Mark Hatfield of Oregon and Charles Goodell of New York. The measure called for a cutoff of all funding for the US military in Cambodia within thirty days of passage, an end of support for efforts in Laos by year's end, and the termination of all funding for military activities in Vietnam by July 1, 1971. On May 12, 1970, the group took the unprecedented step of purchasing a half hour of airtime on NBC to make their case for the resolution, which had twenty Senate sponsors by this time. During the TV broadcast, each of the five senators appearing—Hughes, McGovern, Hatfield, Church, and Goodell—delivered their antiwar messages. Calling the invasion of Cambodia "the straw that broke the camel's back," Hughes said the war was creating a "spiritual scarring of our own nation" and was "brutalizing us internally." He charged that Vietnamization was not a change in policy at all but a strategy that meant "the war will go on and continue to go on for years to come." The time had come, he said, for the United States to exit this war. He noted that the mail received by his office was ten to one against Nixon's position on Vietnam. Hughes ended with a plea: "But for Lord's sake, don't be quiet. Write, support or oppose, but do something in this critical time."[9]

Not one to simply give speeches, Hughes led a peace march in Des Moines on May 17 that numbered several thousand. He marched for five blocks at the head of the unusually quiet crowd, flashing the peace sign. When they reached the state capitol, Hughes spoke for half an hour in favor of the End the War Amendment. After reading the fourteen-page speech, he turned to the crowd and asked, "Do you believe in peace?" "Yes," they cried. "Then find peace in your own heart. If we have to bring peace to the world, we must love our brothers as we love ourselves." After the rally, he sat down on the statehouse steps and chatted for several minutes with about twenty-five students. He told them, "The next time you have a rally, bring your mothers and fathers. They would realize that we're feeling the same things."[10]

Hughes may have had the crowd on his side that day, but he did not have the majority of Iowans behind him. A *Des Moines Register* poll released on May 31 showed that 55 percent of Iowans approved of Nixon's move into Cambodia, with 35 percent disapproving. When asked about the president's overall conduct of the war, Iowans approved 51 to 37 percent. Early in his Senate term, Hughes was fighting uphill against his fellow Iowans on this controversial issue. However, by the middle of July—in response to his televised request for written input—his office had received hundreds of letters from Iowans and others throughout the United States. In all, they were running thirteen to one in favor of Hughes's position.[11]

By the summer of 1970, the antiwar senators' legislation had been divided into the Cooper-Church and McGovern-Hatfield amendments. The first, named for Senators John Sherman Cooper of Kentucky and Frank Church, would cut off funds for the Cambodian invasion; the second, named for Senators McGovern and Hatfield, mandated a full funding cutoff for the Vietnam War by the middle of 1971. On June 30, 1970, the Cooper-Church amendment passed the Senate by a vote of 58–37, but it was a moot point; Nixon had just announced that all American troops had left Cambodia, and the brief incursion was over. (The House voted in July to kill the Cooper-Church amendment, 237–153.) Even so, this was the first direct challenge to presidential war powers since the beginning of the Indochina conflict. Hughes said, "I'm very much encouraged" because it boded well for the McGovern-Hatfield amendment, but, he admitted, "it's still an underdog."[12]

Leading up to the vote, Hughes was at the center of the debate. On July 9 he was the principal force behind a daylong conference of prestigious war critics in Washington. Present were veteran ambassador Averell Harriman and about forty senators and congressmen who supported the McGovern-Hatfield amendment. They argued that a fixed timetable, along with a negotiated agreement to ensure the release of prisoners, was now the only feasible way to extricate the United States from the war. Hughes saw the conference as a way to give the public "the other side of the case," to explain that withdrawal is "feasible as well as desirable, that our troops can be pulled out safely and systematically." He again stressed that the main roadblock to negotiations was "the dance of death in which we are locked with the Thieu-Ky regime, a military dictatorship whose stock in trade is the harsh repression of the freedoms we Americans prize and the brutal treatment of non-Communist political opponents of their unrepresentative regime." According to the *Des Moines Register*'s James Risser, who covered the event, Hughes "has begun to emerge this week as the leading activist and spokesman for Senate war critics."[13]

As leader, Hughes headed an effort to convince the Federal Communications Commission (FCC) to allow critics of the war to respond to Nixon's repeated national addresses to US citizens. In a letter to FCC commissioner Dean Burch on July 30, 1970, Hughes wrote—on behalf of himself, the Amendment to End the War Committee, and a bipartisan group of thirteen other senators—that they sought "access to the airwaves so that we may present our unique point of view opposing the President's views on the Indochina war." On August 15 the FCC ruled 3–2 that the television networks had to allow opponents of Nixon to reply in prime time. The *New York Times* described this decision as "the first of its kind and appeared likely to alter Mr. Nixon's use of the medium."[14]

As the vote on the McGovern-Hatfield amendment neared, it was obvious to backers that they did not have the support to pass it, but they pressed ahead anyway. In a speech on the Senate floor in favor of the effort, Hughes repeated his arguments that the ongoing war was "senseless and destructive of our national interests." He added, "In my own state, the untold story, as I see it, is of the peace movement that has emerged in the small communities of Middle America—not among the youth, who were already with it, but among the calm and established adult citizens of these communities."[15]

On September 1 the Senate rejected McGovern-Hatfield by a vote of 55–39. Said Hughes, "Thirty-nine is a significant number of votes and if I were the administration, I would pay pretty close attention to it." The *Des Moines Register* agreed in an editorial titled "39 Senators Make a Point." Although the final vote was a win for Nixon, the paper argued that it "was, in a way, a victory for the anti-war senators. . . . The senators who have led this fight, including Harold Hughes of Iowa, deserve the nation's gratitude for bringing the war issue to focus in responsible debate—in the forum where it should be debated."[16]

The war would continue for years, with little constraint on Nixon and his national security adviser Henry Kissinger. The administration would announce troop withdrawals, continue fighting with the troops that remained, and support that action with aerial bombing in South Vietnam, as well as secretly in North Vietnam and elsewhere in Indochina. But the administration would not do this with a blank check from the legislative branch, especially the US Senate. Powerful forces—led by Hughes and others—were clearly applying pressure to the White House to end US involvement and to do it as quickly as possible.

18 | Democratic Party Reformer and Presidential Candidate

Hughes came to Washington, DC, as one of the leading voices for reform of the Democratic Party's process for selecting a presidential nominee. As governor, Hughes had been recruited into this effort by those who were upset that Humphrey won the 1968 Democratic presidential nomination without facing voters in any significant primaries. The result was a dramatic transformation in how Democrats chose their presidential nominee.

In the summer of 1968 McCarthy supporters in Connecticut were particularly incensed over their scant delegate totals at the state convention, where they won only nine of forty-four delegates, despite widespread grassroots support for McCarthy throughout the Democratic Party. The problem was that delegates were selected under party rules that gave overwhelming power to party elites, who favored Humphrey. The aggrieved McCarthy supporters in Connecticut formed the Commission on the Democratic Selection of Presidential Nominees to force the party to adopt a more open and fairer process. The group cast a net around the country for a prominent Democratic politician to serve as chairman and eventually connected with Harold Hughes in late July. He seemed like an ideal candidate, based on his recent support of outside activists at the Iowa caucuses—primarily antiwar McCarthy supporters—and his interest in party reform. The group had a chairman and an informal name: the Hughes Commission.[1]

Specifically, Hughes was approached to head the effort by Connecticut delegate Anne Wexler at the suggestion of Iowan Bill Sueppel. He was initially hesitant because he had little time to spare, "but they said they'd do the work. . . . I did it at their request. . . . It was not at my instigation." He added, "I am sure they were looking for someone with enough stature in the party to command some respect and I expect as a Governor I had that symbolically to them, and I was willing to do it." As he became more involved in the effort, Hughes's interest and passion for reform increased.[2]

Hughes and Wexler announced the formation of the commission at a press conference on August 4 in Chicago. A week later, Hughes conducted the first and only meeting of the commission at a private home in Winnetka, Illinois. The group developed an eighty-page document—dubbed *A Democratic Choice*—with proposals to bring "the nominating process more closely into harmony with essential democratic principles." On August 22 Hughes testified before the Democratic Party's rules committee prior to the opening of the convention. Laying out the unfair practices that prevented grassroots votes from translating into delegates, he pointed out that more than 20 percent of the delegates were appointed by persons who had not faced the voters in two years, 20 percent were directly appointed by party officials, and few states applied the one-man, one-vote principle in choosing delegates. "The existence of such pervasive affronts to democratic principles and other similar abuses is indefensible," he argued. He presented recommendations to reform both the national delegate selection process and convention procedures. These included opening up the process to guarantee that all voters have meaningful access to participation and eliminating the "unit rule," under which state delegations vote as a bloc. He advocated a one-man, one-vote rule so that delegates reflected state populations, as well as more open representation of minorities and poor people. Hughes asserted that "the political convention system is on trial," and unless it is reformed, the present two-party system could be destroyed.[3]

After long and arduous debate, the rules committee adopted a majority resolution to set up a commission to discuss general rules and present recommendations to the 1972 Democratic convention. This mandate was vague and did not go far enough for members of the Hughes Commission. Led by commission staff members Geoff Cowan and Simon Lazarus, the group drew up a more detailed minority plank calling for the party to create "procedures open to public participation" a year in advance of the next convention, giving voters "full and timely opportunity to participate." It also specifically prohibited the unit rule, which allowed party elites to force state delegations to back only one candidate. The stage was set for a showdown between a majority report with an indefinite direction on party reform and a minority report with a more concrete directive to open up the party's delegate selection process.[4]

On the second day of the tumultuous 1968 Chicago convention, delegates voted 1,350 to 1,206 to pass the minority plank resolution on party reform supported by the Hughes Commission, marking the only McCarthy victory at the convention. There were several reasons it passed. First, the Hughes Commission staff implemented a disciplined, well-ordered lobbying campaign, led by Wexler, to convince delegates to support reform, arguing that it would be unjust for Humphrey to get the nomination without winning any significant primaries. Second, the Humphrey forces did not contest the resolution, believing the nomination was theirs and they would be in control of setting the rules anyway. Third, party elites seemed content to give this victory to the insurgents to pacify them. In the words of Wexler, "Many people felt that this was a way to throw the liberals a bone." Finally, Hughes's personal standing among Democratic governors and his work as chairman of the Democratic Governors Conference accounted for some defections from the Humphrey wing. After getting the Iowa delegation to support the minority plank, Hughes got the entire Missouri delegation to vote for it by asking Governor Warren E. Hearnes for a personal favor; when that favor was granted (thus taking advantage of the elite, top-down control Hughes was fighting), the Iowan gave Hearnes a big bear hug on the convention floor. The Iowa and Missouri votes alone helped ensure victory. David Broder of the *Washington Post* credited Hughes's work on passing the plank, calling him "one of the country's most valuable young political leaders."[5]

This victory was little noted in media coverage of the convention, however. Few who voted for the reform plank amidst the sound and fury of the 1968 Chicago convention knew it would significantly change how Americans nominated presidential candidates. According to Byron E. Shafer, who wrote an exhaustive history of this effort, it initiated "a revolutionary change in the mechanics of presidential selection, the greatest systematically planned and centrally imposed shift in the institutions of delegate selection in all of American history." This momentous transformation was brought about in part through the aggressive support of Iowa's Harold Hughes.[6]

Armed with passage of the minority plank, Hughes wrote two letters to Larry O'Brien, Democratic national chairman, urging immediate action on the reform commission, but to no avail. Time, he argued, was running short because some actions required state legislative approval, and many legislatures would be meeting soon. Appearing on ABC's *Issues and Answers* on January 26, 1969, Hughes said, "I thought that we should have started out on the reform measures last fall and not waited until after the campaign. . . . It is already too late, in my opinion, and every day that goes by is going to mean we are in that much more difficulty of having a smooth convention process in 1972."[7]

After the 1968 election, new Democratic Party chairman Fred Harris, a senator from Oklahoma, finally announced the formation of the reform commission in early February 1969, but the lineup was not completely to Hughes's liking. He had been lobbying aggressively to become chairman—and had the support of reformers calling themselves the New Democratic Coalition—but some saw Hughes as too intensely tied to reform and an unsteady "irritant to party regulars." One complaint was that Hughes had not supported the national ticket aggressively enough in the last campaign. According to one Democratic insider, Harris "did not regard Hughes as a person with whom one could have a rational discussion." Instead, Harris named Senator George McGovern of South Dakota chairman of the Commission on Party Structure and Delegate Selection, with Hughes as vice chairman. Hughes accepted this position in the interest of party harmony. (It was initially known as the McGovern Commission, but when McGovern left to run for president in early 1971, Congressman Donald Fraser of Minnesota became chairman. It was later known as the McGovern-Fraser Commission.)[8]

McGovern assembled a commission with twenty-six other members, aided by a staff and consultants. He integrated key figures from the Hughes Commission, which had prompted the reform movement. The overall thrust of the commission was to reform the party process to avoid what had happened in 1968: a candidate getting the nomination behind closed doors by courting party insiders.[9]

At the inaugural meeting of the commission on March 1 in the Caucus Room of the Old Senate Office Building, Hughes set the moral tone, adopting his stance as the perennial outsider. "For too long now, national conventions have largely been the private domain of the rich, the white, and the party regular," he said. Although he favored preserving the national party convention, he insisted that its procedures and those leading up to it "must be modernized. We must ensure that delegates who attend carry a fresh mandate from the people."[10]

Following this initial meeting, the staff—Eli Segal, Bob Nelson, and Ken Bode—moved the commission's work forward. The group assembled research on individual states' party rules, organized seventeen regional input meetings that also publicized the group's efforts, and built alliances and support among the Democratic Party faithful. McGovern and Hughes raised funds for these activities in the spring and summer of 1969.[11]

Hughes also spoke vociferously and often about the reform effort, prodding it forward in no uncertain terms. At a dinner of the New Democratic Coalition on May 24, he said, "The truth is that our political parties have become corroded and boss-controlled, and are neither accessible nor responsible to the rank and file of the constituents." He admitted that reforms might alienate some people, but it was worth the risk to address the great issues of "peace, poverty, and equality." Hughes said, "We can't be strong and right on the great moral questions and expect to retain hard-liners who don't give a damn about anything but power."[12]

McGovern was chairman of the reform commission, but Hughes was the more powerful force for change. According to commissioner George Mitchell—later a US senator from Maine—Hughes was the man with "real leadership" on the commission. "McGovern gets credit for all these rules, but the fact is that McGovern never took much part," Mitchell said. "*Hughes* was the outstanding guy on the Commission." As the person who lent his name to the initial call for party reform, Hughes commanded greater loyalty from the commission staff, and according to Shafer, "Hughes necessarily became the commissioner around whom the more extreme reform proposals were organized. His blunt personal style, finally, did nothing to mitigate any of this."[13]

Much of the day-to-day work was done by the commission's staff—Segal, Bode, and Nelson—who, for the most part, were reform sympathizers dedicated to opening up the party's nominating process and therefore limiting the power of established party elites. The staff organized recommendations, consulted regularly with McGovern and Hughes, and ran their ideas through the commission's executive committee. Most of the proposed rules reflected this reformist bias. All this led to an important two-day meeting in Washington beginning on November 19, 1969. This gathering of the commission, wrote Shafer, "capped the most thorough efforts at recommendations for party reform in the history of the world's oldest continuing political party."[14]

Commission members vigorously debated the rules, recommendations, and mandates over two long days, prompting energetic discussions, compromises, and clashes. The major thrust of these mandates represented real and significant reform of the Democratic Party's presidential nominating process; they were, in Shafer's words, "unprecedented and monumental." The commission adjourned with eighteen guiding principles to shape the upcoming nominating process.[15]

One of the key requirements was for "state parties to extend [to] the process of nominating delegates all guarantees of full and meaningful opportunity to participate which apply to the delegate selection process." No one could be shut out of the process, including those who had never participated before. The commission recommended that delegates represent the proportion of support for presidential candidates in each state. Also, the commission approved "affirmative steps to overcome past discrimination, including minority presence." Although the group rejected hard quotas, it sought greater participation by racial minorities, women, and young people. It reaffirmed the abolition of the unit rule, the practice of requiring all delegates to vote for one candidate after he or she had received a majority of votes; in other words, it abolished "the practice of instructing delegates to vote against their preferences at any stage of the delegate selection process." (This rule was not always followed, such as in California in 1972.) In a move to prevent secret gatherings, it urged state parties "to provide for easy access and frequent opportunity for party enrollment by unaffiliated and non-Democrats." In another slap at party leaders, the commission recommended that "state parties not permit any part of the delegation to be selected by party committees." It mandated that delegate selection occur within the calendar year of the national party convention. All told, the recommendations of the commission directed the party's presidential nomination process toward greater openness and inclusiveness through more democratic measures.[16]

It was one thing to state these ideals as goals. It was another to transform them into practice. The commission staff prepared a booklet, titled *Mandate for Reform,* and released it in April 1970. Around this time, former Democratic national chairman Larry O'Brien returned to the job, replacing Harris, and, in a key move, gave his support to the reform movement. Then, activity turned toward the individual states and territories. These reforms were aided by the 1970 elections, which resulted in a number of new Democratic governors—seventeen in all, including Jimmy Carter from Georgia—who led their state parties and, for the most part, vigorously supported party reform. In February 1971 the Democratic National Committee accepted the reforms—the eighteen guiding principles—of the McGovern-Fraser Commission essentially intact and made them party policy.[17]

With this action, the goals of party insurgents and reformers became the official policy of the Democratic Party. What began as a call by Hughes and others to open up the party and reduce control by party bosses was now the party's guiding principle. The transformation got relatively little media attention, and few members of the Democratic Party really understood the changes. Said Segal, "We were always waiting for some people to wake up and say, 'Hey, they're stealing our party from us,' and it never happened." Now, the opponents of reform were on the defensive.[18]

The ultimate enforcement of the new policy would come at the national convention in 1972. Toward that end, state parties got letters from the national party about the need to adhere to the reform principles, and reform groups and individuals applied grassroots pressure to follow the new rules. Media coverage of the issue increased as 1972 approached, and for the most part, it was supportive of the reformers.[19]

Hughes threw himself into an intense battle between party regulars and reformers in the fall of 1971 when he ran for temporary chairman of the credentials committee for the next year's Democratic convention. Selected by a vote of the Democratic National Committee, this position was key to seating state delegations and enforcing the new rules. Against Hughes, party regulars backed activist Patricia Harris, an African American woman associated with the Humphrey wing of the party. The contest between Hughes and Harris marked, according to R. W. Apple of the *New York Times*, "the important split in the preconvention maneuvering between the old guard and the reformers who fought bitterly in 1968."[20]

The contest between the two received national media attention. In Shafer's words, "The orthodox and alternative Democratic coalitions were locked in a conflict as intense and extensive as any in the lifetime of current committee members." Committee members faced a concentrated telephone lobbying campaign from both sides. Several Democratic presidential candidates, including George McGovern, supported Hughes; another, Representative Shirley Chisholm of New York, nominated him for the post. Labor organizations, feeling that the reforms shut them out of party decisions, strongly backed Harris; some labor leaders threatened to withhold donations to campaigns next fall if delegates supported Hughes. Though he publicly supported party reform, O'Brien opposed Hughes for the sake of "party unity." Shafer wrote that O'Brien and his staff opposed Hughes because of "his personal style, especially his reputation for being quixotic and for having a fiery temper," seeing him as a symbol of the "militant reformers." As the contest progressed, O'Brien threatened to resign if the Iowa senator was elected chairman, and he called national committee members directly and lobbied them to vote against Hughes.[21]

The result was that Hughes lost by a vote of 73–29 on October 13, 1971. Afterward, he lamented his defeat at the hands of a "political bulldozer" and claimed that organized labor had waged a campaign of "internal savagery," with spokesmen "telling people that I'm some kind of liberal nut." In his defense, Hughes added, "I'm not some kind of nut out to ruin the Democratic Party. I've been trying to rebuild and strengthen the party for three years."[22]

The loss did nothing to curtail Hughes's support for party reform. In a speech in Iowa City on November 20, 1971, he pledged to work for "the elimination of bossism and discrimination in all of the political party processes." Hughes said he intended to "fight for an open Democratic Party with all of the strength I possess and in every way that I can, whatever the political consequences to me may be." In a special hit at Chairman O'Brien's renewed hesitancy toward reform, Hughes said, "It is not enough to espouse 'party reform' in the abstract and then resort to the old politics when a specific situation develops."[23]

The party regulars may have won this battle, but they were losing the war. Although the Hughes-Harris contest got most of the media coverage, the Democratic National Committee approved rules for delegate selection that supported reform. Over the next year, the process to select convention delegates became more open. In states that chose delegates by convention, party regulars were forced to welcome any professed Democrat who wanted to participate, including those who had been shut out before. Open presidential primaries proliferated; 60 percent of the 1972 convention delegates were chosen in primaries, compared with 40 percent in the prior cycle. In these primaries, the practice of running favorite-son candidates ended, and participants voted directly for presidential candidates. The reforms abolished delegate selection that rewarded party service, and they offered more seats—often using outright quotas—to women, racial minorities, and the young. In 1972 the number of female and minority delegates tripled from four years earlier, and those younger than thirty increased tenfold.[24]

No longer would party leaders alone select candidates. The party became less important, and the organizations of individual candidates became more crucial, allowing "outsiders" to gain the presidential nomination. It is probable that neither McGovern in 1972 nor Carter in 1976 would have won the Democratic nomination under the old system. This new system was not without problems, and there were certainly reasons to lament the loss of some aspects of the old party-ruled days. As the party itself became less important, political consultants and media specialists rose to prominence, as did the need for expensive advertising and organizational networks. This made raising money a much higher priority for candidates and cast a potentially corrupting shadow over the process.

The goals that Hughes and others fought for were fairness, openness, and enhanced participatory democracy. In 1968 they saw how unfair the process could be and sought a better way. Through these reforms, they believed they had found that better way.

Few politicians arrive in Washington, DC, without the simmering dream of seeing themselves as president of the United States one day. Harold Hughes was no exception. Thanks to his personal magnetism, raw directness, and dogged work ethic, he immediately attracted attention as an aspirant to the highest office in the land.

One of the first mentions of Hughes as a presidential candidate came in August 1969 from Robert Walters of the *Washington Evening Star* in a column titled "Hughes a Dark Horse for 1972." The journalist described Hughes as someone "who is emerging as 'the man to watch,'" owing to his work on Democratic Party reform and the antiwar movement. "Perhaps most important," wrote Walters, "he has charisma. Ruggedly handsome and deep-voiced, Hughes looks and sounds like a leader. On television, he is, in the words of a female political admirer, 'a knockout.'" And at a recent Democratic fund-raiser—with McGovern and Edward Kennedy on the program—"the only spontaneous standing ovation of the evening went to Hughes."[25]

This attention to Hughes became a common theme among national political commentators. A month later Thomas Foley, Washington correspondent for the *Los Angeles Times*, wrote that "some prominent and some not-so-prominent Democrats are beginning to look with interest at Sen. Harold Hughes." Mentioning that Hughes was attracting student leaders from McCarthy's former political army, Foley added, "In this, Hughes is not unlike others. But [he] is unlike them in the charisma and dynamism that attach to him." *Newsday* columnist Nick Thimmesch called Hughes "star material" for the upcoming national ticket because "he has strong appeal to the very heartland and Western folks that went big for President Nixon." Late in 1969 David Broder of the *Washington Post*, the dean of national political correspondents, wrote, "Senator Hughes is the only Democrat around who excites the kind of personal enthusiasm the Kennedys used to generate." In the January 1970 issue of *Esquire* magazine, Hughes was listed as one of the leading dark-horse candidates for the presidency.[26]

Hughes did not downplay the presidential talk. "It's fun to be asked," he told Thimmesch. The presidential chatter was loud enough for the *Des Moines Sunday Register* to run a front-page story on December 14, 1969, titled "Hughes Dark-Horse Candidate in '72?" James Risser wrote that Hughes had "acquired somewhat of a national reputation and is often mentioned as a dark-horse Democratic candidate for president," though he added that the senator was realistic enough to know that his chances were remote. "If the lightning strikes, that's fine," said one aide. But Risser cited evidence that Hughes was positioning himself as a likely candidate—accepting national speaking engagements and national TV appearances and linking himself with organizations that could fund a presidential campaign.[27]

The Hughes presidential campaign was more than just talk and media speculation. It is unclear when Hughes gave the go-ahead, but behind the scenes, organizers were building a serious and aggressive effort to elect Hughes president. By early 1971, longtime fund-raiser Joe Rosenfield was collecting money for the campaign; he was joined in the effort by Robert Pirie, a Boston lawyer who had been deputy manager of McCarthy's presidential campaign in 1968. Rosenfield also brought in another financial heavyweight—Warren Buffett—with whom he served on the Grinnell College board of trustees. In a letter to Hughes in early January 1971, Rosenfield expressed Buffett's interest in supporting the campaign, writing, "Harold, here is a real opportunity for you, and I again urge you to act."[28]

Pirie opened an office at 41 Ivy Street, SE, in Washington, DC, with a small staff dedicated to performing background work on issues that would be vital if and when Hughes became an announced candidate. The staff contacted people around the country who supported the nascent campaign and appointed state coordinators. In an undated memo from the office written on "Hughes 72" stationery, state coordinators were told that "Senator Hughes is very seriously considering the possibility of seeking the [presidential] nomination." They were told to collect information on their respective state's delegate selection process and list the most influential party leaders, workers, and contributors, together with a plan of action for winning delegates. This was not a campaign waiting for lightning to strike; it was creating its own bolts.[29]

Publicly, Hughes dismissed these efforts as the actions of others. When asked, he said he was undecided about running and added that some people were "urging and exhorting, pushing, sometimes shouting. I'm not trying to stop it. A lot of what I do will depend on if there is enough activity to encourage me to make the try."[30]

National media coverage of the Iowa senator continued throughout early 1971, emphasizing his charisma and political appeal—as well as his strong religious beliefs. One writer called him the "liberal's Billy Graham" and "a cornfield Robert Kennedy who can unite the hardhats and convince the kids, a giant figure who could pull together the disparate forces of the Democratic party." Iowa native Hugh Sidey of *Time* magazine observed there was "a mystique about him" and added, "No man in the Senate, except perhaps Teddy Kennedy, creates the stir that Hughes does." Reporters noted that Hughes kept his distance from crowds and avoided "pressing the flesh," unlike many other politicians. In a lengthy feature on Hughes in the *Washington Post*, reporter Myra MacPherson quoted a source: "When he walks into a room, he doesn't make you feel comfortable—like 'here's a pal'—he makes you feel there is a very special presence in that room."[31]

The prospective Hughes candidacy was taken seriously by Democratic Party leader O'Brien, who invited the Iowa senator to a meeting of other potential candidates—all US senators—at the Sheraton Park Hotel in Washington in early February 1971. The three-hour meeting included McGovern, Humphrey, Kennedy, Edmund Muskie of Maine, Henry Jackson of Washington State, and Fred Harris of Oklahoma; Birch Bayh of Indiana was traveling and had met with O'Brien earlier. The Democratic chairman stressed to the candidates that their campaigns should be against Nixon, not against one another, in the hope of avoiding intraparty squabbles. One attendee characterized the meeting as one of "optimism, enthusiasm, and a total absence of backbiting." They all agreed to continue this attitude—until, of course, they did not.[32]

In early 1971 Hughes initiated a well-publicized seven-state speaking tour that included Illinois, California, and Texas. One reason for this excursion was financial: he needed the money. While governor, Hughes had made about $30,000 a year and lived rent free in the governor's mansion. As senator, he made the same amount but had monthly mortgage payments for a house he had purchased in Virginia and unexpectedly large income tax bills. Honoraria from these speeches went toward those expenses.[33]

On this tour, Hughes certainly sounded like a presidential candidate. An entourage of half a dozen Washington reporters accompanied him, and he was interviewed by local media. He was open about the potential cost of a campaign, estimating he would need $10 million. Discussing the other candidates, Hughes said he knew he might have to battle McGovern within the liberal wing of the party and lamented, "Well, that's a problem, because if George and I went against each other, the only thing people would have to judge us on would be voice and looks and personality, and I don't want that." But he offered no solution.[34]

The tour merited coverage in the *New York Times* and *Washington Post.* Apple of the *Times* called Hughes "an old-fashioned orator, one of those who hushes a hall rather than rousing it to frenzy." Broder of the *Post* gave the Iowa senator a backhanded compliment by writing, "Hughes has made no major boo-boos on this trip" and "nothing happened to make the notion of his running for President seem ridiculous." The *Des Moines Sunday Register* ran a front-page story about Hughes in March 1971. Nearly all the press coverage mentioned his unconventional rhetoric about love and reconciliation. In Chicago, for instance, Hughes said, "It is time for the resurrection and rebirth of the human spirit, so that even the least of these, the abandoned poor, the unwanted, and helpless can be helped. I ask you to reach out to each other, to know each other to love each other." Said one attendee, "This guy has the lost man in his heart. He's not thinking of himself." This was a different kind of presidential candidate.[35]

On March 20 a Hughes for President headquarters opened on Walnut Street in Des Moines. Watson Powell Jr., president and chairman of the board of the American Republic Insurance Company, was chairman of the effort, and attorney William Wimer was treasurer. Powell said more than one hundred Iowa businesspeople, labor leaders, housewives, farmers, educators, and minority group representatives were associated with the movement to elect Hughes. Wimer's wife, Connie, was in charge of the day-to-day operations of the office, which functioned primarily as a fund-raising center. One technique developed by

Bill Knapp was asking contributors to make small monthly payments to ensure a more consistent cash flow. He also established a Republicans for Hughes fund-raising effort. Together, these activities generated $20,000 a month.[36]

Iowans were evenly divided on whether Hughes should be the Democratic nominee—43 percent for and 43 percent against—according to a *Des Moines Register* poll in late March 1971. Hughes trailed Nixon 41 to 39 percent among Iowans when the two were matched in the presidential race. The only Democrat ahead of Nixon in Iowa was Muskie, 39 to 37 percent. Nationally, it was a different story. A Gallup poll in May showed Hughes with only 1 percent support. Likewise, in the all-important state of New Hampshire, where the first primary would be held, only 1 percent supported Hughes.[37]

In May the campaign hired as director and coordinator Edward A. McDermott, a Washington attorney and Iowa native who had been John Kennedy's Iowa coordinator in the 1960 presidential campaign. Sensing an unfocused campaign, McDermott gathered key supporters in Washington on June 7 with the goal of deciding whether Hughes was willing to mount "a professional effort" or should withdraw. McDermott cited a number of problems, including confusion created by Hughes's insistence on handling his own scheduling and conflicts with his Senate duties. Hughes said after the meeting, "The problem is that there is too much enthusiasm for the campaign, and too much demand on my time." He said the discussions involved "whether I should pay attention to what I consider my major responsibility here in the Senate, or whether I should get both eyes on the White House and the nomination." Ultimately, the meeting resolved nothing.[38]

It was not politics that ended the Hughes presidential campaign. It was Harold Hughes himself.

Far more than most politicians, Hughes was vocal about his religious views. His strong Christian faith had been central to his recovery from the depths of alcoholism, and he freely discussed his faith with others—in person and publicly in speeches. Often he defined his liberalism in Christian terms, occasionally quoting Bible passages to justify government programs for the needy. This made some people uncomfortable. After one Hughes speech, a leader of New York's intellectual left was overheard remarking to a friend, "I didn't mind the God bit but this eternity crap is too much for me."[39]

In his memoir, Hughes detailed what could be described as a "born-again" Christian experience leading to his recovery from alcoholism, although he did not use that term. Hughes was a Methodist, which is generally considered a mainstream denomination. Hughes believed in a personal relationship with Christ and in the power of prayer. He was not a Christian fundamentalist, if that term is defined as a belief that every word of the Bible is true and salvation is available only through a belief in Christ. He acknowledged that the Bible contains a lot of mythology and that other religions offer deliverance and redemption to sincere believers. Christianity was simply *his* religion. About the impact of his faith on politics, he said, "It helps me refine my own being by better understanding myself and other beings, their concerns. It inspires me to believe in the brotherhood of man. I believe in . . . love rather than fear, that there is a place for everyone, the blind, lame, poor, convict, alcoholic. Isn't that a measurement of civilization, how man cares for his brother?"[40]

Though much of Hughes's Christian faith was conventional, some of it was not, and he adopted beliefs from other realms. Referring to Hughes, his friend Vance Bourjaily wrote, "There are guys who just won't stop growing." When Dwight and Pat Jensen were deciding whether to accompany Hughes to Washington after his election to the Senate, Pat and Hughes spent some time together discussing the move. She recalled that the conversation soon turned to theology, and Hughes admitted that he questioned several aspects of conventional Christianity. According to Pat, "It was not that [Hughes said] 'I'm absolute about this or absolute about that. I'm trying to find more. I want to know more.' It was more the questioning and pondering." His library contained a number of books on philosophy, religion, mysticism, and metaphysics. He freely admitted to reporters that he believed in extrasensory perception (ESP). According to Hughes's daughter Phyllis, one person who assisted Hughes in exploring alternative religious beliefs was Gene Kieffer, a communications specialist from Des Moines who worked on several campaigns.[41]

Hughes, like most Christians, believed in the immortality of the soul and that a moral life lived according to Christ's teachings will be rewarded with eternal salvation in heaven. He also believed in talking with God through prayer and in divine intervention in everyday life. In addition, he showed an interest in spiritualism, the belief that people can communicate with deceased loved ones. In 1967 Hughes and Russell Wilson attended a meeting of the Spiritual Frontiers Fellowship in Chicago, a gathering of paranormal enthusiasts such as psychics, faith healers, and spiritual mediums. The pair participated in séances conducted by Arthur Ford, a prominent medium, and Irene Hughes (no relation), a columnist on psychic phenomena. Ford claimed to contact a spirit who spoke to Wilson about his work on ICAP and wished him well; after the session, Hughes revealed that he knew this person, who had worked with alcoholics. Irene Hughes claimed to speak for former vice president Henry Wallace, who urged the governor to run for the Senate and seek aid from Wallace's son, who was living in Des Moines.[42]

At the mid-1971 meeting called by McDermott, Hughes discussed these unconventional views, including his belief that God spoke to him directly. Sherwin Markman, now a Washington attorney and legal adviser to the presidential campaign, was present and recalled, "That conversation, which was quite private in his office, was overheard in the ductwork." Shortly afterward, the exchange became a topic of conversation among Washington journalists and was linked with other stories about Hughes participating in séances and talking with departed souls.[43]

This raised the interest of the Washington office of the *Des Moines Register.* "We had been hearing some rumors," recalled reporter Risser, "not whispering campaigns, but there were people around who were saying things like they understood that Hughes believed that he talked to dead people." Risser and fellow *Register* correspondent George Anthan approached Park Rinard, who was initially hesitant to grant an interview on the subject. "We kind of wanted to do it in a responsible way," said Risser:

> We didn't want to go in and just try to do something sort of flamboyant and perhaps in some way wreck his career. But if people were going to talk about his beliefs in spiritualism and so forth and, if he was possibly going to be a candidate for president, this information was going to have to come out at some point anyway. I think we convinced Hughes and his people that we would do it in a responsible way. . . . Hughes was not happy with us doing the story in the first place but I think he understood that this was going to have to come out and he was better off talking to us than the *National Enquirer* or whatever.[44]

The interview was granted, and the result was a story on the front page of the July 11, 1971, edition of the *Des Moines Sunday Register* that effectively ended Hughes's presidential campaign. The key revelation, buried several paragraphs into the story, was that Hughes believed he had talked, through a medium, with the spirit of his dead brother Jesse for about an hour. "It seemed real to me," he said, confirming that he had taken part in several séances. The senator said he had heard things through the medium that only his brother would know; the medium also provided other information that Hughes did not know about but later found out was correct. He expounded on his belief in ESP, faith healing, and spiritualism, including his belief that certain people have the ability to predict the future. "What are the prophets of the Bible if not looking into the future?" he asked. He reaffirmed that he belonged to the Spiritual Frontiers Fellowship and the British Psychic Research Foundation. At one point, Hughes said of his admissions, "If these are a block to me becoming president, then so be it. I've left too many footprints all over the country to deny it even if I wanted to, which I don't."[45]

Four days later, Hughes announced at a Washington press conference that he was ending his undeclared presidential campaign. He ignored the religious issues and insisted that he was withdrawing because he could not be a presidential candidate and a US senator at the same time. "My legislative efforts have been hampered, and my public statements have been discounted by imputation of presidential motives," he said. "I am now convinced that my greatest value to my country and to my state is to pursue the goals to which I am committed as a United States Senator, unimpeded by the label of presidential candidate."[46]

Mary McGory of the *Washing Evening Star* may have put it best: "While Hughes wanted to be president, he didn't want to be a presidential candidate." Hughes was sincerely torn between campaigning for president and working on his alcohol and drug assistance programs. He also intensely disliked personal fund-raising, although money did not seem to be a problem. Only days before his announcement, Hughes had been approached by two wealthy contributors from California who offered him significant funds each month until the convention. In return, they wanted only a firm commitment that he would remain in the race. But some people found his direct manner off-putting. At one point, Bill Knapp and Hughes were at a fund-raiser with Jewish supporters of Israel in New York City, and Hughes said to them, "I appreciate your help, but if you think I'm going to give Israel a blank check, you've got the wrong guy." Knapp recalled, "You could have heard a pin drop." Hughes also felt hemmed in by a diverse group of supporters who were constantly urging him to adopt political strategies not attuned to his political style.

Harold Hughes was being pressured to not be Harold Hughes, and he did not like it.[47]

Also, a presidential campaign would have been rough on Hughes's family life. According to daughter Phyllis, Eva was "in a downward spiral emotionally"; her mother "required a lot of maintenance at that point" and "was not up to the task at all." Hughes's middle daughter, Carol, also had health problems. Ultimately, said Phyllis, "he just didn't have the fire in the belly for it."[48]

Hughes thought his every action was seen through the prism of a possible presidential candidacy. When he was in Harlem investigating street drugs, one reporter asked whether Hughes had made the trip to gain publicity for his presidential campaign. Said one staffer, "I looked at the expression on Hughes's face and I knew right there that the presidential campaign was over."[49]

The religious revelations in the *Des Moines Register* may not have been the cause of his withdrawal. By that time, he may have already decided to end the campaign. One supporter said, "When he decided to give that interview, I decided that the presidential thing was over. And Hughes felt like a free man."[50]

19 | Secret Bombing over North Vietnam

On March 3, 1972, a one-page letter arrived in Hughes's Washington office from Lonnie Franks, a twenty-three-year-old Cedar Rapids, Iowa, native and intelligence specialist at the Udorn Air Force Base in Thailand. In the letter, Franks brazenly admitted that he and others "have been falsifying classified reports for missions into North Viet Nam." Moreover, the Iowan wrote, his superior officer had ordered him to lie about bombing missions; that officer, in turn, had been following orders from higher up the chain of command. Franks was unsure where the order to falsify documents originated, but he had been told "the President probably doesn't even know about the situation." Franks wanted Hughes to know what was going on and asked "if this falsification of classified documents is legal and proper."[1]

Hughes was well positioned to act on these revelations because he was, by this time, a member of the Senate Armed Services Committee. He had sought the appointment when a seat opened up after the 1970 elections, and he had been supported by like-minded senators who wanted to add a liberal perspective to the committee. Said Hughes, "Those in the Senate who think we're too military oriented usually have to wait until something is approved by the committee before they can find out much about it, and then have to try to fight it on the floor." With Hughes trading his seat on the Banking and Currency Committee for one on the Armed Services Committee, liberals gained a key, critically placed voice on military issues.[2]

That voice was often lonely. The members of Armed Services were some of the most conservative Senate personalities of the era. The committee was headed by archconservative John Stennis of Mississippi, although he and Hughes bonded and became unlikely friends through the weekly congressional prayer breakfast. Other conservatives on the committee were Barry Goldwater of Arizona, John Tower of Texas, Harry Byrd of Virginia, and Strom Thurmond of South Carolina—strong military supporters all.[3]

The actions described by Franks—US aerial bombing of North Vietnam—had a long and controversial history. Initiated in 1965 as Operation Rolling Thunder, bombing marked a significant escalation of the US military commitment to the Vietnam War. Critics questioned whether bombing—typically used to destroy industrial sites—would have any effect on an overwhelmingly agrarian society like North Vietnam. Its dubious goal was to stop the North Vietnamese from supplying aid to their Vietcong allies in South Vietnam. In March 1968 President Johnson reduced bombing throughout much of North Vietnam as an incentive for peace talks. Later that year, he halted all bombing of the north in a failed effort to reach a peace agreement with the Vietnamese communists. The bombing halt remained in place under President Nixon as peace talks continued in Paris and Henry Kissinger, Nixon's national security adviser, held secret negotiations with the North Vietnamese. By early 1972, the official policy on military action over North Vietnam—the rules of engagement, as they were called—allowed reconnaissance flights to monitor troop movements and military equipment and gather other intelligence. To protect these flights, bombers accompanied them and were allowed to attack targets only if the planes were fired upon or tracked by enemy radar. This was called "protective reaction."[4]

This was the clear and established policy when Lonnie Franks was assigned to interview pilots after they completed their missions and write classified reports. A graduate of Washington High School in Cedar Rapids, Franks attended college in Iowa but decided to join the US Air Force before finishing his degree. Now a staff sergeant, he was assigned to the 432nd Tactical Reconnaissance Wing of Seventh Air Force at Udorn Air Force Base in northern Thailand, where flights over North Vietnam originated.[5]

On January 25, 1972, Franks interviewed a pair of pilots who had just completed a reconnaissance mission. Their accompanying F-4 fighter-bombers had dropped bombs, even though they had encountered no enemy fire. The pilots, however, had been ordered to report that they had been fired upon; Franks, in turn, was ordered to include this false information in his classified report. Disturbed, he checked with his supervisor, who told him to fabricate details about North Vietnamese antiaircraft fire and "make it look real"; he told Franks, "just make up some sort of hostile reaction." After reconfirming this order further up the chain of command, Franks created a story that the reconnaissance plane had been subjected to ten to fifteen rounds of antiaircraft strikes.[6]

As Franks examined the so-called reconnaissance mission, he realized that it had been anything but an intelligence operation. "The mission was pretty well planned," he recalled. "They were military targets—petroleum locations, munitions areas, military materials. Targets were supplies and troops, rather than defensive bombing of surface-to-air missiles or antiaircraft artillery—in violation of the established rules of engagement."[7]

In all, according to Franks, more than seventy-five of these bombing missions were initiated from Udorn, with more than two hundred people involved in falsely reporting the raids. (The air force later claimed there were only twenty-four unauthorized missions.) What particularly distressed Franks was the elaborate three-hour procedure needed to falsify the reports—or, as he put it, to "get the wrong information right." That is when he decided to write the letter to Hughes.[8]

Coincidentally, the day Hughes received the letter, he was scheduled to have a lunch meeting with US Air Force chief of staff John Ryan, a native of Cherokee, Iowa. Less than a week later, Ryan dispatched the air force inspector general, Lieutenant General Louis Wilson Jr., to Southeast Asia to investigate. Wilson interviewed the pilots flying the missions, the commanders, and those reporting the missions, including Franks.[9]

Among those interviewed was General John D. Lavelle, who, only seven months earlier, had begun his job as commander of Seventh Air Force. When presented with the forged documents, Lavelle claimed to be astonished. He explained that he had had a conversation in Saigon with secretary of defense Melvin Laird on December 8, 1971, who gave him permission to make "a liberal interpretation of the rules of engagement in the field." This was reconfirmed through a Joint Chiefs of Staff representative at a meeting in Honolulu the next month, who conveyed the opinion that field commanders were "not nearly as aggressive as they should have been." By this time, the North Vietnamese had deployed sophisticated air defense systems that could detect and lock on to US aircraft, giving pilots little or no warning of a missile attack. Since the pilots could be hit at any time, they were free to drop their bombs without being fired upon, under the "liberal interpretation" implemented by Lavelle.[10]

During a mission on January 23, 1972, Lavelle ordered a preplanned "protective strike" against a North Vietnamese airfield that had been the source of attacks on US ships and planes. As the pilots returned, they radioed that the mission had been successful, with "no enemy reaction," meaning they had not been fired upon. When Lavelle heard this, he snapped to his director of operations that they could not report "no reaction." The pilots, he said, "must report reaction." Lavelle later said that he meant the pilots should report "hostile radar"—that is, they should assume radar was locked on to the US jets and they were therefore free to bomb. However, Lavelle did not explain this clearly. Those under his command took this to mean that they must report enemy action or enemy fire, whether they were fired upon or not. In other words, they felt compelled to lie to meet the rules of engagement requirements. This misunderstanding led to the complex system of falsifying documents that Franks complained about to Hughes.[11] (The bombing-related rules of engagement were removed by President Nixon in May 1972, after the North Vietnamese initiated a spring offensive. At this time, the US military initiated a bombing campaign over North Vietnam that lasted until the end of US involvement in early 1973.)[12]

After Inspector General Wilson submitted his report to Ryan, Lavelle was summoned to Washington, DC, where he was given the choice of retiring or remaining in the military at a reduced rank. He chose retirement—but he still lost two of his four stars. This was an unusual move by the Pentagon, which typically retires generals at their highest rank. The Pentagon initially announced that Lavelle was retiring "for personal and health reasons," but media probing and congressional questioning forced the Pentagon to issue a revised statement on May 15, admitting that Lavelle had been relieved of command due to "irregularities in the conduct of his command responsibilities." To many, this seemed like a cover-up.[13]

That did not sit well with Hughes. Who, he asked, had given the original orders to Lavelle, and how high up did this go? Was Lavelle simply the scapegoat once the unauthorized bombings were uncovered? Behind the scenes, Hughes pushed to get to the bottom of the deceptive bombing reports and the details behind Lavelle's retirement, which Hughes considered a "slap on the wrist." He pressed Stennis again and again to hold hearings before the Armed Services Committee, but the Mississippi senator thought that was unnecessary. Hughes threatened to hold up Lavelle's nomination for retirement as lieutenant general until Stennis agreed to hold hearings. While on a flight to Montana to inspect a military base, the two senators had, in Hughes's words, "a bitter confrontation." Stennis finally relented and scheduled full-scale hearings for September 1972.[14]

On June 12 Generals Ryan and Lavelle testified before a House Armed Services subcommittee. Ryan said that, prior to relieving Lavelle, he was assured there had been no military authorization to break the rules of engagement—despite winks and nods from Secretary Laird and the Joint Chiefs—and there certainly had been no orders to falsify classified reports. Lavelle admitted that his order prohibiting reports of "no reaction" resulted in his subordinates feeling the need to falsify classified documents. Ryan stated there were twenty-eight unauthorized missions; Lavelle contended there were only twenty. Ryan and Lavelle were the only two military officers appearing before the House committee. Left unanswered were questions about why Lavelle was allowed a "liberal interpretation" of the rules of engagement and the origin of that permission within the chain of command.[15]

After these hearings, Hughes took to the floor of the US Senate and asked how "the actions of a single combat commander, authorizing persistent violations of established orders over a period of four months, [can] trigger a spiraling escalation of hostilities?" Citing the nearly thirty violations of the rules of engagement mentioned in Ryan's testimony, Hughes roared that they defied the policy "established by the President, the Secretary of Defense, and the Joint Chiefs of Staff." Hughes said he was "deeply disturbed by a system which permits these unauthorized attacks and then conceals them until a courageous airman writes to a member of the U.S. Senate."[16]

On June 20, when President Nixon nominated Admiral Thomas Moorer for another term as chairman of the Joint Chiefs of Staff and General Creighton Abrams to be army chief of staff, Hughes used his authority as a member of the Armed Services Committee to block action until the nominees could be questioned about the Lavelle case.[17]

In the meantime, life was becoming uncomfortable for Franks at Udorn. A few individuals on the base knew about his letter to Hughes, and some of them, in Franks's words, "made it clear that I should not sleep with my eyes closed." He asked for and received a transfer and ended up in Orlando, Florida, transitioning from an intelligence specialist to a typist —"a bit of punishment," he recalled.[18]

Franks was contacted by dogged investigative journalist Seymour Hersh, who had recently uncovered the massacre of Vietnamese civilians in My Lai by US servicemen. After interviewing Franks for four hours in Orlando and checking with other sources, Hersh outed Franks as the writer of the letter to Hughes in a front-page story in the *New York Times* on September 7, 1972. Hersh provided significant details about the falsification of documents, along with the Iowan's claim that there had been more than seventy-five unauthorized missions, not the twenty to twenty-eight admitted by the air force generals. More importantly, the story described the widespread awareness of the deception at Udorn, including the claim by Franks that more than two hundred individuals had taken part in it. Said one air force officer at Udorn: "All I can say is, yes, we did it. But I didn't like what I was doing."[19]

The Senate Armed Services Committee held hearings on the bombings behind closed doors from September 12 to 19, taking a much deeper look at the controversy than the House committee had. There was finger-pointing and blame thrown back and forth between high-ranking military officials. During his many hours of testimony, Lavelle modified his story, telling the senators that he had received permission from General Abrams, commander of US forces in Vietnam, and Admiral Moorer of the Joint Chiefs to initiate the bombing raids over North Vietnam. Lavelle claimed he had "written instructions" as well as constant verbal urging to be "more aggressive" within the rules of engagement. Outside the closed-door meetings, Hughes said Lavelle's testimony "supported my thesis that higher authorities have major responsibilities" in connection with the unauthorized air strikes.[20]

Following Lavelle, Abrams and Moorer contradicted some of the earlier testimony. Abrams said he had never been told that the controversial raids were unauthorized; he knew about them but did not know they were conducted outside the rules of engagement. Moorer also denied knowledge of the unauthorized strikes.[21]

Testimony from Major General Alton Slay, the intermediary between Lavelle and the air strike forces, laid the blame on Lavelle. "Lavelle knew, sir, that regardless of whether there was a reaction or not, it would be reported that there would be reaction. He knew that because he directed it." Slay, interviewed by the committee in a Denver hospital where he was recovering from surgery, said Lavelle had personally ordered him to stage unauthorized bombing missions into North Vietnam and demanded that the official reports be falsified. He added, "I accepted the fact that General Lavelle would not be such a damned fool to go about this on his own."[22]

Amidst the high-level military blame game, Lonnie Franks testified for more than three hours before the Senate Armed Services Committee on September 14, detailing the extensive efforts he and others exerted to falsify reports. Franks explained that when he protested the filing of false reports to superiors, he was simply told to follow orders and fabricate lies.[23] Said Hughes:

> The testimony of Lonnie Franks makes it very clear that the entire top command of the 7th Air Force was involved in the pre-planning of unauthorized reports and in the conspiracy to hide the unauthorized bombing with false reports. There is no question in my mind that this pattern of pre-planning unauthorized strikes would have continued up until all restrictions were lifted on bombing in the North if Sergeant Franks hadn't blown the whistle.[24]

When the dust settled after the Senate hearings, little was immediately clear. The most common takeaway from the investigation was that the military and its civilian leadership wanted more aggressive aerial attacks over North Vietnam in late 1971 and early 1972 but wanted to stay within the rules of engagement as much as possible. The orders given to Lavelle brought actions to the edge of the policy limits and probably beyond. Lavelle's misstep with his "no reaction" comment led to a chain of events that compelled his subordinates to lie, and Franks's letter exposed that deceit.

In a summarizing speech on the Senate floor, Hughes remarked that, seven months after the air force started its investigation, "we are only beginning to get at the truth." He contended that the "basic issue is whether the civilians have lost control over the military, and the military has lost control over itself." He lamented that the military had initiated unauthorized bombing in defiance of the pause and falsified reports, yet other than Lavelle, no one "has been counseled, admonished, reprimanded, or punished." Furthermore, Hughes said, "nothing of any significance has been done to prevent a recurrence of these improper activities." The senator was sympathetic to Lavelle, who, he said, "was understandably in a bind . . . ordered to be more aggressive, but denied the authority to carry out these orders." Given this dilemma, "he chose to break the rules, and his unit was forced to conceal the actions with falsified reports." Hughes added that the president could have changed the policy to make proactive bombing legal—which he did in May—but chose not to because, "for some reason, it was never the 'proper time' for such a change." In other words, Hughes—without concrete proof—accused the Nixon administration of pressuring the military to initiate proactive bombing over North Vietnam without changing its policy for fear of causing negative public reaction. When the flaunted rules were exposed, Lavelle became the scapegoat.[25]

Hughes continued to pressure the Department of Defense to investigate the disparity between civilian policy and the execution of that policy in the field, as well as look into the forced retirement of Lavelle. On October 11 Hughes announced he would block the promotions of all navy and air force officers who participated in air operations during the period of the unauthorized strikes unless the navy and air force fully investigated and disclosed their findings.[26]

Ultimately, his efforts were to no avail. On October 24 the secretary of the air force dismissed all charges against Lavelle, contending that the punitive effect of removing the general from command was sufficient to discourage any future acts. Shortly thereafter, Laird issued a statement that "no further inquiry by the Department is necessary to determine the facts." As far as the Pentagon was concerned, the book was closed on the issue. Hughes disagreed and protested, but there was little he could do. He eventually released his mass hold on promotions.[27]

More than three decades later, with the declassification of Nixon's Oval Office tapes and Joint Chiefs of Staff message traffic, it was revealed that senior military officials had approved the strikes ordered by Lavelle, and they later received "unequivocal authorization" from President Nixon. The military documents show that on November 8, 1971, Admiral Moorer personally approved proactive bombing, giving Lavelle the go-ahead. In 1972, when asked why Lavelle had been relieved of command, Moorer responded, "a violation of instructions." In fact, the instructions were very clear: dramatically bend the rules and bomb North Vietnam. The records show similar approvals by Laird and Abrams in December. There is no direct evidence that Nixon knew about the expanded bombing at this stage, although it is likely that he did. However, in a White House meeting on February 3, 1972, Nixon approved expansion of "the definition of protective reaction" in front of Kissinger and Ambassador Ellsworth Bunker, US envoy to South Vietnam, who was in overall charge of all US operations in Vietnam. Nixon told Bunker to instruct Abrams that he could proactively hit sites in North Vietnam. "But he is not to do it with a public declaration," said Nixon. "All right?

And, if it does get out, to the extent it does, he says it's a protective re-action strike."[28]

The military had received direct orders from the president to bend—if not break—the rules set by Nixon himself. But, given that 1972 was an election year, he wanted these orders kept secret, fearing a strongly negative public reaction to an escalation of the war. When the secret did "get out," the US military turned on Lavelle and blamed him for violating policy. Hughes strongly suspected that Lavelle was a scapegoat but, given military intransigence, could not prove it at the time. The whole episode might have been swept under the rug if not for the honesty of a brave young man from Cedar Rapids and the tenacity of a US senator from Iowa.

20 | Election Defeats and Victories and a Maverick War Critic

Throughout 1972, Hughes remained a staunch critic of the Vietnam War, reflected in the legislation he supported and the speeches he made around the country. As President Nixon sought reelection that year, he was largely successful at reducing US combat deaths through his Vietnamization policy and troop withdrawals, decreasing much of the negative media coverage and taking Americans' minds off the war. That changed when North Vietnam launched what became known as the Easter offensive and the administration responded with an intense bombing campaign to pressure the communists to give up and talk peace.[1]

The escalation in bombing, combined with the mining of North Vietnam's Haiphong Harbor, generated an immediate response from Hughes. He said these actions put the United States "at the brink of World War III." He believed this would prompt a response by the Soviet Union or China and turn the war into "a confrontation with the great nuclear super-powers." Hughes lamented that the United States was "perpetuating the killing to preserve a corrupt dictatorship in Saigon" and called for Congress to cut off all funds for the war. Hughes was clearly wrong about the international response. After Nixon's celebrated trip to China in early 1972, the Asian giant virtually ignored the bombing escalation. The Soviets did much the same, welcoming Nixon to Russia for a summit after mildly criticizing the enhanced US military effort.[2]

Protests against the expanded bombing—on Capitol Hill and on American streets—did little to change Nixon's conduct of the war. If the president's policy could not be changed, reasoned Hughes, it was time to change the president. With Hughes himself out of the presidential picture, he endorsed Senator Edmund Muskie of Maine as his choice for the Democratic nomination. On January 18, 1972, one week before the Iowa caucuses, Hughes held a joint press conference with Muskie in Des Moines and said the former vice-presidential candidate possessed "the guts and poise of leadership." Hughes revealed that he had initiated the endorsement: "I called him—he didn't call me." "It is apparent," remarked Hughes, "that Senator Muskie has stood the acid test of the front-runner."[3]

At the time, this appeared to be true. Muskie was leading in the polls among Democrats and had pulled even with Nixon, 43 to 43 percent, in a national Harris poll. He was the favorite among many establishment Democrats and was certainly more popular than George McGovern, who was challenging Muskie from the party's liberal wing. While campaigning in Iowa, McGovern had asked for Hughes's endorsement, and Hughes refused. McGovern was reportedly "bitterly disappointed," believing he would receive his colleague's backing. In an article he wrote for *New Republic*, Hughes said he had endorsed Muskie in the hope of avoiding the divisive nomination fight of 1968. "No Democrat wants a replay of that nightmare," he noted. In typical Hughes fashion, he admitted that Muskie's campaign "has not always turned me on," and he did not know if his explanations "will please the Muskie campaign staff or reassure my liberal friends who are supporting other candidates." Nevertheless, he believed a Muskie nomination, representing the moderate wing of the party, would best unify Democrats.[4]

Held on January 24, 1972, the Iowa caucuses—as they would so often in the future—upset conventional political expectations. Although Muskie won the largest share of delegates—35.5 percent to McGovern's 22.6 percent—the win, according to R. W. Apple of the *New York Times*, was "clouded by the unexpectedly strong showing of Senator George McGovern." Apple noted that the win was big enough to show that Muskie was not stumbling but not big enough to indicate a bandwagon psychology, especially as one-third of the delegates were uncommitted to any candidate. Given the more open presidential selection process, many saw Iowa as a loss for Muskie.[5]

This was the first of several setbacks for the Muskie campaign in the months ahead, caused by his own stumbling and "dirty tricks" later revealed to originate from the Nixon campaign. For example, the Nixon tricksters sent a fake letter to a newspaper, claiming that Muskie had laughed at a pejorative reference to French Canadians as Canucks. Muskie responded to this false report at a tear-filled press conference in New Hampshire. This breakdown was seen as a sign of weakness, and it doomed the Muskie campaign there.[6]

In the meantime, Hughes stumped for Muskie in Illinois, Ohio, and Michigan but failed to lift the flagging campaign. Muskie lost the Florida and Wisconsin primaries, and McGovern, benefiting from the support of antiwar organizations and the reform effort that aided insurgent candidates, rolled closer to the nomination. In early April, after Muskie suffered a series of second-place finishes, Hughes and Missouri senator Thomas Eagleton, another key supporter, traveled to Muskie's home in Maine and urged him to limit his active campaigning to several key primaries rather than competing hard in all of them. After twin defeats in Massachusetts and Pennsylvania later that month, Muskie faced the inevitable and suspended his campaign on April 27 due to a lack of funds. On the day of the announcement, Muskie called Hughes three times, the last to inform him of his decision. "He did exactly the opposite of what I advised him," said Hughes. "I advised him to go on, whether he has any money or not, and do the best job he can." Hughes said he would still support Muskie "unless he is eliminated completely as a candidate."[7]

McGovern continued to collect delegates, but many Democrats feared a landslide loss if he was their standard-bearer in the fall. Thus, Muskie started to look more attractive as the convention neared. Muskie asked Hughes to attend a governors' conference in Houston in early June to assess the political sentiment and the possibility of a convention deadlock leading to a revival of Muskie's candidacy. After meeting with a number of governors, Hughes walked away with the consensus that Muskie should sit tight as an inactive candidate and await further developments. There was no effort to take any active steps on his behalf. The irony was that Hughes, the leader of party insurgents in 1968, was now working on behalf of the more traditional Democratic hopeful.[8]

Despite McGovern's victory in the California primary in June, he was still short of the delegates needed to win the nomination. Days later, Muskie announced his decision not to bow out of the race in a speech at the National Press Club in Washington. He paid tribute to Hughes's "leadership" and blasted McGovern's positions as "unacceptable to a very large portion of our people." Hughes issued a statement after the speech, saying, "I will continue my support of the senator from Maine."[9]

At a press conference on June 14 with Hughes at his side, Muskie announced that he was reigniting his campaign in a quixotic effort to offer himself as a "viable alternative" if the Miami Beach convention deadlocked. Said one Muskie aide, borrowing Hughes's earlier language, "If lightning strikes, we want to be the tree." The two senators then boarded a small chartered jet for a weeklong ten-state tour, targeting states with uncommitted delegates and those that had not yet elected delegates. By this time, McGovern was estimated to have 1,350 of the 1,500 delegates needed for the nomination, and any chance of stopping him was a long shot at best.[10]

Hughes had taken complete control of the Muskie campaign organization and directed Park Rinard, Bill Knapp, Martin Jensen, Ed Campbell, Sherwin Markman, and other associates to work on the effort. Publicly, the Iowa senator said he was continuing to back Muskie because he stood a better chance against Nixon in the fall. Behind the scenes, some politicos charged that Hughes resented McGovern. Said one former Hughes aide now working for McGovern, "Hughes is kicking himself all over the place for dropping out of the president race so soon, because he now sees McGovern as being where he could have been." Another former Hughes worker said, "Now that McGovern has done so well, Hughes is a bit jealous because he views himself as more forceful and dynamic than McGovern, in every way better suited to be president than McGovern. He does not intend to be anti-McGovern but there's some ego involved." Hughes denied all this speculation, saying, "I don't know of any strife between us on anything. I have nothing against George McGovern, and if he gets the nomination, I'll support him to the full extent I can."[11]

Hughes dedicated himself to the Muskie effort up until the convention in Miami, even though he found himself at odds with the candidate over tactics. The anti-McGovern forces, including Muskie, fought to deny the South Dakota senator the entire California delegation, which he had won by finishing first in the primary. The winner-take-all rule remained in place in California, in defiance of party reformers' recommendations. If McGovern retained the California delegates, the nomination was his. Despite his support for Muskie, Hughes firmly opposed the effort to deny McGovern the California delegates, calling it changing the rules after the game had been played. "I've told Senator Muskie how I feel about that," he said. "He understands my feelings."[12]

Conflicted, Hughes gave little leadership to the Iowa delegation, which voted 27–19 to seat the entire California delegation for McGovern. "Hughes is in a terrible box," said Iowa delegate Lee Gaudineer, a state senator from Des Moines. "He's got to vote for McGovern, but he wanted the outcome to go the other way." The convention voted to award McGovern the California delegation, and after the vote, both Muskie and Hubert Humphrey, a recently declared candidate, announced they were dropping out. Like most other Democrats, Hughes endorsed McGovern, who won 36 of 46 Iowa delegates in the final vote and became the Democratic nominee.[13]

Hughes's support for McGovern was qualified and defensive. He could read the polls and, more important, the mood of his state and the country. Yet, in remarks to the Iowa delegation, he denied that McGovern was a liberal "Goldwater-in-reverse" who would drag down state and local Democrats. Hughes disagreed with McGovern on some issues, "or at least [I] am confused by him on some," but he added, "in the coming weeks I am sure he will clearly and accurately state his position on all the issues." In a letter to a constituent in Sioux City, Hughes wrote that McGovern was not the best candidate for the party, but he was the nominee, and it was Hughes's "obligation as titular head of the Party in Iowa to support him to the best of my ability when I can and when called on." This was hardly a rousing endorsement.[14]

It surprised few people when McGovern lost overwhelmingly to Nixon in 1972, carrying only Massachusetts and the District of Columbia. There was a significant surprise in Iowa, however, when a little-known but hardworking and very well-organized Democratic candidate was elected to the US Senate, beating two-term incumbent Jack Miller. This upset win by Dick Clark was assisted, in part, by Hughes and his Senate staff.

A former history professor at Upper Iowa College in Fayette and an aide to Congressman John Culver, Dick Clark spent much of 1971 organizing in Iowa for Culver's potential Senate race against Jack Miller the next year. In addition to organizing party volunteers, Clark helped build a statewide voter identification profile (VIP) system to identify likely Democratic supporters and get them to the polls on Election Day. When Culver decided in early 1972 against running for the Senate and chose instead to seek reelection to the House, Clark decided to use the organization he had helped create to run for the Senate himself. A political unknown, Clark began a well-publicized walk around the state, meeting voters and building his name identification Iowan by Iowan. Still, the Democrat faced an uphill battle against Republican Miller, who had won reelection six years earlier by carrying all ninety-nine counties in Iowa. As late as mid-September 1972, Miller had a 55 percent approval rating among Iowa voters, according to a *Des Moines Register* poll. On October 1 the poll showed Miller ahead of Clark, 58 to 35 percent.

With such a big lead, Miller saw no reason to campaign hard or to take his opponent seriously.[15]

The liberal Hughes and the conservative Miller represented opposite forces in the US Senate, and they often canceled out each other's votes. Miller was known as a loyal Nixon administration supporter, and Hughes stood out as a fierce Nixon critic. It was easy to understand why Hughes looked for opportunities to make Miller's reelection as difficult as possible. One opportunity appeared on the Senate floor when Miller introduced a tax bill amendment that was accepted without vote or discussion. Curious about the amendment, Hughes asked his staff to look into it, and they reported back that the meaning of the arcane amendment was unclear. He then directed senior staffer Martin Jensen to contact the *Register*'s Washington staff, and a reporter contacted Miller to inquire about the amendment. The senator said it was a minor correction of a mistake in the tax code and that he—a former tax attorney—was probably one of the few people who truly understood it.[16]

Unsatisfied with Miller's explanation, the reporter dug further and discovered that the amendment had originated at the request of Tommy "The Cork" Corcoran, a longtime lobbyist who had started his career in the Franklin Roosevelt administration. The amendment benefited a Bermuda reinsurance company to the tune of several million dollars in tax savings and no doubt helped Corcoran as well. The *Register* splashed the exposé on the front page just days before the election, forcing Miller on the defensive. When the dust settled, Clark had won the Senate seat, 55 to 44 percent, in a ticket-splitting vote that saw both Nixon and Republican governor Robert Ray win Iowa handily. Clark's organizational talents and his yearlong walk around Iowa certainly helped him win, as did Miller's overconfidence and lack of a real campaign. But the last-minute Miller scandal—a present from Harold Hughes—also aided the political underdog.[17]

The year 1973 was one of frustration and uphill political battles for Hughes. It began with an announcement by the Nixon administration that an agreement had been reached with North Vietnam to end the US commitment to the conflict, but this came at the price of a fierce and violent bombing campaign. During the twelve-day so-called Christmas bombing to pressure the Vietnamese communists to renew negotiations, Nixon ordered more than thirty-six thousand tons of bombs dropped over North Vietnam, exceeding the tonnage during the entire 1969–1971 period. The bombing destroyed major sections of Hanoi and Haiphong and killed as many as sixteen hundred civilians.[18]

Hughes called the bombing an "unbelievable holocaust" that "cannot be justified on any grounds." His Senate office received dozens of letters from Iowans and others protesting the bombing. He learned of several protests taking place in Iowa and sent telegrams and letters of support to the demonstrators. "At this point," he said, "I wouldn't believe anything the President says on the war. . . . His credibility has been broken so many times on this issue."[19]

Negotiations in Paris finally resumed on January 8, and later that month, all parties signed a treaty that ended US participation in the Vietnam War. This concluded decades of US efforts to preserve the South Vietnamese government, at the cost of more than fifty-eight thousand US combat deaths and countless American lives shattered in both Vietnam and the United States. During the twelve years of the Vietnam War, 842 Iowans died, including those killed in combat and as a result of nonhostile action. The last Iowa fatality was twenty-four-year-old Dwight Cook, an air force lieutenant from rural Center Point; he was reported missing over Laos on January 17, only ten days before the Paris Peace Accords were signed. Wrote Hughes to a Boone constituent, "Now this long, ghastly ordeal is over and the overriding need is for the unification and reconciliation of our people."[20]

But the Vietnam War was not over for Hughes. The Iowa senator was involved in a lonely campaign to obtain information about the unauthorized bombing of North Vietnam. As a member of the Armed Services Committee, Hughes threatened in early January to hold up air force and navy promotions until the services agreed to produce a full report on unauthorized bombing strikes against North Vietnam between November 1, 1971, and April 1, 1972, including a full list of officers participating. By March, Hughes had targeted the promotions of 158 officers with possible connections to the bombings.[21]

The Pentagon refused to comply, saying that its internal investigation had ended and no further action was needed. When faced with Hughes's ultimatum, the Pentagon reciprocated with its own hardball tactic: it held up 3,000 additional promotions, saying it could not promote those officers without the 158 targeted by Hughes, and it blamed the roadblock on the senator's stubbornness. Hughes's response was, "That is their decision, not mine." The high-profile confrontation continued through early 1973, with the total number of delayed promotions climbing to 5,000 by late March.[22]

In a closed-door meeting of the Senate Armed Services Committee with secretary of the air force Robert Seamans and chief of staff John Ryan, Hughes was pressured to give up the fight. Publicly, he was given one week to develop a case against any of the officers on his blocked promotion list, but that meant little. "There's no use hanging myself by the thumbs on this every week," he said after the meeting, acknowledging that he had no support from his fellow senators. "Everyone wishes this investigation would die but me. If that's the case, I guess we'd better have the funeral and get it over with."[23]

During that week, there was a flurry of correspondence between Hughes, secretary of defense Elliot Richardson, and J. Fred Buzhardt, general counsel to the Department of Defense. The military stood its ground. Buzhardt's reply to Hughes stated, "7th Air Force had no basis upon which to question either the legality of the orders issued by General Lavelle for missions, or the authority of General Lavelle from his superiors to issue such orders." In defiance of evidence to the contrary, he wrote, "Nor is there evidence of an intent to deceive by the crews who were debriefed following the mission in question, as evidenced by the fact that they provided accurate information on the missions in which they participated." The reasoning behind this position was that the military could not prove "the intent to deceive."[24]

In the face of the Pentagon's intransigence, Hughes backed down and released his hold on promotions. The fight was simply too overwhelming for a single senator to carry on.[25]

These external battles merged with Hughes's internal struggles, causing him to question his presence on the Armed Services Committee. Hughes's incessant religious searching and his deeper progression into Christian spiritualism led him to pacifism. He now rejected war itself, seeing it as a last resort. He doubted that he could effectively represent liberals on the committee, the very role for which he had fought. His doubts grew so serious that he approached Senate majority leader Mike Mansfield, who had played a fundamental role in getting Hughes the assignment, and discussed leaving the committee. Hughes felt his only option would be to vote against all future military budgets and weapons systems. The calm, low-key Mansfield said he thought the Iowa senator was doing a tremendous job on the committee, representing views that "have as much right to be represented . . . as those of anyone else." He convinced Hughes to stay, but the conversation was a harbinger of things to come.[26]

In 1973 Hughes found himself involved in another investigation of unauthorized US bombings in Indochina, this time in Cambodia. Senator William Proxmire, a Democratic maverick from Wisconsin, had received a letter from former air force major Hal M. Knight declaring that he had taken part in bombings over neutral Cambodia prior to the US invasion in May 1970 and had been ordered to file at least two dozen falsified reports to hide these missions. Most of the raids—termed Operation Menu—had been concentrated in the Fish Hook area of the Cambodian border, a region the US military widely considered to be a staging area for Vietcong units and supplies. Proxmire passed the letter on to Hughes because he knew the Iowan would treat it seriously.[27]

On March 28, 1973, Hughes asked Secretary Richardson for a complete record of bombings in Indochina since the war began in 1965. Although Richardson knew about the covert Cambodian bombings, the documents released to the Armed Services Committee contained no record of these actions prior to the 1970 Cambodian invasion. A later declassified record of the bombings issued by the Pentagon was also false.[28]

On July 12 General George Brown appeared before the committee, seeking confirmation as air force chief of staff. With information from the Knight letter in hand, Hughes asked Brown, "Did the United States in fact conduct air strikes in Cambodia prior to May 1970, utilizing B-52s or tactical aircraft or both?" Brown, who was under oath, insisted that the committee go into secret session, where he admitted that he knew about the covert bombings and acknowledged that the initial reports had been falsified. Four days later, however, after conferring with others at the Pentagon, Brown clarified his statement in a letter: "I do not believe it is correct to characterize reports under special security precautions directed by higher authority as 'false.' . . . The reason why special security precautions were directed was not a reporting issue so long as the responsible higher authority knew in fact what was done, and judged it to be in accord with instructions." In other words, as long as the air force had been ordered by superiors to conceal information, it was okay.[29]

The issue became public when Knight testified before the Armed Services Committee on July 16, providing details about the secret Cambodian bombings that had started in February 1970, prior to the US invasion. Knight testified that he had received hand-delivered bombing orders twice a week and subsequently burned the orders once the missions were completed. The official—and falsified—reports included only bombings in South Vietnam. This falsification practice stopped with the US invasion of Cambodia, when the bombings there became public. However, the exposure of these secret missions and the complicity of the US military—and the Nixon White House—in these actions stunned the American people.[30]

Hughes pressed for more hearings and additional witnesses to expose the falsehoods. "I think we should get at the truth about these bombings and who ordered them." He told reporters that Knight was ready to turn over the names of at least ten other air force officers who participated in or were aware of the bombings and record falsifications. Hughes was joined in this pursuit by Senator Stuart Symington of Missouri, who was acting committee chairman after Stennis was hospitalized following a shooting in Washington, DC.[31]

The revelations forced newly confirmed secretary of defense James Schlesinger to acknowledge that the United States had secretly bombed sites in Cambodia in 1969 and 1970, while publicly professing its respect for that nation's neutrality. In a letter to the committee, however, the secretary claimed the bombings had been "fully authorized" to protect American servicemen, and "special security precautions" were taken so "the operations would not be compromised." Hughes declared himself "baffled" by the letter because the Cambodian bombings were not mentioned in the Defense Department's official report on all Indochina bombings since 1965, and he called the entire effort a "revelation of the deliberate deception in official information."[32]

On July 17 Defense Department spokesman Jerry Friedheim said that some members of Congress had been informed of the bombings, but others, including Hughes, had been kept in the dark, adding, "I can't explain why." He also revealed that the Cambodian bombing sorties were "deliberately not included" in the report requested by Hughes, a decision made by "senior military and civilian officials." The reason, Friedheim claimed, was that "it would not be particularly useful to include the information at that time." The reason was clear: it was not useful to provide this ammunition to a well-known critic of the Vietnam War.[33]

Hughes was furious and asked publicly why he was considered "untrustworthy as a member of the Senate Armed Services Committee."

Majority leader Mansfield took to the Senate floor to laud Hughes's diligence in exposing the secret bombings, commending the Iowan "for his determination and doggedness in eliciting the facts . . . facts which were unreported, facts which have raised doubts and confusion and concern in the minds of the American people."[34]

With his national profile rising after exposing the Pentagon's deceit, Hughes attracted correspondence from military officers who wanted to confess their own distasteful activities during the Vietnam War. On July 20 Hughes received a handwritten letter from Gerald Greven of Miami, who described his participation in a "massive air war" over Laos and expressed concern that the "American public was being misled about the conflict in Laos." He also reported that US military officials had deliberately bombed enemy hospitals in 1969, recounting that he took part in at least three and possibly six such missions. This was confirmed in another letter Hughes received from Daniel T. Eismann of Caldwell, Idaho, describing a mission that made four or five passes over a hospital to make sure the bombs reached their target. Bombing hospitals was a violation of the Geneva Convention and was also prohibited under the US Army's Code of Land Warfare.[35]

In other correspondence, Hughes learned from retired lieutenant colonel George M. Miller of Brentwood, Tennessee, an air force liaison officer in the Pentagon from 1970 to 1972, that he had received a verbal directive in 1971 to distinguish between "key" and "non-key" congressional inquiries. Those on the "key" list would get the most expeditious turnaround time—less than ten days—while those on the "non-key" list could take as long as three weeks. He wrote, "The only rationale was 'we must stop helping our enemies on the Hill.'" Miller left the impression that Hughes's inquiry was "non-key," making it obvious why the bombing record he received was incomplete. Saying the double standard "did not seem morally right," Miller declared, "by the act of deciding who the Air Force friends were, and attempting to ensure their re-election, while helping defeat others, were we not trying to place military above civilian control?"[36]

In late July Earle Wheeler, former chairman of the Joint Chiefs of Staff, testified before the Armed Services Committee that President Nixon had ordered the 1969 and early 1970 Cambodian bombings and also ordered that they be kept secret. Wheeler justified the bombings because US troops were being threatened by North Vietnamese attacks coming from Cambodia. He denied the charge of falsifying records because the truth had been told to "those with a need to know," including a handful in Congress who supported the war. Hughes completely rejected this rationale, claiming the secrecy had been intended to quiet antiwar efforts. To Wheeler he boomed, "I totally reject the precept of notification of the American people through a few members of Congress. I have been elected by the people of Iowa to represent the people of my state. You have no right to deny this to me."[37]

By this time, it was obvious to Hughes and many others that this deceit by the US military was not just a few isolated incidents but a common practice that permeated the conduct of the war in Indochina. Referring to the earlier unauthorized bombing over North Vietnam, Hughes said, "In point of fact, General Lavelle was not demoted for ordering falsifications, for nearly everybody was doing it. He was demoted after having implemented the falsifications so clumsily that he got caught." For the US military, lying had become "a way of life."[38]

This was confirmed at an August 9, 1973, Armed Services hearing when the Pentagon released a memorandum written by Wheeler, then chairman of the Joint Chiefs of Staff, on November 20, 1969, ordering false reporting of the B-52 raids in Cambodia, initiated by Secretary Laird. Under the system outlined in the memo, the raids were officially reported as having taken place over South Vietnam. Hughes took advantage of the memo to grill deputy secretary of defense William Clements, who was testifying that day:

> Hughes: This is a direct order to enter targets in the record that are not the targets bombed?
> Clements: Yes, sir, it is part of the cover. This is what we said a while ago.
> Hughes: This is an order?
> Clements: That is exactly right.
> Hughes: It is signed by Secretary Laird, isn't it?
> Clements: That is exactly right.[39]

With this memo, Hughes had obtained the first solid written evidence of instructions to falsify bombing targets by entering misleading coordinates. Later, it was revealed that Laird had been following instructions from national security adviser Kissinger, who had been acting on behalf of President Nixon. The goal: to hide the Cambodian bombings from the American public.[40]

Nixon himself defended the bombings and the secrecy behind them in a speech to veterans in New Orleans on August 20. This was the first time he had spoken publicly on the issue. Nixon claimed the bombings were "absolutely necessary" to save lives and move the war to the negotiating table, and he said he "would make the same decision today." To the cheering audience, he deplored the "great anguish and loud protest from the usual critics."[41]

One "usual critic" saw things differently. Sensing the need to explain his actions to some disapproving constituents, Hughes outlined his position in a *Des Moines Register* essay on August 14, beginning with Knight's letter and describing the falsehoods perpetrated by the US military and the White House. He wrote, "When secrecy, deception, and falsification of official reports becomes a way of life in our country's military operations, it scares the hell out of me." He warned of "the ever-present danger, when high government operations are conducted in secrecy, of confusing the nation's national security with a particular administration's political security." No one, he wrote, "can be permitted to make the momentous decision to wage secret warfare while officially deceiving the Congress and the public." That is how "free nations under civilian governance eventually forfeit their freedoms." Hughes ended the essay with a quote from Knight's congressional testimony: "I didn't take an oath to support the military. I took an oath to support the Constitution."[42]

In 1973 Hughes faced an issue that separated him from many fellow Democrats: abortion. In January 1973 the US Supreme Court issued its monumental decision in *Roe v. Wade*, which declared abortion in early pregnancy to be a federal right for women. Prior to this decision, whenever Hughes had been asked about his position, he had always said that he was personally opposed to all abortions, but because it was a state issue, he could not impact it as a US senator. The *Roe* decision changed that. Now that abortion was a federal issue, Hughes decided to take a stand. On May 31, 1973, he joined six conservative Republican senators in sponsoring a federal constitutional amendment criminalizing abortion. Specifically, the amendment extended full constitutional rights to "unborn offspring at every stage of their biological development." It allowed abortions only when the mother's life was threatened.[43]

Citing a "trend toward dehumanization and violence in the human race," Hughes said, "the general acceptance of abortion in cases other than those of medical necessity would dangerously extend this trend toward dehumanization." With this public move, Hughes placed himself in opposition to most Democrats.[44]

In August Hughes received a strongly worded letter from Roxanne Conlin, representing the Iowa Women's Political Caucus, urging him to withdraw his support for the amendment. Hughes replied, "I am not likely to change my position" because "this is a matter on which I have strong feelings," and he reminded the group of his long-standing support for equal rights for women across the board. Hughes's position on abortion prompted serious discussion among several Iowa politicos about challenging Hughes in a primary. One possible candidate was Minnette Doderer of Iowa City.[45]

But, as few people knew at the time, a primary challenge was the farthest thing from Harold Hughes's mind.

21 | Leaving the Senate and Welcoming Charles Colson

"Frustrating" was a word Hughes used often to describe his life as a US senator. "After you've been a chief executive of a state, you make a decision and you do something about it," he said in 1971. "People carry out orders—something happens. Here, you make a decision and you talk about it for two years, and then maybe nothing happens at all." Hughes was clearly dissatisfied. "Saying that I'm completely happy, with this great august body that everyone in the country seems to want to belong to, wouldn't be the truth."[1]

Adding to Hughes's burdens was worry about the health of his middle daughter, Carol, who was in her early thirties and living with her parents after a failed marriage. Early in life, she had been diagnosed with Peutz-Jeghers syndrome, a rare disease that puts patients at increased risk for cancer. Several times she had had growths removed from her intestine, and she had recently been diagnosed with cancer. Following surgery, radiation, and chemotherapy, Carol appeared to have beaten the disease, but she continued to suffer physically. According to many of those close to Hughes, that experience led him to engage in even deeper soul-searching than normal.[2]

Hughes increasingly turned to his Christian faith, seeing it as the guiding force in his life. He often spoke of his faith in public forums and, of course, in his famous 1971 interview with the *Des Moines Register*. Hughes's thoughtfulness and introspection were not new. His good friend Vance Bourjaily described Hughes as someone who was constantly searching, continually looking for new insights, never satisfied with his current thinking. His public and private burdens at this time drove Hughes to rethink his life's path, with his Christian faith driving this focus.[3]

Shortly after Hughes took his seat in the Senate, John Stennis invited him to attend a regular prayer breakfast with twenty to twenty-five fellow senators. Exclusively Christian, the group met at 8:30 on Wednesday mornings in the Vandenberg Room for a thirty-minute breakfast, beginning with a prayer and followed by a fifteen-minute talk and round-table discussion. The gathering was bipartisan and nonideological; attendees included liberals such as Hughes and Mark Hatfield (R-OR), as well as archconservatives such as Stennis and Strom Thurmond (R-SC). In an interview, Hughes said the conservatives in the group were "generally regarded as 'the Neanderthals' by those who embrace new politics." Initially uncomfortable taking part in this fellowship, Hughes eventually grew more at ease praying with his Senate colleagues.[4]

After Hughes's attendance at the Senate prayer breakfast became common knowledge, he was visited by Doug Coe of the Fellowship Foundation. Coe's organization arranged the National Prayer Breakfast held in the nation's capital each February for politicos of all stripes. Coe was interested in Hughes's impression of the weekly gathering of senators, and Hughes replied that he wished there was more prayer and religious discourse. The discussion turned to talk of the power of prayer and a promise between the two men to pray together in the future. This blossomed into a friendship with Coe that would impact Hughes's life.[5]

Coe became an extremely controversial figure in Washington, DC, praised by some as a charismatic disciple of evangelical Christianity and condemned by others as a right-wing power monger who wielded immense influence behind the scenes, both foreign and domestic. A friendly, open man from Oregon, Coe was continuing the tradition of Abraham Vereide, who had started the National Prayer Breakfast in 1953. After Vereide's death in 1969, Coe took over the Fellowship Foundation (which operated under various names over the years); it had a multimillion-dollar budget and was based out of the Foundation House in Washington, DC. As the breakfast matured, it grew into an international gathering of world leaders with days of seminars and meetings, leading to influential connections with powerful figures.[6]

The personal relationship between Hughes and Coe began with shared prayers, sometimes in person and sometimes over the phone. Daughter Phyllis recalled, "I know my father thought a great deal of him, loved him like a brother." Eventually, Coe linked Hughes with other Washington politicians who were interested in gathering for prayers and Bible discussions. They included Al Quie, a Republican congressman from Minnesota, and Graham Purcell, a former Democratic congressman from Texas. Over time, in Hughes's words, "the handshakes became bear hugs," and the group grew close.[7]

Furthering Hughes's religious pilgrimage was a nine-day trip to Israel in early 1973 with Eva, Carol, and Phyllis and twenty other people from the Des Moines chapter of the Jewish Welfare Foundation. The trip, which included visits to sites of significance to Christians, deeply impacted Hughes. He later wrote that it deepened his Christian faith as few other journeys could have.[8]

Outwardly, Hughes seemed to be moving ahead with his reelection campaign. On March 31, 1973, three of his fellow senators—Mike Mansfield, Ed Muskie, and Stuart Symington—journeyed to Des Moines for a fund-raising reception at the Wakonda Club and a dinner at Veterans Auditorium. Speaking at the dinner, Mansfield said of Hughes, "Tonight we begin the process that will assure his return to the Senate less than two years from now."[9]

The *Des Moines Register*, along with many Iowans, was expecting Hughes to run for reelection. In mid-1973 the newspaper conducted a poll pitting three-term Iowa governor Robert Ray against Hughes and found that it was a virtual dead heat, with Hughes having a slight 39 to 37 percent lead. In the same poll, Hughes had a 55 percent positive approval rating versus Ray's 71 percent. Ray had shown no interest in running for the US Senate in 1974, but there was talk within Republican circles that only a man of Ray's stature could credibly take on Hughes, and pressure was mounting for Ray to carry his party's banner into the Senate race in the fall. This was not to be.[10]

Much earlier, Hughes had toyed with the idea of becoming a minister and had even taken some correspondence courses, only to change direction and turn to trucking and then politics. But this calling was never far from his mind. Clearly dissatisfied with his work in the Senate, he saw the lay ministry as a potential new path for his considerable talents.[11]

On September 6, 1973, Harold Hughes shocked the political world by announcing that he would not run for a second Senate term; instead, he would become a religious lay worker for the Fellowship Foundation of Washington, DC, and the International Christian Leadership. He declared, "I can move people through a spiritual approach more effectively than I have been able to achieve through the political approach." Hughes said he had made this decision "after a long period of personal soul-searching and extended discussion with members of my family." He later claimed, "Nothing special triggered it, just a slow, growing understanding that the needs of this world are not political: they're spiritual."[12]

According to Phyllis, there was no doubt that Doug Coe played a "very instrumental role" in her father's decision not to run for the Senate again. "My father always had a very strong spiritual orientation and he [Coe] thought my father would be more fulfilled doing that." On a more nefarious level, there was speculation that Republicans had urged the conservative Coe to convince the liberal Hughes to leave the Senate, but there is no available proof of this claim.[13]

His decision freed Hughes to talk more candidly about his beliefs and his past. In a speech he gave in DeWitt, Iowa, the night before his announcement, he spoke of his near suicide in Ida Grove twenty years ago—something he had never mentioned in public before. In an interview with James M. Wall, editor of *Christian Century*, Hughes said, "Ministering to God through politics and the social order is not enough for me. I have been in public service for 15 years now, and if I ran again for the U.S. Senate, another six years would reduce the number of years I would have left to devote my full time to leading others to Christ." When Wall pointed out how influential he could be as a senator, Hughes responded bluntly, "You are wanting to limit God; other forums may appear for me."[14]

Both the Fellowship Foundation and the International Christian Leadership operated out of the Fellowship House in northwestern Washington, DC, led by Coe. At the time, the foundation had revenue of $350,000 and was mainly known for organizing the annual National Prayer Breakfast in Washington, but it was also involved in similar gatherings in state legislatures and in parliaments in Europe, Africa, and Asia. Individuals working within the foundation were not paid salaries but were typically financed by a group of businesspeople who formed a team around the foundation staffer. This was how Hughes would operate. Coe said, "As part of the Fellowship Foundation, he will do his own thing. Different people do different things."[15]

One of the "different things" Hughes became involved in was completely unexpected: ministering to the spiritual needs of disgraced Nixon aide Charles Colson. Dubbed Nixon's hatchet man, Colson had a reputation of utter ruthlessness and cold political calculation. In a misquote—but one that he relished—Colson reportedly said he was willing to run over his grandmother for Richard Nixon. Many in Nixon's circle described Colson as someone who brought out the moody president's darkest traits. An extremely conservative Republican, Colson represented everything in politics that Hughes was not. One of Colson's tasks in the

White House was to develop Nixon's infamous "enemies list," which included Hughes.[16]

As Nixon's second term began, Colson found himself immersed in the Watergate scandal. This multifaceted, complex episode in US history originated largely from the illegal activities of the Nixon reelection campaign and efforts by those in the White House to cover them up. On June 17, 1972, a group of burglars was arrested for attempting to illegally bug Democratic national headquarters at the Watergate Hotel in Washington, DC. Subsequent investigations tied this group to the Nixon campaign. In addition, they had previously broken into the office of Daniel Ellsberg's psychiatrist. Ellsberg had released the Pentagon Papers, a secret analysis of the Vietnam War by the Department of Defense, to the media. An irate Nixon ordered retaliation against Ellsberg, resulting in the break-in. Colson was involved in that effort.[17]

In early 1973 Colson resigned from the White House. He was facing possible prison time on a charge of obstruction of justice for attempting to defame Ellsberg. During this upheaval, Colson claimed he underwent a born-again Christian conversion and eventually found himself under the tutelage of Doug Coe.[18]

In late September 1973 Coe invited Colson to an evening meeting at Congressman Quie's home, along with Purcell and Hughes. When Coe first broached the topic of Colson with Hughes over the phone, the senator almost hung up on him. "There isn't anyone I dislike more than Chuck Colson. I'm against everything he stands for," said Hughes, who had been intensely critical of the White House's involvement in the Watergate affair. Coe wore him down, and Hughes agreed to attend the gathering. Initially, Hughes and Colson, in the latter's words, "were like two boxers in separate corners," waiting to pounce on each other. Finally, Hughes spoke up in his forthright style: "Chuck, they tell me you have had an encounter with Jesus Christ. Would you tell us about it?" Colson haltingly detailed his religious conversion, and when he was finished, Hughes raised both his arms, brought them down forcefully on his knees, and said, "That's all I need to know. Chuck, you have accepted Jesus and he has forgiven you. I do the same." After the group spent several minutes in solemn prayer, Hughes gave Colson a huge, unexpected bear hug.[19]

Thus began one of the more bizarre friendships in US political history. The relationship became public on December 6, 1973, when Colson invited Hughes to a biweekly prayer breakfast at the White House.

Hughes had been in the White House only once during the Nixon presidency, and the Watergate scandal "was heating to a fever pitch," in Colson's words, making the liberal senator's appearance there even more awkward. Not surprisingly, Hughes was the center of attention among the twenty or so past and present White House aides, and he was asked to expound on his decision to enter the lay ministry. For more than twenty minutes the senator solemnly described his past, his inner conflicts, his recent decision to leave the Senate, and his acceptance of Colson as his "brother in Christ." After he finished, Arthur Burns, Federal Reserve Board chairman and chair of the prayer breakfast meeting, broke the silence and said, "Senator, I just want to say that is one of the most moving and beautiful things I have ever heard from any man." With that, Burns asked Colson to lead the group in prayer, and the breakfast ended.[20]

Hughes's visit to the White House and his connection to Colson soon hit the national media. The Sunday edition of the *Des Moines Register* dedicated a lengthy front-page article to the subject in late December. Hughes strongly defended his new relationship, and not everyone was pleased. Reflecting that attitude was a letter from Eppie Ledere, a Sioux City, Iowa, native who wrote a nationally syndicated advice column under the name Ann Landers. Beginning with the casual "Dear Pack," she cited the recent news coverage and wrote, "If you let this bird use your good name to help him hide behind God in order to get himself off the hook, I'll vomit." Many of Hughes's former associates, as well as daughter Phyllis, were skeptical of Colson, seeing his conversion and his association with Hughes as an effort to redeem himself and avoid prison time.[21]

This was not the attitude of Harold Hughes. He continued to support Colson both publicly and privately. As Colson faced the legal consequences of the Watergate scandal, Hughes remained a stalwart friend. The senator offered his own home as the site for a joint interview with Colson and Mike Wallace of CBS's *60 Minutes*. Wallace and Colson did most of the talking back and forth, with Hughes commenting from time to time on the authenticity of Colson's conversion, strongly supporting him across the political divide. During the interview, Hughes defended some of Colson's ambiguous answers about his faith by saying that he was "a baby in Christ," a Christian who had not reached "full maturity, not full understanding, and having not made the divisions completely with the past." Colson was, said Hughes, still searching.[22]

On a Sunday evening in early June 1974, Hughes, Coe, and others prayed with Colson, who would be facing US District Court Judge Gerhard Gesell the next morning on obstruction of justice charges. Accompanied by Hughes, Colson pleaded guilty and became the first Nixon aide sentenced to prison for Watergate-related crimes. He served seven months at the Maxwell Federal Prison in Alabama.[23]

It is, of course, impossible to know whether Charles Colson truly took a leap of faith, transforming himself from a cutthroat, right-wing hatchet man—or, as the *Washington Post* put it, "a darkly brilliant political strategist"—into a compassionate born-again Christian. However, Colson's actions after leaving prison cannot be denied. He became a leading figure in the evangelical community and founded the Prison Fellowship Ministries in 1976, which grew into an international movement with branches in more than 110 countries. He pushed for prison reform, including opposition to the death penalty, alternatives to incarceration, and rehabilitation programs for prisoners. Some may have doubted Colson's sincerity, but Harold Hughes did not.[24]

Not running for a second term meant that Hughes could direct his considerable energies toward his senatorial duties throughout 1974. In Iowa, the fight for his seat between John Culver of Cedar Rapids and old Hughes foe David Stanley of Muscatine intensified. But in Washington, Hughes continued his investigations into US military secrecy, document falsification, and intrigue between the armed forces and the White House.

Despite his earlier misgivings about serving on the Armed Services Committee, Hughes clearly established himself as a vocal military critic in his final year on the committee. In a summary of Hughes's committee activities by the *Register*'s Clark Mollenhoff, the investigative reporter wrote that the senator "has not been anxious to curry favor from the military hierarchy or from the committee chairman." He described Hughes as a "strong force for greater justice in the military," earning a reputation as "a formidable investigator" who "does his homework" and knows the levers to pull "to make it difficult for a committee chairman to reject a request for an investigation or hearing."[25]

A significant battle developed in early 1974 over the charge that the US military was spying on the Nixon White House, growing from the uneasy relationship between the Pentagon and national security adviser Henry Kissinger, who was now also the secretary of state. Media reports revealed that military aides working on the National Security Council

(NSC) had taken secret White House documents and provided them to select military leaders. After these revelations, Hughes urged a full investigation by the Armed Services Committee. "I want to know what's going on," he said. "There's a thousand questions related to this sort of thing—and they all go to the previous questions this committee has asked regarding who controls the military."[26]

The main question was whether this was a rogue operation—a single officer stealing secret documents from the White House—or a systematic plan directed by the Pentagon to spy on the White House and, specifically, the NSC. All this, of course, was occurring against the backdrop of the Watergate scandal dominating Washington, DC, and the nation.

The relentless Seymour Hersh reported in the *New York Times* in early February that the Pentagon had started spying on the White House in the fall of 1970, more than a year earlier than previously reported, and it involved as many as five high-ranking officers who regularly received classified documents pilfered by a navy yeoman assigned to the NSC staff. This spying was allegedly in retaliation for Admiral Moorer's being denied access to documents, on the orders of Nixon and Kissinger, even though he was a statutory NSC member. These stolen documents included copies of "eyes only" messages intended exclusively for Nixon and Kissinger from ambassadors in Vietnam and Cambodia. Hersh also reported that the special "plumbers" set up to stop information leaks from the White House—and involved in the Watergate break-in—had investigated the copying of documents.[27]

Not content to simply demand hearings, Hughes took to the floor of the Senate and raised the stakes. Even though the issue involved classified documents, the senator demanded open hearings. "No once-over-lightly in executive session with Admiral Moorer or Kissinger is going to suffice," he said. "No objective is more important to the preservation of our democratic system than vigilant maintenance of civilian control over our military establishment. No force poses a greater threat to civilian control than an obsession for secrecy in government beyond rational needs of national security."[28]

Hughes failed to get open hearings, due to the classified nature of the material, but much of the late February testimony became public. The hearings featured testimony from Rear Admiral Robert O. Welander, who denied he had ever "ordered or directed" navy yeoman Robert Radford to steal classified documents; he did admit, however, that he had been "offered" documents by Radford. The yeoman, in turn, testified that Welander and his predecessor, Rear Admiral Rembrandt Robinson, had urged him to pilfer whatever papers "I could get my hands on," contending that it was "an opportunity to do a job for the Joint Chiefs." In the end, in the words of a *New York Times* editorial, it was a case of the military "resorting to improper methods to find some closely regarded details" about the Nixon administration, "rather than a case of the military revolting against those policies and seeking to penetrate and block them." Hughes wrote to Stennis that the "contradictory testimony on military spying has raised serious questions in my own mind," but he failed to get other members of the committee to agree to further investigation.[29]

In March Hughes continued his campaign against military secrecy, accusing the Pentagon of sending troops into Cambodia and Laos from 1970 to 1973 in violation of the Cooper-Church amendment of 1970, which banned the use of US funds to finance such efforts. Using information collected by the Armed Services Committee, he claimed the Pentagon acknowledged it had authorized thirty-two ground operations in Laos in 1970 and 1971, despite Congress barring such activities in December 1969. In Cambodia, the Pentagon admitted to thirty-one missions after they were banned. Knowing that Nixon had initiated these orders, Hughes urged the House Judiciary Committee to investigate these actions as impeachable offenses. It did, but the committee failed to gain a majority vote.[30]

In this battle against government secrecy, Hughes sought legislation granting greater openness in covert military and intelligence operations through expanded congressional oversight. He gained allies following revelations of secret actions by the Central Intelligence Agency (CIA) in Chile, as well as those by the military in Southeast Asia. His efforts were also aimed at stopping executive branch officials—particularly Kissinger—from ordering secret operations without the president's knowledge, an action that became more common in the waning days of Watergate. The result was a 1974 amendment to the Foreign Assistance Act of 1961 that became known as the Hughes-Ryan Act. Initiated in the Senate by Hughes and amended by Representative Leo Ryan (D-CA) in the House, the act required the president to report all secret actions by the CIA to one or more congressional committees in a "timely fashion." It also prohibited funds for covert actions by the CIA or Defense Department unless and until the president had issued an official "finding" to the appropriate congressional committees that such operations were vital to national security. Passed in late 1974 and signed by President Gerald Ford, this act was an imperfect attempt to provide a check on US covert operations until the process was amended in 1980 to create a more comprehensive framework based on years of experience.[31]

Another issue that arose in Hughes's final year in the Senate was one close to his heart: abolishing the death penalty. Since entering public life, he had consistently opposed the death penalty and had succeeded in ending capital punishment in Iowa in 1965. At issue in 1974 was a move by the Nixon administration to revive the death penalty for certain federal crimes. The death penalty as practiced had been ruled unconstitutional by the Supreme Court in 1972 because, in the words of Justice Potter Stewart, it was "so wantonly and freakishly imposed." The legislation before the Senate sought to address the inconsistencies in federal death penalty law brought up by the court.[32]

Hughes led the debate against the death penalty legislation and was pitted against Senator John McClellan of Arkansas, who argued for it. In the words of the *Register*'s George Anthan, Hughes gave "one of the most impassioned speeches of his congressional career," delivered "almost as a sermon." In his deep, solemn voice, Hughes decried "the morbid trip back to the death penalty." Using the same arguments he had made a decade ago in Iowa, he said he opposed capital punishment because "it demeans human society without protecting it." Referring to the Supreme Court's arguments, Hughes claimed the death penalty "is capricious and unjust in its application. It discriminates against the luckless, the poor, and the racial minorities." It is final, he said, with no road back if an executed person is later proved innocent. "Finally, I opposed the death penalty because it is grossly destructive of human hopes for a society more amenable to peace and less dependent on violence for the solution to its problems." The death penalty can only "coarsen and brutalize society." He ended his oration—one that filled twenty-five pages—by saying: "In the name of God, I ask my colleagues to join me in rejecting death, in affirming life; in rejecting vengeance, in affirming redemption."[33]

Despite this valiant effort, the Senate passed the legislation 54–33, with Dick Clark joining Hughes against it. Hughes then introduced an amendment requiring that executions be held in public and even televised to give them the "widest possible exposure." He took his opponents' arguments at face value. If the death penalty was a deterrent to crime, Hughes said, the more people who saw it applied, the greater the deterrent. The measure was defeated, and Hughes admitted the amendment was "repulsive even to me, just as executions are repulsive."[34]

Hughes's final year in the Senate was fraught with the ongoing Watergate scandal and the threatened impeachment of Richard Nixon. When Hughes's foe resigned from the presidency on August 8, 1974, Hughes said, "For Mr. Nixon as a fellow human being I feel very deeply the agony of the decision which he and his family have suffered. I pray that he may know some measure of peace now that the decision has been made." As to Nixon's resignation speech, Hughes noted that it omitted the words, "I am sorry and the blame was mine." Nor, continued Hughes, "was there any expression of compassion or regret for the lives of the men and their families of his own staff that were ruined by Watergate." Hughes opposed amnesty for the former president "while his subordinates are tried and convicted and sent to prison. This is hardly equal justice for all," he said, perhaps thinking of his friend Charles Colson. Days later, however, he seemed to change his mind but retained his call for equal treatment. Saying "vindictiveness is not an American trait," he urged full clemency "not only to the former President but to the individuals who incriminated themselves by doing his bidding."[35]

When President Gerald Ford pardoned Nixon—and Nixon alone—on September 8, 1974, Hughes's response was relatively low-key. He did not contest Ford's right to do so, nor his motives. In replying to the numerous letters his office received on the subject, he wrote, "If it was a mistake it was, in my opinion, a mistake of judgment, not of the heart nor of the constitutional process." He added that the timing was "unfortunate," in light of the other pending cases "and the need to complete the Watergate record of history."[36]

Later that year, Hughes ended his single term in the US Senate, but not before the traditional accolades from his fellow senators. Barry Goldwater, who served with Hughes on the Armed Services Committee and disagreed with him on virtually every issue imaginable, wrote a sincere and heartfelt letter expressing "the admiration I have for you, not just as a Senator, but as a man. What you have done with your life is exemplary. . . . I will relish the remaining days of our association."[37]

On December 20 a special time was set aside to praise Hughes on the floor of the Senate. Some of his colleagues did so excessively. Senator James Allan of Alabama compared Hughes to the Old Testament Abraham, and Senator Peter Domenici of New Mexico compared him to the New Testament Paul: "He has been called just as certainly as Paul was called." Fellow Iowan Dick Clark called Hughes "the conscience of the Senate," pointing to his moral leadership on the Vietnam War and his legislation on alcoholism. "His great compassion illuminates everything he does—in public life or in his daily contacts with the people around him." Massachusetts senator Ted Kennedy said, "I shall miss most of all the commanding presence, the principled debates he led, the powerful voice that was so often the voice of conscience and decency in the Senate." These were typical of the remarks made by fellow senators and the many tributes from conservatives who shared the weekly prayer breakfasts with him.[38]

Hughes refused to resign early to give his successor, John Culver, a seniority advantage over the ten other newly elected members of the Senate. Six years earlier, Hughes had lost seniority due to this practice and considered "such maneuvering to be political expediency, immoral, and against the Constitution." While he worked with Culver extensively to make the transition smooth—including welcoming Park Rinard as the new senator's administrative assistant—Hughes said, "The people of Iowa elected me to service until January, and I intend to fill that responsibility," even though he had resigned the governorship early to take his Senate oath. In January 1975 Harold Hughes became a private citizen for the first time in sixteen years.[39]

22 | Life Past Politics—Almost

"I don't think money ever meant a lot to him," recalled Peg Mikulanec, daughter of longtime Hughes confidant Wayne Shoemaker. "It just wasn't a big deal for him." After leaving the Senate, Hughes's principal income came from voluntary contributions through the Fellowship Foundation and fees from speaking engagements. He also accepted a $12,000-a-year job as a consultant, providing advice to the Senate Judiciary Committee on alcohol and drug problems. Eventually, he gave up that position because he felt he was not doing enough to earn the salary, which he turned over to an "inner city ministry."[1]

His unpaid occupation continued to be counseling alcoholics on Capitol Hill. Speaking in early 1975, he called it "almost a full-time job over the holidays." One person Hughes helped was Wilbur Mills of Arkansas, the powerful chairman of the House Ways and Means Committee and a severe alcoholic. Mills turned to Hughes in late 1974 after being arrested during an infamous drunk-driving episode with stripper Fannie Foxe. His counseling sessions included five or six meetings with Hughes at the Bethesda Naval Medical Center. Mills went public with his alcoholism, resigned his committee chairmanship, and checked into treatment; he eventually left Congress. Mills was only one of many politicians with drinking problems whom Hughes helped—during and after his Senate term.[2]

Given his work with the Fellowship Foundation, Hughes and his family stayed in the Washington, DC, area, moving to a Maryland farm after he left the Senate. Every Wednesday he went to Capitol Hill to conduct a ministry among members of Congress and congressional aides. He still took part in the Senate prayer breakfast.[3]

Tragedy struck the Hughes family in July 1976 when daughter Carol, aged thirty-two, collapsed at home after a long struggle with cancer. She was taken to George Washington University Hospital, where Hughes was undergoing prostate surgery. While recovering from his operation, Hughes hobbled back and forth from his room to Carol's, and she seemed to be rallying. On July 27, however, just after Hughes had visited her and left to tell his oldest daughter, Connie, that Carol was improving, she died. Services were held at the Fellowship House in Washington and the United Methodist church in Ida Grove, where she was buried. Carol's passing further immersed Hughes in his religious faith, as only the death of a child can do.[4]

His ministry included worshipping with the most prominent Christian politician at the time: President Jimmy Carter. Both the president and his wife, Rosalynn, attended a religious retreat at Hughes's home in Maryland, and Hughes accompanied the First Lady on her trip to Southeast Asia to assist Cambodian refugees. While on this trip, Hughes mentioned to Mrs. Carter the importance of prayer during the upcoming Camp David summit involving Carter, Egyptian president Anwar Sadat, and Israeli prime minister Menachem Begin. Rosalynn passed along this suggestion to her husband, who enthusiastically supported the idea and obtained the agreement of the Egyptian and Israeli leaders. Hughes and Coe composed a prayer common to Christianity, Islam, and Judaism, and it was recited at the 1978 summit.[5]

The former senator was also involved—though reluctantly—in the political battles on Capitol Hill related to the funding and managing of federal programs to aid alcoholics and drug addicts. On March 2, 1979, he appeared before the Subcommittee on Alcoholism and Drug Abuse, chaired by Senator Don Riegle of Michigan, and urged additional funding for addicts in need. Admitting that he was no longer knowledgeable about spending levels, current research, and the latest prevention techniques, he spoke movingly about his own struggles and the need to fund programs to help those addicted to alcohol or drugs. Gruffly proclaiming that more had to be done, he declared:

> If at times I sound like an angry and frustrated man, it is because I am. I see this great abundant land of ours with resources beyond compare. . . . But I am sick to my soul by our response to alcoholics. And I am sick to my soul that even when we pass laws to help the alcoholic or the drug addict, we have remained blind to the illness that alcoholism brings to the spouse or the young children in the family.

He was no doubt recalling experiences from his youth and early adulthood. Hughes ended by describing his own struggles with drinking, including his suicide attempt and self-resurrection, to a silent congressional chamber. At the end of his passionate testimony, attendees broke out in a round of applause—a rare occurrence at a congressional hearing.[6]

Full disclosure was not limited to congressional testimony. In 1979

Hughes published his autobiography, ghostwritten by Dick Schneider and published by Chosen Books of Lincoln, Virginia, a Christian publishing house. It was later retitled and republished in paperback by Zondervan Publishing, another Christian publishing firm. The *Des Moines Register* published a series of excepts from the book, which was less a political biography than a Christian testimonial. The book's tone mirrored his deep faith, and the narrative often glossed over important aspects of his political life.[7]

During this time, his work at Fellowship House was not living up to expectations. The vast majority of Christians involved with Fellowship House were on the conservative end of the political spectrum, which became more prominent with the growth of the Christian Right in the late 1970s. As a liberal Democrat, Hughes felt increasingly uncomfortable interacting with such individuals. "There was always a little bit of discomfort there because the Fellowship was always very conservative and Republican-oriented," recalled Phyllis. "My father was one of the first, if not *the* first, liberal Democrat to have penetrated their inner sanctum. There was always some discomfort on both sides due to the philosophical divide." Hughes also became uncomfortable with the vast funds Fellowship House had at its disposal. "The source of money was anything but transparent," said Phyllis. "If my father asked questions, it was very hard to get an answer." Never a wealthy man himself, Hughes collected limited revenue from his work at the Fellowship Foundation, forcing him to rely on honoraria from speeches he made around the county, which meant that he was constantly on the road.[8]

For these reasons, Hughes decided to return to Iowa in early 1981 and bought a house on five acres outside of Norwalk, south of Des Moines. He accepted a position as vice president at Iowa Realty through long-time friend and financial supporter Bill Knapp. Hughes admitted to the *Des Moines Register* that he was struggling financially and was tired of "hustling to make a living" and "speaking for my supper." The job offered by Knapp was nebulously defined as serving a "pastoral function" and counseling employees at Iowa Realty on personal, family, and spiritual problems. Essentially, it was a favor to a friend experiencing financial difficulties.[9]

Hughes's return to Iowa immediately sparked speculation that he would run for governor in 1982, twenty years after first being elected to the office. This was fueled by his active immersion in Democratic Party affairs, such as a fund-raiser for John Culver. With this charismatic figure returning to the state, Iowa Democrats craved a winning candidate after several disappointing efforts in recent years. Republican Robert Ray had been governor of Iowa for fourteen years—elected to three two-year terms and two four-year terms—and was seemingly invulnerable to Democrats' attempts to defeat him. In two consecutive US Senate races in 1978 and 1980, liberal Democratic incumbents Dick Clark and John Culver were defeated by conservative Republicans Roger Jepsen and Charles Grassley, respectively.[10]

Political pundit Jim Flansburg of the *Register* wrote about a topic that was on the minds of many: the possibility of a contest between Ray and Hughes for the governorship in 1982. He decried the concept of bringing "Harold Hughes out of mothballs," which "smacks of bringing the 1962 Kentucky Derby winner decidedly back from his pasture to run in a 1982 sweepstakes." He added that "Hughes would be the first to argue that it's flimsy politics—that ideas, and a desire to do something first impelled him into politics and not some desire to be the nimbus of a great man." Referring to the progressive ideology of both Hughes and Ray, he noted that it would be interesting "if the two found something they could disagree on."[11]

Indeed, in many ways, Ray's administration had continued the policies of Hughes in terms of state government reform and aid to the less fortunate. A Polk County native and graduate of Drake University and its law school, Ray represented the moderate wing of the Iowa Republican Party—still divided since the days of Allison and Cummins—and won a three-way battle in the 1968 primary when two other candidates split the conservative vote. Early in his tenure as governor, Ray led an effort to modernize state finances and worked to create the Iowa Department of Transportation out of five different agencies. He later pushed for a revision of the Iowa criminal code, revamped the Employment Security Commission, expanded property tax relief, revised open-meeting laws, and endorsed several environmental bills, including lobbying publicly for a nickel deposit on returnable cans and bottles.[12]

Like Hughes, Ray showed a special compassion—in defiance of public opinion—for the needy. Responding to a direct appeal from President Gerald Ford, Ray established the Governor's Task Force for Indochinese Resettlement, which welcomed ten thousand Indochinese refugees to Iowa in late 1975. Even though a *Des Moines Register* poll showed that 51 percent of Iowans opposed the resettlement, Ray charged ahead, believing "it was the right thing to do." Three years later, moved by media coverage of the Vietnamese "boat people," Ray organized a statewide and national effort through religious and humanitarian organizations to find homes for these people. After visiting a refugee camp in Thailand in October 1979, the Iowa governor initiated Iowa Sends Help to Aid Refugees and End Starvation (Iowa SHARES), which eventually raised more than half a million dollars to provide food for refugee camps. Summarizing these efforts, historian Matthew R. Walsh wrote, "Ray is one of the most overlooked humanitarians of the twentieth century."[13]

All these endeavors came together to rank Ray—along with Grimes, Cummins, and Hughes—as one of Iowa's most significant governors.

Hughes indicated in late summer 1981 that he was open to the possibility of running for governor, regardless of who his opponent might be. In an interview he said, "I didn't return to Iowa with any thought in my head of running for public office, but I do want to be open-minded about what way I can serve with my life." Bill Knapp and former Hughes aide Ed Campbell, now chairman of the Iowa Democratic Party, were leading the effort to convince the former governor to run for his old job. Flansburg wrote that the pair's goal was to walk "on tiptoes" and not "intentionally leave fingerprints" because "they don't want Hughes to get sore at the idea of being manipulated, refusing in a huff to run." But Hughes was taking the initiative on his own; in late August he had a three-hour lunch with staffers at the Iowa Democratic Party, asking them what they thought he should do. He also sought counsel from his old Iowa allies, with the same question in mind.[14]

There was not universal celebration at the idea of a Hughes candidacy. Several other Democrats were irritated that Hughes was forcing them to cool their heels and wait in the wings until he made a decision, including Des Moines attorney and activist Roxanne Conlin, Iowa attorney general Tom Miller, and Congressman (future US senator) Tom Harkin. All but Conlin had placed their potential campaigns for governor on hold. Many cautioned that a Hughes candidacy would block new and emerging leaders such as these individuals. Others questioned whether Hughes, who had been living elsewhere for more than a decade, was familiar with current issues in the state.[15]

But the idea was gaining traction among grassroots Democrats. At least two county Democratic central committees—Monona in western Iowa and Story in central—passed resolutions in the fall of 1981 calling for Hughes to run. A Davenport group was already distributing Hughes bumper stickers ("HEH in 82"), and there were reports that $1,000 contributors were funding an exploratory committee. In a front-page *Register* poll released on September 27, Hughes was the two-to-one choice among Iowa Democrats over second-place Harkin, and he was the only Democrat running ahead of Republican lieutenant governor Terry Branstad, a potential candidate. In a face-off with Ray, however, Hughes was behind 52 to 37 percent.[16]

By mid-October, Hughes had established an exploratory committee and opened an office in Des Moines. The committee was headed by Lorne Worthington, a Des Moines insurance executive. Members included Margaret Collison of Oskaloosa, former head of the Iowa Board of Regents; Julianna Holm, former member of Hughes's Senate staff; John Crystal, state banking superintendent under Hughes; Wayne Shoemaker, pastor of Grace United Methodist Church in Des Moines; and Rachel Fulton, Democratic Party activist and wife of former lieutenant governor Robert Fulton.[17]

Hughes still claimed he was only leaning toward running, but his schedule certainly looked like that of a full-time candidate, filled with appearances through March 1982. The Hughes committee scheduled a series of meetings with groups representing farmers, businesspeople, religious leaders, teachers, and others. The main thrust of these discussions, Hughes remarked, "is that there is a leadership element missing. We need someone we can look up to, someone who offers hope, someone who can bring us together again with motivation and direction. They believe I can do that."[18]

All these activities came to a screeching halt in late November when doubts emerged about Hughes's residency. John Law, full-time director of the Hughes committee, had been researching the requirements for nominating petitions and discovered that the Iowa Constitution required a person elected for governor to be a resident of the state for the preceeding two years. Hughes had returned to Iowa in May 1981, falling short of this constitutional requirement for the 1982 election. "I have never considered myself anything other than an Iowa resident," said Hughes, but the issue became central to his potential political resurrection. Complicating matters was the discovery that Hughes had voted in Maryland in November 1980 and signed a voter registration oath that he was a Maryland citizen. During this time, he also paid Maryland, not Iowa, state taxes.[19]

The issue, however, was open to debate. Some argued that case law and court decisions supported the claim that residency boiled down to intent. If Hughes intended to return to Iowa and claim it as his residence, then he was a resident. Hughes had maintained a church membership in Iowa, used an Iowa bank, and had publicly declared his intention to return. Iowa secretary of state Mary Jane Odell, a Republican who also served as state commissioner of elections, requested an opinion from attorney general Miller, who recused himself because he had consulted with the Hughes campaign. Hughes and his allies then pressed Odell for an opinion, which she issued on December 28. Ruling against Hughes, she declared her decision was based on "logic and common sense. It is my belief that an individual . . . cannot vote and swear residency in the state of Maryland and on the same day claim that he was a resident of Iowa." Hughes now had to decide whether to challenge this ruling in court.[20]

He was unwilling to do this. On January 7, 1982, at a press conference at the Hotel Savery, Hughes announced that he was ending his short-lived candidacy. He said the residency question threatened "to disrupt orderly party procedures and the election process" and predicted that any court challenge would take the issue well into the campaign year. This would give his opponents the ability to dispute whether he was a true Iowa citizen, and if the courts ruled against him, the party would be left without a legitimate nominee. He would not subject the Iowa Democratic Party to this risk for the sake of his own candidacy.[21]

It was later revealed that the problem was one of his own making. In 1978 Hughes had deliberately changed his legal residence to Maryland to stop supporters in Iowa from putting his name on the ballot for governor. They were fed up with the relatively weak Democratic candidates lining up to oppose Ray, who was running for a fifth consecutive term. Not wanting to reenter politics at the time, Hughes had reasoned that a public announcement would embarrass the party, so he registered to vote in Maryland. Up to that point, he had remained an Iowa resident, voting via absentee ballot in Ida Grove. When he contemplated the gubernatorial run in 1982, he gave little thought to the two-year residency requirement until it ultimately ended his campaign.[22]

This would be the last time Hughes seriously considered running for office, although he admitted the effort excited him and he was disappointed not to be plunging into a new campaign. "Once I finally made the decision that I was going to be a candidate, the fires have really started burning again." After he withdrew, Hughes got involved in the gubernatorial candidacy of former aide Ed Campbell. The Fort Dodge native lost the 1982 Democratic primary to Roxanne Conlin, who in turn lost to Republican Terry Branstad that fall.[23]

Hughes moved on and committed himself to helping his fellow alcoholics, essentially dedicating the remainder of his working life to that effort. He spoke on behalf of alcoholics and set up treatment programs. In 1984 he established the Harold Hughes Center for Alcohol and Drug Treatment, which was linked with Des Moines General Hospital and the Woman's Resource Center there. The effort expanded to Monticello and Mount Ayr, in association with local hospitals in these cities.[24]

During this time, Hughes's marriage collapsed. His and Eva's relationship had suffered for years under difficult circumstances. Although Eva gave reluctant support to his political activities, she was rarely part of them. In many ways, she remained a small-town girl while her husband took to the national and international stage. Many close friends termed it a loveless marriage. Said Bill Knapp, "I heard him on the phone talking to her and every time he'd say he loved her. Well, he didn't love her." According to the couple's daughter Phyllis, "At no time during my experience would I characterize their relationship as an easy one. It was always difficult." She called her mother "emotionally fragile" and believed "she clearly had some kind of mental illness . . . or personality disorder." Eva frequently accused women on Hughes's staff of having affairs with him, causing embarrassment whether the allegations were true or not.[25]

One of these accusations was certainly true. By the mid-1980s, Hughes was deeply involved in an extramarital affair with Julianne (Julie) Henry Holm, who was twenty years his junior. Hughes first met Julie when she was a sixteen-year-old waitress in a small town and he was running for the Commerce Commission post. Originally from Fort Dodge, Julie grew up in a house next to Ed Campbell. She married Lennis Holm at a young age and moved to Iowa City, where Lennis completed a history degree and was accepted at Georgetown University Law School during Hughes's Senate term. After moving to the Washington, DC, area, Lennis got a job as a Capitol policeman through Campbell, and Julie worked on Hughes's Senate staff. After Lennis graduated from law school, the couple moved back to Iowa, where he practiced law in Winterset and later in Creston, where he grew up.[26]

Julie lived in Des Moines while she completed her college degree, and she volunteered for the Hughes presidential campaign. During this time, she became involved in Iowa Democratic politics, and when Hughes created his gubernatorial exploratory committee in 1981, Julie was one of the six members appointed to advise him on the campaign's direction. It was around this time that the relationship between them deepened. As Hughes later described it, there was no "hanky-panky." He said, "It was not a matter of me trying to make a hit on Julie or Julie trying to make a hit on me, or the two of us wanting to jump in bed somewhere. That didn't happen. It was a matter of life. Difficulty. Pain on both sides. Sharing. Over a long period of time."[27]

The relationship exploded into the public arena on October 24, 1984, when the *Des Moines Register* published an article about the divorce trial of Julie and Lennis Holm. Lennis's attorneys had subpoenaed Hughes but agreed to allow him to submit a deposition rather than testify in court. Once the divorce was granted, few details became public. When asked about it, the normally outspoken Hughes said, "I have no comment about anything regarding that divorce case. No comment, no comment." But the widespread coverage made it quite clear that Julie Holm and Harold Hughes were having an affair.[28]

The final curtain fell on the Hugheses' marriage on December 22, 1986. All in all, the divorce proceedings were an unpleasant affair. Eva had been ill for some time, which made their parting especially difficult. Hughes called it "the most awesome decision of my life" and added, "one of the greatest problems for me was the fact that I knew the pain it was bringing her." Eva was granted Hughes's US Senate pension. Six weeks after the divorce was final, Hughes and Julie Holm were married by a justice of the peace in Phoenix, Arizona, where they lived. The dry climate helped Hughes's escalating lung problems caused by a lifetime of smoking.[29]

He continued to manage the Hughes treatment centers in Iowa, as well as one in Texas. Then, in the late 1980s, Hughes and several of his evangelical allies established a treatment center near Ligonier, Pennsylvania, a twenty- to thirty-acre estate with five houses open to both adolescent and adult addicts and alcoholics. Eventually, the institution ran into financial problems; managed care and changes in insurance laws made reimbursement for services difficult, and the center closed.[30]

Hughes returned to Iowa to face an emotional body blow. While in Pennsylvania, he had placed his oldest daughter, Connie Otto, in charge of the Hughes center's finances, and she had embezzled a large amount of money. The crime was never made public, but it nearly destroyed the center, which survived on a shoestring budget. Needless to say, it broke Hughes's heart.[31]

Still dedicated to aiding addicts, Hughes helped launch the Society of Americans for Recovery (SOAR) in July 1990. Its goal was to end financial, social, legal, and health care discrimination against chemically dependent persons and their families by mobilizing a political constituency focused on advocacy and post-treatment employment for alcoholics and addicts. Based in Arlington, Virginia, it began with one thousand individual members and claimed to have eleven thousand within three years. In 1993 Hughes addressed SOAR regional conferences in Baltimore, St. Louis, Atlanta, and Los Angeles, although attendance was disappointing. Despite high hopes, the organization dissolved in early 1995 due to management problems and the challenges of getting alcoholics and addicts publicly involved in a recovery program.[32]

These setbacks did not stop Hughes from helping friends in very personal ways. Bonnie Campbell shared one example. She had worked on Hughes's Senate staff and married his aide Ed Campbell. The couple moved to Iowa, where Bonnie got a law degree, was elected Iowa attorney general, and won the 1994 Democratic nomination for governor. At one point, the Campbells separated due to Ed's drinking problem, and Bonnie was absolutely furious at him. One cold, snowy winter night, Bonnie answered a knock on her door and found Hughes and Julie standing there. Hughes got right to the point: "You know my friend Ed is an alcoholic. Are you just going to let him die or are we going to do something?" "I don't care if he does die," Bonnie responded. "That's a lie and you know it," said Hughes. "That's a bunch of bullshit." Bonnie did not know what to do, but Hughes did. Together they organized an intervention and got Ed into treatment, and he never had another drink. "Our marriage was better than it ever had been," said Bonnie. "He did this for senators and other people, but he also did it for just about anyone who came to his attention."[33]

For income, Hughes once again relied on honoraria from speaking engagements around the country. He spoke three or four times a month and received between $10,000 and $15,000 each. These speeches were primarily about alcoholism, stressing that it was a disease requiring treatment and that those suffering from it needed sympathy, not condemnation. Hughes relied on Julie and her twin daughters, Jennifer and Jacqui, to help with travel arrangements and, just as important, to act as his ears. Although Hughes's voice was still a strong asset, his hearing was failing as he aged—caused, he thought, from his gunner days in World War II—and he needed help carrying on conversations, listening for speaking cues, and hearing announcements at airports. The group called themselves his "hearing aid brigade."[34]

Hughes's religious views continued to evolve, reflecting his lifelong search for religious truth, including views that went beyond conventional Christianity. Prior to his divorce, he spent time with a Native American tribe in Utah, possibly driven by the story of his Cherokee great-grandmother. He participated in religious ceremonies, smoked a pipe with the Native Americans, and was accepted into their graces by a medicine man representing seventeen tribes. In an interview, he proudly noted that this "is not very often done with what they consider a white man." He added that none of this affected his traditional Christianity, "but it did unite me much closer in brotherhood with men and women that I love and admire a great deal." About his mystic search he asserted that "all religion is mystical" and noted, "if you take mysticism out of the Bible, you have a shell." Still, the strong Christian evangelicalism he espoused in the 1970s was gone from his rhetoric. Both of Hughes's stepdaughters, who had grown close to him, said the outspoken Christian beliefs expressed in his 1979 memoir did not resemble the man they knew in his later years. Said Jennifer, "Organized religion was never attractive to him. It was all the spiritual base, not only in Christianity, but also the Indian-based faith. His theology pulled from all different religions."[35]

One outcome of his second marriage was that Julie convinced Hughes to quit smoking, which daughter Phyllis thought helped to extend his life ten years. Julie also insisted on a healthier diet. Despite these efforts, Hughes's health began to fail in 1994; he was suffering from severe emphysema and was forced to retire from day-to-day operations at the Hughes treatment centers. The Mount Ayr and Monticello centers had closed in the late 1980s, and Des Moines General Hospital assumed operation of the remaining rehabilitation center there. The couple moved to Phoenix full time, and Julie became her husband's caretaker.[36]

The last time Hughes appeared in the public arena was in a bitter legal fight with ex-wife Eva over unpaid alimony and other issues related to their 1987 divorce. The battle was extensively covered in the *Des Moines Register* in late 1995 and 1996. Hughes asserted that because of his declining health and diminished income, it was impossible for him to meet the financial commitments of their earlier settlement. In recent years, he had cut back on alimony payments to Eva—gradually reducing them from $2,000 to $500 a month—and she had difficulty paying her bills while living in a small apartment in West Des Moines. In an open hearing in August 1996, Hughes testified via phone "in a gravelly voice"—the once powerful rhetorical lion had nearly been silenced—and pleaded, "It's a very humiliating, debilitating set of circumstances I find myself in." Now seventy-five years old, he was broke and dying, confined to a wheelchair and dependent on oxygen tanks to breathe. Hughes petitioned the court to decrease or eliminate his alimony payments. The judge reviewing the case had little sympathy for the former governor and US senator—who, as Eva pointed out, was living in a $121,000 home in Arizona—and ordered him to pay nearly $15,000 in back alimony, monthly health insurance premiums for his ex-wife, and slightly reduced alimony of $1,750 a month.[37]

These financial burdens lasted only a couple of months. On Wednesday, October 23, 1996, Hughes and Julie enjoyed a picnic on that warm Arizona day. When they returned home, he decided to take a nap, and later that evening, he died in his sleep.[38]

Reflecting his respect for Native American mysticism, Hughes requested that his body lie in state for five days so his spirit could leave his body. A simple man to the end, he also requested a stark burial with nothing fancy; his body was shipped back to Iowa in a cardboard box. After memorial services, Harold Hughes was laid to rest in the Ida Grove cemetery.[39]

Epilogue

James Flansburg, the cynical, hard-bitten political reporter and columnist for the *Des Moines Register,* covered generations of Iowa politicians. He wrote of Harold Hughes at his death in 1996: "He was the purest of his kind—his flaws even had a kind of majesty—and he never tried to fool himself or pretend to be something he wasn't." Comparing Hughes to contemporary politicians, Flansburg continued: "That simple lack of guile is so foreign to politics today that I wonder if those who didn't know and watch Hughes figure I'm speaking in tongues."[1]

With an honesty and directness rare among politicians of his era, Hughes made a difference—particularly in his state, but in the nation as well. His accomplishments were many, and the actions he took reverberate to this day.

In Iowa, Hughes altered the political and governmental landscape through his leadership and personality. No opinion polls guided him. The liquor-by-the-drink issue in 1962 and 1963 was ultimately a minor one, but it showed that strong and articulate leadership can defy political lethargy. Hughes succeeded in this effort where others had tried and failed. Although the unfair rural dominance in the Iowa legislature certainly would have been overturned by the courts, Hughes's successful fight against the Shaff Plan in 1963 took the issue of equitable representation to the people of Iowa and made the change easier for them to accept. And his leadership in dealing with the Amish school issue—a seemingly unsolvable local problem for years—showed that talking to individuals and finding common ground can overcome hardened, impassioned positions—a lesson for our current age. Although the Iowa Democratic Party was already on the rise when Hughes entered politics, he provided greater leadership, making Iowa a two-party state after years of Republican dominance and offering Iowans wider political choices.

It was in the realm of state government reform that Hughes left his strongest legacy, tackling challenges that had been untouched for decades. "In Iowa," Flansburg wrote, "virtually every aspect of government was modernized or set in motion for modernization by Hughes." He was certainly not alone in striving for this goal; nor was it fully accomplished when Hughes left for Washington. However, he—together with aide Park Rinard—was clearly a driving force behind the effort. The need for property tax reform had been debated for years, but nothing had been done. Hughes's leadership in 1967 broke this inertia, leading to a fairer tax system for Iowans and more equitable funding for local schools. His call for reform led to the abolition of the antiquated three-member state commissions in the areas of social services and taxation, creating institutions with greater professionalism. Likewise, Hughes's civil service reform replaced political appointees with more skilled state employees. He clearly established his leadership in abolishing the death penalty in Iowa. And in campaign after campaign, Hughes advocated for an advanced vocational training program, resulting in the Iowa community college system, which offers low-cost educational opportunities to its citizens to this day.[2]

Hughes's efforts on a national scale were not as impactful, but they were significant. There is no better example than his work to create and fund the National Institute of Alcohol Abuse and Alcoholism. Tackling the issue like a tenacious bulldog, Hughes succeeded where others had failed. This institution still operates today, providing aid to alcoholics and funding research to support this effort. Perhaps more important, Hughes's crusade publicized the principle that alcoholism is a disease, not a personal moral failure. Through his efforts, Hughes made a profound, positive difference in the lives of thousands upon thousands of alcoholics over the years.

Within the national Democratic Party, Hughes worked to implement a more open process for selecting presidential nominees. The McGovern-Fraser Commission did not bear Hughes's name, but it manifested his ideas. For better or worse, presidential candidates would be chosen not by party leaders behind closed doors but by party voters in a more public arena, the trade-off being that campaigns became more expensive with the use of advertising and professional consultants.

Like many other Americans, Hughes turned against the Vietnam War, believing that it flouted American ideals. Unlike many others, however, Hughes articulated his opposition in a clear and impassioned manner that stirred others. He became a sincere spokesman for the antiwar movement. In a similar vein, Hughes was a particular thorn in the Pentagon's side, uncovering its covert actions that defied established policy. Though Hughes was often unsuccessful in getting public admissions of these misdeeds, those in the US military knew they faced a well-prepared and harsh critic in Hughes.

Leadership aside, Hughes's story is one of individual inspiration. He successfully fought the demon of alcoholism and used his experience to counsel countless others and help them overcome this potentially life-threatening disease. In addition to relying on personal will power and help from friends to recover, he relied on his Christian faith. Some aspects of his theology may have seemed unconventional to some, but he never veered from the spiritual command to care for the least of his brethren. His personal Christian outlook, modified over the years, resulted from an intense, lifelong journey into the deep river of his soul. Unlike others whose Christianity led them to political conservatism, Hughes's theology guided him to the left of center. This unique trait, together with his ability to change his mind after serious reflection, makes him an individual worth exploring.

Harold Hughes's political career spanned the so-called Long Sixties, providing a rich perspective into this period. As both governor and senator, Hughes was directly involved in the issues and events that defined this era—the civil rights movement, the growth of the liberal state, the Vietnam War and the antiwar movement, the transition of the Democratic Party, and other elements that combined to make this a singular age in US history. Examining this man's life—this thunder from the prairie—helps us better understand this era.

Notes

Abbreviations

CRG	*Cedar Rapids Gazette*
DMR	*Des Moines Register*
DMT	*Des Moines Tribune*
HEH-G	Harold E. Hughes Gubernatorial Papers, Special Collections and Archives, University of Iowa, Iowa City
HEH-S	Harold E. Hughes Senatorial Papers, Special Collections and Archives, University of Iowa, Iowa City
Mitchell Papers	Donald J. Mitchell Papers, Special Collections and Archives, University of Iowa, Iowa City
NYT	*New York Times*
WP	*Washington Post*

Introduction

1. Bruce I. Godbersen, ed., *A History of Ida County* (Ida Grove, IA: Midwest Industries, 1977), 504; interview with Phyllis Hughes Ewing; William Hedlund and Russell Wilson, *In His Own Words: The Harold Hughes Story* (Bloomington, IN: LifeRich Publishing, 2020), 9.

2. One work that considers this span of years a single period is Christopher Strain, *The Long Sixties: America, 1955–1974* (Hoboken, NJ: Wiley-Blackwell, 2016). Many other works on this period do not use the term "Long Sixties," but they often begin with the civil rights movement in the 1950s and end with Watergate in 1974.

3. Vance Bourjaily, *Country Matters* (New York: Dial Press, 1973), 238.

4. Nick Kotz and James Risser, "Messiah from the Midwest?" *Washington Monthly* 2, 3 (May 1970): 44.

5. Kotz and Risser, 44.

1. Youth, War, and Alcohol

1. Harold Hughes with Dick Schneider, *Harold E. Hughes: The Man from Ida Grove; a Senator's Personal Story* (Lincoln, VA: Chosen Books Publishing, 1979), 22, 25; interview with Phyllis Hughes Ewing.

2. Hughes, *Man from Ida Grove*, 22, 25; Ewing interview; William Hedlund

and Russell Wilson, *In His Own Words: The Harold Hughes Story* (Bloomington, IN: LifeRich Publishing, 2020), 10.

3. Hughes, *Man from Ida Grove*, 22; Ewing interview.

4. Ewing interview; Hedlund and Wilson, *In His Own Words*, 10.

5. Hughes, *Man from Ida Grove*, 22; Hedlund and Wilson, *In His Own Words*, 14.

6. Bruce I. Godbersen, ed., *A History of Ida County* (Ida Grove, IA: Midwest Industries, 1977), 504; Ewing interview; Hedlund and Wilson, *In His Own Words*, 10, 19, 24.

7. Ewing interview.

8. Hughes, *Man from Ida Grove*, 28.

9. Hedlund and Wilson, *In His Own Words*, 12.

10. Hughes, *Man from Ida Grove*, 23; Hedlund and Wilson, *In His Own Words*, 24; Ewing interview.

11. Hughes, *Man from Ida Grove*, 24.

12. Hughes, 30; Godbersen, *History of Ida County*, 504.

13. Hughes, *Man from Ida Grove*, 24–25; Hedlund and Wilson, *In His Own Words*, 11.

14. Godbersen, *History of Ida County*, 454, 455, 504.

15. Godbersen, 504; Hedlund and Wilson, *In His Own Words*, 26.

16. Godbersen, *History of Ida County*, 505.

17. Hughes, *Man from Ida Grove*, 34–35.

18. Hedlund and Wilson, *In His Own Words*, 29.

19. Hedlund and Wilson, 30–31.

20. Hughes, *Man from Ida Grove*, 36, 37.

21. Hughes, 38; Hedlund and Wilson, *In His Own Words*, 32.

22. Ewing interview; Hughes, *Man from Ida Grove*, 38.

23. Hughes, *Man from Ida Grove*, 38.

24. Hughes, 39; Hedlund and Wilson, *In His Own Words*, 32.

25. Hughes, *Man from Ida Grove*, 40.

26. Hughes, 42–43; Hedlund and Wilson, *In His Own Words*, 35.

27. Hughes, *Man from Ida Grove*, 44.

28. Hughes, 46, 47.

29. Hughes, 49; *Etowah County (AL) Messenger*, September 3, 2019.

30. For a complete history of the North African campaign, see Rick Atkinson, *An Army at Dawn: The War in North Africa, 1942–1943* (New York: Henry Holt, 2002).

31. Hughes, *Man from Ida Grove*, 50.

32. Hughes, 50–51.

33. Hughes, 52–53.

34. Hughes, 54. For a detailed summary of the American landing at Gela, Sicily, see Rick Atkinson, *The Day of Battle: The War in Sicily and Italy, 1943* (New York: Henry Holt, 2007), 75–83.

35. Hughes, *Man from Ida Grove*, 54–55; Atkinson, *Day of Battle*, 79.

36. Hughes, *Man from Ida Grove*, 55; Atkinson, *Day of Battle*, 109.

37. Hughes, *Man from Ida Grove*, 56; Atkinson, *Day of Battle*, 158.

38. Hughes, *Man from Ida Grove*, 57.
39. Hughes, 57–58; Atkinson, *Day of Battle*, 204–207.
40. Hughes, *Man from Ida Grove*, 59–60.
41. Hughes, 60; Atkinson, *Day of Battle*, 145–146.
42. Hughes, *Man from Ida Grove*, 60–62.
43. Hughes, 62–64.
44. Hughes, 64–68.
45. Hughes, 69–70.
46. Hughes, 70–78; Ewing interview; Godbersen, *History of Ida County*, 493, 505.
47. Hedlund and Wilson, *In His Own Words*, 39.
48. Hughes, *Man from Ida Grove*, 80–82.
49. Hughes, 82–86.
50. Hughes, 85–86.
51. Hughes, 87, 89.
52. Hughes, 90–92.
53. Hughes, 97–98.
54. Hughes, 99.
55. Hughes, 99.
56. Hughes, 99–100; Ewing interview. Until Hughes published his memoir in 1979, he repeatedly referred to waking up in a hotel room in Des Moines after a long binge as the event that prompted him to give up drinking. See, for example, Fletcher Knebel, "One Man's Triumph," *Look*, October 6, 1964, 97–108. In *Man from Ida Grove*, however, he tells a different and much more dramatic tale.
57. Hughes, *Man from Ida Grove*, 100–103.

2. *Business Success and Statewide Office*

1. Harold Hughes with Dick Schneider, *Harold E. Hughes: The Man from Ida Grove; a Senator's Personal Story* (Lincoln, VA: Chosen Books Publishing, 1979), 106.
2. Hughes, 107; William Hedlund and Russell Wilson, *In His Own Words: The Harold Hughes Story* (Bloomington, IN: LifeRich Publishing, 2020), 50.
3. Interview with Peg Shoemaker Mikulanec.
4. Interview with Russell Wilson.
5. Hughes, *Man from Ida Grove*, 110.
6. Hughes, 111–112.
7. Hughes, 112–114.
8. Hughes, 93–95. After hearing Hughes give an obscenity-laden oration to the fiercely independent truckers—no strangers to coarse language—Gordon Hinrichs recommended that he curb himself in future talks. This was only the beginning of a long process toward that end.
9. Hughes, 97–98.
10. Hughes, 107.

11. Hughes, 118–119.

12. Hedlund and Wilson, *In His Own Words*, 51.

13. Hughes, *Man from Ida Grove*, 117; Wilson interview; interview with Phyllis Hughes Ewing.

14. Hedlund and Wilson, *In His Own Words*, 51.

15. Hughes, *Man from Ida Grove*, 119.

16. Hedlund and Wilson, *In His Own Words*, 43–44.

17. Hedlund and Wilson, 43–44.

18. Hedlund and Wilson, 122; Wilson interview.

19. Hedlund and Wilson, *In His Own Words*, 122; Wilson interview.

20. Jim Larew, *A Party Reborn: The Democrats of Iowa, 1950–1974* (Iowa City: Iowa State Historical Society, 1980), 53–56.

21. Larew, 124.

22. David Yepsen, "The Little Man behind Some of Iowa's Giants," *DMR*, March 10, 1991.

23. Yepsen.

24. Yepsen.

25. Vance Bourjaily, *Country Matters* (New York: Dial Press, 1973), 228, 230; Nick Kotz and James Risser, "Messiah from the Midwest?" *Washington Monthly* 2, 3 (May 1970): 45.

26. Hughes, *Man from Ida Grove*, 124; Yepsen, "Little Man behind Some of Iowa's Giants."

27. Wilson interview; Hedlund and Wilson, *In His Own Words*, 91.

28. Hughes, *Man from Ida Grove*, 124.

29. Hughes, 126.

30. Hedlund and Wilson, *In His Own Words*, 53.

31. Hedlund and Wilson, 126–127.

32. Hedlund and Wilson, 128; *Iowa Official Register, 1959–1960* (Des Moines: State of Iowa, 1960), 31.

33. Hedlund and Wilson, *In His Own Words*, 128; Wilson interview; Ewing interview; *Iowa Official Register*, 30.

34. *Iowa Official Register*, 358.

35. Hughes, *Man from Ida Grove*, 129.

36. Hedlund and Wilson, *In His Own Words*, 73.

37. Hedlund and Wilson, 128.

38. Hedlund and Wilson, 130; *Iowa Official Register*, 370.

39. *Iowa Official Register*, 130–131; Ewing interview; transcript of remarks, Governor Hughes Recognition Dinner, Waterloo, February 1, 1966, box 16, HEH-G Papers.

3. Running for Governor

1. Harold Hughes with Dick Schneider, *Harold E. Hughes: The Man from Ida Grove; a Senator's Personal Story* (Lincoln, VA: Chosen Books Publishing, 1979), 131.

2. Jim Larew, *A Party Reborn: The Democrats of Iowa, 1950–1974* (Iowa City: Iowa State Historical Society, 1980), 23; US Census Bureau, Census of Population and History, Census of Population: 160-VI-Part 17, General Population Characteristics—Iowa. The 1960 census showed that 53 percent of Iowans lived in urban areas and 47 percent in rural areas; in 1950, these percentages had been 47.6 percent urban and 52.4 percent rural. For a more detailed discussion of this transition in the Midwest, see Cornelia Butler Flora and Jan L. Flora, "Midwestern Rural Communities in the Post-WWII Era to 2000," in *The Rural Midwest since World War II*, ed. J. L. Andersen (De Kalb: Northern Illinois University Press, 2014), 103–125.

3. For an overview of the technological advances in American agricultural in the late nineteenth and twentieth centuries, see R. Douglas Hurt, *American Agriculture: A Brief History*, rev. ed. (West Lafayette, IN: Purdue University Press, 2002). For a more detailed discussion of how technology transformed American agriculture in the postwar years, see J. L. Anderson, *Industrializing the Midwest: Agriculture, Technology, and Environment, 1945–1972* (De Kalb: Northern Illinois University Press, 2009). For a discussion of postwar government aid to American agriculture, see J. L. Anderson, "Uneasy Dependency: Rural and Farm Policy and the Midwest since 1945," in Anderson, *Rural Midwest since World War II*, 126–159.

4. Larew, *Party Reborn*, 26. For a detailed summary of the meatpacking and farm implement businesses in early twentieth-century Iowa, see Charles E. Connerly, *Green, Fair, and Prosperous: Paths to a Sustainable Iowa* (Iowa City: University of Iowa Press, 2020), 4–16.

5. Larew, *Party Reborn*, 26; Wilson J. Warren, "Beyond the Rust Belt: The Neglected History of the Rural Midwest's Industrialization after World War II," in Anderson, *Rural Midwest since World War II*, 77–79.

6. Leland Sage, *A History of Iowa* (Ames: Iowa State University Press, 1974), 84–91, 120–121.

7. Morton M. Rosenberg, *Iowa on the Eve of the Civil War* (Norman: University of Oklahoma Press, 1972), 90, 128–131; Sage, *History of Iowa*, 134–138; Dorothy Schwieder, *Iowa: The Middle Land* (Ames: Iowa State University Press, 1996), 72; Robert Cook, *A Baptism of Fire: The Republican Party in Iowa, 1838–1878* (Ames: Iowa State University Press, 1994), 65–68.

8. Sage, *History of Iowa*, 204–210.

9. Sage, 219–232. For background on Allison, see Leland Sage, *William Boyd Allison: A Study in Practical Politics* (Iowa City: State Historical Society of Iowa, 1956).

10. Sage, *History of Iowa*, 222–225.

11. Sage, 225–228, 230–241. See Ralph M. Sayre, "Albert Baird Cummins and the Progressive Movement in Iowa" (Ph.D. diss., Columbia University, 1958). The Allison-Cummins conflict is also fully explored in Sage, *William Boyd Allison*.

12. See George William McDaniel, *Smith Wildman Brookhart: Iowa's Renegade Republican* (Ames: Iowa State University Press, 1995).

13. Sage, *History of Iowa*, 285–286, 303–304, 305–308.

14. Larew, *Party Reborn*, 53–58; Thomas Ryan, "The Early Years of the Iowa Democratic Revival, 1950–1956," *Annals of Iowa* 46, 1 (Summer 1981): 51, 58; Wilson J. Warren, *Struggling with "Iowa's Pride": Labor Relations, Unionism, and Politics in the Rural Midwest since 1877* (Iowa City: University of Iowa Press, 2000), 85–102.

15. Ryan, "Early Years of the Iowa Democratic Revival," 58.

16. F. T. Nye, "The 1956 Election," *Palimpsest* 38, 11 (1957): 453; Ryan, "Early Years of the Iowa Democratic Revival," 51.

17. Neal Smith, *20th Century Politics in Iowa and the Emergence of the Democratic Party* (Des Moines: Iowa Democratic Party, 1998), 13–21, 32–34; Larew, *Party Reborn*, 42–45.

18. Larew, *Party Reborn*, 42–43, 71; memo to officers, County Democratic Central Committees of Iowa, from Democratic State Central Committee and signed by Lex Hawkins, November 21, 1960, box 10, Correspondence and Democratic Literature—Oct. 1, 1960–December 30, 1960, Mitchell Papers.

19. Interview with Lex Hawkins by Tom Henderson, October 22, 2013, https://www.youtube.com/watch?v=6dwWdFcY4n8; *Iowa Official Register, 1959–1960* (Des Moines: State of Iowa, 1960), 35–36; Smith, *20th Century Politics in Iowa*, 43–46.

20. Hughes, *Man from Ida Grove*, 131; Nick Kotz and James Risser, "Messiah from the Midwest?" *Washington Monthly* 2, 3 (May 1970): 45.

21. Interview with Phyllis Hughes Ewing; Hughes, *Man from Ida Grove*, 132–133.

22. Hughes, *Man from Ida Grove*, 135.

23. *Omaha World Herald*, May 4, 1960, box 10, Correspondence and Democratic Literature—April 1, 1960–May 30, 1960, Mitchell Papers.

24. Hughes, *Man from Ida Grove*, 136; "Hughes Cites Principle in Party Choice," *DMR*, June 4, 1960; interview with Bill Sueppel.

25. Hughes, *Man from Ida Grove*, 137; *Iowa Official Register, 1961–1962* (Des Moines: State of Iowa, 1962), 352.

26. Hughes, *Man from Ida Grove*, 139–140.

27. George Mills, "'Liquor by Drink' in 2/3 of Iowa!" *DMR*, May 6, 1962; George Mills, "Many Varied Forces Vie in Liquor Fight," *DMR*, May 13, 1962.

28. For a complete history of liquor legislation in Iowa in the nineteenth and early twentieth centuries and attempts at enforcement, see the three-part series of articles by Dan Ebert Clark: "The History of Liquor Legislation in Iowa, 1946–1861," *Iowa Journal of History and Politics* 6 (1908): 55–87; "The History of Liquor Legislation in Iowa, 1861–1878," *Iowa Journal of History and Politics* 6 (1908): 339–374; "The History of Liquor Legislation in Iowa, 1878–1908," *Iowa Journal of History and Politics* 6 (1908): 503–608. For a summary of liquor issues in Iowa since then and the entire liquor-by-the-drink debate, see Jerry Harrington, "Iowa's Last Liquor Battle: Governor Harold E. Hughes and the Liquor-by-the-Drink Conflict," *Annals of Iowa* 76, 1 (Winter 2017): 1–46.

29. Harrington, "Iowa's Last Liquor Battle," 8; Mills, "Many Varied Forces Vie in Liquor Fight."

30. Charles Wiggins, "The Post World War II Legislative Reapportionment Battle in Iowa Politics," in *Patterns and Perspectives in Iowa History*, ed. Dorothy Schwieder (Ames: Iowa State University Press, 1973), 403–430. The overwhelming power of rural forces in the House was evident: the six least populous counties in 1960 (Adams, Ringgold, Clarke, Davis, Van Buren, and Wayne) had a total of six House seats, representing 52,377 people; the three most populous counties (Polk, Linn, and Black Hawk) also had six House seats but represented 525,696 citizens. Harrington, "Iowa's Last Liquor Battle," 9–10.

31. Hughes, *Man from Ida Grove*, 158.

32. Press release, May 26, 1962, box 25, Press Releases 1962, HEH-G Papers. According to former Iowa congressman Neal Smith, Lex Hawkins contracted with a young Lou Harris to conduct a poll among Iowa Democrats prior to the 1962 gubernatorial primary. It showed Hughes running neck and neck with Lewis Lint, who had the support of Jake More and the Democratic Old Guard. Smith and Hawkins showed the poll to Hughes and urged him to come out for liquor by the drink to draw a distinction between himself and his opponent in the primary. Smith wrote, "It was the blast needed to gain that advantage (especially in a Democratic primary) and he won that primary handily." Whether this urging prompted him or not, the decision was Hughes's alone. Smith, *20th Century Politics in Iowa*, 26.

33. Interview with Nick Kotz; interview with Sherwin Markman.

34. *Iowa Official Register, 1963–1964* (Des Moines: State of Iowa, 1964), 363. Democratic Party chairman Lex Hawkins later contended that he strongly supported Hughes in the primary behind the scenes, using party machinery and money and contributing to Hughes's win in 1962. Frank Nye, "Endorsing by Demos Is Voted," *CRG*, June 11, 1966.

35. *Iowa Official Register, 1961–1962*, 4; George Mills, "Erbe, as a Candidate, Talks about His Record as Governor," *DMR*, October 14, 1962.

36. Mills, "Erbe, as a Candidate, Talks." Iowa's "weak governor" stemmed from state constitutional provisions allowing the election of several executive positions independently of the governor. At the time, these included the lieutenant governor, attorney general, secretary of state, state treasurer, state auditor, and secretary of agriculture.

37. "State Democratic Convention, July 28, 1962," box 27, Speeches—July–Sept. 1962, HEH-G Papers.

38. "First Poll: Erbe, Hickenlooper Lead," *DMR*, October 7, 1962.

39. Hughes, *Man from Ida Grove*, 161.

40. "Remarks at Boone, Iowa, Sept. 1, 1962," box 27, Speeches—July–Sept. 1962, HEH-G Papers; George Mills, "He'd Enforce Liquor Law, Hughes Says," *DMR*, October 3, 1962.

41. Nick Lamberto, "Iowa Restaurant Owners Favor Liquor-by-Drink," *DMR*, October 16, 1962.

42. "Remarks at Des Moines Rotary Club, July 12, 1962," box 27, Speeches—July–Sept. 1962, HEH-G Papers; David Faber, *The Age of Great Dreams: America in the 1960s* (New York: Hill & Wang, 1994), 26–27.

43. "Governor Candidates View Additions to Gasoline Tax," *DMR*, Septem-

ber 9, 1962; George Mills, "Erbe, Hughes in a Peaceful Meeting Here," *DMR*, September 21, 1962.

44. Nick Kotz, "Hughes: Erbe Ducks Issues," *DMR*, September 14, 1962; press release on speaking at a Democratic barbeque in Denison, October 2, 1962, and press release on speech in Fort Dodge, October 15, 1962, box 25, Press Releases 1962, HEH-G Papers.

45. Hughes, *Man from Ida Grove*, 163–164.

46. Nick Kotz, "Hughes Plea to Clergy on Liquor Issue," *DMR*, October 17, 1962; "Support for Erbe from Iowa 'Drys,'" *DMR*, October 21, 1962; "Erbe, Hughes Clash over Aid to Schools," *DMR*, October 27, 1962; press release on speech in Corning, October 23, 1962, box 25, Press Releases 1962, HEH-G Papers.

47. "Erbe for Governor," editorial, *DMR*, October 28, 1962; "Hughes for Governor: He Is Bellwether for Democrats," editorial, *Davenport Morning Democrat*, October 31, 1962.

48. "Disagrees on 'Drink' Issue, but Backs Hughes," *DMR*, October 22, 1962; "Final Poll: Erbe, Hickenlooper Still Lead," *DMR*, November 4, 1962.

49. Frank Nye, "Hughes 'to Work, No Banquets,'" *CRG*, November 11, 1962.

50. *Iowa Official Register, 1962–1963* (Des Moines: State of Iowa, 1963), 4; George Mills, "Hughes Wins, Upset Stuns Republicans," *DMR*, November 7, 1962.

51. "Hughes—Liquor Mandate," *CRG*, November 7, 1962; Nye, "Hughes 'to Work, No Banquets'"; Arlo Jacobson, "'Won Because We Had a Program,' Says Hughes," *CRG*, January 5, 1963; "Hughes Hope Is Peace with Legislature," *DMR*, December 16, 1962.

52. Larew, *Party Reborn*, 90; Drake Mabry, "Hughes Wins by 40,000," *DMT*, November 7, 1962; "Hughes Sees 'Timing' as Win Factor," *Davenport Morning Democrat*, November 8, 1962; George Mills, "Call for Liquor-by-Drink," *DMR*, July 29, 1962; George Mills, "Republicans Keep Grip in Most Areas," *DMR*, November 10, 1962; Nick Kotz, "Spotlight on Hughes and Liquor Laws," *DMR*, November 11, 1962. See also Warren, *Struggling with "Iowa's Pride,"* 85–102.

4. 1963's Political Battles

1. George Mills, "Hundreds Greet Hughes in Homecoming at Ida Grove," *DMR*, November 18, 1962.

2. Mills.

3. George Mills, "Republicans Keep Grip in Most Areas," *DMR*, November 10, 1962; George Mills, "Hughes Eyes a Bipartisan Liquor Plan," *DMR*, November 29, 1962; Nick Kotz, "Hughes Asks 'Wets' to Be More Vocal," *DMR*, January 20, 1963.

4. Jerry Harrington, "Iowa's Last Liquor Battle: Governor Harold E. Hughes and the Liquor-by-the-Drink Conflict," *Annals of Iowa* 76, 1 (Winter 2017): 23.

5. Jerry Gross, "State Agents Get Set for Liquor Drive," *CRG*, December 11, 1962; Nick Kotz, "Hughes Set to 'Dry up' Iowa," *DMR*, January 4, 1963.

6. Harrington, "Iowa's Last Liquor Battle," 25–27.

7. Interview with Dwight Jensen.

8. Dwight Jensen interview; press release, January 8, 1963, box 25, Press Releases January–June 1963, HEH-G Papers.

9. Dwight Jensen interview; press release, February 11, 1963, box 25, Press Releases January–June 1963, HEH-G Papers. Unlike Jensen, Boyd left before Hughes's first term was up. Tragically, he later took his own life.

10. Dwight Jensen interview.

11. Jim Larew, *A Party Reborn: The Democrats of Iowa, 1950–1974* (Iowa City: Iowa State Historical Society, 1980), 81; interview with Elva Pittman; William Hedlund and Russell Wilson, *In His Own Words: The Harold Hughes Story* (Bloomington, IN: LifeRich Publishing, 2020), 84.

12. Harold Hughes, inaugural address, January 17, 1963, box 27, Speeches, Jan.–Feb. 1963, HEH-G Papers.

13. Hughes inaugural address; George Mills, "School Bus Proposal Surprises Legislature," *DMR*, January 18, 1963.

14. Hughes inaugural address.

15. "5,000 at Inaugural," *DMR*, January 18, 1963.

16. "Erbe to Leave Mansion Today," *DMR*, January 11, 1963; Harold Hughes with Dick Schneider, *Harold E. Hughes: The Man from Ida Grove; a Senator's Personal Story* (Lincoln, VA: Chosen Books Publishing, 1979), 163.

17. Tall Corn Broadcasts (Radio) 1–25, January–July 1963, box 26, HEH-G Papers.

18. Dwight Jensen interview.

19. Nick Kotz, "Liquor Drive Aid Pledged by Hultman," *DMR*, January 24, 1963.

20. Harrington, "Iowa's Last Liquor Battle," 28–31.

21. Harrington, 31–32, 36.

22. Harrington, 32–34.

23. Harrington, 37.

24. Harrington, 37–38.

25. Harrington, 39–40.

26. Harrington, 44–45.

27. Harrington, 45.

28. *Iowa Official Register, 1963–1964* (Des Moines: State of Iowa, 1964), 98; Allan Hoschar, "Assembly Ends, Kills Tax Rise," *DMR*, May 19, 1963; "Iowa Legislators Go Home," *CRG*, May 19, 1963.

29. Hoschar, "Assembly Ends, Kills Tax Rise."

30. *Iowa Official Register*, 100.

31. Charles Wiggins, "The Post World War II Legislative Reapportionment Battle in Iowa Politics," in *Patterns and Perspectives in Iowa History*, ed. Dorothy Schwieder (Ames: Iowa State University Press, 1973), 408–409; Frank Nye, "A Statement on Legislative Apportionment in Iowa and Questions and Answers on the Shaff Plan," October 1, 1963, box 13, Shaff Plan Materials 1963, HEH-G Papers.

32. Wiggins, "Post World War II Legislative Reapportionment," 408–411.

33. Wiggins, 412–413.

34. Wiggins, 415–418; *Iowa Official Register*, 98.

35. "Shaff Plan First Step?" *DMR*, July 20, 1963; interview with Martin Jensen.

36. Tall Corn Broadcasts (Radio) 1–25; memo by Kirk Boyd, administrative assistant, on the Shaff Plan referendum, August 15, 1963, box 13, Shaff Plan Materials 1963, HEH-G Papers.

37. Press release, September 2, 1963, box 25, Press Releases July–December 1963, HEH-G Papers; "Hughes: Shaff Plan a 'Roadblock,'" *DMT*, September 27, 1963.

38. Marvin Braverman, "Hughes Fights Shaff Plan," *DMT*, August 29, 1963.

39. Harrison Weber, "Demos Take No Stand on Shaff Remap Plan," *CRG*, September 26, 1963; "Shaff Plan Assailed by Democrats," *DMR*, September 29, 1963. In the second legislative session, the state senate approved the Shaff Plan by a vote of 31–19, with 29 Republicans and 2 Democrats voting for it. The vote in the Iowa house was 77–28, with 66 Republicans and 11 Democrats voting for it and 10 Republicans and 18 Democrats voting against it. George Mills, "5 Top G.O.P. Leaders Support Shaff Plan," *DMR*, November 6, 1963.

40. Drake Mabry, "Beck Heads Committee to Fight for Shaff Plan," *DMT*, September 12, 1963.

41. Marvin Braverman, "Hughes Says Shaff Plan Sells Iowans Down River," *DMT*, October 23, 1963; remarks of Governor Harold E. Hughes, Iowa Bankers Convention, October 23, 1963, box 13, Shaff Plan Materials 1963, HEH-G Papers. Hughes had planned to give a more mundane speech to the bankers, but when he heard that David Shaff was giving a speech promoting the plan at the same convention, the governor threw away his prepared remarks and spoke emotionally against the amendment. "The Shaff Plan and Governor," *DMR*, November 2, 1963.

42. Mills, "5 Top G.O.P. Leaders Support Shaff Plan."

43. Allan Hoschar, "Beck: Union Bosses Seek Shaff Defeat," *DMR*, November 20, 1963; "Beck Assails Hughes on Shaff Plan," *DMT*, November 14, 1963; Harrison Weber, "Shaff Expects Victory," *CRG*, November 18, 1963.

44. Memo from Dwight Jensen to Harold Hughes, November 5, 1963, box 13, Shaff Plan Materials 1963, HEH-G Papers. Other materials generated by Hughes's staff can be found in the same place.

45. Wiggins, "Post World War II Legislative Reapportionment," 418; Drake Mabry, "Ruling in Shaff Plan Case Awaits Iowa Vote on Dec. 3," *DMT*, November 13, 1963. The federal panel voted 2–1 not to rule on the Shaff Plan; the lone judge who voted in favor of deciding the issue said he would like to rule against the Shaff Plan and save the people of Iowa $250,000 in election costs.

46. "Issues in Shaff Plan Aired across State," *CRG*, November 21, 1963; Drake Mabry, "Go Aloft in Shaff Plan Fight," *DMT*, November 29, 1963.

47. Wiggins, "Post World War II Legislative Reapportionment," 418; George Mills, "Voters Beat Shaff Plan," *DMR*, December 4, 1963.

48. "Court Acts Next on Remap," *CRG*, December 4, 1963.

5. Helping the Downtrodden

1. Frank Nye, "Political Notes," *CRG*, August 18, 1963.

2. Ed Helms, "Gov. Hughes Regrets Time Spent on Ceremonial Trips," *DMR*, October 1, 1963.

3. Interview with Dwight Jensen; "The Governor Is Right," editorial, *CRG*, October 2, 1963.

4. Harold Hughes, inaugural address, January 17, 1963, box 27, Speeches, Jan.–Feb. 1963, HEH-G Papers; Nick Kotz, "Hughes Plea to Kennedy for Feguer," *DMR*, April 26, 1964.

5. *Iowa Official Register, 1963–1964* (Des Moines: State of Iowa, 1964), 100; Kotz, "Hughes Plea to Kennedy."

6. Kotz, "Hughes Plea to Kennedy."

7. Kotz.

8. Interview with Nick Kotz.

9. Kotz interview; Dwight Jensen interview.

10. Press release, January 9, 1965, box 25, Press Releases, January–June 1965, HEH-G Papers; George Mills, "Hughes Spares Life of Tice," *DMR*, January 10, 1965; "Death Penalty Lifted," editorial, *DMR*, January 12, 1965.

11. "Tice Parents Are Elated," *DMR*, January 11, 1965.

12. Gene Raffensperger, "Lifer, 15, and His Questions Jolt Hughes," *DMR*, May 30, 1963.

13. Raffensperger; Harold Hughes with Dick Schneider, *Harold E. Hughes: The Man from Ida Grove; a Senator's Personal Story* (Lincoln, VA: Chosen Books Publishing, 1979), 176–178.

14. Don Finley, "Report on Anamosa Prison Riot," *CRG*, November 8, 1963; Marvin Braverman, "Hughes Demands Full Story of Anamosa Riot," *DMT*, November 4, 1963; "Hughes: Must Decide on Prisons," *DMT*, November 6, 1963.

15. Interview with Russell Wilson.

16. Wilson interview; "Hughes: Must Decide on Prisons"; "Governor to Broaden Prison Plan," *CRG*, November 6, 1963.

17. "Hughes: Must Decide on Prisons"; "Governor to Broaden Prison Plan."

18. George Mills, "Smash Windows at Prison," *DMR*, November 9, 1963; Hughes, *Man from Ida Grove*, 178.

19. Mills, "Smash Windows at Prison"; "Hughes Ends Brief Revolt by Prisoners," *CRG*, November 9, 1963; Hughes, *Man from Ida Grove*, 178.

20. Dwight Jensen interview; Mills, "Smash Windows at Prison"; "Two Penologists to Study Reformatory, State Prison," *CRG*, November 20, 1963.

21. Marvin Braverman, "Hughes' 'Modern' Penal Idea," *DMT*, November 14, 1963.

22. "Penologists' Iowa Prison Study Filed," *CRG*, January 3, 1964; "Call Prison Guards Poorly Trained, Under-paid," *CRG*, January 7, 1964.

23. "Call Prison Guards Poorly Trained"; "Sad Chapter in Penology," *CRG*, June 10, 1964.

24. Marvin Braverman, "Firm Hughes Prison Stand," *DMT*, May 13, 1964.

25. Subcommittee Hearings of the Committee on Appropriations, House of

Representatives, 98th Congress, second session, April 3, 1984, 1638; "Hughes Backs Baer's Program," *DMR*, June 9, 1964; Donald Finley, "Link Powerful Politicians to Baer Resignation," *CRG*, June 10, 1964.

26. Finley, "Link Powerful Politicians to Baer Resignation"; "Hughes' Views on Baer Case," *DMR*, June 16, 1964.

27. Wilson interview.

28. "Hughes: End Our Own Bias," *DMT*, July 13, 1963; Nick Kotz, "Gov. Hughes Names 35 to Rights Group," *DMR*, July 24, 1963.

29. "Apply for Road Patrol, Hughes Urges Negroes," *CRG*, July 30, 1963; "Hughes: For Bans on Housing Bias," *DMT*, October 16, 1963.

30. "Many Critics of Welfare Programs Unfair—Hughes," *CRG*, September 22, 1963.

31. Marvin Braverman, "Hughes Blames '63 Legislature," *DMT*, October 3, 1963; Marvin Braverman, "Protest to Hughes on ADC Cuts," *DMT*, October 9, 1963; "G.O.P. Responsible for Budget Cut, Governor Says," *CRG*, October 3, 1963.

32. Marvin Braverman, "Hughes Sets Weekly 'Gripe Day' for Visitors," *DMT*, August 19, 1963.

33. Drake Mabry, "Hughes Hears Citizens' Complaints," *DMT*, September 4, 1963; "Guards Visit, Thank Hughes," *DMT*, September 11, 1963; Ron Speer, "Governor Hears Father's Plea at First Open House," *CRG*, September 4, 1963; Hughes, *Man from Ida Grove*, 206.

34. Donald R. Finley, "Hughes to Continue 'Open Door,'" *CRG*, November 1, 1963; Dwight Jensen interview.

6. Reapportionment and Reform

1. Charles W. Wiggins, "The Post World War II Legislative Reapportionment Battle in Iowa Politics," in *Patterns and Perspectives in Iowa History*, ed. Dorothy Schwieder (Ames: Iowa State University Press, 1973), 419; Marvin Braverman, "Court Orders Reapportion and Sets out Guidelines," *DMT*, January 15, 1964.

2. "Court Orders Iowa Remap," *CRG*, January 15, 1964; George Mills, "Special Session Feb. 24," *DMR*, January 18, 1964. One issue that had to be settled before the beginning of the special session was representation from Johnson County, home of Iowa City and the University of Iowa. Its Democratic representative, Scott Swisher, was in federal prison in Missouri, serving time for tax evasion. Swisher resigned, and a special election was held to fill the post. The new representative from Johnson County was Minnette Doderer, who soon established herself as a prominent leader in Iowa politics. "3 Iowa Seats to Democrats," *DMR*, February 19, 1964.

3. Message to Special Session of Sixtieth General Assembly by Honorable Harold E. Hughes, Governor of Iowa, Joint Session, February 24, 1964, box 12, Reapportionment, 1963–1964, HEH-G Papers.

4. *Iowa Official Register, 1963–1964* (Des Moines: State of Iowa, 1964), 468.

5. George Mills, "Vote for 6 More Senators," *DMR*, March 10, 1964; Drake Mabry, "Bitter G.O.P. Wrangle," *DMT*, March 10, 1964.

6. Nick Kotz, "Ray of G.O.P. Asks Backing for His Plan," *DMR*, February 12, 1964; "G.O.P. Unit Backs Ray's Remap Plan," *CRG*, February 13, 1964.

7. George Mills, "Iowa G.O.P. Group Urges Senate of 56," *DMR*, March 16, 1964.

8. George Mills and Alan Hoschar, "Senate 'No' on 56-Seat Plan," *DMR*, March 12, 1964; Nick Kotz, "Warns that Senate Plan Defies Court," *DMR*, March 12, 1964; Drake Mabry and Marvin Braverman, "House Insists on Own Plan," *DMT*, March 12, 1964.

9. Drake Mabry, "That Was the Week that Was Wrangling," *DMT*, March 14, 1964.

10. Alan Hoschar, "G.O.P. Rural Bloc Kills 55-Senator Plan," *DMR*, March 17, 1964; George Mills, "Vote Today on Apportion Compromise," *DMR*, March 18, 1964.

11. Drake Mabry and Marvin Braverman, "Hughes: Compromise OK," *DMT*, March 18, 1964; Marvin Braverman, "Hughes Signs Reapportionment Bill," *DMT*, March 23, 1964; George Mills and Alan Hoschar, "Redistricting Bill Passes," *DMR*, March 19, 1964; George Mills, "Iowa's New Legislature Is Approved," *DMR*, March 28, 1964.

12. George Mills and Alan Hoschar, "'Permanent' Plan Passed," *DMR*, April 9, 1964.

13. Statement of Governor Harold Hughes, April 9, 1964, box 12, Reapportionment, 1963–1964, HEH-G Papers.

14. Drake Mabry, "Hughes and Hultman Assail Apportion Plan," *DMT*, April 9, 1964.

15. Reynolds v. Sims, 377 U.S. 533 (1964); "Apportion Plans Upset!" *DMT*, June 15, 1964.

16. "Apportion Plans Upset!"; "Both Houses on Population—May Force Changes in Iowa Remap," *CRG*, June 15, 1964.

17. "Face Problems of Government," *DMT*, January 16, 1964.

18. "Hughes 'Idea Exchange,'" *DMT*, February 8, 1964; "Use Advice of Iowa Leaders, Hughes Urges," *CRG*, May 26, 1964.

19. "Hughes: Education Is Key," *DMT*, February 18, 1964.

20. State of Iowa, Department of Public Instruction, Des Moines, "Problems of Vocational Post–High School, Community College, and Technical Institute Education," April 16, 1964, box 12, Public Instruction, 1964–1967, HEH-G Papers.

21. Frank Nye, "Hughes Asks Improvement in Education," *CRG*, February 21, 1964.

7. LBJ's "Favorite Governor" and Reelection

1. "Hultman Hitchhikes Partway to D. M.," *CRG*, December 30, 1963.

2. Frank Nye, "Hultman in Race; Cites Remap Issue," *CRG*, December 30,

1963; Drake Mabry, "Hultman Enters Governors Race," *DMT*, December 30, 1963.

3. John Bleakly, "Ray's Call to G.O.P.: Back Hultman," *DMT*, March 25, 1964.

4. "Hughes Draws 57% Approval in Poll," *DMR*, January 19, 1964; "Hughes 51%, Hultman 21%, Undecided 28%," *DMR*, March 8, 1964; Donald Finley, "Gov. Hughes Named UPI's Man of Year," *CRG*, January 2, 1964.

5. George Mills, "Hughes to Run for Second Term," *DMR*, January 19, 1964; "Hughes Seeks Second Term as Governor," *CRG*, January 19, 1964.

6. Ron Speer, "Hughes, Hultman to Keep Contact during Campaign," *CRG*, January 3, 1964.

7. "Hultman Tax Plea Derided by Governor," *DMR*, April 23, 1964; Drake Mabry, "Hultman Comes out Swinging," *DMT*, April 25, 1964.

8. Interview with Dwight Jensen; interview with Martin Jensen.

9. Harold Hughes to Hugh McGuire, Holstein, December 10, 1959, box 6, Personal—Hughes, 1959–1968, No. 1, HEH-G Papers; Lyndon Johnson to Harold Hughes, July 26, 1963, box 6, Governors Conference 1963, HEH-G Papers.

10. "Hughes, Johnson Discuss Imports, Hunting," *CRG*, January 24, 1964; Harold Hughes with Dick Schneider, *Harold E. Hughes: The Man from Ida Grove; a Senator's Personal Story* (Lincoln, VA: Chosen Books Publishing, 1979), 187.

11. For a concise summary of American mid-twentieth-century liberal ideology, see James T. Patterson, *Grand Expectations: The United States, 1945–1974* (New York: Oxford University Press, 1996), esp. 524–561.

12. Nick Kotz, "Hughes and Family White House Guests," *DMR*, July 29, 1964; Hughes, *Man from Ida Grove*, 187–188.

13. Hughes, *Man from Ida Grove*, 187; Frank Nye, "Seconding Speech by Hughes Set," *CRG*, August 26, 1964; interview with Phyllis Hughes Ewing.

14. The story of the Mississippi Freedom Democratic Party and its controversial mission to seat itself has been covered in many studies. One of the more detailed discussions is found in Taylor Branch, *Pillar of Fire: America in the King Years, 1963–1965* (New York: Simon & Schuster, 1998), 454–476. See also David Faber, *The Age of Great Dreams: America in the 1960s* (New York: Hill & Wang, 1994), 111.

15. Interview with Sherwin Markman; Branch, *Pillar of Fire*, 469.

16. Frank Nye, "Iowans May Be in Thick of Democratic Fight," *CRG*, August 23, 1964.

17. Hughes, *Man from Ida Grove*, 189.

18. Hughes, 189–190; Branch, *Pillar of Fire*, 473; Drake Mabry, "Johnson's Pressure on Hughes Is Told," *DMT*, August 28, 1964.

19. George Mills, "Hughes Sees Democratic 'Crop' in Seconding Speech," *DMR*, August 27, 1964; Drake Mabry, "A Stellar Role for Hughes," *DMT*, August 27, 1964.

20. Press release, August 31, 1964, box 25, Press Releases July–September 1964, HEH-G Papers.

21. For a detailed summary of the Goldwater campaign and its place in

American history, see Rick Perlstein, *Before the Storm: Barry Goldwater and the Unmaking of the American Consensus* (New York: Nation Books, 2001).

22. George Mills, "Iowa's Ray to Vote for Scranton," *DMR*, July 15, 1964; George Mills, "Hickenlooper 'Incensed' over Rift," *DMR*, July 16, 1964.

23. George Mills, "Lively Clash by Hultman and Hughes," *DMR*, September 20, 1964. Interestingly, Ray's vote against his party's nominee did not cost him the Iowa Republican Party chairmanship. The conservatives' dethroning of Ray would have required the support of Hultman, and the two men had been close for years. The general consensus among party leaders was that it was not the right time for a divisive fight over the chairmanship. George Mills, "Ray Passed Bid to Serve as Seconder," *DMR*, July 17, 1964.

24. "Issues Are Clear, Says Governor," *CRG*, July 18, 1964.

25. "Hughes Vows to Fight Hard," *DMR*, September 2, 1964.

26. Rosenfield quoted in "Iowa Democrats Cite G.O.P. Aid to Hughes," *DMT*, August 28, 1964; "Hughes Lead Strong, but Hultman Gains," *DMR*, July 26, 1964; "Hughes Widens Lead over Hultman in Poll," *DMR*, August 16, 1964.

27. Mills, "Lively Clash by Hultman and Hughes."

28. Ros Jensen, "Hultman Spells out His Program," *DMR*, July 12, 1964; "Two Talks by Hultman," *DMT*, July 4, 1964; Drake Mabry, "Who'll Outshake and Outleg Whom?" *DMT*, August 8, 1964.

29. Ros Jensen, "Hughes Opens Copter Tour of Iowa," *DMR*, October 20, 1964; "Iowa Poll: Goldwater Gains, but Lags, 37–57," *DMR*, November 1, 1964

30. Hughes, *Man from Ida Grove*, 190–191.

31. Fletcher Knebel, "One Man's Triumph," *Look*, October 6, 1964, 97–108; Hughes, *Man from Ida Grove*, 189–190; Fletcher Knebel to Harold Hughes, September 28, 1964, box 9, Look Magazine Story—Hughes, 1964–1965, HEH-G Papers.

32. Letters to Hughes from individuals in California, Florida, Ohio, Maine, Georgia, Massachusetts, and Iowa, box 9, Look Magazine Story—Hughes, 1964–1965, HEH-G Papers; Hughes, *Man from Ida Grove*, 190–191.

33. George Mills, "Hultman Repudiated by Moody," *DMR*, November 1, 1964.

34. Interview with Bill Sueppel.

35. Hughes, *Man from Ida Grove*, 194–195.

36. Hughes, 195; George Mills, "Hultman Reveals Arrest of Hughes as Drunk Driver," *DMR*, October 31, 1964.

37. Hughes, *Man from Ida Grove*, 196; Mills, "Hultman Reveals Arrest of Hughes."

38. Markman interview.

39. "Hultman Charge Brings Critical Reaction—G.O.P.," *CRG*, October 31, 1964; Mills, "Hultman Repudiated by Moody"; phone calls backing the governor, October 30, 1964, box 7, Hughes-Hultman Debates 1964, HEH-G Papers.

40. James A. Socknat, *Governor Harold E. Hughes and Social Crisis in Iowa: A Study of the Exercise of Gubernatorial Power for Human Resources Development* (Ames: Iowa State University, 1969), 9.

41. *Iowa Official Register, 1965–1966* (Des Moines: State of Iowa, 1966), 401;

George Mills, "Worst Loss for G.O.P. in Iowa History," *DMR*, November 4, 1964; Dwight Jensen interview.

42. *Iowa Official Register*, 107; George Mills and Allan Hoscher, "'Democratic' Legislature Convenes Today," *DMR*, January 11, 1965. In addition to sweeping state legislative and executive offices, Iowa Democrats elected six of seven congressional candidates. The lone Republican, conservative H. R. Gross from northeastern Iowa, won by a narrow margin.

8. The Historic 1965 Iowa Legislature

1. George Mills and Alan Hoschar, "'Democratic' Legislature Convenes Today," *DMR*, January 11, 1965.
2. Kenneth Rystrom, "New Legislators Younger than in 1963," *DMR*, January 10, 1965; "Newcomers," caption, *DMT*, January 11, 1965; Frank Nye, "Major Legislation," *Palimpsest* 46, 6 (1967): 459.
3. Interview with Nick Kotz.
4. William Eberline, "Hughes Says Iowa Surging Ahead," *CRG*, January 12, 1965.
5. Messages to the Sixty-First General Assembly by the Honorable Harold Hughes, 1965, box 22, General Assembly 62 Legislation 1965–66, HEH-G Papers.
6. Drake Mabry, "Hughes: Aid for Scholars," *DMT*, January 14, 1965; Frank Nye, "Goals for Iowa Set by Hughes," *CRG*, January 14, 1965.
7. Messages to the Sixty-First General Assembly by Hughes.
8. Frank Nye, "Computer Is Key to Iowa Remap Plan," *CRG*, January 31, 1965; interview with Dwight Jensen.
9. George Mills, "Hughes Man Is Elected Speaker of the House," *DMR*, November 14, 1964.
10. "Strengthening Local Government," editorial, *DMR*, January. 1, 1965.
11. "Open Legislature," editorial, *DMR*, January 14, 1965.
12. George Mills, "Democrats Streamline Legislature," *DMR*, November 18, 1964.
13. Alan Hoschar, "School Bus Bill to Iowa Legislators," *DMR*, February 5, 1965; Harrison Weber, "Private School Closings Keep Public School Enrollment Up," *CRG*, April 5, 1965.
14. George Mills, "Vote School Bus Bill, 66–56," *DMR*, April 7, 1965; Frank Nye, "Tempers Flare during School Bus Bill Debate," *CRG*, April 7, 1965.
15. Frank Nye, "Pupil Ride Bill Beaten in Senate," *CRG*, April 23, 1965; Alan Hoschar, "Bus Ride Bill Loses, 39–19," *DMR*, April 23, 1965.
16. State of Iowa, Department of Public Instruction, Des Moines, Problems of Vocational Post–High School, Community College, and Technical Institute Education, April 16, 1964, box 12, Public Instruction, 1964–1967, HEH-G Papers.
17. Interview with Bill Hedlund; William Hedlund and Russell Wilson, *In His Own Words: The Harold Hughes Story* (Bloomington, IN: LifeRich Publishing, 2020), 111–112.

18. Janice Nahra Friedel, "Engines of Economic Development: The Origins and Evolution of Iowa's Comprehensive Community Colleges," *American Educational History Journal* 37 (2010): 211, 213.

19. For information on Iowa's fifteen community colleges, see https://educateiowa.gov/community-colleges; *Iowa Official Register, 1985–1986* (Des Moines: State of Iowa, 1986), 292; Hedlund and Wilson, *In His Own Words*, 112. The Iowa Board of Regents, representing the state university system, was initially opposed to allowing community colleges to offer liberal arts and science courses, seeing this as competition for state university students. The board successfully lobbied for a strictly vocational curriculum at community colleges. Later, when the board and university management saw the advantages of using community colleges as a feeder system for four-year colleges, they welcomed expansion of the curriculum. Hedlund interview.

20. Friedel, "Engines of Economic Development," 215–217.

21. Charles Wiggins, "The Post World War II Legislative Reapportionment Battle in Iowa Politics," in *Patterns and Perspectives in Iowa History*, ed. Dorothy Schwieder (Ames: Iowa State University Press, 1973), 419–420; "Apportionment Now a Must," editorial, *DMR*, February 14, 1965.

22. Frank Nye, "Action on Many Key Bills Due This Week," *CRG*, April 18, 1965.

23. Nye, "Computer Is Key"; "Enlarging the Legislature," editorial, *DMR*, April 28, 1965.

24. George Mills, "End Voting 'at Large,' Hughes Asks," *DMR*, January 5, 1965; Drake Mabry, "Governor Put in Odd Position," *DMT*, March 13, 1965.

25. "House Kills Remap Plan on 64–53 Vote," *DMR*, June 4, 1965; "Remap Vote Irks Hughes," *DMT*, June 4, 1965.

26. *Iowa Official Register, 1965–1966* (Des Moines: State of Iowa, 1966), 107–108; Frank Nye, "Kudos and Kicks for Assembly," *CRG*, June 6, 1965.

27. "Right-to-Work Foes Stronger, Fight Looms," *DMR*, January 31, 1965.

28. Ros Jensen, "Showdown on Right-to-Work," *DMR*, February 7, 1965.

29. Jensen.

30. "Builders Back Curb on Unions," *DMR*, January 6, 1965.

31. Jensen, "Showdown on Right-to-Work"; Drake Mabry, "Hughes Press Conference," *DMT*, March 6, 1965.

32. Drake Mabry, "Democrats' Union Stand Irks Hughes," *DMT*, January 28, 1965.

33. Nick Kotz, "Hughes' Victory over Union Pressure," *DMR*, April 16, 1965.

34. Ros Jensen, "Hughes Bill Shocks Industry," *DMR*, March 14, 1965.

35. "One-Sided Labor Bill," *DMR*, March 25, 1965; Peter H. Kuyper, president, Rolscreen Company, Pella, Iowa, to Harold Hughes, March 26, 1965, box 16, Trade Mission to Europe—Right-to-Work and Labor Letters, HEH-G Papers.

36. Drake Mabry, "Hughes Labor Law Plea," *DMT*, May 5, 1965; Frank Nye, "Labor Law Pinpointed by Hughes," *CRG*, May 5, 1965.

37. Mabry, "Hughes Labor Law Plea."

38. George Mills, "Union Shop Passes, 75–46," *DMR*, May 19, 1965.

39. Alan Hoschar, "Defeat Union Shop, 31–27," *DMR*, May 22, 1965.

40. Governor Harold E. Hughes, broadcast—Tall Corn Network, March 15, 1963, box 26, Tall Corn Broadcasts (Radio) 1–25, January–July 1963, HEH-G Papers; "Death Penalty Lifted," editorial, *DMR*, January 12, 1965.

41. "An End to Legal Hangings," editorial, *DMR*, February 20, 1965.

42. "Abolishing the Death Penalty," editorial, *DMR*, February 6, 1965; "Lauds Vote Banning Death Penalty," *DMR*, February 19, 1965; "Death-Ban Bill Signed," *DMT*, February 24, 1965.

43. Frank Nye, "End Death Penalty in Iowa," *CRG*, February 18, 1965.

44. Adam Fairclough, *To Redeem the Soul of America: The Southern Christian Leadership Conference and Martin Luther King* (Athens: University of Georgia Press, 1987), 242–243.

45. Western Union telegram to the Honorable George Wallace, governor of Alabama, March 13, 1965, box 1, Alabama Race Riots, 1965, HEH-G Papers; Drake Mabry, "'Disgrace,' Says Hughes to Wallace," *DMT*, March 12, 1965. Hughes was not alone in expressing his revulsion for the state troopers' attack on the defenseless marchers in Selma, Alabama. Telegrams poured into the White House from across the nation. Pickets outside the Justice Department in Washington, DC, demanded federal intervention in Selma. Congressmen and senators decried the brutal actions on the floors of their respective chambers. The event prompted President Johnson to address Congress and the nation days later, ending with his famous words, "And we shall overcome." All this pressure contributed to passage of the federal Voting Rights Act of 1965. See Kevin Boyle, *The Shattering: America in the 1960s* (New York: W. W. Norton, 2021), 189–192, 208.

46. "Proposed Civil Rights Act for Iowa," *DMR*, January 20, 1965.

47. Marvin Braverman, "State Civil Rights Unit Voted," *DMT*, March 24, 1965; *Iowa Official Register, 1965–1966*, 107.

48. Alan Hoschar and George Mills, "Iowa Legislature Finally Calls It Quits," *DMR*, June 5, 1965.

49. Hoschar and Mills.

50. "Hughes Names Firm for Study," *DMR*, August 20, 1965; Marvin Braverman, "Set a Full Tax Study for Iowa," *DMT*, October 8, 1965.

51. "A Forward Looking Legislature," editorial, *DMR*, June 8, 1965; "Decision Session," editorial, *DMT*, June 7, 1965; Frank Nye, "Kudos and Kicks for Assembly," *CRG*, June 6, 1965.

52. Marvin Braverman, "A Formal End to '65 Assembly," *DMT*, June 10, 1965; Nye, "Kudos and Kicks for Assembly."

9. Where Angels Fear to Tread

1. "Gov. Hughes' Father Dies," *DMR*, March 2, 1965; interview with Phyllis Hughes Ewing.

2. Charles E. Connerly, *Green, Fair, and Prosperous: Paths to a Sustainable Iowa* (Iowa City: University of Iowa Press, 2020), 5–8.

3. Ed Helms, "Pact Sought at Iowa Beef," *DMR*, February 8, 1965; Wilson J. Warren, *Tied to the Great Packing Machine: The Midwest and Meat Packing* (Iowa City: University of Iowa Press, 2007), 23–26; Connerly, *Green, Fair, and Prosperous*, 8.

4. Helms, "Pact Sought at Iowa Beef."

5. Helms.

6. George Anthan, "Fort Dodge Packing Strike," *DMT*, March 6, 1965; Ros Jensen, "Beef Plant Picketing Curbed," *DMR*, March 7, 1965; Nick Lamberto, "Crosses Picket Line 'at Gunpoint,'" *DMR*, March 9, 1965.

7. Frank Nye, "New Labor Bill Backed by Hughes," *CRG*, March 9, 1965.

8. Nick Lamberto, "Hughes Acts in Beef Strike," *DMR*, March 17, 1965.

9. "Hughes Joins Packing Talks," *DMR*, March 26, 1965.

10. "Plans to Open Struck Plant," *DMR*, April 2, 1965; Ed Helms, "Beef Strike Talks Today," *DMR*, April 3, 1965.

11. Jack Gillard, "Strike Talks Deadlocked," *DMR*, April 4, 1965.

12. Harold Hughes with Dick Schneider, *Harold E. Hughes: The Man from Ida Grove; a Senator's Personal Story* (Lincoln, VA: Chosen Books Publishing, 1979), 199.

13. Hughes, 199–200; Jack Gillard, "Iowa Beef Postpones Reopening," *DMR*, April 5, 1965.

14. Ed Helms, "Ratify Pact at Iowa Beef in Ft. Dodge," *DMR*, April 6, 1965.

15. Helms.

16. Dorothy Schwieder and Elmer Schwieder, *A Peculiar People: Iowa's Old Order Amish*, expanded ed. (Iowa City: University of Iowa Press, 2009), xi, 5, 98.

17. "Liens to Be Served during Amish Truce," *CRG*, November 23, 1965; Schwieder and Schwieder, *Peculiar People*, 100.

18. Schwieder and Schwieder, *Peculiar People*, 101–102.

19. Schwieder and Schwieder, 102.

20. Schwieder and Schwieder, 103.

21. Schwieder and Schwieder, 104; "Bus Will Go for Amish Children Again Monday," *CRG*, November 21, 1965.

22. Schwieder and Schwieder, *Peculiar People*, 105.

23. Schwieder and Schwieder, 107.

24. "Not Involved in Amish Dispute, Hughes Stresses," *CRG*, September 29, 1965.

25. "Act to Seize Goods from Iowa Amish," *DMR*, October 30, 1965; "Beliefs More Valuable than Property—Amish," *CRG*, October 31, 1965; "Sympathizers Pay Fines of Amish Father," *CRG*, November 9, 1965.

26. Petition from Amish parochial schools to Harold E. Hughes, October 1965, box 4, Amish—1966, No. 4, HEH-G Papers; Governor Harold Hughes, Iowa Radio Broadcast No. 65-42, November 13, 1965, box 26, Governor's Radio Broadcasts 1965, HEH-G Papers.

27. Schwieder and Schwieder, *Peculiar People*, 107; "Tape Recording of Hughes' Speech Jars Amish Fathers," *CRG*, November 16, 1965; John Robertson, "Roundup of Amish Fails," *CRG*, November 19, 1965.

28. Gene Raffensperger, "After Tears, Anguish, Amish Attend Classes," *DMR*, November 20, 1965.

29. Schwieder and Schwieder, *Peculiar People*, 108; Gene Raffensperger, "Amish Again Defy School," *DMT*, November 22, 1965.

30. Ed Helms, "Hughes Urges Amish Truce," *DMR*, November 23, 1965.

31. Governor Harold Hughes, Iowa Radio Broadcast No. 65-42, November 27, 1965, box 26, Governor's Radio Broadcasts 1965, HEH-G Papers.

32. Art Hough, "Governor Visits Amish Fathers Near Hazleton," *CRG*, January 10, 1966; interview with Bill Hedlund.

33. George Mills, "Hughes Hints Amish Must Obey Law," *DMR*, January 11, 1966; Hedlund interview.

34. Background on governor's role in the Amish situation, n.d., box 1, Alcoholism—Statewide Program—1965–1967, No. 2, HEH-G Papers; "Hughes Meets Oelwein Group," *DMR*, February 4, 1966; Donald Finley, "Asks State Fund for Amish," *CRG*, February 22, 1966.

35. Harrison Weber, "Hughes Tells Views on Amish Issue," *CRG*, February 18, 1966; Finley, "Asks State Fund for Amish."

36. George Mills, "Legislative Battle Seen on Amish Aid," *DMR*, February 23, 1966.

37. George Mills, "Legislators Cool to Amish Aid," *DMR*, February 27, 1966.

38. Schwieder and Schwieder, *Peculiar People*, 110; George Mills, "House Group Cool to Plan to Aid Amish," *DMR*, February 3, 1967; James Flansburg, "For Amish Schools, a New Idea," *DMR*, April 2, 1967; James Flansburg, "Urge Waiving School Standards for Amish," *DMR*, April 15, 1967.

39. "Amish Win School Battle," *DMR*, July 1, 1967; Schwieder and Schwieder, *Peculiar People*, 114–115.

40. Schwieder and Schwieder, *Peculiar People*, 114, 116; Hedlund interview.

10. Vietnam, State Politics, and Aid to Alcoholics

1. Stephen Seplow, "98 Iowans Gave Lives in Vietnam," *DMR*, December 18, 1966.

2. Marvin Braverman, "D.C. Briefing Bolsters Hughes Viet Stand," *DMT*, July 30, 1965; press release, August 2, 1965, box 25, Press Releases, July–December 1965, HEH-G Papers.

3. "Weekend of Viet Protests—Students in Iowa Also Take Part," *DMR*, October 16, 1965; "Student at U. of I. Burns Draft Cards," *DMR*, October 21, 1965; "Students to Demonstrate on Vietnam," *CRG*, October 15, 1965.

4. Interview with Tom Harkin.

5. "Hughes Sees Attack on Reds," *DMT*, November 6, 1965; "Hughes Sees U.S. Bombing of Viet Cong," *DMR*, November 7, 1965; "Hughes Visits a U.S. Carrier," *DMR*, November 8, 1965; "Hughes Leaves Viet for Okinawa," *DMR*, November 9, 1965; "Hughes, Other Governors to Visit Frontline Units," *CRG*, November 8, 1965.

6. Transcript of press conference concerning governor's trip to Japan and Vietnam, November 11, 1965, box 16, HEH-G Papers.

7. *Meet the Press*, NBC, April 4, 1971, box 196, Press—Pending, June–July 1971, HEH-S Papers; interview with Phyllis Hughes Ewing.

8. Interview with George Drake; George Drake, *Mentor: Life and Legacy of Joe Rosenfield* (Des Moines, IA: Business Publications Corporation, 2019), 145; Nick Kotz and James Risser, "Messiah from the Midwest?" *Washington Monthly* 2, 3 (May 1970): 52.

9. "Hughes Rakes S.N.C.C. Stand," *DMR*, January 8, 1966; "We'll Survive 'Godawful Music' of Youth: Hughes," *DMR*, February 18, 1966.

10. Clark Mollenhoff, "Hughes: Work out Disputes," *DMR*, February 10, 1966.

11. Nick Kotz, "Johnson: We'll Never Run—Vows Firm Viet Nam Stand in Speech Here," *DMR*, July 1, 1966; "Hughes Says Visit to Iowa Aided Johnson's Strength," *DMR*, July 6, 1966; remarks of the president, Veterans Auditorium, Des Moines, Iowa, June 30, 1966, box 12, Presidential and Vice Presidential Correspondence, 1964–1968, HEH-G Papers.

12. James Flansburg, "Democrats to Take Sides in Primaries," *DMR*, July 15, 1965.

13. Ron Speer, "Demo Plan Is Lashed by Hughes," *CRG*, July 15, 1965; press release, July 15, 1965, box 25, Press Releases, July–December 1965, HEH-G Papers.

14. Letter to Donald J. Mitchell from most of the executive council, July 16, 1965, Correspondence and Democratic Literature—Jan. 9, 1964–Dec. 21, 1965, Mitchell Papers.

15. "Primary 'Compromise' Is Backed by Hughes," *DMR*, July 18, 1965.

16. Jack Gilliard, "Hughes and Hawkins Not Feuding," *DMR*, August 4, 1965.

17. Frank Nye, "Endorsing by Demos Is Voted," *CRG*, June 11, 1966; George Mills, "Lex Hawkins Resigns as Demo Chief," *DMR*, June 12, 1966.

18. Jim Larew, *A Party Reborn: The Democrats of Iowa, 1950–1974* (Iowa City: Iowa State Historical Society, 1980), 116.

19. James A. Socknat, *Governor Harold E. Hughes and Social Crisis in Iowa: A Study of the Exercise of Gubernatorial Power for Human Resources Development* (Ames: Iowa State University, 1969), 12–13.

20. Socknat, 13–14.

21. US Department of Labor press release, June 4, 1965, box 9, Manpower Development 1965, HEH-G Papers; news bulletin of the Iowa State Manpower Development Council, n.d., box 9, Manpower Development 1965, HEH-G Papers.

22. Press release, January 5, 1966, box 25, Press Releases, January–July 1966, HEH-G Papers; Iowa State Manpower Development Council, Third Progress Report, March 15, 1966, to May 15, 1966, box 9, Manpower Development 1966, No. 2, HEH-G Papers.

23. Socknat, *Governor Hughes and Social Crisis in Iowa*, 14–15.

24. Socknat, 16; activities of the Iowa State Manpower Development Council, January 1967, box 9, Manpower Development 1967, HEH-G Papers.

25. Maurice Isserman and Michael Kazin, *America Divided: The Civil War*

of the 1960s, 3rd ed. (New York: Oxford University Press, 2008), 115; Jerry Szumski, "Hughes and Shriver Meet Privately Today," *DMR*, January 21, 1966.

26. Szumski, "Hughes and Shriver Meet Privately Today"; Jerry Szumski, "Denies Wider Poverty Role for Governor," *DMR*, January 22, 1966; interview with Russell Wilson.

27. Wilson interview; William Hedlund and Russell Wilson, *In His Own Words: The Harold Hughes Story* (Bloomington, IN: LifeRich Publishing, 2020), 124; Socknat, *Governor Hughes and Social Crisis in Iowa*, 15.

28. Wilson interview.

29. Wilson interview; Harold Hughes to Sargent Shriver, April 15, 1966, box 1, Alcoholism—Statewide Program—1965–1967, No. 2, HEH-G Papers; Harrison Weber, "Unique Iowa Alcoholism Program," *CRG*, July 12, 1966.

30. "Says Alcoholics Fall off Referral Merry-Go-Round," *CRG*, April 5, 1966; press release, July 12, 1966, box 25, Press Releases, January–July 1966, HEH-G Papers.

31. Donald Finley, "Plans for Alcoholism Treatment Centers, Halfway Houses Aired," *CRG*, August 26, 1966.

32. Memorandum from Russell Wilson to Harold Hughes, January 26, 1967, box 1, Alcoholism—Statewide Program—1965–1967, No. 3, HEH-G Papers; Frank Nye, "Legalizing of ICAP Given House OK," *CRG*, June 19, 1967.

33. Kelsey Ensign, "From Iowa to the Nation: Harold Hughes and the Politics of Alcoholism Treatment," *Annals of Iowa* 81 (Summer 2022): 227–228.

34. Harold Hughes to Sargent Shriver, director, OEO, February 9, 1968, box 1, Alcoholism—ICAP, 1967–1968, No. 1, HEH-G Papers.

35. Hugh P. Finerty, city attorney, Council Bluffs, to Harold Hughes, February 5, 1968; Mac A. Leaming, Fort Dodge, to Harold Hughes, February 6, 1968; P. Keith Simpson, DO, director, Harrison Treatment and Rehabilitation Center, to Harold Hughes, February 9, 1968, all in box 1, Alcoholism—ICAP, 1967–1968, No. 1, HEH-G Papers.

36. Memorandum from Leo E. Chester to William G. Hedlund, May 21, 1968; Wayne Shoemaker to Harold Hughes, April 4, 1968, both in box 1, Alcoholism—ICAP, 1967–1968, No. 1, HEH-G Papers.

37. Sargent Shriver, director, OEO, to Harold Hughes, February 26, 1968, box 1, Alcoholism—ICAP, 1967–1968, No. 1, HEH-G Papers.

11. Third-Term Reelection

1. George Mills, "Hughes Will Seek Third Term," *DMR*, January 9, 1966; "Hughes (55%), Miller (52%) Win Heat," *DMR*, February 6, 1966.

2. Mills, "Hughes Will Seek Third Term."

3. Dorothy Schwieder, *Iowa: The Middle Land* (Ames: Iowa State University Press, 1996), 303; "Democrats Still Lead, G.O.P. Gains in Poll," *DMR*, May 1, 1966; "Hughes Still Leads, but Drops 9%," *DMR*, May 22, 1966; Drake Mabry, "Campaign Issue in One Word," *DMT*, June 17, 1966.

4. Mabry, "Campaign Issue in One Word"; Jerry Szumski and David Eastman, "Democrats Ask Income Tax Refund," *DMR*, March 29, 1966.

5. Drake Mabry, "How Tax Became a Campaign Issue," *DMT*, March 31, 1966.

6. "G.O.P. Leaders Raps Hughes' Tax Statement," *CRG*, March 28,1966.

7. James H. Schweiker, "Surplus Not Too Large, Say Demos," *CRG*, March 27, 1966.

8. "Hughes Sees No Prospect of a Rebate," *DMT*, April 13, 1966.

9. Harrison Weber, "Iowa Tax-Take up $93 Million in 1966," *CRG*, July 8, 1966; George Mills, "State Boost in School Tax Aid to Farms," *DMR*, August 5, 1966.

10. *Iowa Official Register, 1967–1968* (Des Moines: State of Iowa, 1968), 395.

11. Drake Mabry, "Calm Race by Two in G.O.P.," *DMT*, August 13, 1966; George Mills, "Face-to-Face on Tax 'Forgiveness,'" *DMR*, September 1, 1966.

12. *Iowa Official Register, 1967–1968*, 395; "1,370 Lead to Murray," *CRG*, September 7, 1966; George Mills, "Beck Yields, Pledges Aid to Murray," *DMR*, September 8, 1966.

13. Advice to Governor Hughes from Park Rinard, August 1966, box 3, Campaign 1966, HEH-G Papers.

14. Ed Heins, "Hughes Sees Danger to State's Future in Tax Refund Proposal," *DMR*, September 9, 1966.

15. George Mills, "The Iowa Campaign Issue: Surplus vs. Taxes," *DMR*, September 11, 1966; George Mills, "Some G.O.P. Coolness to Tax Refund," *DMR*, September 19, 1966; Stephen Seplow, "4 G.O.P. Hopefuls Shun Refund," *DMR*, September 20, 1966; Frank Nye, "Party Chiefs Argue Surplus," *CRG*, September 12, 1966.

16. Frank Nye, "Says Murray Phasing out Refund Plan," *CRG*, September 25, 1966; Drake Mabry, "Hughes Assails Refund, Murray Calls for More Industry," *DMT*, September 26, 1966.

17. "Poll Finds Hughes, Miller Leading," *DMR*, October 9, 1966; "Most Would Spend Surplus for Needs," *DMR*, October 16, 1966.

18. James Flansburg, "The Iowa Campaign—Hughes Assails 'Vote Buying,'" *DMR*, October 26, 1966.

19. Drake Mabry, "Hughes Asserts Tax Fears Are Premature," *DMT*, October 25, 1966; Drake Mabry, "Hughes Aims at Victory—That's Total," *DMT*, October 29, 1966; "Hughes, Miller Lead in Final Iowa Poll," *DMR*, November 6, 1966.

20. *Iowa Official Register, 1967–1968*, 414; George Mills, "Five Seats in Congress Won by G.O.P.," *DMR*, November 9, 1966; Frank Nye, "Freshmen Hold Key to 1967 Legislature," *CRG*, January 8, 1967; interview with Robert Fulton.

21. Drake Mabry, "Hughes, Miller Victors," *DMT*, November 9, 1966.

22. Robert Dallek, *Flawed Giant: Lyndon Johnson and His Times, 1961–1973* (New York: Oxford University Press, 1998), 335–339.

12. Presidential Confrontation and State Reform

1. Harold Hughes with Dick Schneider, *Harold E. Hughes: The Man from Ida Grove; a Senator's Personal Story* (Lincoln, VA: Chosen Books Publishing, 1979), 224–225.

2. Hughes, 225; interview with Dwight Jensen.

3. Hughes, *Man from Ida Grove*, 226; Dwight Jensen interview.

4. Nick Kotz, "Hughes Blames Johnson," *DMR*, December 16, 1966; Jack Bell, "Demos Train Guns on Johnson," *CRG*, December 16, 1966.

5. Kotz, "Hughes Blames Johnson"; interview with Sherwin Markman.

6. Nick Kotz, "Hughes in U.S. Spotlight," *DMR*, December 18, 1966.

7. George Mills, "Hughes Confronts Johnson," *DMR*, December 22, 1966; Hughes, *Man from Ida Grove*, 228; William Hedlund and Russell Wilson, *In His Own Words: The Harold Hughes Story* (Bloomington, IN: LifeRich Publishing, 2020), 119; Dwight Jensen interview; interview with Bill Hedlund. The other governors present at the presidential meeting were Warren E. Hearnes, Missouri; John Connally, Texas; Dan Moore, North Carolina; Robert McNair, South Carolina; Hulett Smith, West Virginia; Philip Hoff, Vermont; Mills Goodwin, Virginia; and Karl Rolvaag, Minnesota.

8. Mills, "Hughes Confronts Johnson"; Vance Bourjaily, *Country Matters* (New York: Dial Press, 1973), 226.

9. Minutes of Advisory Commission on Governmental Reorganization, June 14, 1966, box 17, Government Reorganization 1966, HEH-G Papers.

10. Advisory Commission minutes.

11. Administrative Organization of the Executive Branch of Iowa, "A Survey Report, Part One, Public Administration Service, Chicago," November 28, 1966, box 6, Government Reorganization, 1965–1967, No. 1, HEH-G Papers.

12. Executive Order 6, November 7, 1966, box 6, Executive Orders, 1963–1970, HEH-G Papers.

13. Administrative Organization of the Executive Branch of Iowa, "Survey Report"; Harrison Weber, "One Social Service Dept. Urged," *CRG*, December 7, 1966.

14. "Hughes O.K.'s State Plan Goal," *DMT*, November 18, 1966.

15. Messages to the Sixty-Second General Assembly by the Honorable Harold Hughes, 1967, box 22, General Assembly 62 Legislation 1966–67, HEH-G Papers; Frank Nye, "Iowa's Future Unlimited, Says Hughes," *CRG*, January 10, 1967; Frank Nye, "Hughes Asks Big Program," *CRG*, January 12, 1967; "Hughes Action Program," editorial, *DMR*, January 14, 1967.

16. Charles Wiggins, "The Post World War II Legislative Reapportionment Battle in Iowa Politics," in *Patterns and Perspectives in Iowa History*, ed. Dorothy Schwieder (Ames: Iowa State University Press, 1973), 421–422.

17. Wiggins, "Post World War II Legislative Reapportionment," 423; "Legislators, Hughes Confer," *DMR*, January 6, 1967.

18. Wiggins, "Post World War II Legislative Reapportionment," 423–430.

19. "Chaotic Tax Situation," editorial, *DMR*, July 5, 1966; "Says Tax Structure Inequitable," *CRG*, July 11, 1966.

20. George Mills, "See Record Property Tax Rise," *DMR*, August 7, 1966.

21. Report of the Tax Study Advisory Committee to Governor Harold E. Hughes, January 1967, box 14, Tax Study 1965–1967, No. 2, HEH-G Papers.

22. Drake Mabry, "Hughes Predicts Surplus of $90 Million Plus," *DMT*, January 16, 1967; Frank Nye, "No Boost in State Tax Asked," *CRG*, January 19, 1967; George Mills, "Hughes Asks 'Basic Tax Reform,'" *DMR*, January 20, 1967.

23. Drake Mabry, "Again, Session-End Confusion," *DMT*, June 24, 1967.

24. Mabry; Hedlund interview.

25. Frank Nye, "School Aid Pact Made by Leaders," *CRG*, June 27, 1967; Hedlund interview.

26. George Mills and Allan Hoschar, "$100-Million Iowa Tax Plan," *DMR*, June 28, 1967; Frank Nye, "House Votes School Aid," *CRG*, June 28, 1967.

27. Alan Hoschar, "Senate Votes Tax Bill, 48–13," *DMR*, June 29, 1967; George Anthan, "House Votes School Aid," *DMT*, June 28, 1967; Drake Mabry, "Tax Bill Is Near Final O.K.," *DMT*, June 29, 1967.

28. Drake Mabry, "Governor Points to 'Major Job' Ahead: To Explain and Defend Tax Program," *DMT*, June 30, 1967; Governor Harold E. Hughes, Iowa Radio Broadcast No. 67-20, July 1, 1967, box 26, Governor's Radio Broadcasts 1967, HEH-G Papers.

29. Governor's Office, excerpts from special press briefing on property tax replacement bill and tax bill for funding it, July 21, 1967, box 14, Tax Bill 1967, No. 1, HEH-G Papers.

30. *Iowa Official Register, 1967–1968* (Des Moines: State of Iowa, 1968), 119; James Risser, "Plan 33% Income Tax Boost," *DMR*, May 7, 1967; Harold Hughes to Daniel J. Evans, governor of Washington, July 27, 1967, box 11, Planning and Programming Office—Advisory Committee of the Department of Social Services, HEH-G Papers.

31. Proposal to US Department of Labor, Project G-R-E-A-T, submitted by Iowa Merit Employment Department, State House, Des Moines, Iowa, November 1967, box 10, Merit Employment Department (Iowa) 1967, HEH-G Papers; "Job Merit Bill Sent to Hughes," *DMT*, May 25, 1967; "Governor Signs Civil Service Bill into Law," *CRG*, June 20, 1967.

32. *Iowa Official Register, 1967–1968*, 119.

33. Press release, July 9, 1963, box 25, Press Releases, July–December 1962, HEH-G Papers; Hedlund interview.

34. Press release on Edward Campbell, July 12, 1965, box 11, Personnel—Governor, 1963–1969, HEH-G Papers.

35. Dwight Jensen to Marvin Selden, July 28, 1967, box 11, Personnel—Governor, 1963–1969, HEH-G Papers; press release, June 4, 1966, box 25, Press Releases, May–August 1968, HEH-G Papers; Dwight Jensen interview.

13. Civil Rights, Crisis Conferences, and a Senate Candidacy

1. Urban violence in Black communities in 1965–68 was generally limited to the summers. Historians and social scientists debate whether this violence

was caused by unmet expectations, racism, urban poverty, police violence, or a combination of factors. For a more detailed summary of the shift in the civil rights movement, see Allen J. Matusow, *The Unraveling of America: A History of Liberalism in the 1960s* (New York: Harper & Row, 1984), especially 180–216. For a discussion of why unrest emerged in Black urban communities in this period, see Godfrey Hodgson, *America in Our Time* (New York: Random House, 1976), especially 429–462. See also David Faber, *The Age of Great Dreams: America in the 1960s* (New York: Hill & Wang, 1994), 111; Maurice Isserman and Michael Kazin, *America Divided: The Civil War of the 1960s*, 3rd ed. (New York: Oxford University Press, 2008), 183–186.

2. Isserman and Kazin, *America Divided*, 210.

3. Charles E. Connerly, *Green, Fair, and Prosperous: Paths to a Sustainable Iowa* (Iowa City: University of Iowa Press, 2020), 98–99.

4. Connerly, 101. For a fuller explanation of the role of abolitionists in the emerging Iowa Republican Party, see Robert Cook, *A Baptism of Fire: The Republican Party in Iowa, 1838–1878* (Ames: Iowa State University Press, 1994), especially chaps. 4 and 5.

5. Connerly, *Green, Fair, and Prosperous*, 101–103; Leland Sage, *A History of Iowa* (Ames: Iowa State University Press, 1974), 174.

6. Connerly, *Green Fair, and Prosperous*, 104–105.

7. Connerly, 109–111, 114; Sage, *History of Iowa*, 173.

8. Sage, *History of Iowa*, 173; Nikole Hannah-Jones, *The 1619 Project: A New Origin Story* (New York: One World/Random House, 2021), 8.

9. Connerly, *Green, Fair, and Prosperous*, 111–113.

10. Dick Spry and Stephen Seplow, "Youths Battle Police Here," *DMR*, July 5, 1966; Jerry Szumski and Stephen Seplow, "Good Park Unrest: What's Behind It?" *DMR*, July 7, 1966; "Governor of Iowa Starts Negro Aid," *NYT*, August 8, 1967.

11. "Parents Should Act—Hughes," *CRG*, September 13, 1966.

12. Chad Skaggs, "Damage Is Heavy in Waterloo Disturbance," *CRG*, July 10, 1967.

13. Father Cyril F. Engler, Evaluation of Community Problems, Waterloo Area, July 19, 1967, box 9, Manpower Development 1967, No. 1, HEH-G Papers; Jerry Szumski, "Finds Gulf between Races in Waterloo," *DMR*, July 23, 1967.

14. James Risser, "Hughes Visits S.E. Bottoms," *DMR*, July 22, 1967; Harold Hughes with Dick Schneider, *Harold E. Hughes: The Man from Ida Grove; a Senator's Personal Story* (Lincoln, VA: Chosen Books Publishing, 1979), 232–233.

15. Risser, "Hughes Visits S.E. Bottoms."

16. "Secret Tour by Gov. Hughes of Waterloo Area," *CRG*, August 1, 1967; "Hughes Sees Waterloo Negro Plight," *DMT*, August 1, 1967.

17. "Governor Looks for Himself," editorial, *DMR*, August 8, 1967; "Hughes Tours Negro Area in Davenport," *CRG*, August 8, 1967.

18. Governor Harold Hughes press conference, August 9, 1967, box 16, Transcripts—Press Conference, 1967–1968, HEH-G Papers.

19. "Seek Roots of Iowa Racial Unrest," *DMR*, August 13, 1967.

20. Harrison Weber, "Housing and Jobs Stressed by Governor," *CRG*, August 15, 1967; John Armstrong, "Private Youth Work Program Gains in D.M.," *CRG*, August 15, 1967.

21. Proposal to US Department of Labor Manpower Administration, submitted by Harold E. Hughes, governor, state of Iowa, January 2, 1968, box 5, Crisis Meeting 1968, No. 2, HEH-G Papers; report to Thomas N. Urban, mayor of the city of Des Moines, February 5, 1968, box 4, Community Improvement Incorporated, 1967–1968, HEH-G Papers.

22. Hughes, *Man from Ida Grove*, 232; James A. Socknat, *Governor Harold E. Hughes and Social Crisis in Iowa: A Study of the Exercise of Gubernatorial Power for Human Resources Development* (Ames: Iowa State University, 1969), 29–30; interview with Peg Shoemaker Mikulanec; interview with Russell Wilson.

23. Conference on Iowa's crisis (a summons to action), January 1968, box 5, Crisis Meeting 1968, No. 1, HEH-G Papers; James Beaumont, "A Challenges to Hughes on Social Ills," *DMR*, January 22, 1968: Socknat, *Governor Hughes and Social Crisis in Iowa*, 31.

24. Socknat, *Governor Hughes and Social Crisis in Iowa*, 28.

25. Paul H. King, executive secretary, Iowa Council of Churches, to Harold Hughes, February 19, 1968, box 5, Crisis Meeting 1968, No. 1, HEH-G Papers; Louis Milton Thompson Jr., "The Communication and Decision-Making Processes, Environmental Factors in Harold E. Hughes' 1968 Campaign for the U.S. Senate" (master's thesis, Iowa State University, 1969), 82.

26. Thompson, "Communication and Decision-Making Processes," 92.

27. Proposal to US Department of Labor Manpower Administration; Jerry Szumski, "7 Cities Plan Job Program for Dropouts," *DMR*, January 11, 1968; Bill Hedlund, memo on discussion meeting with governor, January 31, 1968, box 5, Crisis Meeting 1968, HEH-G Papers.

28. Gene Raffensperger, "Hughes Maps Cure to Riots," *DMR*, March 7, 1968.

29. Raffensperger; William Simbro, "Hughes Challenges C.R. Officials to Aid Minorities," *DMR*, March 21, 1968; conversation with Russ Wilson—governor's staff, March 14, 1968, box 5, Crisis Meeting 1968, HEH-G Papers; Socknat, *Governor Hughes and Social Crisis in Iowa*, 43.

30. Memo from Bill Hedlund to Harold Hughes, April 19, 1968, box 5, Crisis Meeting 1968, No. 1, HEH-G Papers; crisis follow-up meetings by Russell Wilson, April 18, 1968, box 5, Crisis Meeting 1968, HEH-G Papers; Teamwork for Human Rights, 1968, Eight Iowa Programs during the International Human Rights Years, Prepared by Dr. W. H. Stacy, Iowa State University, Human Rights Committee, Iowa Division, United Nations Association, USA, December 1969, box 8, Judiciary, Civil Rights, 1969, HEH-S Papers; Socknat, *Governor Hughes and Social Crisis in Iowa*, 63–64.

31. James Flansburg, "35 U. of I. Students Chase CIA Recruiter," *DMR*, January 18, 1967; "CIA Protest Signs Taken by Officials," *DMR*, January 19, 1967.

32. "Peace Pickets at Parsons Sprayed with Deodorant," *DMR*, January 20, 1967; James Beaumont, "Protest Viet in D.M. March," *DMR*, April 16, 1967; photo caption, *CRG*, May 25, 1967.

33. Al Nelson, "Melee on Iowa U. Campus," *CRG*, November 1, 1967; "8 Pickets March in CIA Protest," *DMR*, January 20, 1967; "Strife on Iowa Campus!" *DMR*, November 2, 1967; James Flansburg, "A Bad Day at Iowa City— Protestors Attempt to Halt Job Interviews," *DMR*, December 6, 1967.

34. "61 Pct of Iowans against Johnson in War," *DMR*, September 3, 1967. Of course, disapproval of Johnson's policy meant different things to different people. Some respondents wanted a full withdrawal, others wanted a dramatic escalation for a quick end to the conflict, and still others urged a negotiated settlement. In any case, dissatisfaction with Johnson's Vietnam policy was significant in Iowa by 1967.

35. James Risser, "Hint Hughes to Take Top Business Job," *DMR*, August 4, 1967; "Hughes Plans Not Set Yet," *DMR*, August 6, 1967.

36. *Iowa Official Register, 1967–1968* (Des Moines: State of Iowa, 1968), 40; Nick Kotz, "Stanley Puts Senate Campaign in Gear," *DMR*, June 16, 1967.

37. Kotz, "Stanley Puts Senate Campaign in Gear"; "It's Official: Stanley Seeks Senate Seat," *CRG*, June 26, 1967.

38. "Poll Shows Hughes 47–40 over Hickenlooper," *DMR*, October 22, 1967.

39. Thompson, "Communication and Decision-Making Processes," 48.

40. Kevin Boyle, *The Shattering: America in the 1960s* (New York: W. W. Norton, 2021), 255–256. For a detailed summary of the personal conflict between Robert Kennedy and Lyndon Johnson, see Jeff Shesol, *Mutual Contempt: Lyndon Johnson, Robert Kennedy, and the Feud that Defined a Decade* (New York: Norton, 1998).

41. Hughes, *Man from Ida Grove*, 237; Thompson, "Communication and Decision-Making Processes," 53–54.

42. Thompson, "Communication and Decision-Making Processes," 54.

43. Thompson, 238–240.

44. Thompson, 242; interview with Pat Deluhery.

45. "Hughes Announces He Will Run for U.S. Senate," *DMR*, December 17, 1967.

46. George Mills, "G.O.P. Delight in Hughes Bid," *DMR*, December 19, 1967.

47. George Mills, "Hickenlooper Retirement Aids Hughes," *DMR*, December 29, 1967.

14. Political Upheaval in Iowa and the Nation

1. Interview with Pat Jensen.

2. George Mills, "Iowans Back McCarthy by 46–1 Vote," *DMR*, December 3, 1967; George Mills, "Demos Told: 'Bolt Party over Vietnam,'" *DMR*, December 11, 1967.

3. George C. Herring, *America's Longest War: The United States and Vietnam, 1950–1975*, 2nd ed. (New York: Alfred A. Knopf, 1986), 198–202.

4. George Mills, "Kennedy Jars Iowa Democrats," *DMR*, March 17, 1968;

Louis Milton Thompson Jr., "The Communication and Decision-Making Processes, Environmental Factors in Harold E. Hughes' 1968 Campaign for the U.S. Senate" (master's thesis, Iowa State University, 1969), 40.

5. Mills, "Kennedy Jars Iowa Democrats."

6. Stephen Seplow, "Hughes Says Johnson 'No' Shocks Him," *DMR*, April 1, 1968.

7. George Mills, "Demos Set for Hot Time in Caucuses," *DMR*, March 25, 1968; George Mills and James Flansburg, "Anti-Johnson Trend in Iowa," *DMR*, March 26, 1968; George Mills, "Major Johnson Defeat in Iowa Caucuses," *DMR*, March 27, 1968.

8. George Mills, "Urges Demo Delegation Challenges," *DMR*, April 4, 1968.

9. "Democratic Caucuses Stir Rift among Party Leaders," *DMR*, April 5, 1968.

10. George Mills, "Battle Begins among Iowa Demo Units," *DMR*, April 2, 1968; Frank Nye, "Kennedy Visits with 900 to 1,000 Iowa Delegates," *CRG*, May 15, 1968; Thompson, "Communication and Decision-Making Processes," 53.

11. George Mills, "Kennedy Wins Iowa Majority," *DMR*, May 26, 1968.

12. Harold Hughes with Dick Schneider, *Harold E. Hughes: The Man from Ida Grove; a Senator's Personal Story* (Lincoln, VA: Chosen Books Publishing, 1979), 248–249; Jon Van, "U.S. Has Malignancy, but It Can Be Cured: Hughes," *DMR*, April 6, 1968.

13. "Iowans Shocked, Stunned by Tragedy of Dr. King's Slaying," *DMR*, April 5, 1968.

14. Stephen Seplow, "Thousands Mourn King Here," *DMR*, April 8, 1968; Nick Lamberto, "Riot Drill for Guardsmen," *DMR*, April 9, 1968; Jack Hovelson, "Break Panes in Waterloo," *DMR*, April 10, 1968; Maurice Isserman and Michael Kazin, *America Divided: The Civil War of the 1960s*, 3rd ed. (New York: Oxford University Press, 2008), 237–238.

15. Seplow, "Thousands Mourn King Here."

16. Jerry Szumski, "Hughes, Turner Collide over Federal Fund Use," *DMR*, April 22, 1967; George Anthan, "Governor Briefed on His Rights," *DMT*, June 2, 1967; "Senate Gets Bill on Aid to Drinkers," *DMT*, June 19, 1967.

17. Anthan, "Governor Briefed on His Rights"; Allan D. Vestal, Murray Professor of Law, to Wade Clark, June 26, 1967, box 7, Highway Safety Act of 1966, 1966–1967, No. 1, HEH-G Papers.

18. George Mills, "New Turmoil on Tax Plan as Groups Rebuff Turner," *DMR*, September 28, 1967; George Mills, "3% Service Tax Goes into Effect at Midnight," *DMR*, September 30, 1967.

19. Richard Turner to Harold Hughes, September 27, 1967, box 2, Attorney General, 1967–1968, HEH-G Papers.

20. "Defer Buying of Iowa Plane," *DMR*, October 14, 1967; memorandum from staff to governor, initialed by Dwight Jensen, October 25, 1967, box 1, Airplane—Hughes, 1966–1968, HEH-G Papers.

21. Dale Kueter, "'Bending the Law' Warning by Turner," *CRG*, December 8, 1967.

22. "Hughes: No Special Session; Lauds Tax Bill, Hits Opponents," *CRG*,

November 16, 1967; Drake Mabry, "Hughes Praises Tax Law," *DMT*, November 16, 1967.

23. Drake Mabry, "Reply to Hughes on Tax," *DMT*, November 2, 1967; Drake Mabry, "A Tax Break Problem," *DMT*, November 25, 1967; Drake Mabry, "A Closer Look at Tax Returns if Claims for Credit Pour In," *DMT*, November 28, 1967; Dale Kueter, "Cronin: Tax Situation Threat to Iowa Growth," *CRG*, December 8, 1967.

24. "Bldg. Tax Suit Urged by Hughes," *CRG*, December 19, 1967.

15. The 1968 Democratic Convention and Senate Race

1. George Mills, "Bobby Warns of Crisis Facing Nation," *DMR*, March 10, 1968; Allen J. Matusow, *The Unraveling of America: A History of Liberalism in the 1960s* (New York: Harper & Row, 1984), 409–410.

2. Harold Hughes with Dick Schneider, *Harold E. Hughes: The Man from Ida Grove; a Senator's Personal Story* (Lincoln, VA: Chosen Books Publishing, 1979), 254–255; "State Period of Mourning," *DMT*, June 6, 1968; "Hughes, Sueppel to Attend Rites for Sen. Kennedy," *CRG*, June 7, 1968.

3. George Mills, "Battle for Iowa Delegates," *DMR*, June 26, 1968.

4. George Mills and Jerry Szumski, "McCarthy vs. Humphrey in Iowa," *DMR*, June 30, 1968.

5. Mills and Szumski.

6. Mills and Szumski; Hughes, *Man from Ida Grove*, 254–255.

7. Drake Mabry, "Humphrey Has It Won? Not Yet, in Hughes' View," *DMT*, July 10, 1968; "Hughes Eyes Ted Kennedy," *DMR*, July 24, 1968.

8. "Hughes Joins Group Urging Views of RFK," *CRG*, August 5, 1968; Roland Evans and Robert Novack, "Hughes: 'Forget It, George'; McGovern Runs Anyway," *DMR*, August 14, 1968.

9. Hughes, *Man from Ida Grove*, 254; Louis Milton Thompson Jr., "The Communication and Decision-Making Processes, Environmental Factors in Harold E. Hughes' 1968 Campaign for the U.S. Senate" (master's thesis, Iowa State University, 1969), 104–105.

10. Clark Mollenhoff, "Sees Move by Hughes as Midwest Key," *DMR*, August 22, 1968.

11. Thomas S. Smith, "The Vietnam Era in Iowa Politics," *Palimpsest* 63, 5 (September–October 1982): 139–140.

12. Matusow, *Unraveling of America*, 411–416.

13. George Mills, "Hughes to Nominate McCarthy," *DMR*, August 25, 1968; George Mills, "Hughes Urges Bombing Halt without Ties," *DMR*, August 26, 1968.

14. Mills, "Hughes to Nominate McCarthy"; Mills, "Hughes Urges Bombing Halt"; Drake Mabry, "The Divided Iowans," *DMT*, August 28, 1968; Thompson, "Communication and Decision-Making Processes," 111.

15. "Iowans Pooped after Session," *DMR*, August 28, 1968.

16. Senator Tom Harkin, insertion of "Eulogy for Park Rinard" by John Culver, *Congressional Record*, December 5, 2000, 26271.

17. George Mills, "Hughes Acclaims M'Carthy as Leader Born of Crisis," *DMR*, August 29, 1968; nomination speech for Senator Eugene J. McCarthy by Governor Harold Hughes of Iowa, Democratic National Convention, Chicago, August 28, 1968, box 25, Press Releases, 1968, May–August, HEH-G Papers.

18. Drake Mabry, "When McCarthy Candidacy Rested in Hughes' Hands," *DMT*, September 26, 1968.

19. Mabry.

20. "19½ Iowa Votes to McCarthy," *DMR*, August 29, 1968; Drake Mabry, "Hughes Rakes 'Riotous' Parley," *DMT*, August 31, 1968.

21. "Opposing Candidates in Tuesday's Primary," *DMR*, September 1, 1968; George Mills, "Hughes Gets Democratic Senate Nod," *DMR*, September 4, 1968; "Stanley vs. Hughes," editorial, *DMR*, September 5, 1968.

22. "Against Bombing-Halt, Troop Pull-out," *DMR*, October 27, 1968.

23. Thompson, "Communication and Decision-Making Processes," 74; "Nixon, Stanley Gain in Iowa Poll," *DMR*, October 13, 1968; interview with Martin Jensen.

24. "Conversations with Senator Harold Hughes," *Addictions* 92 (1997): 143.

25. "Conversations with Senator Harold Hughes," 143.

26. George Mills, "Viet Clash by Stanley and Hughes," *DMR*, September 9, 1968.

27. "Hughes Endorses Viet Statement," *DMR*, October 1, 1968; Drake Mabry, "Hughes—Welcomes Bombing Halt Statement," *DMT*, October 1, 1968.

28. Thompson, "Communication and Decision-Making Processes," 137.

29. Interview with Pat Deluhery.

30. "Hughes Is Ill, Staying at Home," *DMR*, October 4, 1968; "Illness Keeps Hughes Sidelined," *DMT*, October 7, 1968; Hughes, *Man from Ida Grove*, 260.

31. Hughes, *Man from Ida Grove*, 260–261.

32. Thompson, "Communication and Decision-Making Processes," 136, 152.

33. Deluhery interview.

34. "Hughes Leads Stanley, 50–46%, in Iowa Poll," *DMR*, October 13, 1968; "Hughes Urges Viet Change," *DMR*, October 16, 1968.

35. Governor Harold E. Hughes, Iowa Radio Broadcast No. 68-6, October 13, 1968, box 26, Governor's Radio Broadcasts 1967 & 1968, HEH-G Papers.

36. Drake Mabry, "Stanley Asks U.S. Consider Seizure of North Korea Ships," *DMT*, October 15, 1968; Drake Mabry, "Stanley's Pueblo Idea Is Attacked," *DMT*, October 17, 1968; George Anthan, "Hickenlooper Expresses His Support of Stanley," *DMT*, October 29, 1968; "Thoughtless Suggestion by Stanley," editorial, *DMR*, October 17, 1968.

37. James Flansburg, "Hughes Hits Hard at War in Campaign," *DMR*, October 20, 1968.

38. Thompson, "Communication and Decision-Making Processes," 175.

39. George Mills, "How Iowans View Halt in Bombing," *DMR*, November 1, 1968; Robert Dallek, *Flawed Giant: Lyndon Johnson and His Times, 1961–1973* (New York: Oxford University Press, 1998), 587–588.

40. "Hughes, Stanley Spar on Vietnam, Pueblo, Guns," *CRG*, November 3, 1968; "Nixon Still Leads in Iowa, Humphrey Gains—Hughes Holds Narrow Lead," *DMR*, November 3, 1968.

41. George Mills, "Hughes Wins Senate Seat, Ray Elected Governor," *DMR*, November 6, 1968; *Iowa Official Register, 1969–1970* (Des Moines: State of Iowa, 1970), 350, 352. Hughes's margin of victory was not the smallest. In 1938 Democrat Guy Gillette of Cherokee defeated Republican Lester Dickinson by fewer than twenty-eight hundred votes for a US Senate seat.

42. Mills, "Hughes Wins Senate Seat"; "Hughes Is Winner by Thin Edge," *CRG*, November 6, 1968.

43. Smith, "Vietnam Era in Iowa Politics," 141.

44. "Hughes Is Winner by Thin Edge."

45. George Mills, "Fear Iowans Face More Tax Boosts," *DMR*, September 29, 1968; George Mills, "State Short of Money to Pay Aid to Schools," *DMR*, October 16, 1968.

46. George Mills, "Service Tax Is Upheld by Iowa Court," *DMR*, November 13, 1968; *Iowa Official Register, 1969–1970*, 605.

47. "Interview with Frank Nye," *CRG*, December 11, 1968, box 16, Transcripts 1968, HEH-G Papers; Harrison Weber, "Governors' Problems: Past and Present; Hughes Weighed Tax Bill Risks," *CRG*, December 12, 1968; Frank Nye, "Hughes Cites Iowa Change in Attitude," *CRG*, December 29, 1968.

48. George Mills, "Hughes Quits as of Jan. 2," *DMR*, December 21, 1968.

16. The Hughes Act and Federal Aid to Alcoholics

1. Harold Hughes with Dick Schneider, *Harold E. Hughes: The Man from Ida Grove; a Senator's Personal Story* (Lincoln, VA: Chosen Books Publishing, 1979), 14–19.

2. Hughes, 17–19, 263–266; interview with Dwight Jensen; interview with Martin Jensen. An experience during Hughes's third term as governor prompted this late-night visit. After he had gone to bed, Hughes received a call from a former staffer and fellow AA member who was out of work and despondent. Tired after working for days with little sleep, the governor asked the caller to come to his office in the morning. The next day, Hughes learned that the person had committed suicide. Shaken, Hughes vowed never again to turn down an individual's call for help—no matter how late the hour. William Hedlund and Russell Wilson, *In His Own Words: The Harold Hughes Story* (Bloomington, IN: LifeRich Publishing, 2020), 53.

3. Dwight Jensen interview; Martin Jensen interview; interview with Bill Hedlund.

4. Hughes, *Man from Ida Grove*, 267; Senator Harold E. Hughes, speech at Iowa Regional Medical Program's annual luncheon meeting, Des Moines, June

27, 1969, box 126, Press Releases—Misc. 1969, HEH-S Papers; "First-Choice Committee Assignments to Hughes," *DMR*, January 11, 1969.

5. William L. White, *Slaying the Dragon: The History of Addiction Treatment and Recovery in America* (Bloomington, IL: Chestnut Health Systems/Lighthouse Institute, 1998), 265; Kenneth R. Warren and Brenda Hewitt, "NIAAA: Advancing Alcohol Research for 40 Years," *Alcohol Research and Health* 33, 1–2 (January 2010): 6; Nick Kotz, "Hughes to Head Probe of Alcoholism and Drug Use," *DMR*, April 17, 1969.

6. "Conversation with Harold Hughes," *Addictions* 92 (1997): 142, 144; letter from Ralph Yarborough, chairman, Labor and Public Welfare Committee, March 27, 1969, box 135, A & N Correspondence, April 1969, HEH-S Papers; Nancy Olsen, *With a Lot of Help from Our Friends: The Politics of Alcoholism* (Lincoln, NE: Writers Club Press, 2003), 16.

7. Kotz, "Hughes to Head Probe"; "Conversation with Harold Hughes," 144; Warren and Hewitt, "NIAA: Advancing Alcohol Research for 40 Years," 7.

8. "Conversation with Harold Hughes," 144; Harold Hughes to Wallace Miller, Overland Park, KS, August 15, 1969, box 135, A & N Correspondence, August 12–15, 1969, HEH-S Papers. According to Bill Hedlund, an aide to Jacob Javits told him that Hughes was wasting his time trying to pass alcoholism legislation. Hedlund suggested that the two senators talk, and they eventually "became the best of friends." Hughes had the advantage of not knowing what could not be done, and in typical Hughes fashion, he charged ahead to do it. Hedlund interview.

9. "Conversation with Harold Hughes," 144.

10. Donald Ronning, Park River, ND, to Harold Hughes, March 4, 1969, box 11, Labor & Public Welfare, Health, Misc., HEH-S Papers; transcript—*Tonight Show*, January 5, 1970, box 165, Transcripts from Broadcast Appearances, 1969–70, HEH-S Papers.

11. Opening remarks—Harold E. Hughes, chairman, Open Hearings on Alcoholism and Narcotics, Washington, DC, July 23, 1969, box 165, Press Releases & Opening Statement—Alcoholism Hearings, HEH-S Papers.

12. Nick Kotz, "Hughes, Harrison Turn Spotlight on Alcoholism," *DMR*, July 24, 1969; White, *Slaying the Dragon*, 266; Subcommittee on Alcoholism and Narcotics, August 6–8, 1969, box 165, News Release on August Drug Hearings, HEH-S Papers.

13. "Questions Aid to Alcoholics," *DMR*, July 26, 1969.

14. "Conversation with Harold Hughes," 145.

15. Ralph Yarborough to Harold Hughes, August 5, 1969, box 125, A & N Correspondence, August 1969, 2, HEH-S Papers.

16. The letters are in box 136, A & N Correspondence, August 26–30, 1969, HEH-S Papers.

17. James I. Davidson, executive director, Alcoholism Council of Greater Los Angeles, to Harold Hughes, September 30, 1969, box 136, A & N Correspondence, October 1–16, 1969, HEH-S Papers; press release, October 1, 1969, box 166, Press Release for N.Y. Trip, HEH-S Papers; James Risser, "Hughes Hits Harsh 'Pot' Penalties," *DMR*, October 2, 1969; Brenda Holt, "The Creation

of the National Institute on Alcohol Abuse and Alcoholism," *Alcohol Health & Research World* 19 (1995): 12–16.

18. "Hughes Alcohol Bill Passes Senate in Unanimous Vote," *DMR*, August 11, 1970; Comprehensive Alcohol Abuse and Alcoholism Prevention, Treatment, and Rehabilitation Act of 1970, Public Law 91-616, *U.S. Statutes at Large* 84 (1970): 1851–1852; Kelsey Ensign, "From Iowa to the Nation: Harold Hughes and the Politics of Alcoholism Treatment," *Annals of Iowa* 81 (Summer 2022): 234–236.

19. White, *Slaying the Dragon*, 266; remarks of Senator Harold E. Hughes regarding S. 3835, the Comprehensive Alcohol Abuse and Alcoholism Prevention, Treatment, and Rehabilitation Act of 1970, US Senate, August 10, 1970, box 190, Speeches, 7/6/70–8/10/70, HEH-S Papers; "Hughes Alcohol Bill Passes Senate in Unanimous Vote," *DMR*, August 11, 1970; Warren and Hewitt, "NIAA: Advancing Alcohol Research for 40 Years," 7.

20. "Hughes Wants to Know—Will Administration Implement New Alcoholism Bill?" press release, March 16, 1971, box 169, HEH-S Papers.

21. "Hits Lag on Alcoholism," *DMR*, March 17, 1971; George Anthan, "Senators Hit HEW Stall on Alcoholism," *DMR*, March 19, 1971.

22. Remarks of Senator Harold E. Hughes, US Senate, Washington, DC, March 25, 1971, box 192, Speeches, 3/6/71–4/21/71, HEH-S Papers.

23. Release on alcoholism bill, March 8, 1973, box 173, HEH-S Papers.

24. Harold Hughes to Dr. John C. MacQueen, associate dean, College of Medicine, University of Iowa, Iowa City, March 27, 1973, box 148, A & N Correspondence, General, January–May 1973, HEH-S Papers; Harold Hughes to Nathan S. Seriff, Jamaica, NY, October 2, 1973, box 148, A & N Correspondence, General, September–October 1973, HEH-S Papers.

25. Remarks of Senator Harold E. Hughes, Lutheran General Hospital's First International Symposium on Alcoholism and Alcohol Problems, Chicago, April 30, 1973, box 195, Speeches, 4/9/73–4/27/73, HEH-S Papers.

26. National Institutes of Health, "Important Events of NIAAA History," https://www.nih.gov/about-nih/what-we-do/nih-almanac/national-institute-alcohol-abuse-alcoholism-niaaa; "In Memoriam: Remembering Harold Hughes," http://www.well.com/user.woa/harolde.htm.

27. White, *Slaying the Dragon*, 266; Harold Hughes to Albert Lasker, New York, NY, December 28, 1970, box 140, A & N Correspondence, December 1970 (2), HEH-S Papers.

28. Warren and Hewitt, "NIAA: Advancing Alcohol Research for 40 Years," 5, 7.

29. Ensign, "From Iowa to the Nation," 205–206.

30. "Senate Drug Bill Passes," *DMR*, October 8, 1970; James Risser, "Vote Hughes Drug Abuse Bill, 86–0," *DMR*, November 25, 1970.

31. Harold Hughes to Mrs. Lawrence V. Cluer, Key West, FL, September 2, 1970, box 139, A & N Correspondence, September 1970, HEH-S Papers.

32. "My Trip to the Far East," memo from Julian Granger to Harold Hughes, September 18, 1970, box 26, Health—Drugs, HEH-S Papers.

33. Remarks of Senator Harold E. Hughes, Preventive Psychiatry Con-

ference, Washington, DC, February 9, 1971, box 191, Speeches, 12/17/70–2/12/71, HEH-S Papers.

34. "Hughes Releases Report on Drug Abuse in Armed Forces," press release, April 19, 1971, box 169, HEH-S Papers.

35. "Hughes Charges Military Not Equipped to Handle Drug Problem," press release, June 9, 1971, box 169, HEH-S Papers; James Risser, "OK Hughes Move to Curb GI Viet Drug 'Epidemic,'" *DMR*, June 10, 1971; James Risser, "Drug Plan Vote in Senate Timely Boost for Hughes," *DMR*, June 12, 1971.

36. Risser, "OK Hughes Move"; Risser, "Drug Plan Vote in Senate."

37. James Risser, "Soldiers Steal for Heroin, Vets Tell Senate Hearing," *DMR*, June 16, 1971.

38. George McArthur, "Compulsory Heroin Tests for Viet GIs," *DMR*, June 19, 1971; James Risser, "Hughes Unit Rakes Nixon Drug Plan," *DMR*, June 23, 1971.

39. James Risser, "Hughes Charges Military Is 'Branding' Drug Users," *DMR*, March 1, 1972.

40. "Hughes: Get GIs out of Vietnam," *DMR*, June 4, 1971.

17. Angry Dove on the National Stage

1. Transcript, *Issues and Answers*, January 26,1969, box 165, Transcripts from Broadcast Appearances, 1969–70, HEH-S Papers; Harold Hughes to Robert E. Horsfall, superintendent, Webster City Community Schools, April 10, 1969, box 1, Approp.–Labor, HEW, 1969—#2, HEH-S Papers.

2. Remarks by Senator Harold E. Hughes, Vietnam speech on US Senate floor, June 20, 1969, box 165, HEH-S Papers.

3. Stanley Karnow, *Vietnam: A History* (New York: Viking Press, 1983), 582; George C. Herring, *America's Longest War: The United States and Vietnam, 1950–1975*, 2nd ed. (New York: Alfred A. Knopf, 1986), 222–225.

4. Speech by Senator Hughes, Greater Hamilton County Democratic Party meeting, Chattanooga, TN, January 24, 1970, box 166, HEH-S Papers; speech by Senator Harold E. Hughes, Conference for Business Executives on Federal Government Operations, New Senate Office Building, Brookings Institute Advance Study Program, Room 1318, February 2, 1970, box 166, HEH-S Papers.

5. Testimony of Senator Harold E. Hughes, Committee on Foreign Relations, US Senate, February 3, 1970, box 166, HEH-S Papers.

6. James Risser, "Hughes Urges Rekindling of Peace Effort," *DMR*, March 13, 1970.

7. Reaction by Senator Harold E. Hughes to American invasion of Cambodia, May 1, 1970, box 166, Press Releases—Misc., 1970, HEH-S Papers.

8. James Risser, "Hughes: War Is to Blame for 4 Students' Deaths," *DMR*, May 5, 1970; "Hughes Urges: No Violence," *DMR*, March 7, 1970.

9. Transcript, Harold Hughes on WRC, Washington, DC, broadcast with McGovern, Hatfield, Goodell, and Church, May 12, 1970, box 164, Media Reference: Printed Press, Broadcast, Photo, March–October 1969, HEH-S Papers;

Nick Kotz, "Today's Schoolboys Might Fight in Vietnam, Hughes Warns on TV," *DMR*, May 13, 1970.

10. Stephen Seplow and Michael Sorkin, "Peace March Held in D.M.," *DMR*, May 18, 1970; remarks of Senator Harold E. Hughes, peace rally at state capitol, Des Moines, May 17, 1970, box 190, Speeches, 5/16/70–6/27/70, HEH-S Papers.

11. "55% of Iowans Approve Move into Cambodia," *DMR*, May 31, 1970; Harold Hughes to Mrs. Ed Darst, Clearfield, IA, July 20, 1970, box 190, Vietnam, July 11–30, HEH-S Papers.

12. James Risser, "Chances Improve for End-War Amendment," *DMR*, July 2, 1970.

13. James Risser, "Hughes Leads Attack on Nixon's Plan to End War," *DMR*, July 10, 1970.

14. Harold Hughes to Dean Burch, chairman, Federal Communications Commission, July 30, 1970, box 19, Communications, HEH-S Papers; Christopher Lydon, "F.C.C. Orders TV to Set Prime Time for War Critics," *NYT*, August 15, 1970.

15. James Risser, "Senate End-War Amendment Vote Today; Sponsors Hopeful," *DMR*, September 1, 1970.

16. James Risser, "Senate Approves Military Weapons Bill—'End the War' Plan Rejected," *DMR*, September 2, 1970; "39 Senators Make a Point," editorial, *DMR*, September 3, 1970.

18. Democratic Party Reformer and Presidential Candidate

1. Byron E. Shafer, *Quiet Revolution: The Struggle for the Democratic Party and the Shaping of Post-Reform Politics* (New York: Russell Sage Foundation, 1983), 13–20.

2. McCarthy Historical Project/Oral Interview Series, 1969, Sen. Harold Hughes, August 11, 1969, box 288, HEH-S Papers.

3. Nick Kotz, "Hughes Asks Reforms, Warns 2-Party System Is Endangered," *DMR*, August 23, 1968; Louis Milton Thompson Jr., "The Communication and Decision-Making Processes, Environmental Factors in Harold E. Hughes' 1968 Campaign for the U.S. Senate" (master's thesis, Iowa State University, 1969), 104, 106; Shafer, *Quiet Revolution*, 21–25.

4. Shafer, *Quiet Revolution*, 29–33.

5. David Broder, "Rules Victory for Hughes," *DMR*, August 28, 1968; Shafer, *Quiet Revolution*, 34–37.

6. Shafer, *Quiet Revolution*, 4.

7. "Hughes Stresses Reform," *DMT*, December 9, 1969; Shafer, *Quiet Revolution*, 47.

8. "Demos Put Hughes, Franklin on Convention Reform Units," *DMR*, February 9, 1969; Roland Evans and Robert Novak, "Insurgent Demos Make Hughes Rallying Point," *DMR*, February 14, 1969; Shafer, *Quiet Revolution*, 60, 302–303.

9. Shafer, *Quiet Revolution*, 68–71.

10. Remarks by Senator Harold E. Hughes, Commission on Party Structure and Delegate Selection, Caucus Room, Old Senate Office Building, March 1, 1969, box 189, Speeches, 2/28/69–5/8/69, HEH-S Papers.

11. Shafer, *Quiet Revolution*, 109–111.

12. "Urges Demos: Face Issues," *DMR*, May 25, 1969.

13. Shafer, *Quiet Revolution*, 123–124.

14. Shafer, 161.

15. Shafer, 194.

16. Shafer, 541–545.

17. Shafer, 254, 241–268, 309, 368.

18. Shafer, 393–394.

19. Shafer, 396–427.

20. R. W. Apple, "Democratic Reformers, Old Guard Split over Filing '72 Convention Post," *NYT*, October 8, 1971.

21. Apple; R. W. Apple, "Muskie May Back Reform Bloc in a Key Preconvention Dispute," *NYT*, October 9, 1971; R. W. Apple, "Mrs. Harris Wins Democratic Post," *NYT*, October 14, 1971; George Anthan, "Hughes Loses Bid for Party Post, 72–31," *DMR*, October 14, 1971; Shafer, *Quiet Revolution*, 429–430, 435, 456.

22. Anthan, "Hughes Loses Bid for Party Post"; Shafer, *Quiet Revolution*, 450.

23. Remarks of Senator Harold E. Hughes, Des Moines, Iowa, November 20, 1971, State Democratic Jefferson-Jackson Day Dinner, box 170, HEH-S Papers.

24. Shafer, *Quiet Revolution*, 526; Maurice Isserman and Michael Kazin, *America Divided: The Civil War of the 1960s*, 3rd ed. (New York: Oxford University Press, 2008), 291.

25. Robert Walters, "Hughes a Dark Horse for 1972," *Washington Evening Star*, August 18, 1969, box 165, Press Clippings, 8/69–6/71, HEH-S Papers.

26. Thomas J. Foley, "An Illogical Candidate . . . ," *Los Angeles Times*, September 15, 1969; Nick Thimmesch, column, *Louisville (KY) Courier-Journal*, September 26, 1969, box 136, A & N Correspondence, Sept. 26–30, 1969, HEH-S; Inland Daily Press Association, Members Service Bulletin, Chicago, October 2, 1969, box 164, Notes on Interviews Done, HEH-S Papers; Nick Kotz, "'72 Dark Horse Ranking Is 'Flattering' to Hughes," *DMR*, January 13, 1970.

27. James Risser, "Hughes Dark Horse Candidate in '72?" *DMR*, December 14, 1969.

28. Myra MacPherson, "Probe Deeper into Hughes' Bid in '72," *DMR*, January 10, 1971; James Doyle, article from *Washington Star*, in *Iowa City Press Citizen*, February 1, 1971, box 165, Press Clippings, 8/69–6/71, HEH-S Papers; Joe Rosenfield, Des Moines, Iowa, to Harold Hughes, January 14, 1971, box 46, Political Misc., #2, HEH-S Papers.

29. Robert Phelps, "Senator Hughes Quietly Pushes 1972 Presidential Bid," *NYT*, October 29, 1970; memo to state coordinators from Hughes Committee, n.d. (probably early 1971), box 231, Office Memos, 1971–72, HEH-S Papers.

30. MacPherson, "Probe Deeper into Hughes' Bid."

31. MacPherson; Doyle article; Louis Swartzwalder, "See Hughes in No. 2 Spot in '72," *DMR*, January 20, 1971.

32. R. W. Apple, "Democratic Rivals Agree Not to Feud in Presidency Bids," *NYT*, February 11, 1971; George Anthan, "Secret Demo Parlay by 7 Potential '72 Candidates," *DMR*, February 11, 1971.

33. Larry King, "Harold Hughes: Evangelist from the Prairie," *Harper's*, March 1969, 50–57; R. W. Apple, "The Mood Changes When Senator Hughes Speaks," *NYT*, March 3, 1971.

34. Apple, "Mood Changes When Senator Hughes Speaks."

35. Apple; David Broder, "Hughes Looking Like a Real Candidate," *DMR*, March 7, 1971; George Anthan, "Hughes Paves Way for '72 President Bid," *DMR*, March 7, 1971.

36. Press release, Hughes for President headquarters, March 20, 1971, box 6, Harold, Hughes E. (Ida Grove), Frank Nye Papers, Special Collections, University of Iowa Libraries; William B. Friedricks, *The Real Deal: The Life of Bill Knapp* (Des Moines, IA: Business Publications Corporation, 2013), 87; interview with Connie Wimer.

37. "Muskie Leads Nixon, Hughes Close; Other Democrats Trail Far Behind," *DMR*, March 28, 1971; "Poll Finds Kennedy Is Top Choice for '72 Nomination," *DMR*, May 16, 1971.

38. R. W. Apple, "Hughes Presidency Bid at Crossroads," *NYT*, June 10, 1971; Clark Mollenhoff, "Hughes Denies Candidacy All but Dead," *DMR*, June 11, 1971.

39. Paul Wieck, "For God and Country: The Presidential Campaign of Harold Hughes," *New Republic* 164 (May 15, 1971): 19–24.

40. Wieck, 19–24; interview with Phyllis Hughes Ewing.

41. Vance Bourjaily, *Country Matters* (New York: Dial Press, 1973), 284; MacPherson, "Probe Deeper into Hughes' Bid"; interview with Pat Jensen; Ewing interview.

42. William Hedlund and Russell Wilson, *In His Own Words: The Harold Hughes Story* (Bloomington, IN: LifeRich Publishing, 2020), 60.

43. Interview with Sherwin Markman.

44. Interview with James Risser.

45. James Risser and George Anthan, "'Personal' Religion of Senator Hughes," *DMR*, July 11, 1971.

46. Statement by Senator Harold E. Hughes, July 15, 1971, box 170, Press Release, Statement of Announcement, HEH-S Papers.

47. Mary McGory, "Why Did Hughes Drop Out?" *Washington Evening Star*, July 16, 1971; Nick Kotz, "Hughes Quits Contest for 1972 Nomination," *WP*, July 16, 1971; interview with Bill Knapp.

48. Ewing interview.

49. George Anthan, "Drugs Key Issue in Hughes' Decision Not to Enter Race," *DMR*, July 16, 1971.

50. Kotz, "Hughes Quits Contest."

19. Secret Bombing over North Vietnam

1. Lonnie Franks to Harold Hughes, APO San Francisco, February 25, 1972, box 162, Testimony Info, Aug. 13, 1973—Nov. 1974, HEH-S Papers.
2. Clark Mollenhoff, "The Controversy over Cambodia—Iowa's Lawmakers Tell Concern," *DMR*, January 27, 1971.
3. John Stennis to Harold Hughes, February 11, 1971, box 34, Armed Services, Misc. #2, HEH-S Papers.
4. John T. Correll, "Lavelle," *Air Force Magazine*, November 2006, 58–64.
5. Interview with Lonnie Franks.
6. Franks interview; Correll, "Lavelle," 62.
7. Franks interview.
8. Franks interview; Seymour Hersh, "Sergeant Says 200 Men Helped Falsify Bomb Data," *NYT*, September 7, 1972.
9. Correll, "Lavelle," 62; Dale Van Atta, *With Honor: Melvin Laird in War, Peace and Politics* (Madison: University of Wisconsin Press, 2008), 400.
10. Correll, "Lavelle," 60, 62.
11. Aloysius Casey and Patrick Casey, "Lavelle, Nixon and the White House Tapes," *Air Force Magazine*, February 2007, 87; Correll, "Lavelle," 62.
12. George C. Herring, *America's Longest War: The United States and Vietnam, 1950–1975*, 2nd ed. (New York: Alfred A. Knopf, 1986), 246–249.
13. Herring, 58, 62.
14. Harold Hughes with Dick Schneider, *Harold E. Hughes: The Man from Ida Grove; a Senator's Personal Story* (Lincoln, VA: Chosen Books Publishing, 1979), 305–306; Harold Hughes to John Stennis, May 8, 1972, box 51, Armed Services—Misc., HEH-S Papers.
15. Correll, "Lavelle," 62.
16. Press release on speech regarding Lavelle case, June 14, 1972, box 171, HEH-S Papers.
17. Box 51, General Chronology, Testimony & Related Info, 1971–1973, HEH-S Papers.
18. Franks interview.
19. Franks interview; Hersh, "Sergeant Says 200 Men Helped Falsify Bomb Data."
20. Seymour Hersh, "Lavelle Is Reported to Tell Senators Abrams and Moorer Approved Raids," *NYT*, September 13, 1972; Clark Mollenhoff, "Abrams Testifies on Role in 'Unauthorized' Raids," *DMR*, September 14, 1972; Seymour Hersh, "Senators Assert Abrams Disputes Lavelle on Raids," *NYT*, September 14, 1972.
21. Hersh, "Senators Assert Abrams Disputes Lavelle."
22. Correll, "Lavelle," 63; "3 Senators Pin Blame on Lavelle," *DMR*, September 20, 1972; Seymour Hersh, "Aide Says Lavelle Ordered Bombings," *NYT*, September 20, 1972.
23. Franks interview.
24. Clark Mollenhoff, "Iowan: False Raid Reports," *DMR*, September 15, 1972.

25. Statement by Senator Harold E. Hughes, October 11, 1972, box 172, US Senate—Support of Abrams Nomination—October 11, 1972, HEH-S Papers.

26. Box 151, General Chronology, Testimony & Related Info, 1971–1973, HEH-S Papers.

27. Box 151, General Chronology, Testimony & Related Info, 1971–1973; press release on Laird's response to command and control—Washington, DC, November 1, 1972, box 172, HEH-S Papers.

28. Casey and Casey, "Lavelle, Nixon and the White House Tapes," 86–88; John Finney, "Moorer Says Navy Did Not Violate Rules on Bombing," *NYT*, September 30, 1972.

20. Election Defeats and Victories and a Maverick War Critic

1. George C. Herring, *America's Longest War: The United States and Vietnam, 1950–1975*, 2nd ed. (New York: Alfred A. Knopf, 1986), 223–224, 231–233, 246–249.

2. Remarks by Senator Harold E. Hughes, Emergency Convocation to End the War, Washington, DC, May 10, 1972, box 194, Speeches, 5/6/72–6/14/72, HEH-S Papers.

3. Senator's endorsement of Muskie, press release, January 17, 1972, box 170, HEH-S Papers; James Flansburg, "Muskie Sees 'Bargaining' by Farmers," *DMR*, January 19, 1972.

4. James M. Naughton, "Muskie Wins Support of Senator Hughes of Iowa," *NYT*, January 18, 1972; R. W. Apple, "Iowa Democrats Hold Caucuses, First Step in Picking Delegates," *NYT*, January 25, 1972; Harold Hughes, "Why I'm for Muskie," *New Republic*, February 12, 1972, 15–18.

5. James Flansburg, "Democrats in Iowa Vote in Precincts," *DMR*, January 25, 1972; R. W. Apple, "Muskie Is Victor in Iowa Caucuses," *NYT*, January 26, 1972.

6. Theodore H. White, *The Making of the President 1972* (New York: Atheneum Press, 1973), 105–106.

7. James Risser, "Hughes Reaffirms Support for Candidacy of Muskie," *DMR*, April 8, 1972; James Flansburg, "State Democratic Leaders See Muskie out of Race," *DMR*, April 28, 1972.

8. Warren Weaver Jr., "Dakotan Woos Governors," *NYT*, June 6, 1972.

9. Clark Mollenhoff, "Muskie Lauds Hughes in Decision to Stay in Race," *DMR*, June 10, 1972.

10. Jack Rosenthal, "Muskie's New Goal: Viable Alternative," *NYT*, June 15, 1972.

11. James Risser, "Hughes and McGovern: Unlikely Foes," *DMR*, July 2, 1972.

12. George Anthan, "Hughes and Muskie Plot Fifth Ballot Victory," *DMR*, July 8, 1972.

13. James Flansburg, "Iowans Vote 27–19 to Seat Californians," *DMR*, July 11, 1972; Clark Mollenhoff, "S.D. Senator on Brink of Nomination," *DMR*, July 11, 1972; James Flansburg, "McGovern Gets Backing of Hughes," *DMR*, July 12, 1972.

14. Remarks to Iowa delegation at Miami convention, July 11, 1972, box 171, HEH-S Papers; Harold Hughes to John Reback, Sioux City, October 3, 1972, box 200, Personal Correspondence, 1972, HEH-S Papers.

15. Jim Larew, *A Party Reborn: The Democrats of Iowa, 1950–1974* (Iowa City: Iowa State Historical Society, 1980), 116, 168–170; "Hughes, Miller Win Approval for Their Work in the Senate," *DMR*, September 13, 1972; Dick Clark, *Iowa and the World: Memoirs of Dick Clark* (State College, PA: Editions Enlaplage, 2017), 51.

16. Clark, *Iowa and the World*, 52; Pat Deluhery interview.

17. Clark, *Iowa and the World*, 52–54.

18. Herring, *America's Longest War*, 254.

19. James Risser, "Hughes Urges Priority for Legislation to End War," *DMR*, January 3, 1973; Harold Hughes to Helen Schechter, Miami Beach, Florida, January 10, 1973, box 70, Foreign Relations, Vietnam—January, HEH-S Papers.

20. Herring, *America's Longest War*, 255–256; "842 Iowans Died during War in Viet," *DMR*, January 24, 1973; Harold Hughes to Mr. and Mrs. Raymond Ahrens, Boone, Iowa, March 8, 1973, box 70, Foreign Relations, Vietnam—February–April, HEH-S Papers.

21. Harold Hughes to John Stennis, January 17, 1973, box 66, Armed Services, Misc., HEH-S Papers; Harold Hughes to Barry Goldwater, March 21, 1973, box 66, Armed Services, Misc., HEH-S Papers.

22. Hughes to Goldwater, March 21, 1973; George Anthan, "Hughes Bars Promotion for 5,000," *DMR*, March 23, 1973.

23. Anthan, "Hughes Bars Promotion for 5,000"; Seymour Hersh, "Senate Unit to End Promotions Delay," *NYT*, March 23, 1973.

24. Harold Hughes to Elliot Richardson, Secretary of Defense, Washington, DC, March 28, 1973, box 66, Armed Services, Misc., HEH-S Papers; J. Fred Buzhardt, general counsel to the Department of Defense, to Hughes, March 28, 1973, box 151, Pending Nominations, HEH-S Papers.

25. Press release on statement before Armed Services Committee with regard to nominations and their connection with Lavelle case, March 29, 1973, box 173, HEH-S Papers.

26. Harold Hughes with Dick Schneider, *Harold E. Hughes: The Man from Ida Grove; a Senator's Personal Story* (Lincoln, VA: Chosen Books Publishing, 1979), 307–308.

27. William Shawcross, *Sideshow: Kissinger, Nixon and the Destruction of Cambodia* (New York: Simon & Schuster, 1979), 287; Seymour Hersh, "Cambodian Raids Reported Hidden before '70 Foray," *NYT*, July 15, 1973.

28. Shawcross, *Sideshow*, 287; Hersh, "Cambodian Raids Reported Hidden."

29. Shawcross, *Sideshow*, 287–288; George Brown, General USAF, Com-

mander, Air Force Systems Command, to Stuart Symington, acting chair, Armed Services Committee, July 16, 1973, box 152, Testimony–July 1973, HEH-S Papers.

30. Hersh, "Cambodian Raids Reported Hidden"; Ted Frederickson, "Bombing Cover-up Charged," *DMR*, July 16, 1973.

31. Frederickson, "Bombing Cover-up Charged."

32. Seymour Hersh, "U.S. Confirms Pre-1970 Raids on Cambodia," *NYT*, July 17, 1973; release on Pentagon deceiving Congress on Cambodia bombing, Washington, DC, July 17, 1973, box 174, HEH-S Papers.

33. "Hughes Demands Full Probe of 'Lies' on Cambodian Bombing," *DMR*, July 18, 1973.

34. Capital Cloakroom, CBS News, July 18, 1973, box 228, Interview Transcripts, 1973–1974, HEH-S Papers; "Laud Hughes for Exposing of Bombings," *DMR*, July 21, 1973.

35. Gerald J. Greven, Miami, Florida, to Harold Hughes, July 20, 1973, box 151, General Chronology, Testimony & Related Info, 1971–73, HEH-S Papers; George Anthan, "Hospitals Bombed, Yank Says," *DMR*, July 23, 1973; Daniel T. Eismann, Caldwell, Idaho, to Harold Hughes, July 24, 1973, box 152, Testimony–July 1973, HEH-S Papers.

36. George M. Miller, retired Lt. Col., USAF, Brentwood, Tennessee, to Harold Hughes, July 23, 1973, box 152, Testimony–July 1973, HEH-S Papers.

37. Statement of Earle Wheeler, US Army, retired, before Senate Armed Services Committee, July 30, 1973, box 152, Testimony of Gen. Wheeler, Clements & Moorer—7/73, HEH-S Papers; James Risser, "Wheeler: Nixon Ordered Secrecy-Veil on Bombing," *DMR*, July 31, 1973.

38. Release on bombing falsification drops, request for reports on official promotions, Washington, DC, August 2, 1973, box 174, HEH-S Papers.

39. Shawcross, *Sideshow*, 290; Seymour Hersh, "Laird Approved False Reporting of Secret Raids," *NYT*, August 10, 1973.

40. Shawcross, *Sideshow*, 290–291.

41. John Herbers, "Nixon Says Raids on Cambodia in '69 Were Necessary," *NYT*, August 21, 1973.

42. Harold Hughes, "Hughes—Peril to Democracy in Secret Military Policies," *DMR*, August 14, 1973.

43. Statement by senator in support of amendment on abortion, May 31, 1973, box 173, HEH-S Papers; "Buckley Pushes Curb on Abortion," *NYT*, June 1, 1973.

44. Statement by senator in support of amendment on abortion.

45. Harold Hughes to Roxanne Barton Conlin, chairperson, Iowa Women's Political Caucus, Des Moines, August 23, 1973, box 71, Judiciary Constitutional Amendments, HEH-S Papers; James Flansburg, "A Primary Fight for Hughes?" *DMR*, June 4, 1973. Hughes may have changed his position on abortion later in life. After his retirement from the Senate, during a conversation with Pat Jensen, Hughes apologized for taking such a strong stand on an issue that was important to her and explained that, after reflection, he had changed his mind.

The strongly pro-choice Jensen took this to mean that he had changed his position on abortion. Interview with Pat Jensen.

21. Leaving the Senate and Welcoming Charles Colson

1. Interview with *Overdrive Magazine*, October 22, 1971, box 221, Biography, HEH-S Papers.
2. Harold Hughes with Dick Schneider, *Harold E. Hughes: The Man from Ida Grove; a Senator's Personal Story* (Lincoln, VA: Chosen Books Publishing, 1979), 314–315, 325–326; interview with Bonnie Campbell; interview with Phyllis Hughes Ewing.
3. Vance Bourjaily, *Country Matters* (New York: Dial Press, 1973), 282–286.
4. Harold Hughes to Dorsie Buck, Fairfax, Virginia, July 1, 1971, box 200, Personal Correspondence, 1971, HEH-S Papers; Myra MacPherson, "Probe Deeper into Hughes' Bid in 1972," *DMR*, January 10, 1971; "Ignoring God's Laws: Hughes," *DMR*, July 17, 1971; Hughes, *Man from Ida Grove*, 269–270.
5. Hughes, *Man from Ida Grove*, 269–270.
6. Jeff Sharlet, *The Family: The Secret Fundamentalism at the Heart of American Power* (New York: Harper Perennial, 2008), 21–25.
7. Hughes, *Man from Ida Grove*, 275–276; Ewing interview.
8. Hughes, *Man from Ida Grove*, 310–312; James Risser, "Hughes: Israelis Sorrow over Libyan Jet Crash," *DMR*, March 1, 1973.
9. "Senators Here for Hughes Fete," caption, *DMR*, April 1, 1973; remarks by Senator Mansfield at Democratic dinner in Des Moines, March 31, 1973, box 173, HEH-S Papers.
10. "A Toss-up if Ray and Hughes Vied for the Senate," *DMR*, June 17, 1973.
11. Interview with Russell Wilson; Hughes, *Man from Ida Grove*, 117.
12. Senator's withdrawal from running for reelection in '74, September 6, 1973, box 174, HEH-S Papers; Jerry Szumski and Steven M. Johnson, "Iowa Politics in Turmoil—Hughes: God's Work Comes First," *DMR*, September 7, 1973; Clark Mollenhoff and George Anthan, "How Colson 'Found Jesus,'" *DMR*, December 23, 1973.
13. Ewing interview.
14. Szumski and Johnson, "Iowa Politics in Turmoil"; James M. Wall, "A Senator's Faith and Vocation," *Christian Century*, September 26, 1973, 931–932.
15. Szumski and Johnson, "Iowa Politics in Turmoil."
16. Michael Dobbs, "Charles Colson, Nixon's 'Dirty Tricks' Man, Dies at 80," *WP*, April 21, 2012.
17. For a more complete history of the Watergate scandal, see Stanley I. Kuster, *The Wars of Watergate: The Last Crisis of Richard Nixon* (New York: Alfred A. Knopf, 1990).
18. Colson's experiences—both political and religious—are detailed in Charles Colson, *Born Again* (Grand Rapids, MI: Chosen Books, 2008); Dobbs, "Charles Colson."

19. Colson, *Born Again*, 160–165.

20. Colson, 175–177; "Colson, Hughes at Prayer Meeting," *DMR*, December 8, 1973.

21. Mollenhoff and Anthan, "How Colson 'Found Jesus'"; Eppie/Ann Landers to Hughes, December 14, 1973, box 235, Political Decision/Religion, 1973, HEH-S Papers; Ewing interview.

22. *60 Minutes* transcript, CBS Television Network, May 26, 1974, box 228, Interview Transcripts, 1973–1974, HEH-S Papers.

23. Colson, *Born Again*, 249–250; Clark Mollenhoff, "Colson Prays with Hughes, Then He Enters Guilty Plea," *DMR*, June 4, 1974.

24. Dobbs, "Charles Colson."

25. Clark Mollenhoff, "Hughes Plays Major Role in Probe of Pentagon Spying," *DMR*, February 25, 1974.

26. "Stennis, Moorer Hold Private Talk," *NYT*, January 24, 1974.

27. Seymour Hersh, "Spying in the White House Said to Have Begun in '70," *NYT*, February 3, 1974.

28. Seymour Hersh, "Senator Hughes Asks Public Military Spy Hearings, Breaks with Stennis Closed Session for Kissinger," *NYT*, February 4, 1974; dateline Washington, DC, Report to Iowa from Senator Harold E. Hughes, winter 1974, box 85, Judiciary—Amnesty, HEH-S Papers.

29. Seymour Hersh, "Admiral Denies Telling Yeoman to Take Highly Classified Data," *NYT*, February 22, 1974; Seymour Hersh, "Nixon Said to Have Balked Charges in Secrets Theft," *NYT*, February 23, 1974; Harold Hughes to John Stennis, February 27, 1974, box 81, Armed Services, Misc. (1), HEH-S Papers.

30. Seymour Hersh, "Nixon Is Assailed on Ground Raids," *NYT*, March 28, 1974.

31. Interview with Martin Jensen; Legislative History of the Senate Select Committee on Intelligence, Congressional Research Service, August 6, 1978, 9; Covert Action: Legislative Background and Possible Policy Questions, Congressional Research Service, April 10, 2013, 1.

32. Sisyphus, "Children of Cain?" *Commonweal*, April 5, 1974, 107–108.

33. George Anthan, "Clash over Death Penalty," *DMR*, March 13, 1974; remarks of Senator Harold E. Hughes, regarding S. 1401, a bill to restore capital punishment as an authorized penalty for certain crimes, US Senate, Washington, DC, March 12, 1974, box 195, Speeches—Hughes, 11/30/73–3/13/74, HEH-S Papers.

34. "Senate Votes to Restore Death Penalty," *DMR*, March 14, 1974.

35. "Iowa Politicians Express Relief, Sadness at Nixon's Resignation," *DMR*, August 9, 1974; Senator Harold E. Hughes's comments on immunity for former president Nixon, Cedar Rapids, August 16, 1974, box 85, Judiciary—Impeachment, HEH-S Papers; statement by Senator Harold Hughes on the resignation of the president, August 9, 1974, box 151, Armed Services Committee, 7/74–12/74, HEH-S Papers.

36. Harold Hughes to Michael McCormick, Keokuk, and others, September 30, 1974, box 85, Judiciary—Amnesty, HEH-S Papers.

37. Barry Goldwater to Hughes, November 28, 1974, box 234, HEH-Political, 1974, HEH-S Papers.
38. James Risser, "Colleagues Bid Good-bye to Hughes," *DMR*, December 21, 1974.
39. Clark Mollenhoff, "Hughes 'Won't Quit Early,'" *DMR*, November 27, 1974.

22. Life Past Politics—Almost

1. Interview with Peg Shoemaker Mikulanec; Clark Mollenhoff, "$12,000 Senate Post for Hughes," *DMR*, January 3, 1975; Joseph Lelyveld, "Ex-Senator Conducts a Ministry at Capitol," *NYT*, December 9, 1975.
2. Lelyveld, "Ex-Senator Conducts a Ministry"; Clark Mollenhoff, "Tell of Hughes' Influence in Sobriety Vow by Mills," *DMR*, January 10, 1975; interview with Bill Hedlund; interview with Dwight Jensen.
3. Lelyveld, "Ex-Senator Conducts a Ministry"; William Simbro, "Hughes Seeks Greener Pastures," *DMR*, February 20, 1981.
4. Harold Hughes with Dick Schneider, *Harold E. Hughes: The Man from Ida Grove; a Senator's Personal Story* (Lincoln, VA: Chosen Books Publishing, 1979), 330–331.
5. Nancy Olsen, *With a Lot of Help from Our Friends: The Politics of Alcoholism* (Lincoln, NE: Writers Club Press, 2003), 442; "Camp David: An Outpouring of Prayer," *Christianity Today*, October 6, 1978, 48.
6. Olsen, *With a Lot of Help from Our Friends*, 371–385.
7. Hughes, *Man from Ida Grove*; Harold Hughes with Dick Schneider, *The Honorable Alcoholic: A Senator's Personal Story*, paperback ed. (Grand Rapids, MI: Zondervan Publishing, 1983); Dwight Jensen interview.
8. Interview with Phyllis Hughes Ewing; interview with Jennifer Cooper and Jacquie Holm-Smith; interview with Bonnie Campbell.
9. Simbro, "Hughes Seeks Greener Pastures"; interview with Bill Knapp; William B. Friedricks, *The Real Deal: The Life of Bill Knapp* (Des Moines, IA: Business Publications Corporation, 2013), 152. Roxanne Conlin, a contender for the 1982 Democratic nomination for governor, claims Hughes moved back to Iowa with the clear intention of running for governor, prompted by supporters Bill Knapp and Ed Campbell. The goal, she says, was to prevent her from getting the Democratic nomination and taking over the party. Interview with Roxanne Conlin.
10. David Yepsen, "Hughes, Culver Say Don't Turn Back on Heritage," *DMR*, February 22, 1981; James Flansburg, "The Draft-Ray, Draft-Hughes Plan," *DMR*, June 8, 1981.
11. Flansburg, "Draft-Ray, Draft-Hughes Plan"; James Flansburg, "The Democratic Collapse: In the Nation and in Iowa," *DMR*, July 19, 1981.
12. For the most complete summary of Robert D. Ray's life and accomplishments as governor, see Jon Bowermeister, *Governor: An Oral Biography of Robert D. Ray* (Ames: Iowa State University Press, 1987).

13. Matthew R. Walsh, *The Good Governor: Robert Ray and the Indochinese Refugees of Iowa* (Jefferson, NC: McFarland, 2017), 2.

14. "Hughes: No Plan to Run Again, but . . . ," *DMR*, August 28, 1981; James Flansburg, "Drafting Hughes without Leaving Fingerprints," *DMR*, September 7, 1981.

15. James Flansburg, "Miller Avoiding Race as Long as Hughes May Run," *DMR*, September 19, 1981; David Yepsen, "Doubts Surface on Wisdom of Hughes Run for Governor," *DMR*, September 26, 1981.

16. James Flansburg, "Top Democrats Laying Odds on Hughes Bid for Governor," *DMR*, September 25, 1981; Lawrence M. Paul, "Hughes Top Democratic Choice in Poll," *DMR*, September 27, 1981.

17. James Flansburg and David Yepsen, "Hughes Gives Nod to Group Exploring Election Chances," *DMR*, October 16, 1981.

18. Flansburg and Yepsen, "Hughes Gives Nod"; David Yepsen, "Hughes Says He's Leaning toward Candidacy," *DMR*, October 25, 1981.

19. David Yepsen, "Hughes Says He'll Run, but Faces a Legal Snag," *DMR*, November 20, 1981; James Flansburg, "A 1981 Version of the Fitted-Bedsheet Debate," *DMR*, December 21, 1981.

20. "Needless Delay on Hughes," editorial, *DMR*, December 22, 1981; David Yepsen, "Odell Rules against Bid by Hughes," *DMR*, December 29, 1981. The decision by Iowa attorney general Tom Miller to recuse himself was controversial. Harkin later argued that Miller should have asserted his authority as attorney general and ruled that, based on solid case law and the former governor's intent to return to Iowa, Hughes had always been a resident. Then Miller could have dared others to prove him wrong. Miller's decision, claims Harkin, gave the issue to the Republicans (Odell). "How do you think she's going to decide?" asked Harkin. Interview with Tom Harkin.

21. David Yepsen, "Hughes Withdraws from 1982 Race," *DMR*, January 8, 1982.

22. James Flansburg, "How 'No' to '78 Iowa Race Made Hughes a Marylander," *DMR*, January 10, 1982.

23. Ken Sullivan, "Hughes Withdraws with Dignity," *CRG*, January 10, 1982; David Yepsen, "Campbell to Resign Top Democratic Post," *DMR*, January 10, 1981.

24. Ewing interview; Cooper and Holm-Smith interview.

25. Knapp interview; Ewing interview.

26. Cooper and Holm-Smith interview; Lisa Collins, "The Hughes for All Seasons Has a New Life," *DMR*, March 6, 1988.

27. Collins, "Hughes for All Seasons."

28. Nick Lamberto, "Hughes' Deposition Entered in Divorce Trial of Lawyer," *DMR*, October 24, 1984.

29. Anne Carothers-Kay, "Harold Hughes and Wife, Eva, Granted Divorce," *DMR*, December 23, 1986; Collins, "Hughes for All Seasons."

30. Carothers-Kay, "Harold Hughes and Wife, Eva, Granted Divorce"; Collins, "Hughes for All Seasons"; Cooper and Holm-Smith interview.

31. Ewing interview.

32. Ewing interview; Pat Taylor, Tom Hill, and William White, "Chronology of the Addiction Recovery Advocacy Movement," May 2013, http://www.william whitepapers.com.

33. Campbell interview.

34. Cooper and Holm-Smith interview.

35. Collins, "Hughes for All Seasons"; Cooper and Holm-Smith interview.

36. Cooper and Holm-Smith interview.

37. Thomas Fogarty, "Hughes, Ex-Wife in Money Feud," *DMR*, November 19, 1995; Dan Eggen, "$14,850 Alimony Bill Comes Due to Hughes," *DMR*, August 27, 1996.

38. In Memoriam, Remembering Harold Hughes, box 229, Memorials, Eulogies and Obituaries, 1996, HEH-S Papers.

39. Cooper and Holm-Smith interview.

Epilogue

1. James Flansburg, "Hughes' Faith in Democracy," *DMR*, November 3, 1996.

2. Flansburg.

Bibliography

Books, Articles, Theses, and Dissertations

Anderson, J. L. *Industrializing the Midwest: Agriculture, Technology, and Environment, 1945–1972.* De Kalb: Northern Illinois University Press, 2009.

———, ed. *The Rural Midwest since World War II.* De Kalb: Northern Illinois University Press, 2014.

Atkinson, Rick. *An Army at Dawn: The War in North Africa, 1942–1943.* New York: Henry Holt, 2002.

———. *The Day of Battle: The War in Sicily and Italy, 1943.* New York: Henry Holt, 2007.

Bourjaily, Vance. *Country Matters.* New York: Dial Press, 1973.

Bowermeister, Jon. *Governor: An Oral Biography of Robert D. Ray.* Ames: Iowa State University Press, 1987.

Boyle, Kevin. *The Shattering: America in the 1960s.* New York: W. W. Norton, 2021.

Branch, Taylor. *Pillar of Fire: America in the King Years, 1963–1965.* New York: Simon & Schuster, 1998.

"Camp David: An Outpouring of Prayer." *Christianity Today,* October 6, 1978, 48.

Casey, Aloysius, and Patrick Casey. "Lavelle, Nixon and the White House Tapes." *Air Force Magazine,* February 2007, 86–90.

Clark, Dan. "The History of Liquor Legislation in Iowa, 1861–1878." *Iowa Journal of History and Politics* 6 (1908): 339–374.

———. "The History of Liquor Legislation in Iowa, 1878–1908." *Iowa Journal of History and Politics* 6 (1908): 503–608.

———. "The History of Liquor Legislation in Iowa, 1946–1861." *Iowa Journal of History and Politics* 6 (1908): 55–87.

Clark, Dick. *Iowa and the World: Memoirs of Dick Clark.* State College, PA: Editions Enlaplage, 2017.

Colson, Charles. *Born Again.* Grand Rapids, MI: Chosen Books, 2008.

Connerly, Charles E. *Green, Fair, and Prosperous: Paths to a Sustainable Iowa.* Iowa City: University of Iowa Press, 2020.

Cook, Robert. *A Baptism of Fire: The Republican Party in Iowa, 1838–1878.* Ames: Iowa State University Press, 1994.

Correll, John T. "Lavelle." *Air Force Magazine,* November 2006, 58–64.

Dallek, Robert. *Flawed Giant: Lyndon Johnson and His Times, 1961–1973.* New York: Oxford University Press, 1998.

Drake, George. *Mentor: Life and Legacy of Joe Rosenfield.* Des Moines, IA: Business Publications Corporation, 2019.

Ensign, Kelsey. "From Iowa to the Nation: Harold Hughes and the Politics of Alcoholism Treatment." *Annals of Iowa* 81 (Summer 2022): 203–238.

Faber, David. *The Age of Great Dreams: America in the 1960s.* New York: Hill & Wang, 1994.

Fairclough, Adam. *To Redeem the Soul of America: The Southern Christian Leadership Conference and Martin Luther King.* Athens: University of Georgia Press, 1987.

Friedel, Janice Nahra. "Engines of Economic Development: The Origins and Evolution of Iowa's Comprehensive Community Colleges." *American Educational History Journal* 37 (2010): 207–220.

Friedricks, William B. *The Real Deal: The Life of Bill Knapp.* Des Moines, IA: Business Publications Corporation, 2013.

Godbersen, Bruce I., ed. *A History of Ida County.* Ida Grove, IA: Midwest Industries, 1977.

Hannah-Jones, Nikole. *The 1619 Project: A New Origin Story.* New York: One World/Random House, 2021.

Harrington, Jerry. "Iowa's Last Liquor Battle: Governor Harold E. Hughes and the Liquor-by-the-Drink Conflict." *Annals of Iowa* 76, 1 (Winter 2017): 1–46.

Hedlund, William, and Russell Wilson. *In His Own Words: The Harold Hughes Story.* Bloomington, IN: LifeRich Publishing, 2020.

Herring, George C. *America's Longest War: The United States and Vietnam, 1950–1975.* 2nd ed. New York: Alfred A. Knopf, 1986.

Hughes, Harold. "Why I'm for Muskie." *New Republic,* February 12, 1972, 15–18.

Hughes, Harold, with Dick Schneider. *Harold E. Hughes: The Man from Ida Grove; a Senator's Personal Story.* Lincoln, VA: Chosen Books Publishing, 1979.

Hurt, R. Douglas. *American Agriculture: A Brief History.* Rev. ed. West Lafayette, IN: Purdue University Press, 2002.

Isserman, Maurice, and Michael Kazin. *America Divided: The Civil War of the 1960s.* 3rd ed. New York: Oxford University Press, 2008.

Karnow, Stanley. *Vietnam: A History.* New York: Viking Press, 1983.

King, Larry. "Harold Hughes: Evangelist from the Prairie." *Harper's,* March 1969, 50–57.

Knebel, Fletcher. "One Man's Triumph." *Look,* October 6, 1964, 97–108.

Kotz, Nick, and James Risser. "Messiah from the Midwest?" *Washington Monthly* 2, 3 (May 1970): 43–54.

Kuster, Stanley I. *The Wars of Watergate: The Last Crisis of Richard Nixon.* New York: Alfred A. Knopf, 1990.

Larew, Jim. *A Party Reborn: The Democrats of Iowa, 1950–1974.* Iowa City: Iowa State Historical Society, 1980.

Matusow, Allen J. *The Unraveling of America: A History of Liberalism in the 1960s.* New York: Harper & Row, 1984.

McDaniel, George William. *Smith Wildman Brookhart: Iowa's Renegade Republican.* Ames: Iowa State University Press, 1995.

National Institutes of Health. "Important Events of NIAA History." https://www.nih.gov/about-nih/what-we-do/nih-almanac/national-institute-alcohol-abuse-alcoholism-niaaa.

Nye, F. T. "The 1956 Election." *Palimpsest* 38, 11 (November 1957): 453–454.

Olsen, Nancy. *With a Lot of Help from Our Friends: The Politics of Alcoholism.* Lincoln, NE: Writers Club Press, 2003.

Patterson, James T. *Grand Expectations: The United States, 1945–1974.* New York: Oxford University Press, 1996.

Perlstein, Rick. *Before the Storm: Barry Goldwater and the Unmaking of the American Consensus.* New York: Nation Books, 2001.

Rosenberg, Morton M. *Iowa on the Eve of the Civil War.* Norman: University of Oklahoma Press, 1972.

Ryan, Thomas. "The Early Years of the Iowa Democratic Revival, 1950–1956." *Annals of Iowa* 46, 1 (Summer 1981): 43–63.

Sage, Leland. *A History of Iowa.* Ames: Iowa State University Press, 1974.

———. *William Boyd Allison: A Study in Practical Politics.* Iowa City: State Historical Society of Iowa, 1956.

Sayre, Ralph M. "Albert Baird Cummins and the Progressive Movement in Iowa." Ph.D. diss., Columbia University, 1958.

Schwieder, Dorothy. *Iowa: The Middle Land.* Ames: Iowa State University Press, 1996.

———, ed. *Patterns and Perspectives in Iowa History.* Ames: Iowa State University Press, 1973.

Schwieder, Dorothy, and Elmer Schwieder. *A Peculiar People: Iowa's Old Order Amish.* Expanded ed. Iowa City: University of Iowa Press, 2009.

Shafer, Byron E. *Quiet Revolution: The Struggle for the Democratic Party and the Shaping of Post-Reform Politics.* New York: Russell Sage Foundation, 1983.

Sharlet, Jeff. *The Family: The Secret Fundamentalism at the Heart of American Power.* New York: Harper Perennial, 2008.

Shawcross, William. *Sideshow: Kissinger, Nixon and the Destruction of Cambodia.* New York: Simon & Schuster, 1979.

Shesol, Jeff. *Mutual Contempt: Lyndon Johnson, Robert Kennedy, and the Feud that Defined a Decade.* New York: Norton, 1998.

Sisyphus. "Children of Cain?" *Commonweal,* April 5, 1974.

Smith, Neal. *20th Century Politics in Iowa and the Emergence of the Democratic Party.* Des Moines: Iowa Democratic Party, 1998.

Smith, Thomas S. "The Vietnam Era in Iowa Politics." *Palimpsest* 63, 5 (September–October 1982): 138–141.

Socknat, James A. *Governor Harold E. Hughes and Social Crisis in Iowa: A Study of the Exercise of Gubernatorial Power for Human Resources Development.* Ames: Iowa State University, 1969.

Strain, Christopher. *The Long Sixties: America, 1955–1974.* Hoboken, NJ: Wiley-Blackwell, 2016.

Taylor, Pat, Tom Hill, and William White. "Chronology of the Addiction Recovery Advocacy Movement." May 2013. http://www.williamwhitepapers.com.

Thompson, Louis Milton, Jr. "The Communication and Decision-Making Processes, Environmental Factors in Harold E. Hughes' 1968 Campaign for the U.S. Senate." Master's thesis, Iowa State University, 1969.

Van Atta, Dale. *With Honor: Melvin Laird in War, Peace and Politics*. Madison: University of Wisconsin Press, 2008.

Wall, James M. "A Senator's Faith and Vocation." *Christian Century*, September 26, 1973, 931–932.

Walsh, Matthew R. *The Good Governor: Robert Ray and the Indochinese Refugees of Iowa*. Jefferson, NC: McFarland, 2017.

Warren, Kenneth R., and Brenda Hewitt. "NIAAA: Advancing Alcohol Research for 40 Years." *Alcohol Research and Health* 33, 1–2 (January 2010): 5–17.

Warren, Wilson J. *Struggling with "Iowa's Pride": Labor Relations, Unionism, and Politics in the Rural Midwest since 1877*. Iowa City: University of Iowa Press, 2000.

———. *Tied to the Great Packing Machine: The Midwest and Meat Packing*. Iowa City: University of Iowa Press, 2007.

White, Theodore H. *The Making of the President 1972*. New York: Atheneum Press, 1973.

White, William L. *Slaying the Dragon: The History of Addiction Treatment and Recovery in America*. Bloomington, IL: Chestnut Health Systems/Lighthouse Institute, 1998.

Wieck, Paul. "For God and Country: The Presidential Campaign of Harold Hughes." *New Republic* 164 (May 15, 1971): 50–57.

Personal Interviews

Bonnie Campbell, Senator Hughes's staff member; November 11, 2017

Dick Clark, US senator from Iowa; January 27, 2020

Roxanne Conlin, Iowa political activist; June 15, 2021

Jennifer Cooper, Hughes's stepdaughter; May 17, 2019

Pat Deluhery, Senator Hughes's aide; May 31, 2021

George Drake, author of Joe Rosenfield biography; September 13, 2017

Phyllis Hughes Ewing, Hughes's daughter; June 25, 2017, and February 27, 2021

Lonnie Franks, US Air Force intelligence specialist at Udorn Air Force Base, Thailand, in 1972; June 19, 2018

Fran Frazier, Governor Hughes's secretary; September 18, 2018

Robert Fulton, Iowa lieutenant governor, 1965–69; October 26, 2019

Tom Harkin, US senator from Iowa; December 14, 2020

Bill Hedlund, Governor and Senator Hughes's staff member; August 15, 2017, and July 12, 2018

Jacquie Holm-Smith, Hughes's stepdaughter; May 17, 2019

Dwight Jensen, executive assistant to Governor Hughes and press secretary to Senator Hughes; June 15 and August 29, 2017

Martin Jensen, WMT News reporter and Governor and Senator Hughes's staff member; September 14, 2018

Pat Jensen, wife of Dwight Jensen and Hughes's friend; October 30, 2020

Bill Knapp, Hughes's confidant; July 20, 2017

Nick Kotz, *Des Moines Register* and *Washington Post* reporter; August 20, 2018

Sherwin Markman, Hughes's legal adviser and confidant; December 11, 2018

Peg Shoemaker Mikulanec, daughter of the Reverend Wayne Shoemaker; June 7, 2017

Elva Pittman, Governor Hughes's secretary; August 2, 2019

Clark Rasmussen, 1960s Iowa Democratic Party chairman; June 24, 2021

James Risser, *Des Moines Register* reporter; August 31, 2018

Bill Sueppel, Hughes's associate and legal adviser; June 17, 2017

Russell Wilson, Hughes's friend, appointed to Iowa Board of Control; August 15, 2017, and January 15, 2019

Connie Wimer, staffer in Hughes's presidential campaign office; August 15, 2017

Index

Page references in *italics* indicate an illustration.